# The Romance of China

# The Romance of China
## Excursions to China in U.S. Culture, 1776–1876

*John Rogers Haddad*

www.gutenberg-e.org

COLUMBIA UNIVERSITY PRESS

NEW YORK

Columbia University Press
*Publishers Since 1893*
New York    Chichester, West Sussex
Copyright © 2008 Columbia University Press

Library of Congress Cataloging-in-Publication Data

Haddad, John Rogers.
The romance of China : excursions to China in U.S. culture, 1776–1876 /
John Rogers Haddad.
p. cm.
Includes bibliographical references.
ISBN 978-0-231-13094-3 (cloth : alk. paper)—ISBN 978-0-231-50404-1 (e-book)
1. Americans—Travel—China—History—19th century.   2. United States—
Civilization—Chinese influences.   3. United States—Intellectual life—19th
century.   4. China—Foreign public opinion, American—History—19th century.
5. China—Civilization—Public opinion—History—19th century.
6. Public opinion—United States—History—19th century.
7. China—Description and travel.   8. China—In popular culture.
9. United States—Relations—China.   10. China—
Relations—United States.   I. Title.
E183.8.C5H175 2008
973.9—dc22
2008037637

Columbia University Press books are printed on permanent
and durable acid-free paper. This book is printed on paper
with recycled content. Printed in the United States of America.

c 10 9 8 7 6 5 4 3 2 1

References to Internet Web sites (URLs) were accurate at the time
of writing. Neither the author nor Columbia University
Press is responsible for URLs that may have expired
or changed since the manuscript was prepared.

# CONTENTS

# ACKNOWLEDGMENTS

While working on this book, I have incurred numerous debts, which I am pleased to acknowledge here. First, I would like to thank my wife, Minhui, who has been an endless well of support and patience through the years. Though most of the book was written by the time my son came along, William's cheerful demeanor helped immeasurably during the final stages of revision (though he does not yet comprehend the morale boost he provided!). I owe a similar debt of gratitude to my parents, Richard and Betsy Haddad, and to my brother and his wife, Rich and Sandy Haddad. My in-laws in China all wished me well from afar; thank you, Wang Qingyi and Yang Xiurong. I would also like to thank Daniel Medwed, a good friend who kept my spirits high and who certainly feels like family.

Next, I would like to single out the contribution of my dissertation adviser, William H. Goetzmann. Whether it was reading a chapter for the third time, recommending a seemingly obscure book that turned out to be pivotal, or offering encouragement over lunch, Dr. Goetzmann showed a boundless generosity with his time and intellect without which this dissertation would not have been possible. Dr. Goetzmann, I appreciate all that you have taught me over the years. I would also like to thank the other members of the dissertation committee, each of whom contributed in an important way. Edward Rhoads provided invaluable assistance, both by reading chapters and by helping me grasp

Chinese history. Mark Smith provided excellent advice in structuring the work. Janet Davis generously offered her expertise in popular culture, as did John Park in the field of Asian American Studies.

Turning a doctoral dissertation into a book posed a new and daunting challenge. This effort was aided greatly by the American Historical Association, which, in conjunction with Columbia University Press, awarded me the Gutenberg-e award in 2002. To say that this award put wind in my sails would be an egregious understatement. All of a sudden, I became welcome in a true community of history scholars and publishing professionals; this group provided the intellectual, financial, editorial, and moral support necessary to complete a project begun in graduate school. Here I would like to give special mention to Nicholas Frankovich, who brought tremendous care, thoughtfulness, and precision to his job as copy editor.

Since this dissertation required substantial archival research, I was fortunate enough to receive fellowships from three institutions, the University of Texas, Winterthur Library, and the McNeil Center for Early American History. I also owe a debt to all of the archivists and research librarians at the following institutions who took an interest in my project and brought countless sources to my attention: Winterthur Library, the Peabody Essex Museum, the Department of Anthropology at the American Museum of Natural History, the New York Public Library, the New-York Historical Society, the Cooper-Hewitt Museum, the various reading rooms at the Library of Congress, the Manuscripts and Archives department at Yale University, the Smithsonian Museum of American History, the Library Company of Philadelphia, the Historical Society of Pennsylvania, the Free Library of Philadelphia, the Chester County Historical Society, and the Humanities Research Center at the University of Texas at Austin. I would also like to extend my gratitude to Susan Roeckle and the other wonderful people of the Inter Library Loan Office at the University of Texas who

Finally, I would like to thank friends, colleagues, and staff at Penn State Harrisburg—in particular Charlie Kupfer, Simon Bronner, Michael Barton, Catherine Rios, Sue Etter, and Cindy Leach—who have provided good advice, good coaching, and (most importantly) good humor!

# INTRODUCTION

China was once romantic to me. Back in 1994, when I decided that I wanted to travel overseas, I had two reasons. First, I possessed the sort of wanderlust that seizes many recent college graduates; I desired to break out of the comfortable sphere I had inhabited for more than two decades, see part of the world, and enjoy an adventure. Second, I had decided I wanted to teach for a living, and I thought that a temporary position at an overseas university would provide me with much-needed experience in front of a classroom. As I surveyed the wide array of possible countries, something peculiar took place. All the candidate nations quickly fell away—all except China, that is, which rose before me as the only real choice. Why did China alone beckon? I was not exactly sure, but I believe its attraction had something to do with the challenge afforded by its epic size, with my perception that its culture was intriguingly different and exotic, and with the aura of mystery that hovered over a once-closed communist country now opening up to the world. In sum, I chose China because it was, in a word, *romantic.*

Though I enjoyed living and teaching in the People's Republic of China for many reasons, the country's romance turned out not to be among them. In truth, shortly after I had arrived in Tianjin, the romantic aura that had lured me evaporated into thin air. China, I discovered, was not romantic at all; it had only seemed so from my vantage point in the United States. Instead, China was a country like any other where the people quietly went about their own business. In this way, I learned what a lot of dreamers learn when they visit a place previously viewed from afar. The romance of China had resided entirely in my own mind.

Later, in graduate school, faculty members and fellow students occasionally asked me about my experiences in China. From their line of questioning, I could gather that they also considered China to be a romantic place. And as I was casting about for a dissertation topic, I began to contemplate China's attractive force. What, I asked myself, was the source of China's ability to enjoy a powerful hold over the collective imagination of Americans? To answer this question, I began to trek backward in time, reading the popular works of literature and journalism in which China had been presented to Americans: John Hersey's novels set in China, Henry Luce's coverage of China in Time and Life magazines, Edgar Snow's Red Star over China, Pearl Buck's The Good Earth, and Carl Crow's 400 Million Customers. Working backward in time, I eventually reached the start of the twentieth century. Though I was greatly pleased to have read so many influential works, I had not located to my satisfaction the source of China's romance. And so I delved further into the past, where, at last, I found the object of my search.

Later, in graduate school, faculty members and fellow students occasionally asked me about my experiences in China. From their line of questioning, I could gather that they also considered China to be a romantic place. And as I was casting about for a dissertation topic, I began to contemplate China's attractive force. What, I asked myself, was the source of China's ability to enjoy a powerful hold over the collective imagination of Americans? To answer this question, I began to trek backward in time, reading the popular works of literature and journalism in which China had been presented to Americans: John Hersey's novels set in China, Henry Luce's coverage of China in *Time* and *Life* magazines, Edgar Snow's *Red Star over China*, Pearl Buck's *The Good Earth*, and Carl Crow's *400 Million Customers*. Working backward in time, I eventually reached the start of the twentieth century. Though I was greatly pleased to have read so many influential works, I had not located to my satisfaction the source of China's romance. And so I delved further into the past, where, at last, I found the object of my search.

For Americans alive at the dawn of the nineteenth century, the world beyond the nation's boundaries seemed intriguing and new. Their era would be one in which Europeans and Americans would fan out across the globe, traversing oceans and enduring inhospitable climes, to reach destinations that were either completely unknown to them or known but largely unexamined. These voyages were launched with different objectives, a mixture of the noble and the morally problematic—to seize colonies, to open up new markets, to slaughter whales and seals, to convert "the heathen" to Christianity, to map uncharted regions, to study unknown civilizations, and to document and record new species. By the latter half of the nineteenth century, this flurry of exploratory activity had succeeded in leaving very little of the globe untouched by Western influence, for good or for ill; the Antarctic continent was discovered, Japan was opened to Western intercourse, much of the interior of Africa was explored, and North America was mapped, conquered, and settled. Taken collectively, these efforts generated an astounding amount of contact between the different cultures of the world.[1]

Though explorers and merchants had been plying the seas for centuries, ordinary men and women could not easily follow their peregrinations and share in their discoveries until the first half of the nineteenth century. In the United States, several factors combined to provide Americans with access to newly acquired information about distant lands and cultures. The federal government sponsored exploring expeditions, to the American West and other parts of the globe, that seized the nation's attention. A revolution in transportation resulted in a network of roads, turnpikes, canals, and railroads that reconfigured the natural landscape while it accelerated the flow of people, machines, commodities, and information. In the 1830s, penny newspapers and other print media proliferated as a result of innovations in printing, including the steam-driven cylinder press. Furthermore, the advent of lithography, by facilitating the mass reproduction of images, to a great extent democratized the visual image itself. Working synergistically with these technological breakthroughs, advances in literacy further increased the demand for information, as did the emergence and expansion of a middle class possessing enough disposable income to purchase books and newspapers and other periodicals. By the antebellum era, Americans' fascination with the outside world was generating a vogue for travel writing.[2]

What was the effect of these works on the individuals who read them? For some impressionable readers, accounts of expeditions proved so irresistible as to prompt action. In the mid 1850s, Samuel Clemens, twenty-one years old and living in Keokuk, Iowa, read Lieutenant Lewis Herndon's account of his exploration of the Amazon River for the U.S. Navy. As Clemens recalled later in life, when he was better known as Mark Twain, the effect of this narrative on his youthful mind was profound:

> Among the books that interested me in those days was one about the Amazon. The traveler told an alluring tale of his long voyage up the great river . . . through the heart of an enchanted land, a land wastefully rich in tropical wonders, a romantic land where all the birds and flowers and animals were of the museum varieties. . . .

I was fired with a longing to ascend the Amazon. . . . During months I dreamed that dream, and tried to contrive ways to get to Para. . . .

Herndon's account not only piqued Clemens's intellectual curiosity but also captivated his imagination. He was enthralled by the possibility that the Amazon region was an "enchanted land" full of "tropical wonders." Not content with his fantasies, Clemens yearned to see this "romantic land" with his own eyes. He traveled by riverboat to New Orleans, where he hoped to board a vessel bound for Para, Brazil. Discovering that no such ship existed, he instead sought out the riverboat pilot he had met on his journey from Iowa and implored the man "to teach me the river." Rather than ascending the Amazon River, Clemens turned to the Mississippi, which would prove to be central to his writing career.[3]

Inspired by the literature of exploration, Samuel Clemens "dreamed that dream" of seeing exotic locales for himself. Though his desire to travel was common, his ability to act on this impulse was exceptional, as most Americans could not extricate themselves from their obligations to family, community, and place of work. Indeed, for them the new availability of information was not without one concomitant frustration: Reading about the exploits of others in faraway places, though pleasurable, only served to intensify their sense of their own stasis. For this reason, their reading tantalized them by providing them with a second-hand view of a fascinating world they could never expect to see for themselves.

Clemens also notes, interestingly, that "the birds and flowers and animals" described in Herndon's work "were of the museum varieties." In other words, he had seen exotic flora and fauna on exhibit and, somewhat paradoxically, writes as if the real South American specimens were mere imitations of originals found in American museums. From this comment, we see that Clemens regarded museum exhibits as legitimate portals to the outside world. And he was not alone. Many Americans firmly believed that a museum stocked with artifacts, pictures, and stuffed wildlife could generate a pleasing illusion of travel and therefore serve as a surrogate for real sightseeing.

In the 1830s, a young girl named Caroline Howard King made numerous visits to the East India Marine Society in Salem, Massachusetts. Salem was a thriving center of maritime commerce and ships departed from it daily for destinations all over the world. When sea captains returned home bearing artifacts, they deposited them in the Society's museum, East India Marine Hall. The collection was especially strong in artifacts from China, India, the East Indies, and the Pacific Islands, and so the Hall provided visitors with a new and intriguing way to experience Asia without venturing far from home.

King relished her encounters with Asia. In fact, in memoirs composed later in life, she reminisced about the magical attraction these exhibits held:

> . . . the Museum had a mysterious attraction for me and indeed it was an experience for an imaginative child to step from the prosaic streets . . . into that atmosphere redolent with the perfumes from the east, warm and fragrant and silent, with a touch of the dear old Arabian Nights. . . . I . . . was greeted by the solemn group of Orientals [referring to several life-size statues] who, draped in eastern stuffs and camel's hair shawls, stood opposite the entrance. . . . the hours were full of enchantment, and I think I came as near fairyland as one can in this workaday world. . . . And in those days the Spice Islands seemed to lie very near our coast.[4]

Like Clemens, King used the exhibits to contemplate an escape from everyday life—the "prosaic streets" and the "workaday world" of Salem. She enjoyed a flight of fancy that liberated her, albeit briefly, from the dullness of the quotidian world and allowed her to experience wonder and "enchantment." Yet unlike Twain, who planned to escape to a real destination (the Amazon), King used her imagination to fashion a new world. The museum's arrangers intended the exhibits to offer an object lesson in the customs, arts, costumes, and religious practices of Asian cultures, but Caroline happily defied their wishes. For she knew that, once the sights and scents of Asia entered her mind, she was free to do with them as she pleased. With this license, she chose to invent her own personal Asia. This Asia was exactly the sort of place one might expect "an imaginative child" to create: It was "fairyland," and it was all her own.

For dreamers like Caroline, China existed as perhaps the most alluring of all destinations in the world because it was enshrouded in mystery. China is "the great unknown," wrote an American missionary in 1843, because "foreigners know but little more of it than they do of the moon." [5] This remoteness resulted largely from the Qing government's restrictive policy regarding the West. In 1760, Emperor Qianlong, desiring to control the empire's foreign intercourse, confined all Westerns to the southern port of Canton; they were strictly forbidden from visiting any other part of the country. In this way, China afforded foreigners only a glimpse, as if through a keyhole, of the vast and intriguing land that lay beyond Canton. Rather than squelching Westerners' nascent interest in China, this containment strategy only fanned the flames of their curiosity, compelling them to yearn for more information.[6] In 1830, William Wood, a merchant who had lived in Canton, wrote that any traveler returning home from China suffered "considerable annoyance at the multitude of questions" from the lips of curious Americans. A "romantic illusion," he said, had enveloped China in the minds of Americans.[7]

Wood was correct. During much of the nineteenth century, mystery lent China a romantic aura in the West. In trying to engage the mystery, the Western mind split into two and proceeded to engage China on separate intellectual planes. At one level, the Western imagination used the absence of information as a license to spin wonderful Oriental fantasies (as Caroline Howard King had done) which could then be projected onto China's geographic blankness. At a second level, the mystery provoked restless discomfort for the more rationally minded side of the West; it sought (like Clemens considering the Amazon) to see China for itself so as to inscribe empirical knowledge into the intolerable empty space. Thus, in the Western mind, China existed in a state of tension caused by the presence of two contrary impulses: the imagination's need to create fictional lands and the rational mind's inexorable quest to demystify the real world.

In the United States and Europe, that fictional land was known as Cathay. Hugh Honour, in his study on European Chinoiserie, offers a vivid description of Cathay: "Of this mysterious and charming land, poets are the only historians and porcelain painters the most reliable topographers. They alone can give an adequate impression of the beauty of the landscape with its craggy snow-capped mountain ranges, . . . cities of dreaming pagodas," and "meandering rivers whose limpid waters bear delicately wrought junks." It is a landscape of "perpetual spring" filled with "weeping willows," "bamboo," "chrysanthemums," and "forests of gnarled trees." On branches "gaudy birds with rainbow-hued plumage" perch; "butterflies the size of puffins" flutter through gardens; and in murky ponds "diaphanous-tailed goldfish" swim about "amidst the water lilies." As for the denizens of Cathay, they are a serene, contemplative people who possess long curling fingernails and wear robes embroidered with gold. In short, Cathay was a wholly unrealistic, yet wonderfully kaleidoscopic, vision of a country.[8]

In 1873, Gideon Nye, a retired China trader, offered an insight that is helpful in explaining exactly why China, as a subject of Western contemplation, could deliver so much romantic pleasure. Looking back wistfully on the first half of the nineteenth century, Nye wrote: "The very name of China—the distant Cathay,—was, at that day, pregnant of the Romance of History; and suggested imaginative dreams. . . ." [9] With these words, Nye had made a critical observation: Americans failed to draw a clear distinction between real China and dreamy Cathay, choosing instead to leave the two in a state of splendid conflation. In other words, much of China's romance flowed out of the imagination's ability to take the early lead on the rational mind: A fantasy world had been invented but had not been discredited. As a result, dreamers could justifiably enjoy believing that their imagined ideal was real.

But China could also be romantic in that it attracted a second kind of dreamer—Americans possessing ambitions of epic proportions. For these individuals, China beckoned in the same way that Mt. Everest calls to mountain climbers. Viewing China as one of the great challenges of their age, these bold individuals hoped to demystify it by penetrating into the heart of China's vast unknown territory and becoming the first to return to the United States with accurate descriptions of the country and its people. That the Qing government had erected obstacles to block their efforts only served to increase the challenge and, therefore, augment the significance of the quest. Indeed, this was no task for either the small-minded or the fainthearted. Thus, the large-scale project of describing China often attracted romantic individuals with grandiose ambitions.

In the nineteenth century, these two different kinds of dreamers would frequently meet. During this time period, merchants, missionaries, diplomats, engineers, painters, and travel writers journeyed to China. While there, they recorded their observations, gathered artifacts, collected specimens, met inhabitants, and sketched scenes. On returning home, they reconstituted their experiences overseas into cohesive cultural productions—re-creations of China that were designed to educate, amaze, and amuse American audiences. Because of these cultural productions, ordinary people could do more than merely visit Cathay in their minds; they could confront China through the various acts of reading texts, inspecting objects, viewing pictures, attending lectures, and meeting actual Chinese people.

In fact, many Americans went so far as to claim that their experience with virtual China was tantamount to visiting China itself. Of course, these virtual tourists were not seeing China so much as a construction of China. Though nearly all of the individuals who created these cultural productions aspired for accuracy and sincerely believed they had attained it, their manner of perceiving China was in fact shaped by their personal background, the times in which they lived, their systems of belief, and the demands of the fickle marketplace. Indeed, when we penetrate to the core of these constructions, we see the great extent to which they were colored by religious faith, views on technology, scientific paradigms, sexual orientation, financial issues, personal anxieties, or pseudoscientific theories. And so in each case a unique combination of biographical, ideological, historical, and commercial factors circumscribed the attempt to describe China truthfully.

However, though the truth on China proved elusive, these individuals did impart their knowledge of China to American audiences. Knowledge, which is distinct from truth, refers to the coherent set of ideas, observations, and images that results when the factors listed above merge with the individual's attempt to understand China. Since the factors necessarily varied from one individual to the next, knowledge of China was (and still is) far from being fixed and stable. In fact, constructions of China were as diverse as the people who created them.

In the nineteenth century, this diversity helped make China the topic of a rich national debate. Each American who journeyed to China understood the country in his own way. After returning to the United States, he would fashion a unique construction of China and, perfectly convinced of his own accuracy, would often identify serious flaws both in the portrayals by his rivals and in the American public's understanding of China. And so Americans vied with one another for influence in the marketplace of ideas. Of course, a few merely duplicated prevalent stereotypes for commercial gain, yet most chose not to act in complicity with their lesser-informed audiences because they were too ambitious to sacrifice originality for profit. In fact, some were inexorably driven by an overweening pride that approached hubris. They sought to add to world knowledge and to make a name for themselves in the process, both by disabusing their audiences of erroneous stereotypes and by actively dissenting against whatever the accepted view on China was. After all, what was the point of traveling all the way to China only to repeat what others have already said? Not surprisingly, when we look at constructions of China we find that, as a group, they are characterized by an exciting amount of conflict, competition, and contestation—not by a dull consensus.

It will also come as no surprise that we also find ample evidence of racism. The individuals who described the Chinese sometimes understood the latter as being inferior. And even when an individual's portrayal was informative and respectful, audience members proved capable of overriding a positive message by choosing to see only what they wanted to see (as Caroline Howard King did in Salem). Indeed, a large portion of the ordinary Americans who took virtual journeys to China exhibited neither a salutary curiosity nor a spirit of open-mindedness; instead, we find manifest in their reactions only a smug belief in the preeminence of their own civilization and a disappointing intolerance for a way of life that differed from their own. Some Americans would attend a virtual China only to subject Chinese people and customs to the basest forms of mockery and ridicule.

That said, there was one factor that often worked to mitigate racism—the Chinese themselves. The historian Arif Dirlik has argued that, in Western representations of Easterners, power was seldom concentrated exclusively in Western hands; rather, it tended to be dispersed, with much of it in the possession of Easterners. By locating both power and a voice in the East, Dirlik's theory represents a significant departure from one previously articulated by Edward Said. In *Orientalism*, Said had argued that the West possessed all of the power and the only voice. He defined Orientalism as "a Western style for dominating, restructuring, and having authority over the Orient." In Said's formulation, the Easterners who were being represented came across as passive and silent.[10]

The findings from my research fall more in line with Dirlik's model of representations than with Said's. The evidence suggests that constructions of China did not emanate solely from a white American consciousness and reflect only the views, needs, and prejudices of white people; instead, they were generated by the cultural, commercial, and diplomatic interactions that took place in what Mary Louise Pratt has called "contact zones"—loci of Eastern and Western encounters and relationships.[11] Out of these contact zones, constructions of China emerged that reflected the input of both parties. Not only did Americans in China rely heavily on the Chinese. Sometimes their constructions were actually *made possible* by the latter's assistance. The Chinese served as tour guides and translators, executed paintings of Chinese life, acted as cultural interpreters, and even worked as collecting agents by traversing their own country in search of artifacts. And on at least one occasion the Chinese even assembled their own exhibit, which they transported to the United States.

Sometimes, China's participation amounted to what Dirlik has called "self-orientalization." That is, the Chinese constructed themselves, accurately or otherwise, in a manner intended to advance their own interests. They viewed self-description for an overseas audience as a beneficial way to increase exports, improve relations with other nations, or refute damaging stereotypes. In sum, the Chinese are far from being passive or silent in this story. Rather, in overt or subtle ways, they exerted real control over their own representation in the United States and, in doing so, often provided a countervailing force that could hold anti-Chinese sentiment somewhat in check.

At least two other scholarly works have explored American representations of China and the Chinese, though these mostly cover different sources from those included in the present study. Both agree that the chief historical relevance of these representations is their ability to elucidate an unfortunate event in American history: the Chinese Exclusion Act of 1882. This act, which prohibited the entry of Chinese laborers into the United States, was the first federal law designed to block the immigration of individuals of a specific nationality.

Stuart Creighton Miller was the first to treat this topic, in *The Unwelcome Immigrant: The American Image of the Chinese, 1785–1882*. Miller's project, as stated in his own words, was "to trace systematically the evolution of the unfavorable image of the Chinese in nineteenth-century America and to examine the role of this image in the national decision to exclude the Chinese from the melting pot." To accomplish this objective, Miller read extensively from a wide variety of American writers—missionaries, traders, diplomats, journalists—who were responsible for generating images of the Chinese. In his view, anti-Chinese sentiment in America resulted from the gradual accretion of disparate and unrelated negative images. For instance, he claims that the China trader and the missionary both cast the Chinese in an unflattering light but did so for entirely different reasons. After computing the aggregate of these images, Miller concluded that, by 1882, Americans had received an overall impression of the Chinese that was decidedly negative.[12]

My purpose is not so much to refute Miller as to present new sources which show that representations of China were not as uniformly negative as he claims. Anti-Chinese views, though common, were always contested and failed to monopolize the marketplace of ideas. With the sole purpose of his research being to locate the cause for the Exclusion Act, Miller was quite possibly drawn to negative representations to the point of overlooking the many that were positive, innocent, admirable, hopeful, and even comical. With this work, I hope to present many of these lost narratives, stories of Sino-American cultural contact, so as to broaden our understanding of how Americans interacted intellectually and creatively with China.

The next historian, John Kuo Wei Tchen, used New York as his case study in *New York Before Chinatown: Orientalism and the Shaping of American Culture, 1776—1882*. Like Miller, Tchen conferred vast importance on the role played by representations of the Chinese, going so far as to state that they were "intrinsic to American social, economic, and political life." Unlike Miller, Tchen understood representations not as disparate and unrelated but rather as unified by a consistent and disturbing theme permeating mainstream American culture—the need of white Americans to define themselves in opposition to an Oriental "other." In his attempt to "adapt Said's concept [of Orientalism] to the United States," Tchen argued that the Chinese provided white Americans with the "otherness" they needed to define "who they were and were not." "The formulators of U.S. identity," Tchen asserted, "sought to advance a unique form of American nationalism that often used China and the Chinese symbolically and materially." At times, the Chinese were "mimicked, simulated, and reproduced," for the purpose of "provoking laughter, assuaging fear, and forging solidarity between members of a paying audience by formulating a pan-European occidental identity in juxtaposition to the stereotype of yellow face." The Exclusion Act was the inevitable consequence of this nationwide fixation on self-definition.[13]

Tchen offered an intriguing theory: that representations of China were actually indirect forms of *self*-representation. In other words, the curiosity for China that prompted Americans' outward-looking gaze masked what was really an ugly and narcissistic exercise in defining the national character in an exclusionary fashion. I do not disagree entirely with this conclusion; some Americans clearly did use the perceived difference of Chinese culture as a means either to attain self-understanding or, much worse, to assert self-superiority. Yet I do not think a nation's obsession with itself can account for the abundance of intellectual and imaginative energy that Americans spent on China. In other words, there truly was a vast reservoir of American curiosity about China in the nineteenth century, and not all of it was vile.

Instead, a variety of needs and desires motivated Americans to turn their collective gaze toward China—not just one. Many were motivated by a healthy and laudable yearning to know more about the outside world. They were capable of demonstrating an exciting open-mindedness to the cultural offerings of the Chinese and enthusiastically sought to spread their discoveries to others. Others journeyed to China only after failing to build a career in the United States. Since China had provided them with a fresh opportunity to start anew, they chose to view it with tolerance and even respect. For another group, who never left the United States, China offered a chance to exercise a fertile imagination. Using the multiple images of China that were adrift in American culture, American women and children constructed their own Oriental wonderlands, which they could visit while daydreaming. For them, China served as a kind of mental theme park, an imagined destination where bored but creative people could romp with childlike delight as they escaped the monotony of their domestic setting. Though they clearly described China erroneously, they were not consumed by a nationalistic fervor to assert the superiority of their own culture. Instead, they harbored a desire that stands as the polar opposite of the chauvinistic and narcissistic impulse: escapism or the desire to temporarily flee one's own life and society.

In sum, I see neither a high degree of unity among those who constructed China nor the presence of a consistently anti-Chinese message in their cultural productions. For this reason, I contend that the United States was not headed all along on a misguided course that would lead inevitably to the Exclusion Act of 1882. Instead, I see Americans as being engaged in a rich and lively debate in which presenters of China, their audiences, and the Chinese themselves each possessed a strong voice. Even when Americans seemed to collectively turn against China at the end of the Opium War in 1842, the Chinese were never without their defenders and were never completely silenced. Because of that debate, I do not believe that the Exclusion Act was inevitable.

Yet, sadly, that debate, though fertile, did not evolve into a wise and benevolent immigration policy. Starting in the 1870s, the economic and political landscape shifted in a profound way. The massive industrialization that followed the Civil War brought about an epic clash between two titans—labor and capital—and Chinese immigrants experienced the extreme misfortune of becoming a political football in this confrontation. However, prior to this unfortunate chapter in Chinese-American history, the contested nature of China in the public discourse meant that multiple trajectories were at least possible.

The period under study encompasses the first one hundred years of the United States, from 1776 to 1876. Before 1776, British merchants and officials

handled all intercourse with China. Thus, we cannot really speak of a construction of China in Colonial times that was distinctly "American." Yet just
months after the signing of the Treaty of Paris, American independence began
to express itself through commerce as traders sought to establish their own relationship with the Chinese. The first American trading vessel bound for
China, the *Empress of China*, embarked in 1784. The success of this business
venture inaugurated a commercial exchange that would alter the American
landscape, both materially and intellectually. By directing a flood of Chinese
goods into the American market, the China trade caused a concomitant stream
of images to flow into the American mind at a time when China loomed as a
colossal mystery.

This book proceeds chronologically. In each chapter I examine either a single construction of China or a small cluster of related ones. As a quick scan of
the table of contents suggests, the subjects of the chapters reflect the central argument that these constructions were shaped by a rich diversity in perspectives:
an eccentric diplomat, women and children at home interacting creatively with
their porcelain, tea merchants advertising their product on the market, a China
trader with grand dreams, an enterprising sea captain, a missionary, an engineer, a painter, a showman, and a famous travel writer. I have chosen to conclude the study at 1876 for a handful of reasons. This date allows me to explore
China's large contribution at the Centennial Exposition in Philadelphia and to
gauge American reaction to it, just six years prior to the passage of the Exclusion
Act in 1882. The inclusion of this event is important also because the Chinese
become the primary architects of a Chinese exhibit intended for American audiences. Thus, to our set of representative voices, we add one that is distinctly
Chinese.

I would like to emphasize the term *representative voices* because I do not
pretend to offer a comprehensive study. For if one attempted to cover all the
books, magazine articles, and newspaper stories devoted to China, the project
would swell to unmanageable proportions. Rather, this work has taken a large
temporal swath, isolated a handful of fertile and influential constructions of
China, and attempted to show the remarkable diversity in thought that animated both the creators and their audiences. That we find in the United States
not one construction but many different ones is in fact fitting for a country that
has never been homogeneous. And though none of the individuals could be
said to have "gotten China right," their efforts show that most did possess integ-
rity: They tried to do more than dip into pools of accepted stereotypes and
please audiences. Rather, equipped with their own systems of belief, they confronted China and proceeded to construct the country as they saw it and as they
hoped truly curious Americans would see it too.

NOTES

1. William H. Goetzmann, *New Lands, New Men: America and the Second Great Age of Discovery* (New York: Penguin, 1986), 1.

2. Carl Bode, *The Anatomy of American Popular Culture, 1840–1861* (Berkeley: University of California Press, 1959), 223; Michael Schudson, *Discovering the News: A Social History of American Newspapers* (New York: Basic Books, 1978), 31–39; Goetzmann, 1–2.

3. Mark Twain, "The Turning Point in My Life," *Harper's Bazaar* (February 1910), 118–19.

4. Caroline Howard King, *When I Lived in Salem, 1822–1866* (Brattleboro, Vt.: Stephen Daye Press, 1937), 28–30; and Walter Muir Whitehill, *The East India Marine Society and the Peabody Museum of Salem: A Sesquicentennial History* (Salem, Mass.: Peabody Museum, 1949), 37–38, 45–46.

5. *Chinese Repository* (January 1843), 6. According to the historian Kenneth Latourette, China in the early part of the nineteenth century "was almost as remote from ordinary American life as the planet Mars." Kenneth Scott Latourette, *The History of Early Relations between the United States and China, 1784–1844* (New Haven: Yale University Press, 1917), 124.

6. Jonathan D. Spence, *The Search for Modern China* (New York: Norton, 1990), 121.

7. William Wood, *Sketches of China: With Illustrations from Original Drawings* (Philadelphia: Carey and Lea, 1830), vii, x–xi.

8. Hugh Honour, *Chinoiserie: The Vision of Cathay* (New York: E. P. Dutton, 1961), 1–7.

9. Gideon Nye, *The Morning of My Life in China: Comprising an Outline of the History of Foreign Intercourse from the Last Year of the Regime of Honorable East India Company, 1833, to the Imprisonment of the Foreign Community in 1839* (Canton, 1873), 4. Nye delivered these words during a lecture on the evening of 31 January 1873

10. Arif Dirlik, "Chinese History and the Question of Orientalism," in "Chinese Historiography in Comparative Perspective," ed. Axel Schneider and Susanne Weigelin-Schwiedrzik, special issue, *History and Theory* 35 (December 1996), 96–118; and Edward Said, *Orientalism* (New York: Pantheon, 1978), 3.

11. Mary Louise Pratt, *Imperial Eyes: Travel Writing and Transculturation* (London: Routledge, 1992), 6.

12. Stuart Creighton Miller, *The Unwelcome Immigrant: The American Image of the Chinese, 1785–1882* (Berkeley: University of California Press, 1969), ix.

13. John Kuo Wei Tchen, *New York before Chinatown: Orientalism and the Shaping of American Culture, 1776–1882* (Baltimore: Johns Hopkins University Press, 1999), xvi, 125, 292–295. Robert Lee has also published a study in the area of representations, though he has not limited his study to the treatment of the Chinese. Lee's

work is sweeping in scope, examining all groups of Asian descent and covering the entire history of the United States. However, like Tchen, Lee makes the argument that the mainstream used depictions of Asians in popular culture to "define American nationality" and decide "who 'real Americans' are." Robert G. Lee, *Orientals: Asian Americans in Popular Culture* (Philadelphia: Temple University Press, 1999), 6.

# 1. XANADUAN

## Envoy at the Throne of a Monarch

First, a success. On February 22, 1784, a rise in temperature finally melted some of the ice in New York's East River, opening this channel for commerce. At long last, the *Empress of China* was free to depart for Canton, and the American China trade was officially underway. Along with its cargo of ginseng and Spanish silver dollars, the vessel carried dreams—the dreams of American merchants who saw in the China trade vast potential for wealth accumulation. Their dreams were realized. When the Empress returned in 1785, it released a flood of merchandise onto the markets of New York and Philadelphia: tea, silks, nankeens, and porcelain. The ship did not, however, bring much information on China, as the captain and crew had seen very little of the country itself—only a small commercial zone on the Canton waterfront. The vessel was an importer not so much of knowledge as of dreams. Many of the goods were emblazoned with idyllic images of China, and so American consumers could savor the dream that China was a romantic land of great beauty. Since numerous American merchant vessels would embark for Canton in the wake of the *Empress's* success, the flow of images that amounted to a mere trickle in 1785 would grow into a torrential current by the close of the eighteenth century, as will be shown in chapters 2 and 3.[1]

Second, a failure. In 1794, Andreas Everardus van Braam Houckgeest left Canton and traveled north to Peking to appear before the emperor inside the Forbidden City. Although Houckgeest was a naturalized U.S. citizen, on this particular embassy he was representing the country of his birth, Holland. The winter weather was formidable, but the Dutch American envoy was able to tolerate it because he too was possessed by a dream: to see and catalog China. Throughout the journey, Houckgeest's attention was fixed on the landscapes, the plants and animals, the countryside and towns, and the people. All of these provided inexhaustible sources of fascination. In Houckgeest's day, China stood as a colossal mystery in the Western mind. This dearth of reliable information resulted largely from the Qing government's restrictive policy toward the West. In 1760, Emperor Qianlong, whom Houckgeest would meet, had confined all Western traders to the southern port of Canton in order to keep China's intercourse with the outside world at a minimum.[2]

Given these historical circumstances, Houckgeest knew that the Dutch embassy of which he was a part presented him with an opportunity few Westerners before him had enjoyed, and he was determined to take full advantage. While the embassy headed north, his pen remained in a state of perpetual motion as he endeavored to capture, in words and in sketches, everything that passed before his eyes. After moving to Philadelphia less than two years later, he combined these observations and images with his Chinese paintings, natural specimens, and cultural artifacts to form a grand Chinese collection that he temporarily exhibited in the city. Houckgeest's reconstruction of China on American soil was so thorough that visitors felt as if they had been magically transported to the Far East. Americans now finally enjoyed access to an educational venue designed to instruct them about a country they knew almost nothing about. At last, China had been demystified.

Or had it? The problem with Houckgeest's exhibit is that precious few people saw it. Not only was the exhibit of a transient nature, being open for just a few months in the summer of 1796, but its owner was not overly committed to educating ordinary people—guests at the exhibit consisted mainly of the city's scientific elite. The grand Chinese collection came and went, attracting scant public notice and achieving little lasting influence. This was indeed a pivotal failure. By neglecting to disseminate his knowledge, Houckgeest allowed images that were far more idealized to take hold of the popular imagination. In other words, the limited influence of his exhibit contributed to the proliferation of an idyllic, even fantastical image of China in the early nineteenth century.

## A TRIP THROUGH CHINA

The epitome of eighteenth-century worldliness, Andreas Everardus van Braam Houckgeest was born in Utrecht, Holland, in 1739. As a young man, he served in the Dutch navy and later lived in China for fifteen years while working for the Dutch East India Company. In the early 1780s he moved to South Carolina to represent his government as the Dutch consul to the American South. Finding the warm climate and the slower lifestyle of South Carolina to be increasingly agreeable, he decided that his seafaring days were finished and that it was time to settle down. Toward this end, he purchased a rice plantation, brought his wife and children over from Holland, and, in 1784, became a naturalized citizen of the young United States.[3] At the time his life might have seemed to being entering a happy period of productive routine and stability, but he would soon be in for a rude awakening.

Tragedy intruded on his bucolic bliss when a diphtheria epidemic claimed his four youngest children. To make matters worse, the state of his personal finances collapsed when he entrusted his money to an individual who turned out to be a "false friend." Filled with sorrow and on the verge of bankruptcy, Houckgeest could not bear to remain in South Carolina. When he received an offer in 1790 to return to China to occupy his former post with the Dutch East India Company, he bid farewell to his wife and sailed for Canton. There he would discover that the greatest adventure of his life was in fact not behind him but in the years just ahead.[4]

While living and working in the great Asian port city, Houckgeest longed to see other parts of China. He chafed at the rigid restrictions imposed on him by the Qing government. Not surprisingly, when the opportunity arose in 1794 to accompany the Dutch ambassador on an official journey to Peking, Houckgeest seized the chance. In November of that year, the embassy commenced its lengthy journey to the north under the leadership of several Chinese officials. The early stages were accomplished on boats with little trouble, but in December the embassy encountered subzero temperatures that had frozen China's natural and man-made waterways. Abandoning the idea of water travel, the Chinese officials responsible for conveying the Dutch delegation presented each of its members with a palanquin and proceeded to hire teams of bearers. Grunting in unison, the bearers assigned to Houckgeest hoisted him into the air—no easy task, given his substantial girth—and the embassy resumed its slow trek to the capital.[5]

But this mode of transportation only posed new problems as the palanquin bearers kept deserting the party. Though Houckgeest speculated that the bitter cold had driven some of them away, he also believed that corrupt Chinese officials had pocketed government funds earmarked for the bearers. Whatever the true reason, the Chinese officials encountered great difficulty enlisting new men, and so the journey was prone to frequent and prolonged delays. Worse still, Houckgeest did not believe that the officials were equitable in distributing provisions. On days that he went hungry, he observed, they were "in want of nothing."[6] Though he could not condone their behavior, he understood corruption to be universal rather than a peculiarly Chinese problem. "But where is there a place in the universe without corruption?" he asked rhetorically. "Would it not be the same thing in Europe? Let us not then judge too severely the Chinese."[7]

Though perturbed by the shortage of food, the cold weather, the corruption, and the slow progress, Houckgeest decided not to sit in his palanquin and pout. Instead, according Moreau de Saint-Mery, a friend from France who later edited Houckgeest's account of this embassy, the Dutch American chose to capitalize on the rarity of this moment, when "a vast extent" of China was "laid open to his view." He used the extra time to sketch scenes and describe places that, as he claimed, "never yet were marked with the footstep of an European." This constant activity with the brush and quill, in addition to providing Houckgeest a much-needed diversion from the hardships of travel, brought him closer to the fulfillment of a personal ambition. He aspired to create the most accurate and complete depiction of the Middle Kingdom in history.[8]

Priding himself on his objectivity, he recorded only those stimuli that had passed through his own sensorium and refused to allow "a single line borrowed from any traveller or writer" to enter his journal. He was also aware of the subtle distortions of which the human memory was capable, and he therefore faithfully recorded all observations on the same day they were made. Sometimes he worked late into the night, despite frigid temperatures, to finish drawings and descriptions because, as he explained, "I thought it far better to lose a few hours rest, than to let a single remarkable object escape me." Thus, throughout the journey, his eyes were open, his mind was active, and his "pen and pencil were constantly employed."[9]

As the embassy traversed the countryside, Houckgeest took in the surrounding scenery, most of which possessed a pastoral beauty that greatly appealed to him. "I can venture to say," he observed, "that in all the space my eyes could reach in every direction, there was not a single unpleasant point of view. . . . Externally every thing wore the appearance of prosperity and happiness."[10] In a few isolated locations, the beauty of China was so great as to inspire genuine wonder. For instance, as he beheld the "astonishing spectacle" of "a valley situated between two ridges of mountains," he was so stunned by the beauty that he recorded in his journal, "I could not falsify my eyes." It seems the visual data processed by his eyes surpassed the limits of credibility established by his rational faculties. "Yes, I am sure," Houckgeest wrote of this valley, "that many people in Europe would go a hundred miles to enjoy a prospect so enchanting."[11]

Houckgeest was also impressed by the myriad ways the Chinese had improved on the natural landscape. For instance, by building pagodas on hilltops, the Chinese enhanced what was already "a very beautiful picture." In addition, they had inserted in their rivers waterwheels of a design superior to those used in the United States. These labor-saving devices, Houckgeest asserted, offered "proof of the industry and intelligence of the Chinese." And most remarkably, the Chinese had invented an ingenious way to create additional space for crops by terracing mountains: "The eye of an European is delighted at beholding the industrious application of the Chinese, who, rating difficulties at nothing, convert mountains into fertile fields." In sum, the Chinese had managed to maximize their agricultural output without diminishing—in fact, while augmenting—the aesthetic appeal of the landscape.[12]

As Houckgeest's eyes consumed one amazing sight after another, he was constantly reminded that he himself had become a spectacle. For Westerners were not the only ones who demonstrated a strong curiosity for foreign peoples and cultures. Each time his embassy passed through a village, Houckgeest found himself besieged by "the incredible multitude of people who came crowding to see me." In fact, just to get through the dense crowds of onlookers, the delegation often required the assistance of the Chinese soldiers attached to the embassy, who would clear a path through the throng. Yet as the Chinese pushed and shoved to catch a glimpse of him, he continued to inspect them from his palanquin. Chinese women in particular attracted his attention. The women "who filled all the doors and windows" to watch him pass, he remarked, were often "pleasing" and sometimes even "beautiful."[13]

## THE FORBIDDEN CITY

As fascinating as his journey was, Houckgeest anxiously awaited his arrival in Peking. When the embassy finally reached its destination in January 1795, the envoy found that the streets of the capital offered still more novel sights: "This Spectacle, the noise of the carriages, horses, mules, and dromedaries; the assemblage of so many men and animals; the appearance of new dresses, manners, and faces; every thing, in short, put in its claim upon my curiosity, and captivated my attention." Yet Houckgeest was also physically exhausted; the once portly man discovered to his astonishment that the privations of travel had removed a full five inches from his waistline. He fully expected the food and lodging in the capital to be of a quality befitting an official guest of the emperor, but unfortunately it proved disappointing.[14] And so with weary eyes and with garments hanging loosely on his once ample frame, Houckgeest looked to carry out the embassy's mission, which, somewhat surprisingly, had nothing to do with Sino-Dutch trade negotiations. He had covered well over one thousand miles with no object other than "to congratulate the Emperor on his entry into the sixtieth year of his reign." Houckgeest, it turns out, was little more than a party guest.[15]

Early in the morning on the appointed day, Chinese officials escorted Houckgeest and the Dutch ambassador to the Forbidden City, where they were to appear before the emperor. As his eyes scanned his surroundings, Houckgeest marveled at the "rich gilding," the "brilliant colours," the "rigid symmetry," and the "uncommon grandeur" of the architecture.[16] Yet he was not always pleased by what he saw. As he waited for the arrival of the emperor in the company of envoys from other lands (Tibet, Mongolia, and Korea), he was struck by the disorderliness of the scene. Instead of the expected model of order and civility, a "state of disturbance" prevailed "at the court of the Chinese Monarch." Thoroughly disgusted, he wrote that "one might have imagined himself in the midst of a savage nation, that had never entertained the least idea of civilization." Despite his disappointment, when Emperor Qianlong arrived in his yellow palanquin, Houckgeest showed his respect in the fashion demanded by Chinese protocol. Unlike George Lord Macartney, the ambassador of Great Britain who had elected not to kowtow before the emperor in 1793, Houckgeest prostrated himself in the ruler's presence and bowed his head to the ground three times.[17]

Houckgeest was only the second-ranking member of the delegation, but a fortuitous event brought about the expansion of his role. After an illness incapacitated the Dutch ambassador, he turned to Houckgeest to ask him to perform the ambassador's official duties, which included making several visits to the Forbidden City to appear before the emperor. The ambassador's illness proved to be a blessing in disguise, as Qianlong took an instant liking to Houckgeest. The "old Monarch was very satisfied with us" and with "myself in particular," Houckgeest wrote, because "I had the good fortune to exhibit a physiognomy and a demeanor which captivated" his "good will." Qianlong, it seems, had studied Houckgeest's face and mannerisms and had approved of what he saw.[18]

Houckgeest further endeared himself to the emperor during his visit to the throne room. While attempting to perform "the ceremony of adoration," which involved bowing one's head all the way to the floor, Houckgeest's hat fell off. This comic moment elicited great laughter from Qianlong, who then proceeded to ask Houckgeest whether or not he could speak Chinese. When Houckgeest responded by saying "Poton" ("I do not understand"),[19] the emperor "laughed still more heartily," thinking it quite amusing that his guest had used the Chinese language to express his inability to speak Chinese. Thus, without trying, Houckgeest had became a favorite of the emperor, and poton, his inadvertently humorous expression, quickly gained popularity inside the Forbidden City.[20]

At this same meeting, Houckgeest and Qianlong also enjoyed libations of wine. After the envoy finished delivering his toast to the emperor, something remarkable took place that Houckgeest would never forget.

> I afterwards finished my salute of honour; and when I rose to retire, the Emperor, having his eyes still turned towards me, kept looking at me with a countenance expressive of the greatest kindness. Thus did I receive a mark of the highest predilection, and such as it is even said no Envoy ever obtained before.

Qianlong, it seems, had developed a special fondness for Houckgeest and had, with a mere look, conveyed his warm feelings of friendship. As the envoy journeyed back to Canton, he basked in the knowledge that he had formed a personal connection with the most exalted individual in the Eastern Hemisphere.[21]


## ASSEMBLING A CHINESE COLLECTION

After Houckgeest returned to Canton in May 1795, he promptly met with two Cantonese painters and presented them with an important job—to convert his hastily executed sketches into complete paintings. However, the pictures that resulted from this assignment were not the first that these two artists had painted for Houckgeest. Years earlier, he had hired them to play a role in his grand strategy to circumvent the Qing government's ban on travel by foreigners. He knew that, since the restriction did not apply to them, they could become his eyes in the Chinese interior and see the "places which he had no opportunity of seeing." With this plan in mind, he had charged them with a task that was truly mammoth in scope: They were to travel "throughout the whole of China" entirely at his expense, "in order that they might collect views of everything curious and picturesque which that country contains." Their job, in short, had been to paint China.[22]

That the two painters had executed this objective to the best of their ability was evident in the large corpus of artwork they produced. In the end, they accounted for the vast majority of the two thousand paintings that eventually comprised Houckgeest's burgeoning portfolio. They were clearly its centerpiece, although he also gathered numerous other objects, both manmade artifacts and natural specimens, to represent China's culture and wildlife. And since the Chinese landscape had often entranced him during the long trek to Peking, he also purchased a physical model of a Chinese landscape that contained rocks, pagodas, human figures, flowers, insects, streams, and fruit trees. With dimensions measuring 3 feet high, 22 inches wide, and 26 inches long, the model could rest on a large display table.[23]

This impulse to record China comprehensively through objects, images, and written words grew out of Houckgeest's background in Enlightenment science. He believed that one could perfectly understand any country by placing into categories all observed phenomena from both the man-made and the natural worlds—native crafts, architecture, ceremonies, customs, criminal justice, agriculture, topography, climate, and natural history, among many others. Applying this scientific methodology to China, Houckgeest attempted to fill each category with the appropriate objects, pictures, or precise written descriptions. His efforts here were part of a grand aspiration that suffused his age and flowed from the utopian belief that total knowledge of the cosmos was an ascertainable goal for humankind. Theoretically, once Houckgeest had completed his extensive taxonomical endeavor, the world would possess an authoritative and systematic record of China; at that point, China as a subject for scientific inquiry would be officially closed.[24]

Or so his reasoning went as he set sail from Canton in 1795. His ship, the *Lady Louisa*, was heavily laden with all that he needed to reconstruct China in the United States: nearly two thousand paintings, a vast collection of objects, and—astonishingly—five living, breathing Chinese people. "Never, I will venture to assert," Moreau wrote, "did a foreigner leave China with a like treasure."[25] In contrast to Houckgeest's lofty scientific objectives, his behavior in the realm of human interactions was often far from commendable. On the way home, the vessel dropped anchor at the Cape of Good Hope, where Houckgeest enjoyed an affair with the teenage daughter of his wife's sister; he was more than three decades her senior. Furthermore, under the pretext that the young lady required future instruction, he brought her along when he embarked for Philadelphia.[26]

## CONSTRUCTING CHINA IN PENNSYLVANIA

The *Lady Louisa* arrived in Philadelphia in late April 1796.[27] Houckgeest, who had amassed a small fortune while trading in Canton, immediately began to pursue a profligate lifestyle with monomaniacal zeal. He purchased a plot of 430 acres outside the city for double its actual value, commissioned an architect to design a pagoda-topped mansion, and then paid the workmen twice the going rate to build it.[28] When construction on his property was finished, Houckgeest retired to his new home and promptly started to demonstrate how much his experience in China had altered his identity. He renamed the road leading up to the mansion "China Lane," dubbed the entire estate "China's Retreat," and directed his Chinese servants to use the Chinese collection and decorate the mansion's interior according to the Chinese style. And since he was joined by his wife's niece, who had now become his mistress, he had also apparently embraced a custom practiced by many affluent Chinese males, that of taking on a concubine. (He was still married to his wife, who had moved back to Holland.) As Houckgeest strolled across his grounds, he could observe with tremendous satisfaction that the sinification of an American space was complete, and he proceeded to live in a fashion befitting the world's only self-proclaimed Euro-American Chinese mandarin.[29]

Not surprisingly, he immediately became something of a local celebrity. Wherever he went, he would take his carriage with his five Chinese servants because he relished passing the crowds who would stop to stare at the novel sight. He was also fond of entertaining the visitors who would frequently stop by the estate to receive a guided tour from the eccentric gentleman they called the "Chinese Embassador."[30] A skilled storyteller, Houckgeest would thread his amazing narratives through his belongings, causing the once inert objects to come to life. Guests were pleasantly astonished, even dumbfounded, as China in all its splendor unfolded before their eyes. And with their imaginations stimulated, they began to feel that they had not just seen one man's Chinese collection but had actually journeyed to China itself. "Everything at Mr. Van Braam's reminds us of China," observed Moreau.[31]

## AMERICA'S FIRST CHINESE EXHIBIT

During the summer of 1796, while China's Retreat was under construction, Houckgeest placed his enormous collection on display in Philadelphia.[32] Inside the exhibition space, he entertained a group of individuals who were curious about the world. Moreau referred to them as "amateurs of the sciences." As these guests inspected the collection, met the proprietor's five Chinese servants, and listened to his spellbinding stories, they felt as if they had been transported to China. "It was even impossible to avoid fancying ourselves in China," Moreau wrote of this exhibit, "while surrounded at once by living Chinese, and by representations of their manners, their usages, their monuments, and their arts."[33] Houckgeest presented guests with what must have been a completely novel experience—that of virtual travel.

Indeed, with his Chinese objects, Chinese paintings, Chinese anecdotes, and even Chinese people, he had seemingly reconstructed China itself. Of course, what Houckgeest really offered was not the real China but rather his own construction of it. Although few specifics about this exhibit are known, we can, by piecing together what information we do have, gain some understanding of the sort of cultural presentation Houckgeest offered to his guests. His version of China was conditioned by the historical circumstances he faced in China, the Chinese with whom he interacted, the ideology to which he adhered, and his desire to overturn an earlier intellectual construction of China.

Two major historical circumstances played a role in shaping Houckgeest's construction of China: the Qing government's confinement of foreigners to Canton and the celebration commemorating the sixtieth anniversary of Qianlong's ascension to the throne. For Houckgeest, these two circumstances worked in tandem, like a lock and key. While the former effectively sealed off most of China from a foreigner's view, the latter allowed Houckgeest special access. And with that access, the Dutch American was able to provide detailed information on two areas previously enshrouded in mystery—the vast Chinese interior and the majestic Forbidden City itself. And there is yet another reason why the Qing ban and the Dutch embassy were so crucial in shaping Houkgeest's re-creation of China. These two historical circumstances enhanced the importance of the next factor contributing to this re-creation, and that was the participation of the Chinese.

During his embassy to Peking, Houckgeest could not roam freely about the country making sketches and observations. Instead, Chinese officials dictated his every move, deciding where he went, what he ate, whom he met, what he saw, and even how he interpreted what he saw. According to Moreau, Houckgeest was attentive in observing "all that he was *allowed* to see of China" [emphasis added], but he was not permitted to see everything. Similarly, on reaching the capital, Houckgeest was aware that his access to forbidden places depended entirely on the whim of his Chinese hosts. And so he was elated when he heard that "the old Monarch was very satisfied with us." This encouraging report "assured us that we should have an opportunity of seeing things that no foreigner as yet had ever beheld"—the "internal parts of the palace." Indeed, by the time of his departure, Houckgeest estimated that he had seen three-fourths of the Forbidden City. Yet that Houckgeest had special access to rare sights did not mean he necessarily understood what he saw. When questions occurred to him, he invariably turned to the Chinese to supply the answers. In this way, the Chinese fed Houckgeest much of the information that he later used to construct China in the United States.[34]

Why did the emperor allow Houckgeest to see so much? Quite possibly, by granting substantial access to the Dutch envoy, Qianlong was pursuing the interests of his country. With Houckgeest in his presence, the emperor made no secret of both his favorable impression of the Dutch and his strong distaste for the English, with whom he had met less than two years earlier. Indeed, Houck-geest felt certain that the "praise" he had received from the emperor came "at the expense of the English."[35] Just two years earlier, in 1793, George Lord Mac-artney had both refused to honor Qianlong with a kowtow and unilaterally presented the emperor with a list of requests intended to reduce England's trade deficit with China.[36] In contrast, the Dutch envoys had willingly prostrated themselves before the emperor and had elected not to bother him with trade-related issues during their visit. By rewarding the behavior of the Dutch, Qian-long was simultaneously sending a signal to the English: The demeanor of their diplomats was not sufficiently respectful and British insistence on pressing the Chinese government to change its policy was not an effective way to achieve a desired result. In other words, the emperor was quite shrewdly utilizing perhaps the most effective tactic in the Chinese arsenal for dealing with foreigners— playing the interests of one nation against those of another.

In addition, Houckgeest's lack of painterly skills led him to further forfeit to the Chinese the control over his construction of their country. He was an ama-teur with the brush and, since visual representations were integral to his grand ambition to record China, he was compelled to hire the two native painters men-tioned above. As a result, although he formulated his own vision of China, he was not able to transfer it directly into his collection of paintings. That vision had to pass first through the two Chinese artists, who, if they so desired, could make subtle alterations to the vision before finalizing it on multiple canvasses. Further-more, the nature of their assignment was such that they worked with consider-able independence. When Houckgeest sent them on an extensive journey across China, he of course provided them with instructions as to the kind of scene they should reproduce. Nevertheless, when the time came to select specific views, the two artists necessarily made decisions on their own without consulting their employer. Thus, much of Houckgeest's collection of paintings really offered a *Chinese perspective of China*. According to Moreau, this lent the painting more, not less, authenticity. "When we reflect that it is China that is meant to be repre-sented, and that Chinese are the painters," he wrote, "we are disposed to believe that . . . this manner is not without its advantage," as "the more delicate hand of a European" would have robbed "the resemblance" of its genuine quality.[37]

The Chinese molded Houckgeest's construction of China in one final re-spect. At the exhibit in Philadelphia, visitors with questions could speak not only with Houckgeest but also with his five Chinese servants. According to Moreau, they were on hand to "attest the truth of what he [Houckgeest] has re-lated concerning their country."[38] Thus, in these several ways, the Chinese ex-erted substantial influence over a Westerner's attempt to portray their country.

Houckgeest's ideology also played a role in that his experience in China was structed by his faith in the ability of Enlightenment science to demystify the world. He was animated by what Moreau called a "rational curiosity which seeks to penetrate into mysteries under which it imagines useful truths to lie concealed."[39] For Houckgeest, this ideology functioned as a mode of perception or a way of ordering the reality he confronted in China. It equipped him both with the principles he used to construct meanings out of what he saw and with a methodology that could guide his collecting effort. One visitor recalled being impressed by the number of categories exhaustively covered in the collection of artwork: "But what is the most interesting in all this collection is about 60 notebooks of Chinese paintings representing with the greatest accuracy their techniques in arts and crafts, their sciences, their agriculture, ceremonies, criminal code, natural history, botany, geographical maps, etc., etc."[40] Without this faith in Enlightenment science, Houckgeest would not have assembled a collection so encyclopedic in its scope because he would not have felt compelled to fill so many categories.

In sum, I see neither a high degree of unity among those who constructed China nor the presence of a consistently anti-Chinese message in their cultural productions. For this reason, I contend that the United States was not headed all along on a misguided course that would lead inevitably to the Exclusion Act of 1882. Instead, I see Americans as being engaged in a rich and lively debate in which presenters of China, their audiences, and the Chinese themselves each possessed a strong voice. Even when Americans seemed to collectively turn against China at the end of the Opium War in 1842, the Chinese were never without their defenders and were never completely silenced. Because of that debate, I do not believe that the Exclusion Act was inevitable.

Since Houckgeest viewed China through a particular ideological lens, he not surprisingly developed novel views. And like most of the individuals who constructed China, he was keenly aware that his views differed from those offered by his predecessors. In his day, most knowledge of China, what little of it there was, originated in the accounts of Catholic missionaries, written back in the sixteenth and seventeenth centuries. More often than not, these accounts depicted China quite favorably as a benign despotism ably governed by a ruling class of educated elites, or mandarins. For instance, in 1556, Gaspar da Cruz, a Dominican friar, augured success for the Christian mission in China because "the Chinas exceed all others in populousness, in greatness of the realm, in excellence of polity and government, and in abundance of possessions and wealth."[41]

Although Houckgeest was enchanted by much of what he saw in China, he also found a lot to loathe, especially in Peking. In his published account of his journey, he aggressively contested the glowing descriptions left by the Catholic missionaries. "This picture will perhaps accord ill with the brilliant accounts that the Missionaries have sent to Europe of this capital," Houckgeest wrote, "but I paint what I see, and what (I repeat it again) I so little expected to see, that nothing but my own eyes have convinced me of its reality."[42] Convinced of his own objectivity and the soundness of his scientific methods, Houckgeest used his exhibit to refute the conclusions drawn by the Catholic missionaries. In the place of their largely exuberant account, he offered an assessment that mixed sincere praise with scathing criticism.

Concerning the latter, he found serious fault with the closed nature of Chinese civilization, believing quite strongly that China could greatly improve itself by learning from the outside world. Having himself resided in Europe, North America, and Asia, Houckgeest had developed an unwavering belief in international exchange; when people, inventions, and ideas crossed borders, all countries involved benefited. In fact, when Houckgeest encountered a Chinese invention that could be applied in the West, he did not hesitate to apply it. For instance, after judging the Chinese waterwheel to be far superior to its American equivalent, he promptly introduced this technology to his adopted country after returning home. "I have introduced the use of them into the United States of America," he wrote, "where they are of great utility in rivers." Not surprisingly, he expressed a preference for the Cantonese people over their countrymen in other provinces because they had benefited the most from frequent contact with the Western world: "I will venture to say, that by means of their continual intercourse with Europeans, the Chinese of Canton are in general more civilized than the rest of the nation to whom that advantage is denied."[43]

Though liking the emperor on a personal level, Houckgeest directed most of his criticism toward the members of China's ruling class. In his estimation, their policy of self-isolation was so disastrous as to cause "the profound ignorance of the Emperor of China, and of the people he governs, as to everything that concerns the rest of mankind." After all, he would argue, the state of American waterwheels had undergone marked improvement only because he had been willing to cross national borders, expose his mind to new ideas and inventions, and introduce these in the United States. And yet a "miracle" must take place, he wrote, before "the idea of sending a Chinese as an envoy to other nations can enter the Chinese head." Why should China's rulers deny their people this same opportunity to improve themselves?

They did so, Houckgeest believed, out of excessive pride: Chinese ignorance flowed directly out of Chinese arrogance. When presented with something new, their attitude was simply to ask condescendingly, "How, indeed, is it possible . . . to learn any thing, when we are convinced that our knowledge is already

superior to that of the rest of the world?" And so, even in industry and the mechanical arts, where "our [Western] genius surpasses theirs," the Chinese refuse
to take foreign inventions seriously. Though mechanical devices often provoke
the "astonishment" of the Chinese, their "vanity" is so great that they "do nothing to imitate" the West, choosing instead to dismiss these wonders as mere
"superfluities."[44] If China continued to keep the outside world at bay, it would
ultimately pay the tremendous cost of cultural and technological stagnation.

As harsh as Houckgeest's critique was, it is important to remember that he
was not criticizing Chinese people or the culture so much as the rulers' decision to block any kind of outside stimulus that could help their culture and society evolve. It is also important to consider his condemnation of Qing policy in
the context of China's Retreat, the mere existence of which begs an important
question. Did Houckgeest truly believe in a China without walls, a China that
could adopt the ways of the West? After all, China's Retreat existed only because one man possessed the driving ambition to re-create China in a rural
Pennsylvanian setting. One could argue that the estate was nothing more than
the physical embodiment of its owner's belief in cultural exchange. However,
Houckgeest went to great lengths to transform his property because he yearned
to luxuriate in the exotic opulence afforded by Chinese culture. He found this
culture to be so seductive, irresistible, and intoxicating precisely because he
perceived it as being intensely different from his own. And so he openly decried
China's policy of isolation but simultaneously demonstrated a profound attraction to the rich cultural distinctiveness that the policy had preserved.

In sum, Houckgeest's actions belied his words in a manner that suggests he
himself was truly divided, whether he realized it or not. Most likely, his exhibit
in Philadelphia reflected his unresolved ambivalence. Guests were taken on a
tour courtesy of a man who celebrated the ingenuity, beauty, and exoticism of
Chinese culture, and at the same time they were treated to his excoriation of
China's leaders for enacting measures that preserved the very way of life that he
went to such lengths to put on display.[45]


## DECADENCE AND DEMISE


For about a year, Houckgeest led a life of opulence at China's Retreat. But it was
not long before his extravagant and even wasteful ways soon caught up with
him. He was living so far beyond his monetary means that, by 1797, he had
already depleted his fortune and fallen into arrears. Indeed, his debts grew so

severe that authorities placed him in debtor's prison—a humiliation that the Caucasian mandarin regarded as an affront to his dignity. After his friends found the resources to secure his release, Houckgeest returned to China's Retreat for a brief period during which he learned that his wife in Holland, who had evidently learned of his mistress, had divorced him.[46]

While this downward spiral was in process, China's Retreat received a visit from Julian Niemcewicz, a traveler from Poland. The once ebullient Houckgeest, Niemcewicz reported, had given into despair and was now prone to incessant moaning over the dismal state of his financial affairs. Fearful that his host's despondent mood would prevent him from receiving the greatly anticipated tour of China, Niemcewicz wisely redirected the conversation away from depressing topics and toward a subject steeped in majesty and wonder:

> He spoke of it [his debt] with a heart wounded by grief, and his complaints would never have finished if I had not put him on the subject of the Emperor of China. Immediately his face became radiant. He began to tell us of the lunch to which he was invited by this prince; of the glass of wine and the preserves that the Emperor himself had sent to him, etc. He then showed us his house.

While Niemcewicz was receiving the much coveted grand tour, he became so accustomed to inspecting inanimate objects that, when he unexpectedly encountered a living human being, he mistook her for a porcelain doll. "In truth everything was so much in porcelain," he recalled, "that I thought for a moment that his wife was made of the same material, she was so pale and still. This is his own niece, aged 18, that Mr. Van Braam has just married." With this observation, Niemcewicz pointed out the dark side of Houckgeest's mania for collecting. Consumed by his passion to own, classify, arrange, and display things, he had perhaps forgotten how to treat his youthful bride as a person instead of as one of his lifeless possessions.[47]

Niemcewicz also faulted Houckgeest's acquisitive nature for effecting his rapid demise. Indeed, the tour of the mansion convinced him that Houckgeest's grave pecuniary difficulties were largely self-inflicted. "If he brought us great riches and great curiosities from that country [China]," the Polish traveler wrote, "it seems that in return he has left there all his good sense and all his prudence." Rather than "conforming to the simplicity of the country," he has organized his life with no purpose other than "to flaunt an Asiatic luxury."[48] In making this criticism, Niemcewicz was of course correct; his host truly had fallen prey to his own excesses. In fact, shortly after granting this tour, Houckgeest sold China's Retreat and moved to London, where he auctioned off his collection. In 1801, he died in obscurity in Amsterdam.[49]

## CONCLUSION

With his Chinese collection, Houckgeest was in possession of a rare jewel that, unfortunately, few people were able to enjoy. Interested mainly in delighting select gatherings of friends and travelers, Houckgeest kept the collection largely outside of the public's view. Though he did showcase his collection in Philadelphia while he awaited the completion of his Chinese-themed mansion, the exhibit was open for just a few months and appears to have attracted visitors primarily from the educated and aristocratic ranks of society. For this reason, ordinary Americans never enjoyed an excursion to Houckgeest's China.

While much of this failure was clearly his own doing, the era in which his Chinese collection appeared should bear part of the responsibility. For in Houckgeest's day, the printing, transportation, and market revolutions that would transform American culture in the nineteenth century had yet to happen. In the 1830s, important advances in print technology would increase the affordability of newspapers and widen their circulation. In the 1790s, though, newspapers were comparably more expensive, possessed a smaller readership, and were not written to appeal to a general audience. Thus, they were largely ineffective as organs for generating publicity, and in any case Houckgeest's exhibit apparently received no attention from the press.[50] Even if Americans had been aware of the exhibit's existence, the difficulties inherent to travel in the 1790s would have prevented most interested parties from seeing it. Before railroads, canals, and steamship lines revolutionized transportation in America, people who lived either in the outlying areas of Philadelphia or in other cities lacked a convenient means to visit the exhibit. And finally, the exhibit also appeared well before the market revolution of the Jacksonian era brought about the expansion of the middle class. In Houckgeest's day, most Americans possessed neither the disposable income (in the event an admission fee was required) nor the leisure time to patronize museums, no matter how educational and entertaining the experience promised to be. In short, Houckgeest made his cultural offering in an economic climate that was not yet conducive to success.

This is not to say that any museum erected in the 1790s was doomed to failure; after all, the museum of Charles Willson Peale was flourishing in Philadelphia at this very time. For this reason, much of the onus for the failure of Houkgeest's exhibit must rest squarely on his own shoulders. Moreau was quite fond of his eccentric friend. Nevertheless, he believed that Houkgeest had squandered a wonderful chance to disseminate knowledge through the establishment of a permanent exhibit that could, in time, reach a wide audience. "[I]f Mr. Van-Braam had only exhibited his numerous drawings," he stated, "China would be better known by them alone than by all that has been written concerning it till the present day."[51] Niemcewicz also recognized the enormous educational potential of the paintings; he believed that Houckgeest should have published a book that combined illustrations of China "with a text by a man who has been there." Such a work, he was sure, would supply "precise information on these people so ancient and interesting."[52]

By failing to spread this "precise information," Houckgeest left a gaping void that allowed carriers of imprecise information to enjoy greater influence. Without his guidance, Americans did decide to construct China in the early decades of the nineteenth century, but they did so in an unsupervised fashion—by gathering images from disparate sources and stitching them together into a crazy quilt of oriental fantasy. Most of these images came not from a specific individual with real expertise but rather from impersonal economic forces. Indeed, through channels created by the vast Sino-American trade, idyllic images of China streamed into the United States, appeared on dinner tables and in store windows, and stimulated lively but bored imaginations. As a result, many Americans came to understand China less as a geographical reality and more as an oriental fantasyland. In this way, Houckgeest's failure to instruct had a profound effect on Americans' conception of China. One wonders, for instance, if anyone who had visited his exhibit and seen a substantial portion of his two thousand paintings could possibly continue to believe that the real China resembled the simple blue-and-white pictures found on porcelain. As the next chapter shows, many Americans did exactly that.

## NOTES

1. For a thorough account of this ship's voyage, see Philip Chadwick Foster Smith, *The Empress of China* (Philadelphia: Philadelphia Maritime Museum, 1984), 3–5, 220–34.

2. Jonathan D. Spence, *The Search for Modern China* (New York: Norton, 1990), 121.

3. As an act of allegiance to his adopted country, Houckgeest dedicated to George Washington the account of his embassy to Peking: "I cannot show myself more worthy of the title of Citizen of the United States, which is become my adoptive Country, than by paying a just tribute to the Chief, whose principles and sentiments are calculated to procure them a duration equal to that of the Chinese Empire." M. L. E. Moreau de Saint-Mery, *An Authentic Account of the Embassy of the Dutch East-India Company, to the Court of the Emperor of China in the Years 1794 and 1795 . . . Containing a Description of Several Parts of the Chinese Empire, Unknown to Europeans; Taken from the Journal of André Everard Van Braam* (London: Lee and Hurst, 1798), 1:vi.

4. Charles H. Carpenter, "The Chinese Collection of A. E. van Braam Houck-geest," *Magazine Antiques* (February 1974), 338–40; and Moreau, 1:vii–xii.

5. Edward R. Barnsely, *History of China's Retreat: Paper Read by Edward R. Barnsley before the Bucks County Historical Society at Doylestown, Pa., May 6, 1933* (Bristol, Pa.: Bristol Printing Company, 1933), 6–7.

6. Moreau, 1:119, 132.

7. Moreau, 1:209.

8. Moreau, 1:xi–xii.

9. Moreau, 1:xi–xii.

10. Moreau, 1:91.

11. According to Stephen Greenblatt, one experiences wonder when the "shock of the unfamiliar" compels the mind to register simultaneously two incompatible reactions to a single stimulus: first, that the sight is so amazing that one cannot grant it credibility and, second, that the sight is witnessed firsthand and therefore must be trusted as real. In other words, a sense of wonder results when one cannot resolve the contradiction that something is at once "unbelievable and true." Stephen Greenblatt, *Marvelous Possessions: The Wonder of the New World* (Chicago: University of Chicago Press, 1991), 2, 20–21. Moreau, 1:121–23.

12. Moreau, 1:74–75, 110–11.

13. Moreau, 1:102.

14. Moreau, 1:179–80, 183, 187, 192.

15. Moreau, 1: 2, 8.

16. Moreau, 1:197, 219, 228.

17. Macartney did, however, kneel on one knee, bow his head, and present a gift to the emperor. James L. Hevia, *Cherishing Men from Afar: Qing Guest Ritual and the Macartney Embassy of 1793* (Durham: Duke University Press, 1995), 1. Moreau, 1:188–90, 223.

18. Moreau, 1:202.

19. In Pinyin, *poton* would be *bu dong*.

20. Moreau, 1:238–39, 247.

21. Moreau, 1:239.

22. Moreau, 2:298.

23. Barnsely, 7. Moreau, 2:320–22.

24. Houckgeest's methodology was common for this period. One finds the same tendency to collect and classify in Lord Macartney's 1793 embassy to Peking. Hevia, 84–90.

25. Moreau, 1:xii.

26. Barnsely, 7. Houckgeest's wife was the daughter of the governor of the Cape of Good Hope. William Davis, *History of Bucks County, Pennsylvania*, 1:96–97.

27. Philadelphia Gazette, 26 April 1796.

28. Moreau, xiii.

29. For information on China's Retreat, see the following: "China Retreat, Advertisement for Sale of" (28 July 1801), Historical Society of Pennsylvania; Barnsely, 10; Julian Ursyn Niemcewicz, *Under Their Vine and Fig Tree: Travels in America in*

1797–1799, 1805, with Some Further Account of Life in New Jersey, trans. and ed. Metchie J. E. Budka (Elizabeth, N.J.: Grassmann, 1965), 62–64.

30. Carpenter, 338.

31. Moreau, 2:324.

32. Moreau, 1:xiii.

33. Moreau, 1:xiii.

34. Moreau, 1:x–xiii, xxi, 202–3, 228.

35. Moreau, 1:204.

36. Specifically, Macartney sought the right to establish a diplomatic residence in Peking, the end of the restrictive trading system, and the privilege of conducting trade in ports other than Canton. All of these requests were denied. Spence, 122–23.

37. Moreau, 2:302.

38. Moreau, 1:xiii.

39. Moreau, 1:x.

40. Niemcewicz, 63.

41. Jonathan Spence, The Chan's Great Continent: China in Western Minds (New York: Norton, 1998), 25. In this study, Spence provides an historical overview of the West's view of China, beginning with Marco Polo and ending with Kafka and Borges. His American coverage, which does not overlap with this work, begins with depictions of Chinese immigrants in the second half of the nineteenth century.

42. Moreau, 1:192.

43. Moreau, 1:74–75, 246.

44. Moreau, 1:242–43.

45. Though generally in favor of international exchange, Houckgeest did see one possible drawback. The introduction of Western ideas and inventions into a non-Western society did not necessarily effect an overall improvement in the quality of life. After all, he asked, "are the people of the South Sea islands . . . more happy or more wretched, in consequence of their intercourse with Europeans for the last thirty or forty years? Alas! it is but too true, that we have given them a knowledge and desire of things which their country cannot produce. No doubt, the same cause would produce the same effect in China." Moreau, 1:244.

46. Carpenter, 340–41.

47. Niemcewicz, 62–64.

48. Ibid.

49. Carpenter, 340–41.

50. My search through Philadelphia's newspapers yielded no mention of Houckgeest's exhibit.

51. Moreau's statement seems to imply that Houckgeest did not include his collection of paintings in the temporary exhibit in Philadelphia. However, Moreau possibly meant that the pictures were so instructive as to merit, instead of the brief Chinese exhibit Houckgeest offered in Philadelphia, permanent display in a venue that would attract substantial numbers of visitors. Moreau, 1:xii.

52. Niemcewicz, 62–64.

## 2. ROMANTIC DOMESTICITY

## A Chinese World Invented at Home

Houckgeest enjoyed a rare opportunity to depart the confines of Canton, traverse the Chinese interior, behold new sights and even tread on the hallowed grounds of the emperor that were inside the walls of the Forbidden City. After returning to the United States, however, he squandered this rarest of chances to disseminate knowledge to the public. With his failure, our narrative returns to its dominant storyline—the Qing ordinance barring foreigners from traveling in China. Indeed, this ban acquires tremendous significance when we recall that it took place in an age otherwise known for exploration. In the early decades of the nineteenth century, merchants, missionaries, sea captains, and naturalists were all thwarted in their attempts to explore the interior of China. Thus, at a time when much of the world was opening up to Western eyes, China remained a sealed book.

When men of science proved unable to demystify China, they left behind not only a vacuum of empirical data but also an enticing opportunity. And a rather unlikely group took great delight in stepping into the gaping void. Women and children in Europe and America elected to fashion their own version of China by interacting creatively with sources of imagery that were readily available within their homes: Chinese paintings, porcelain plates, and the volumes of *Arabian Nights*. The China that they created was truly splendid, it being replete with bucolic landscapes, enchanting mountains, picturesque pagodas, bountiful fruit trees, graceful willow trees, exotic birds and fish, meandering streams, and charming wooden fishing junks. Of course, this idyllic land was not China but Cathay. At the smallest whim, women and children could embark on pleasurable excursions to Cathay simply by invoking the strange land in their imaginations [1].

These journeys of fanciful discovery coincided with, but existed in striking contrast to, the more-manly expeditions of scientific exploration. Whereas the latter required that one engage in extensive travel to distant climes, the former took place in the home and might involve nothing more than a trip to the cupboard. And whereas the cognitive tasks inherent in nautical, geographic, and ethnographic work demanded that one use his rational faculties, trips to Cathay required only that one possess a lively imagination. And finally, whereas the professional explorers transmitted their findings to the learned community through scientific tracts and ethnological exhibits, mothers employed entirely different media—playful rhymes and folk stories—to delineate the wonderful land of Cathay before their captive young auditors. In short, women and children seized the blank page of China and happily scrawled on it the imagined geography, topography, and ethnography of Cathay. In doing so, they mimicked in playful fashion the expeditions of scientific exploration then taking place in the men's sphere.

As women and children derived great pleasure from this form of domestic recreation, it is not surprising that Cathay achieved immense popularity in the United States, spreading easily and rapidly from one household to another and from one generation to the next. However, it is emphatically surprising that Cathay also enjoyed a strong measure of credibility. With only scant and unreliable data emanating out of China, many Americans apparently mistook the oriental dream world for the real Asian nation. This tendency of Americans to conflate the two becomes abundantly clear when one reads the reactions of sailors, merchants, travel writers, and diplomats arriving in Canton and confronting China for the first time. As this chapter will show, these worldly men often took what they saw and measured it against what they had expected to see— Cathay. When rational-minded mariners carry quaint images of an oriental paradise in their minds, we begin to understand the profound influence of simple trade objects, like common porcelain and mass-produced Chinese watercolors, and the enchanting stories that imaginative mothers told their young sons.

In this chapter I explain how ordinary people interacted with common household objects, and in that I depart from the typical study of Chinese trade articles, which focuses on luxury items belonging to wealthy Americans. Indeed, for this elite tier of society, objects from China arrived in a striking profusion of color and variety—exquisite porcelain, the finest silks, handsome lacquer ware, dazzling pieces of silver, hand-painted wallpaper, and sculptures carved meticulously from ivory and jade. The attractiveness of these objects notwithstanding, their steep price tags prohibited all but the wealthy few from enjoying them. Consequently, the images of China found on them reached only a small segment of society. Yet despite their modest influence over the American image of China, these finer objects have received considerable attention in books and articles because their age, beauty, and value render them sources of continuing interest for owners, collectors, and museums. In contrast, one finds comparatively little discussion on the more affordable commodities that truly did affect the popular imagination. To rectify this omission, this chapter is limited in scope, covering only those kinds of image-bearing goods that one would find in the typical American home: the inexpensive grades of porcelain and cheap Chinese watercolor paintings. We begin by examining a very common image, one delineated in blue and white, that many Americans encountered several times each day.

## CHINESE EXPORT PORCELAIN

In the 1780s, the English traveler Claude C. Robin during his tour of America observed that "there is not a single person to be found, who does not drink it [tea] out of China cups and saucers."[2] What Robin was witnessing was a sudden spread of Chinese blue and white porcelain that moved both horizontally across geographic regions and vertically through the social classes. Concerning the former, archeological digs, advertisements for auctions in newspapers, and manifests from vessels arriving in American ports all offer testimony to a tremendous proliferation of blue and white porcelain in domestic spaces across the eastern United States.[3]

As for the latter, two key developments contributed to the availability of inexpensive ceramics that Americans at almost any economic level could afford. First, though American traders carried the high grades of porcelain for their select clientele, they also loaded the compartments of their vessels with the commoner grades and even the misfires for very practical reasons. Cheap porcelain provided traders with an ideal cargo to place in the bottoms of ships because it did not suffer from prolonged exposure to moisture; by serving as a bulwark against the encroaching seawater, it protected the more valuable and perishable teas and silks placed on top of it. In addition, these ceramics were heavy and so provided good ballast for the long journey through turbulent seas.[4]

Second, starting in the 1780s, British porcelain manufacturers began to mass produce imitations of Chinese ceramics (with "willow ware" being the most famous example), which initially sold at lower prices than the genuine Chinese varieties. No longer possessing a monopoly, Chinese manufacturers responded with new measures designed to increase the efficiency of their production lines, enhance the appeal of their product, and cut the overall cost. At Jingde zhen, a city devoted entirely to porcelain production, the Chinese painted images on porcelain using a system of division of labor that possessed similarities with the modern assembly-line system. "One man traces the outline of a flower," wrote a foreign observer, "another of a pagoda, while a third is at work upon a river or a mountain" (fig. 2.1). To further simplify production, the Chinese reduced the number of patterns that embellished the pieces. By 1815, between 80 and 95 percent of all pieces bearing landscape views carried a pattern chosen from a select group of just three or four.[5]

Finally, to ensure that the pattern included in this small group appealed to Western tastes, the Chinese examined the British design that had recently appropriated such a substantial portion of their market share—the willow pattern. Though undoubtedly suspicious of its artistic merits, the Chinese nevertheless began offering wares with a similar, though not identical, design.[6] So in a bizarre sequence of events, Chinese porcelain painters now found themselves imitating a bad European imitation of original Chinese designs; as a result, much *authentic* Chinese export porcelain of this era, quite ironically, carried *ersatz* Chinese scenes.[7] Outraged by the sacrifice of aesthetics for marketability, the twentieth-century American porcelain expert Warren Cox described the ludicrous situation: "It got so complicated that the terrible 'willow pattern' sentimentally concocted from Chinese originals was sent back to China to copy. Such is the effrontery of merchants!"[8]

In this fashion, inexpensive Chinese porcelain found its way onto the cupboards of middle- and lower-income families. On a daily basis, fathers, mothers, and their children viewed appealing Chinese scenes on their plates, bowls, saucers, and cups, completely oblivious to the process of cross-fertilization with England that had brought about the formation of this tableware. And what they saw delighted them. Typically, a piece of Chinese-manufactured porcelain carried a landscape design referred to as *shan shui* (hills and streams) by the Chinese. Most such designs included a handful of basic elements: birds, fruit trees, a willow tree, a junk with a fisherman, a bridge, an island, Chinese figures, pagodas, and Chinese houses (fig. 2.2).[9] Although Americans may have purchased the china because it was cheap and functional, they cherished it for its designs.

Why did American families find such simple pictures so alluring? For the individual with an active imagination, these images possessed more than just ornamental value; they offered a portal to a different world, the world they called Cathay. While sipping tea, one could escape household chores, misbehaving children, debilitating illnesses, or the pressures of the workaday world and take a brief flight of fancy to a strange but wonderful realm. The land depicted was one of perpetual spring in which humanity lived in perfect harmony with the natural world. That nature was friendly, unthreatening, and, above all, giving: It bountifully provided fish from the river, gigantic fruit from trees, shade from the sun, and delightful pastoral views on which to gaze. In short, Cathay resembled an oriental Garden of Eden.

In addition, in most households, pieces of china were the only objects that possessed an origin one could classify as exotic. Therefore, people fondly associated their cups and saucers with the romance of swift-sailing vessels, epic voyages through storms and pirate-infested waters, and distant Canton, the great Far Eastern emporium known for its strange people, novel sights, beautiful views, and unusual smells. According to Alice Morse Earle, a late-nineteenth-century collector of porcelain, the residents of American port cities in the past had purchased their dishes and cups on the wharves, directly from the merchants who had recently weighed anchor. There they could watch "the strange picturesque foreign sailors, barefooted and earringed," removing the porcelain from crates with their "bronzed tattooed hands." Purchased in this fashion, the pieces seemed steeped in the mysterious and exotic cultures of the orient. That "old blue Canton [china]" she wrote, must have "savored to the fair buyers" of the "far-away lands and foreign sights" and "the magic and mystery of the sea."

Earle desired so passionately to feel connected to the people and customs of China that she learned enough of the Chinese written language to read the characters on her porcelain: "I too belonged to what is in China the ruling class, the literati." Finally, to while away the dull hours of the day, she invented narratives that explained the various elements in a porcelain design: "I have woven about it and halloed around it an *Arabian Nights* romance of astonishing plot and fancy." As Earle demonstrates, objects shipped from China often played a large role in the imaginative life of a creative individual. "Truly, we of to-day," Earle concluded, "have lost all the romance."[10]

# THE WILLOW PATTERN

Earle was not the first to create a fabulous oriental tale to accompany a picture fired onto a piece of porcelain. At some point around the dawn of the nineteenth century, a spurious Chinese story developed around the famous willow pattern, even though the only porcelain bearing this exact design had its origin in England, not China. After many years and numerous mishaps, British potters in the 1780s finally produced porcelain that had the same physical properties as did the Chinese varieties. Having met Chinese standards, manufacturers next faced the challenge of crafting the appearance of their wares so that these could not only survive but ultimately flourish in a marketplace that continued to embrace Canton china. Using the popular *shan shui* designs as models, English porcelain designers executed landscape scenes in the Chinese style and placed these patterns on bowls, plates, and cups through a mechanical process called transfer printing.[11]

Thomas Turner, working for the Caughley establishment in Shropshire in the 1780s, designed a precursor to willowware.[12] Though his creation resembled the pattern that would eventually conquer the Western world, it could not be strictly classified as authentic willow because it did not possess all of the four elements that would come to define willowware: a willow tree in the central position, three figures crossing a bridge away from the main building, a fence stretching across the foreground, and two birds hovering in the top center (fig. 2.3).[13] Thomas Minton, working for Josiah Spode's pottery manufactory, designed the actual prototype at some later point in the same decade.[14] Despite being the first to sell willowware, Spode did not remain the sole producer for long because, shortly after the pattern's inception, several other porcelain manufacturers obtained copies of it.[15] By the end of the 1780s, numerous porcelain factories were churning out willowware, much of it intended for the American market.[16]

The British-designed willow pattern pleased American consumers for mostly the same reason as the Chinese *shan shui* patterns. Still, with its production in England, willowware lacked one critical attribute that had contributed heavily to the success of its Chinese competitor: the mystique and romance that origin in a distant Far Eastern country could lend to an object? Compensating for this shortcoming, a pseudo-Chinese tale evolved around the non-Chinese willow pattern. This willow legend, like the pattern that inspired it, emerged as a Western attempt to capture a Chinese essence. Whether the legend arose on its own out of the popular imagination or was the result of an ingenious marketing scheme by a British potter, one cannot say for certain. Regardless, the story proved enormously popular in England and soon migrated across the Atlantic to the United States.

The most important feature of this legend, and what contributed to its contagious appeal, was that any piece of porcelain bearing the willow pattern provided the illustrations for the narrative. In an era in which illustrated storybooks were both expensive and rare, the willow legend allowed mothers of modest means to tell a story to their children at bedtime or during meals and even show illustrations. Since the legend mutated as it moved from person to person and from one culture to the next, several versions of the legend eventually came into existence. However, all tell a romantic tale of two star-crossed Chinese lovers—a mandarin's daughter and his lowly bookkeeper.

As the story goes, a powerful mandarin serves the emperor as the customs officer of a great seaport. His position allows him to acquire great wealth because smugglers repeatedly offer him bribes in order to avoid paying customs fees. When word of the mandarin's corruption begins to circulate, he removes himself from his post and retires to his mansion in the countryside, taking only his accumulated wealth, a bookkeeper named Chang, and his daughter, Koong-se. Fearing an official investigation, the mandarin orders Chang to square away his books so that they can bear scrutiny. Chang loyally executes this task, only to find himself summarily discharged by the mandarin upon its completion. However, prior to his dismissal, Chang and Koong-se fall in love.

Knowing that the mandarin would never approve of the union of his daughter with a lowly bookkeeper, the two young lovers meet surreptitiously every night beneath the fruit trees, which are included in the pattern. When the mandarin learns of these clandestine trysts, he confines Koong-se to a room overlooking the river and demands that a strong palisade (pictured on all specimens of willowware) be built all around the mansion grounds to keep Chang away from his daughter. Worst of all, he also makes arrangements for her to wed Ta-jin, a wealthy duke who is her equal in status but far more advanced in age. The wedding is to take place when the peach tree blossoms (pictured). Upon hearing the news of Koong-se's engagement, a despairing Chang realizes that he prefers death to a life without his beloved. To his lover across the river he floats a hollow coconut containing a note in which he vows to commit suicide when the buds on the peach tree open. Though greatly depressed, Chang also formulates a plan to steal Koong-se away.

One evening, Ta-jin arrives at the mansion bearing a box of jewels that he intends as a gift for his fiancée. That same night, Chang appears at the mandarin's doorstep disguised as a beggar seeking alms. Since Chinese custom requires the wealthy to treat the poor charitably, Chang gains entrance into the house and soon finds Koong-se in her room. Down in the main hall, the mandarin and Ta-jin enjoy an evening of entertainment, food, and wine. When the latter induces sleep, Chang seizes the box of jewels and quietly leads Koong-se out of the mansion. Unfortunately, as the lovers attempt to sneak past the mandarin, he awakens, raises the hue and cry, and proceeds to pursue them himself. The two lovers flee cross the bridge as the mandarin, holding a whip, follows closely behind (pictured). It must have been one of the earliest instances of what later became known as a chase scene.

The lovers find a fisherman with a junk (pictured) who is willing to convey them to a nearby island, where they promptly hide in a gardener's hut. The enraged duke, hoping to have Chang put to death for stealing both his fiancée and his jewels, deploys his spies to search the area. When the duke's soldiers arrive on the island, Chang and Koong-se escape onto a boat and sail to another island. To support themselves, they begin to sell off the jewels one by one. But as time passes, the two realize they are safe and begin to build a new life. Chang constructs a house (pictured) and brings the land to a profitable state of cultivation. He also writes a book on gardening, and it brings him a degree of fame. As for the duke, his desire for revenge continues to smolder in his heart. And so, when the literary reputation of Chang reveals his whereabouts, the duke dispatches his soldiers to the island. Chang valiantly resists their advances but is mortally wounded in the process. Greatly distraught, Koong-se flees into the house and lights it on fire with herself inside. At this point, the Chinese gods, who are watching the tragedy unfold from on high, decide to intervene; they place a curse on the vengeful duke and take pity on the unfortunate lovers. As is pictured in the pattern, they turn Chang and Koong-se into kissing doves just before they perish.[17]

With the willow legend, mothers captivated their juvenile audiences by projecting a narrative of love, danger, and adventure onto a make-believe Chinese landscape. And the tremendous popularity of this legend had the effect of creating a vogue for willowware. Since supply in England was able to keep pace with demand in the United States, cups, bowls, plates, and saucers bearing the design soon flooded American society. Ada Walker Camehl, who collected china around the dawn of the twentieth century, found plenty of willowware even out in rural areas of the United States.[18] To the porcelain connoisseur Warren Cox, the proliferation of willowware occurred to the detriment of good taste: "Nothing could better exemplify the utter dearth of aesthetic consciousness than the stupid copying of this design which lacks every element of true Chinese painting and any real claim to beauty whatsoever, and the maudlin stories wrought about it to please the sentimental old ladies of the late eighteenth century."[19]

The "maudlin stories" to which Cox referred are of course the willow legend in its myriad permutations. The story became such an integral part of American folklore that it even found its way into verse. In fact, along with the usual nursery rhymes, a poetical version of the story was commonly recited to children by their mothers:

*So she tells me a legend centuries old*
*Of a Mandarin rich in lands of gold,*
*Of Koong-Shee fair and Chang the good,*
*Who loved each other as lovers should.*
*How they hid in the gardener's hut a while,*
*Then fled away to the beautiful isle.*

*Though a cruel father pursued them there,*
*And would have killed the hopeless pair,*
*But kindly power, by pity stirred,*
*Changed each into a beautiful bird.*

Like any retelling of the willow legend, this poem was clearly designed to be repeated in the presence of a piece of willowware, because it points out the various elements in the pattern that correspond to specific moments in the story: "Here is the orange tree where they talked, / Here they are running away, / And over all at the top you see / The birds making love always."[20]

Henry Wadsworth Longfellow also fell under the magical spell of the willow pattern in his childhood years. However, he did not require the legend to fire his imagination, because the image by itself was sufficient to transport him to an imaginary world. The willow pattern that "we knew / In childhood," he wrote, enabled these "coarser household wares" to transcend their purely utilitarian function. With "its bridge of blue / Leading to unknown thoroughfares," the willow pattern offered a portal to an enchanted world where one could observe the "solitary man," the "white river," the "arches," and the "fantastic trees." So different, novel, and powerful, the willow pattern made an unmistakable impression on the imaginative Longfellow and others like him; it either "filled us with wonder and delight" or "haunted us in dreams at night."[21]

Another poem on the subject suggests that many people actually believed that both willowware and the romantic willow legend came from China, not England. And as the poem indicates, these mistaken origins played an integral role in transforming the dining experience in nineteenth-century America:

*My Willow ware plate has a story,*
*Pictorial, painted in blue,*
*From the land of the tea and the tea plant*
*And the little brown man with a queue.*
*Whatever the food you serve, daughter,*
*Romance enters into the feast,*
*If you only pay heed to the legend,*
*Of the old chinaware plate from the East.*[22]

Since the story sounded Chinese and the design looked Chinese, the willow pattern and the accompanying legend had the combined effect of masking the true origin of the porcelain—just as the English producers had hoped it would. Many Americans who believed that this spurious Chinese legend was authentic told it at the dinner table to imbue an otherwise quotidian meal with the romance and exoticism associated with China.[23] In this way, an ordinary meal could take on an ersatz Far Eastern splendor: "Romance enters into the feast." Since any revelation of willowware's true origin threatened to spoil the enjoyment, Americans tended to consider all blue-and-white porcelain as Chinese and could become testy when apprised of a piece's true English roots.[24] The willow pattern and the accompanying legend achieved such ubiquity in American life that one must consider their pervasive influence if seeking to understand how an idealized vision of China of permeated Americans' thinking in the early nineteenth century.

## WATERCOLORS ON PITH

Americans encountered porcelain far more than any other image-bearing commodity, but one other inexpensive trade article also offered scenes of Chinese life: export watercolors. Although many people mistakenly referred to these as "rice paintings," the actual surface was pith, an inexpensive vegetable-based paper that was light, brittle, and translucent.[25] Unlike the simplistic *blue-and-white shan shui* or willow patterns, these paintings were varied, detailed, and colorful. Executed by Chinese artists, they illustrated Chinese people, customs, ceremonies, plants and animals, trades and industries, and landscapes. Though serving no practical purpose, the paintings nonetheless found their way into many American homes because they were affordable enough to appeal to the individual who desired visual information on China but did not have deep pockets.

Chinese watercolors have a history dating back to the mid-eighteenth century, but it wasn't until the 1830s that they could be purchased in an American store. Before then, they were uncommon enough that a minister looking back on his childhood years in the 1820s recalled his intense fascination with one particular Chinese painting owned by a neighbor:

> Fifty years ago, when the humble parlors of frugal New England possessed but few pictures, and those of little artistic merit, we used to go to a neighbor's, and ask . . . that we might satisfy childish curiosity by gazing upon the portrait of a Chinese lady, done by a native artist in brightest reds and blues, and brought to this country by a sailor friend of the family who had voyaged to Canton. The little feet peeping out beneath the ample folds of the wide pantalets were objects of greatest interest. We were told that said feet were cramped to infantile dimensions by wearing, in infancy, an iron shoe.[26]

In addition to illustrating how starved people were for pictures (which explains some of their fixation on willow and *shan shui* designs), the above extract suggests that, to see a picture of this type, one had to know (or at least be not too many degrees of separation removed from) someone who had visited Canton. Unavailable on the American market, Chinese watercolors were something that traders, sailors, and missionaries brought home in limited quantities as gifts or souvenirs. In 1790, William Bentley, a pastor in Salem, wrote of a strikingly colorful "Image of a Mandarin" presented to him by a sea captain. The trader Robert Bennet Forbes returned from China bearing export watercolors for friends and family. Similarly, John Haskell carried home an album containing pictures of Chinese ships. And Hugh Brown, a missionary, purchased several sets of twelve paintings in Canton for about two dollars each.[27]

Rarities in the earliest decades of the nineteenth century, these paintings became common when merchants began to view them less as souvenirs and more as tradable commodities that could be shipped to the United States in bulk. In the early 1830s, Nathaniel and Frederick Carne began to import Chinese export watercolors to New York. According to one observer, when these paintings reached the American market "they took amazingly."[28] When other traders decided to follow the example of the Carne brothers, the Chinese responded by stepping up production. By 1848, Samuel Wells Williams, an American missionary in China, estimated that the industry employed two thousand to three thousand people.[29]

The most famous and prolific of all Chinese watercolor painters was known to foreigners as Tingqua, though his true name was Kwan Luen Chin. Tingqua was the brother of Lamqua, an accomplished Chinese painter in the Western style who had been the protégé of the English painter George Chinnery. The younger Tingqua chose watercolors as his medium in part out of familial deference to his brother, who worked primarily in oils. In Canton, Tingqua owned a studio where he directed a small stable of watercolorists. Though all paintings produced by this studio are attributed to Tingqua, many never received so much as a single brushstroke from the master painter. He would create original compositions, and his assistants would churn out as many reproductions as the market demanded.[30]

To produce copies quickly and effectively, many watercolor studios employed an operational system in which a sheet of pith paper would pass from one artist to the next, with each responsible for painting a particular element. A French observer visited a studio and described the process:

> Here it is that are painted those little silk covered albums which are sent to England and the United States and even to France. . . . There is no art in this. It is purely a mechanical operation, in which the system of division of labor is faithfully practiced. One painter makes trees all his life, another figures; this one draws feet and hands; that one houses . . . but none of them capable of undertaking an entire painting.[31]

Other studios implemented a transfer printing technique whereby the painter obtained a general outline by tracing a master design through the translucent pith paper and then proceeded to fill in between the lines with color.[32] In this way, the Chinese mass-produced watercolor paintings in much the same fashion as they did images on porcelain.

Though produced solely by Chinese hands, these watercolors bore the imprint of Western tastes. Osmond Tiffany, an American tourist who traveled to Canton in 1844, drew a line of distinction between traditional Chinese art and these export watercolors: "The painters are a numerous class in old and new China streets, and are certainly much better than I expected to find. I mean those artists who have learned to paint in the English style; though the genuine artists, who practice in the native fashion, are very good in their way." One can explain the radical differences between the two aesthetic styles by calling attention to the scientific purpose that these watercolors executed in "the English style" were originally intended to serve.[33]

The Chinese began producing these watercolors well before 1800, at a time when the Western world was awash in the ideals of the Enlightenment. For Westerners with scientific leanings, obtaining knowledge of China entailed the classification of everything found in China according to a strict taxonomy. In this spirit, Europeans communicated to the Chinese their desire to obtain pictorial information on the nation's human society as well as on its extensive flora and fauna. In short, they sought detailed and accurate paintings of any living thing that could be systematically assigned an appropriate place in the Great Chain of Being. To meet this demand, a new type of Chinese painter emerged who operated under what was to him a novel aesthetic, one centered more on realism and possessing none of the subtle or impressionistic qualities of traditional Chinese painting.[34]

With this new objective, Chinese watercolorists soon produced a tremendous corpus of paintings that bordered on the encyclopedic. Osmond Tiffany vouched for their comprehensiveness, saying they depicted "everything enacted in life."[35] Indeed, the paintings provided a pictorial version of the Great Chain of Being, or at least of those links that were indigenous to China. Like the museum of Charles Willson Peale in Philadelphia, where one could view much of creation displayed hierarchically, from the portraits of the founding fathers on down to preserved specimens of beetles, surviving Chinese watercolors show China represented from top to bottom, from the most august examples of human beings on down to insect and plant life.[36]

At the pinnacle rests the emperor himself, seated on the dragon throne, all decked out in his dazzling imperial robes. That he appears before a completely white background suggests he was as much a specimen for scientific inquiry as he was a subject for art (fig. 2.4). Proceeding down the Great Chain, one encounters mandarins and their wives, soldiers, tradespeople, and commoners. In addition to the various classes of human beings on offer from the watercolorists are various zoological, entomological, and botanical subjects: Chinese birds, fish, animals, insects, and flowers. As a further reflection of the scientific interests guiding this artwork, many of the species depicted are provided with Latin names used in the Linnaean system of nomenclature; the name Helubium speciosum, for example, accompanies the picture of a lotus flower.[37] Of course, since the Chinese did not employ the Linnaean system, Europeans and Americans necessarily provided these labels. In fact, Tingqua, upon completing a series, would typically present it to the American missionaries stationed in Canton, who would give each individual composition an appropriate title.[38]

In addition to covering China vertically along the Great Chain, watercolors moved laterally, offering illustrations of the various customs, trades, pastimes, and vices of the Chinese people. Americans could view depictions of a wedding ceremony, a funeral, methods of torture and punishment, sailing vessels, and gambling as well as the various stages involved in the preparation and consumption of opium (fig. 2.5). The artists also depicted the various stages of production in the four major industries of China—silk, rice, tea, and porcelain. Americans particularly coveted sets of watercolors treating the latter two items in that list. Nearly everyone purchased those goods, and so they were curious about the production process. Sets of thirteen paintings (one painting for each step of the process) were the norm, but a masterful composition by Tingqua compacted all stages of tea production into a single view (fig. 2.6).[39] Also popular were the panoramic views of Canton, the famous port from which all tea and porcelain had come (fig. 2.7).[40] These pictures came both in albums and in sets that included a brocaded silk frame with a glass front; with this display apparatus, one could rotate the paintings, perhaps featuring a different one each day (fig. 2.5).[41]

Despite the scientific impetus behind the creation of these paintings, modern scholars have challenged their verity. With respect to the scenes of China's major industries, Craig Clunas, an authority on these watercolors, has argued that the Westerner was not seeing "an accurate piece of reportage" because the artists themselves had probably never visited the locations they depicted. But since the artists did understand the tastes of their customers, the Westerner received his own glamorized preconceptions "reflected back at him by an artist whose sole concern was to please." In particular, the production of porcelain, for which thousands labored in "cramped and primitive workshops," cameacross in these pictures as a delightful cottage industry.[42] And with respect to the panoramic views of Canton, Carl Crossman has written that the landscape is always highly idealized—with clear sky, cottony clouds, and unpolluted water.[43] Concerned more with sales in a highly competitive market than with infallible realism, watercolorists understandably presented a version of China that would entice Westerners. Though not necessarily inaccurate, the paintings did depict a platonic ideal more than a geographic reality.

The idealized nature of these paintings, more than their scientific merit, explains their popularity with the general American public. In the aggregate, all these paintings may have amounted to a Great Chinese Chain of Being, but ordinary people encountered them in a disorganized or piecemeal fashion; they never viewed all of the works at one time arranged in the hierarchical manner prescribed by the Linnaean system. Even if they did, few possessed the scientific background to understand the importance of such an arrangement. Instead, the paintings, when hung on a wall or viewed in an album, were able to stimulate the interest of the beholder for a reason utterly divorced from their underpinnings in science: For families who already owned willowware or Canton china, they provided a more detailed look at Cathay.

## THE REAL CHINA?

Americans clearly enjoyed marveling at the Chinese scenes found on teacups and sheets of pith paper, but to what extent did they believe the world depicted on these commodities reflected the actual China? Were they able to draw a line of distinction between geographical reality and a charming picture on a commodity? Chinese watercolorists embellished their scenes with such subtlety that their works came to enjoy a reputation for unimpeachable accuracy. Osmond Tiffany asserted that actual scenes of Chinese life "all appear in perfect truth in these productions." So confident was Tiffany of their verity that he boldly proclaimed, "He who studies them has a better opportunity of seeing things as they actually exist in China, than if he stayed there ten years."[44] As for porcelain, one might assume that people knew better than to believe that these simplistic designs could reflect the actual landscapes of China. But if Americans did trust that these idyllic images were accurate, then they must also have believed that their vision of Cathay was accurate.

Surprisingly, compelling evidence suggests this was indeed the case. Brantz Mayer, a travel writer from Baltimore who visited Canton in 1827, held porcelain accountable for shaping perceptions of China. "Our general notions of the arts and civilization of the Empire," he observed, "were derived from . . . 'that world before perspective,'—a China plate."[45] In 1845, a writer for the *Boston Atlas* wrote that "our first ideas of China-dom were formed at meal times, and illustrated with *plates*."[46] Samuel Goodrich, the popular author of children's books for young readers, was so certain that children were using Canton china to imagine the country and its people that, in his *Manners and Customs of Nations* (1844), he introduced China by alluding to this commodity: "Everyone is familiar with their dress, personal appearance, and aspect of their houses, from the drawings in their porcelain."[47] Another children's book, *Peter Piper's Tales About China*, instructed young readers to examine Canton china for accurate information on China. "You may form a good idea of the manner in which the Chinese dress upon ordinary occasions," the author advised, "by noticing the figures which they delineate upon their tea-cups, and their other articles of porcelain."[48] As late as 1900, L. C. Meyer, an Englishman, helped his readers visualize the Chinese: "You have seen their pictures, for they often draw pictures of themselves on their china."[49]

With respect to willowware in particular, in 1843 a British writer attested to its instructive value: "The earliest record that we have of Chinese customs, is to be found in the willow pattern plate. From this it would appear that the Celestials are in the habit of fishing from the tops of bridges."[50] In 1887, Carter Harrison, the former mayor of Chicago, used the famous willow pattern to prove his point that frequent and repeated small events, such as the daily exposure to an image, can affect one's outlook: "Men's opinions [are] moulded, or at least colored, by the veriest trifles—colored into prejudices which require time and care to eradicate. He whose mother's treasured porcelain service was of the old blue willow pattern, has, more or less, his impressions of the Celestial Empire fashioned upon the model he studied upon the plates from which he ate."[51] Indeed, at the turn of the twentieth century, the travel literature of Thomas Cook and Son attempted to entice Americans to purchase a packaged tour of China by invoking their collective memory of the willow pattern: "Foochow [Fuzhou] at once reminds us . . . of the renowned 'Willow Pattern' which usually decorated the dinner plates."[52]

Owners of willowware and Canton china, then, apparently took quite seriously these small designs that we now deem unrealistic and purely ornamental. Our next step is to understand why they did. First, one must consider that these patterns first appeared in a historical period in which visual images in general were scarce. At the turn of the nineteenth century, printing technology had yet to achieve a high proficiency in the mechanical reproduction of pictures, so that newspapers were largely devoid of images. And lithography and photography, which would effectively democratize the visual image later in the century, had yet to be invented. As a result, pictures of any kind were hard to come by for those who could not afford paintings and books with engraved illustrations, and so Chinese landscapes on porcelain enjoyed a heightened currency for a brief period during which they received a great deal of attention from their curious owners.

Second, the spread of these objects coincided with a shortage of accessible information on China. In an effort to preserve stability by keeping the outside world at bay, the Qing government confined Westerners to the foreign factories, a small zone designated for international trade located on the waterfront just outside the city walls of Canton. Although this edict proved constraining, the lack of access did not mean that information was entirely unobtainable; in fact, several lengthy works by European authors were available to anyone with the money to buy them, the time to read them, and the education to understand them.[53] However, even those holding such a weighty tomes in their hands might not learn much from it because it forced the reader, in the words of the American trader William Wood, "to wade through such a mass of comparatively uninteresting matter, and tediousness of detail, that few choose to purchase their knowledge of China at the price of so much patient research." In 1830, Wood wrote a book on China partly because a truly accessible source for information on China had yet to appear.[54]

Third, although Americans lacked a trustworthy source for information on China, a literary work highly cherished during that era contained rich descriptions that seemed to corroborate the images on porcelain. Before the Civil War, one of the most common volumes found on American bookshelves was *Arabian Nights* (it also went by the title *The Thousand and One Nights*), a large collection of oral literature compiled over several centuries.[55] For any literate child, these volumes were almost standard reading. According to the preface to a children's edition of 1848, "the *Arabian Nights* are to our childhood what . . . the writings of Shakespeare are in after life."[56] Andrew Carnegie recalled the magical effect of *Arabian Nights* on his childhood imagination in the 1840s. "I was carried into a new world," he wrote. "I was in dreamland as I devoured those stories."[57] Though we in the present tend to think of the work as Middle Eastern, a couple of tales are actually set in China, a fact not overlooked by nineteenth-century readers. They knew, for example, that Aladdin, perhaps the best-known character in the entire work, was Chinese.[58] They also appeared to believe that the book, far from being pure fancy, imparted legitimate ethnographic information about Eastern cultures. Indeed, they were told as much in the introductions to some of the early editions: "The *Arabian Nights*," one translator proclaimed, "is more descriptive of the people, customs, and conduct of Eastern countries . . . than any existing work," and travelers to those parts have confirmed "the correctness and authenticity of this work."[59]

That China and *Arabian Nights* were melded together in the American imagination is supported by numerous references connecting the two. When Caroline Howard King visited the Chinese exhibits at the East India Marine Society in Salem in the 1830s, she described them as having "a touch of the dear old *Arabian Nights*."[60] In 1844, New Yorkers enjoyed a theatrical production called *Aladdin the Wonderful Lamp* that contained characters named Tongluck, Kein Long Fong Whang, and Widow Ching Mustapha.[61] In 1847, the Boston

Museum presented *The Grand Chinese Spectacle of Aladdin of the Wonderful Lamp*, a musical composed by the popular songwriter Thomas Comer.[62] When former president Ulysses S. Grant toured China in 1879, a member of his party described his surroundings as being "like a scene from the *'Arabian Nights.'*"[63] In sum, if trade objects offered an unrealistic view of China, the fantastical scenes from *Arabian Nights* only compounded the problem. Thus, when Alice Morse Earle invented "an *Arabian Nights* romance" to accompany the designs on her Canton china, she probably was not the only one to fuse these two unreliable sources of images into a single enchanting vision.[64]

Fourth, many Americans put credence in Cathay for the simple reason that they wanted to do so. As the imaginative musings of Alice Morse Earle, the poetry of Longfellow, and the popularity of the willow legend all attest, the vision of Cathay filled various psychological needs. Many people had a strong desire to escape their daily lives and enjoy a taste of the exotic, and now they were able to look to china bowls and plates to deliver just such an experience. Of course, the pleasure afforded by these small fantasies hinged on the absence of empirical evidence refuting the existence of Cathay. Since some Americans traveled to China regularly, one would expect their firsthand accounts to puncture the fiction of Cathay, once and for all. What did travelers to China report when they returned home?

## TRAVELERS WEIGH IN

Interestingly, Americans who visited China often made comparisons between the scenes before their eyes in Canton and the idyllic mental images formed by frequent exposure, during their childhood, to pictures on both porcelain and pith. Some travelers expressed disappointment at the failure of the real China to match dreamy Cathay, while in the opinion of others China satisfactorily met all expectations. Regardless, that so many referred to this comparison in their accounts offers testimony to the ability of these pictures to shape attitudes toward China and to etch deep and lasting impressions in the American psyche.

No less of a figure than Commodore Matthew Perry appears to have invested watercolors and blue-and-white china with a degree of credibility. Perry arrived in China in 1853 to use the area of Canton, Macao, and Hong Kong as a temporary Far Eastern station from which he would launch his expedition to Japan. When he gazed on Canton for the first time, the emotion he registered was one of supreme disappointment. According to Francis Hawks, who compiled the official account of the expedition using the commodore's notes and journals, Perry had brought to the experience an inflated idea of the beauty of China, and the actual place failed to match his expectations.

> He had imagined that it would be more striking to a stranger than in his case it proved to be. He expected to behold myriads of boats, decked with gay banners, and moving with cheerful activity in all directions. His fancy had sketched a pleasing picture of beautiful floating domiciles, moored under the banks of the river, and inhabited by a hundred thousand people in variegated costume; he recalled to memory the stories of the lofty pagodas lifting roof above roof, . . . *the snug cottages with the picturesque bridges and the comfortable Chinaman under the shade of a willow, with nothing to do but fish, all of which we have been accustomed to read, and pictures of which served to amuse us in our childhood. . . .* But the sketches of imaginative *boyhood* were . . . dispelled by the sober realities of maturer years. There was nothing of all this beautiful picture of crowded and happy life. There were, indeed, boats and people, pagodas and cottages, bridges and trees; but there were also filth and noise, poverty and misery, lying and roguery, and, in short, anything but a picture of quiet content and Arcadian simplicity. [Emphasis added.] [65]

During the years of his "imaginative boyhood," Perry had clearly constructed China as a bucolic paradise, and his trip to China in his adult years exposed these unrealistic hopes for what they were. That said, one must not overlook that all the elements Perry expected to see did indeed exist; unfortunately, their charm and beauty were spoiled by the presence of less desirable qualities—squalor, noise, penury, and mendaciousness.

But as for the sources that Perry had used to construct his idyllic vision, Hawkes unfortunately makes only a vague allusion to books and "pictures." These pictures very likely included the popular watercolor depictions of Canton that presented an idealized version of the harbor city (fig. 2.7). Indeed, they portrayed the great Chinese port as clean, colorful, happy, and lively—just as Perry had expected. Furthermore, Perry's references to bridges, cottages, pagodas, fishing, and a willow tree all strongly suggest the influence of blue-and-white porcelain china. That Perry would have such images stored in his memory should not come as a surprise. Having been raised in the coastal town of Newport, Rhode Island, he was almost certainly exposed both to Chinese watercolors and to porcelain on a regular basis. Since merchants, sea captains, and sailors regularly brought back views of Canton as souvenirs, the young and curious Perry would have viewed them one way or another. Of porcelain, too, he would have seen plenty, both in storefront displays and on his own dining room table.

Perry's case is most perplexing because, if anyone should have known better, it was the commodore. Though one can understand and forgive his faith in

Chinese watercolors, he was too intelligent, rational, and well-educated to be likely to take seriously the simplistic and unrealistic images on porcelain. More importantly, Perry was unlike most Americans of his time in that he had waded through many of the dull and lengthy books on China. Before his departure, he prepared himself for Asia by subjecting himself to a rigorous study regimen in which he pored over every source he could find on the Far East.[66] Yet somehow, despite this wealth of information, the blue-and-white image not only held its ground but was able to trump the knowledge he had acquired from serious scholarly sources.

However, Perry was not alone in endowing commodities with the power to shape preconceptions, as a log entry from an anonymous sailor approaching Canton indicates:

> I was as happy as any person ever was to see anything. I scarcely believed I was so fortunate as really to be in China. As we sailed up the river I would cast my eyes from side to side: the thoughts and ideas I had pictured in my mind of it were not lessened in brilliancy, rather increased: the immense number of buildings that extended as far as the eye could reach; their fantastic shapes and gaudy colors; their trees and flowers *so like their paintings*, and the myriads of floating vessels; and above all the fanciful dresses and gaudy colors of their clothes, all serve to fix the mind of the stranger, upon his first arrival. [Emphasis added.] [67]

Just as Perry had recalled "pictures" of China, this ebullient sailor refers to "paintings." Judging from his mention of the landscape, vegetation, architecture, sailing vessels, and attire of the people, one can assume that he too was alluding to watercolors on pith, in which such elements were common.

Like the anonymous sailor, the tourist Osmond Tiffany also compared the approach to Canton with what were probably albums of Chinese watercolors. "Now we entered the river proper and had a fair view of the Canton province," he wrote. "Presently we descried the unique and exclusively Chinese towers, the pagodas, such as we had seen in picture books; and we hailed them as old friends and familiar."[68] Like Perry, both the sailor and Tiffany treated these painted views as legitimate conveyors of geographic information. Unlike the commodore, they found to their great delight that reality in China actually conformed to their preconceptions.

Similarly, a sailor named Charles Tyng found that China fared well when compared to images he had seen on commodities. Tyng was only fourteen when, in 1815, he made his first approach to Canton on board the Cordelia, and he found the scenery so striking that he was able to recall it in vivid detail many decades later when he wrote his memoirs (published in 1878).

The scenery along the river, which is thickly settled, is exceedingly interesting, and to one like me, who never saw anything of the kind before, it was wonderful. We passed a pagoda of large size, seven stories high. It was about a mile from the banks of the river. *It is exactly of the same form as pictures* & models of pagodas which I had seen before. . . . The houses were curious, *similar in appearance as those seen on china plates, and other ware.* The country seemed crowded with inhabitants, young and old, all moving about like ants round an ant hill. [Emphasis added.]

The first sight of China must have been exhilarating for a young boy. Using pictures and porcelain as his frame of reference, Tyng could only attempt to comprehend the remarkable sight.[69]

These glowing first impressions notwithstanding, the negative opinion expressed by Perry appears to have been the more typical response of Americans viewing China for the first time. John Latimer of Delaware, a trader in the employ of Russell and Company, resided in Canton for long intervals between 1815 and 1831. He noted the potential of Chinese commodities to mislead. "Canton is seen to most advantage from a great distance," he wrote in 1821. "I mean you form a greater idea of the beauty of it *by viewing its products* than if you were to be here" [emphasis added]. During his prolonged tenure in Canton, Latimer met with enough new arrivals to the city to detect a repeated pattern of behavior: "I never knew a person who was not greatly disappointed on landing and finding everything so different from what he expected." Evidently, those who had never visited China before used images on commodities to form an imaginative construct that, they would late conclude, surpassed the actual place in beauty and charm.[70]

With so many traders sharing this experience, one would expect that word of their disenchantment with China would eventually reach the ears of Americans back home. After all, at the major eastern ports in the United States, ships bearing merchants returning from China arrived on a regular basis. They probably did not communicate their disappointment or disseminate a negative view of China, for three reasons. First, it was clearly not in the economic interests of the traders to puncture the idyllic vision. Since consumers associated Chinese trade articles with their country of origin, merchants knew profits could suffer if the American opinion of China darkened. For example, compare the above description of Commodore Perry's approach to Canton in 1853 with one that appeared the same year in a serialized adventure story set in China and published in P. T. Barnum's *Illustrated News:*

The blue river . . . softly descended to the sea, between two rows of pretty villages, which recalled those on porcelain plates. . . . Far in the distance the eye was lost amid mountains, blue and dreamy as the hues of the setting sun, or among endless collections of rice-fields and gardens. As night came on, all sank in its dark flood. 'China is a painted dream.' [Emphasis added.][71]

Writing for Barnum's paper, the author intended solely for his story to please and entertain; the readers, he knew, wanted to believe that the "porcelain plates" they owned depicted the Chinese landscape correctly. As a result, his description reflected not realities in China but rather the desires of Americans who would never travel there.[72] Merchants in the China trade, like the author of this story, understood these desires quite well and knew they contributed heavily to their commercial success. And so, even if a trader despised China, he simply lacked the economic incentive to broadcast his condemnation to the public.

Second, the merchants withheld their criticism of China because, in the decades before the Opium War, the aforementioned Qing edict prevented them from seeing much of the empire. Major Samuel Shaw, the first American consul in Canton, recorded in his journal that "Europeans, after a dozen years' residence, have not seen more than what the first month presented to view." The "few observations to be made at Canton cannot furnish us with sufficient data from which to form an accurate judgment."[73] John Sword, a disgruntled American trader, decried the small size of the area in which he was sequestered. He added with frustration that he could not give an account of a country he was prohibited from seeing.[74] John Latimer echoed these observations: "From this country it is impossible for me to write any thing descriptive that can be interesting, being debarred the privilege of going in to the Country and even into the city [Canton]. . . . Our business constantly occupies our attention." To ensure that visitors enjoyed at least one authentic Chinese experience during their stay in Canton, Latimer often treated them to expensive feasts served and eaten "in the Chinese style."[75] For Latimer and others, stringent governmental restrictions and their own all-consuming concentration on trade-related matters combined to eliminate almost any chance for a reliable description of China.

Latimer also remarked that, since his arrival, he had had "very little time to gratify my curiosity further than what I found in the stores where my business called me."[76] The stores to which he referred were the Chinese-owned shops that were located beside the foreign factories and that catered to European and American customers. Brantz Mayer, who visited China in 1827, became terribly bored because the Qing law had placed such severe restriction on his movement. Like Latimer, Mayer found himself depending on these stores to supply an educational experience. "Shopping is the only relief for idleness and ennui in Canton," he wrote, "and the daily lounge through such cool and picturesque streets is as entertaining as a museum."[77] Another American tourist, Osmond

Tiffany, also observed that the stores have "the appearance of a museum." And he found the shops that sold watercolors particularly edifying, because he rated displays of these watercolors more instructive than a ten-year residency in China.[78] Even young Charles Tyng described the stores using the term: "In the stores . . . there was everything that one had never seen before," he wrote. "It was like a museum."[79] Finally, B. L. Ball, a physician who toured Canton in 1848, wrote that one of the shops "seemed like a museum, and we streamed along . . . feasting our curious eyes."[80] The experiences of these five individuals suggest the supreme irony of the situation: Men who actually sojourned in China found themselves learning about the country from the local shops that displayed Chinese commodities, many of which were exported to, and therefore available in, the United States.

A third reason traders did not disabuse their countrymen of the idealized visions of China that were then in general circulation is that many of them had visited a real place in China that actually resembled a *shan shui* or willow pattern. While the foreign factories dominated the life of the merchant, one option did occasionally present itself to those eager to see another side of China. That was a trip to the pleasure gardens of the hong merchants. The Chinese government, not wanting to sully its hands in the daily transactions with foreigners, gave a small group of eight to thirteen men the privilege of brokering the entire foreign commerce of the empire. Though these hong merchants paid Peking dearly for this opportunity, they were often able to turn it into astounding profits.

Some hong merchants spent a portion of their personal fortunes building and maintaining luxurious pleasure gardens on Honam Island, located across the Pearl River from the foreign factories. These Chinese gardens were spectacular man-made environments composed of artificial mountains, exotic birds and fish, flowers of brilliant colors, willow and fruit trees, winding pathways, meandering streams, zigzagging bridges, and handsome pavilions. According to Maggie Keswick, who has written extensively on the subject, Chinese gardens possessed an "extraordinary magic" that gave the visitor the effect of being "transported to a fairy landscape quite unlike any other on earth."[81] To give his private gardens this magical quality, Houqua, the wealthiest of all the hong merchants, diverted $200,000 annually toward its upkeep.[82]

On occasion, a hong merchant would allow a group of foreign traders or travelers to enter his artificial world. Since these men knew of the reputation of these gardens and had grown bored by life in the foreign factories, they readily accepted such invitations when they came. Almost without exception, guests described the gardens not only in glowing terms but also using a vocabulary that could just as easily have applied to patterns on porcelain. Some even remarked specifically on the uncanny resemblance between the two. When Brantz Mayer received his invitation in 1827, he seized the chance to spend a day in the private gardens of Manhop:

> Passing . . . through a large circular gateway, we entered an extensive garden of flowers and shrubbery laid out in all the fanciful devices of the East. . . . On every side in the miniature vallies [sic], lakelets spread out filled with lilies . . . and swarming with gold fish that chased each other among the blossoms. Coquettish summer-houses of bamboo and cane, were twisted into every grotesque shape. . . . Light bridges, whose airy lines seemed spun of gossamer, were hung over the narrow streams . . . in this exquisite picture of Oriental fantasy and taste.[83]

Apparently aware that his descriptions defied believability, Mayer insisted on the truthfulness of his account and even gave his stamp of approval to a comparison he knew his readers wanted to make: "Fanciful and beautiful as this might seem to a reader who has never been in the East, yet we assure him, that *in China he would be forced to believe the glowing descriptions of the Arabian Nights are not drawn from the imagination*" [emphasis added].[84]

The *Arabian Nights* to which Mayer referred also contained a description of Chinese gardens. In one tale, "The Princess of China," the daughter of the emperor lives in the palaces of her father, who "has furnished them in the most sumptuous style." Each includes, as one of its most beautiful features, a garden: "Nor has he forgotten to embellish the gardens, which are attached to them, with everything, that can delight the senses; smooth lawns, or pastures enamelled with flowers; fountains, canals, cascades; groves thickly planted with trees, through which the rays of the sun never penetrate, and all differently disposed in each garden." As the story goes, the princess of China loves her palaces and gardens so much that she refuses all of the suitors who would wed her and take her away.[85]

Osmond Tiffany, too, saw China through the lens of *Arabian Nights*. "In the Arabian Tales the central flowery kingdom [China] is considered the land of enchantments," he wrote, and then proceeded to allude to the two tales set in China: "Though I did not fall in love with a princess of China, yet to my vision there were as many wonders displayed as were unveiled by the genie of the lamp of Aladdin."[86] Since Tiffany passed nearly all of his time in China observing life and commerce in the foreign factories, his trip to the legendary estate of the hong merchant Puntinqua almost certainly contributed heavily to his highly idealized view of the country.

Interestingly, at some point before this day trip, Tiffany had stopped into the chinaware shop of Cumchong, a Cantonese merchant. While perusing the displays of porcelain, he paused to examine the variety of Canton china that had been "exported in the millions of sets" to the United States and other Western countries. In describing the pattern, he noted the trees with leaves "like cherries" and the "three men passing over a triangular bridge," details that strongly suggest he was looking at Chinese-designed imitations of willowware. Later, when Tiffany beheld Puntinqua's pleasure garden, the pattern lingered in his memory:

> The house stood in the midst of the water, and was approached by bridges winding about in various directions, and guarded by balustrades as intricate and fantastic as the ivory carvings. There were bridges beginning every where, and ending in nothing at all. . . . Everything was queer, different from any thing we had ever before seen, and perfectly Chinese. *We thus learned that the extraordinary representations on porcelain . . . were not fictitious creations, but faithful realities. The bridge shaped like a truncated triangle on Chinese plates we actually saw. . . .* [Emphasis added.] [87]

Unlike Commodore Perry, Tiffany had visited a Chinese garden and therefore could report the existence of a place that corroborated the idyllic image on blue-and-white porcelain. Thanks largely to this experience, he left China with none of the disenchantment that would characterize Perry's reaction several years later. After all, he had seen Cathay with his own eyes.

Though diplomatic matters occupied the commodore during his stay in China, one member of his expedition found the time to embark on a tour before Perry's squadron embarked for Japan. In 1853, Bayard Taylor, the most celebrated travel writer in antebellum America (and the subject of chapter 8), was able to visit several of China's largest coastal cities because, after the Opium War, the Treaty of Nanjing (1842) made such excursions possible by opening up additional ports to foreign intercourse. In Shanghai, Taylor visited a famous "Tea Garden" and, to help his readers visualize the sight, he made reference to a familiar image. The garden resembled the "old-fashioned plates of blue Liverpool ware," Taylor wrote, alluding to one of the many producers of willowware, "with a representation of two Chinese houses, a willow tree, a bridge with three Chinamen walking over it, and two crows in the air." Though Taylor loathed China, he nevertheless considered a Chinese garden to be "a fair sample of what is most picturesque in Chinese life."[88]

Like the three travel writers—Mayer, Tiffany, and Taylor—traders also described the gardens as splendid, strange, and enchanting. Only the perennially glum John Sword could sound a dour note. Commenting on his visit to the gardens of Houqua, he criticized them as "arranged in very bad taste"and referred to his host as a "miserable looking old wretch."[89] Sword excepted, the traders who visited Honam Island reached a consensus. Written accounts by

William Wood, Charles Manigault, Samuel Shaw, William C. Hunter, and Bryant Parrott Tilden, to name just a few, indicate that they all fell under the spell of Chinese gardens. Tilden even referred to his visit to the gardens of Paunkeiqua as "one of the most happy days of our lives." And on returning to the foreign factories at the end of the day, he was besieged by curious "yankees" who all wanted to know "where I had been, and what I had seen."[90]

Not surprisingly, later in the nineteenth century, when a few well-off Americans were fortunate enough to visit China, they arrived with the *shan shui* and willow patterns deeply ingrained in their memories. Walter Bole, who visited Canton in the 1860s, immediately drew the connection between Chinese gardens and porcelain when confronted with the former. Viewing the gardens at the Temple of Longevity, Boles wrote that "they reminded me forcibly of the old-fashioned wedgewood ware, known as the 'willow pattern.'"[91] As the century progressed, the relationship between Chinese gardens and the famous pattern changed; what had been viewed as a coincidental resemblance became direct causation in travelers' accounts. Francis Clark, a tourist in China in the 1890s, claimed that a specific garden in Canton had actually inspired the ubiquitous willow pattern:

> Let us go into the Guild Hall of the tea merchants. . . . [W]e are especially interested in a little garden behind the Guild Hall, for, *from this garden the famous willow pattern was copied, which is found upon the blue china ware of our grandmothers and great-grandmothers.* The original tree which gave it its name has died, but the other features are the same which have been perpetuated so many scores of millions of times, on the plates and cups and saucers and teapots and teacups, which, in the olden time, were treasured by the mothers and handed down to the daughters with such scrupulous care. [Emphasis added.] [92]

Where did Clark get this notion? She got it from the Cantonese tour guide who organized and led her tour. "We were exceedingly fortunate, on our arrival at Canton, in finding the best guide it has ever been our good fortune to secure," Clark wrote. "Mr. Ah Cum, Jr., deserves to have his name embalmed in history."[93] Ah Cum Jr. belonged to an enterprising family that had dominated the sightseeing business in Canton since 1858 and would continue to do so well into the twentieth century. (The father and founder of the company, "Ah Cum" had taken Walter Boles around Canton three decades earlier.) [94] Quite possibly, the tour guides from this family had listened repeatedly over the years to tourists exclaiming that Chinese gardens bore a striking resemblance to the willow pattern, which they erroneously attributed to Chinese potters. After a while, the family perhaps decided to enhance their tours by making the false claim that a particular garden had served as the model for the famous pottery design. If so, tourists must have relished the opportunity to step inside a three-dimensional version of the famous pattern.[95]

Even if the Ah Cum family did perpetrate this rather benign hoax, the falsehood involved was minor. By tracing back the line of influence, one can see that Chinese gardens did in fact shape the willow pattern, albeit indirectly, through the intermediary of landscape painting. Though all experts on porcelain agree that the actual willow pattern sprang from the mind of an English pottery designer in the 1780s, this individual was clearly attempting to imitate the popular *shan shui* landscapes found on Canton china. The Chinese porcelain painters responsible for these designs had borrowed extensively from the long tradition of landscape painting in China; they employed the same artistic conventions and possessed the same view of man in relation to the natural world. Continuing the chain of influence, landscape painters in China historically played a large role in the development of Chinese gardens, as officials and wealthy men often hired landscape painters to design their private gardens. For these projects, the artists would implement the same art esthetic, conventions, and motifs that animated their paintings.[96]

Nearly all Chinese, rich and poor alike, dreamed of owning a garden that they could use either to entertain friends or to find a pocket of serenity in an otherwise chaotic world.[97] Constructing one, however, was no easy task; a Chinese garden required a tremendous amount of planning, skill, materials, and labor. One had to dig the grottoes; build hollow mountains; excavate lakes or ponds, fill them with water, and introduce varieties of colorful fish; construct various architectural elements including bridges, pavilions, winding paths, and kiosks; and import the recommended vegetation, such as chrysanthemums, peonies, orchids, lotus flowers, peach trees, plum trees, and bamboo. And of course, one could not forget the obligatory willow tree! Finally, one needed to erect the high walls that could block out the dust, noise, and confusion of the outside world.[98]

Even when the construction was complete, this interaction between the garden and the landscape painter did not cease. The finished garden might attract another painter, who would use it as inspiration for his own landscape painting. In this way, the three Chinese art forms—porcelain, paintings, and gardens—developed together and ultimately influenced the English porcelain industry. Painters designed gardens that became the subject of later landscape paintings; porcelain painters transferred these paintings onto a ceramic surface; finally, English potters studied Chinese wares in order to develop designs for their own ceramics. Ah Cum's family, it seems, had not really lied after all.[99]

Though American traders were probably unaware of the centuries-old cross-fertilization that resulted in *shan shui* and willow patterns, their visits to the private gardens of the hong merchants clearly affected their overall outlook on China. These luxurious properties were the only part of China—at least the only part not organized to handle international commerce—that traders saw with their own eyes. Probably, most of them knew better than to believe either that the gardens were microcosms of China itself or that the vast interior of the country resembled on a larger scale these marvelous cultivated landscapes. That said, a garden was no less true to American traders in the sense that they perceived it as being pristine Chinese culture, Chinese culture distilled to its purest essence—a bastion of oriental splendor that broke up the monotony of their purely mercantile existence in the foreign factories. In sum, American traders might not have punctured the exaggerated visions of Cathay held by their countrymen, because they saw only a tiny portion of China that was un-adulterated by contact with the West—and what they saw was truly spectacular. Or, to put it differently, if a potential customer in New York held up a china plate in the company of a merchant and inquired whether or not one could find such a scene in China, the merchant's answer was an emphatic Yes.

# CONCLUSION

Through their interactions with porcelain, Chinese watercolors, and *Arabian Nights*, ordinary Americans—predominantly mothers and housewives—developed an unrealistic construction of China as a pastoral oriental dreamland: the fantastical kingdom of Cathay. If a merchant in the China trade was observant, he could alight on a valuable insight into the psychology of his consumers: Chinese landscape scenes played a large role in the popularity of Canton china. Although people purchased these bowls, plates, and cups out of necessity, they treasured them because their origins in China imbued them with a romantic aura. In short, sales of both Canton china and willowware benefited from what we could call a "China effect."

But not all Chinese goods carried charming landscape scenes. And so the challenge to merchants was somehow to extend the China effect to a commodity such as tea that, since it carried no image, did not necessarily signify China in the popular imagination. In chapter 3, I explore how merchants used aggressive advertising and creative marketing to establish in the minds of consumers a mental association between China and tea—an association that has endured to the present day. And since this effort required merchants to paint a colorful portrait of their subject, they unwittingly made a major and lasting contribution to the American image of China.

## NOTES

1. Although the name *Cathay* can have different meanings, which depend on the context in which it is used, for our purposes it refers exclusively to the imaginary construction of China that was prevalent in Europe and the United States and that was legendary for its beauty, mystery, and exoticism.

2. Nancy Ellen Davis, "The American China Trade, 1784–1844: Products for the Middle Class" (Ph.D. diss., George Washington University, 1987), 114.

3. Davis, 67, 122. Ping Chia Kuo, "Canton and Salem: The Impact of Chinese Culture upon New England Life during the Post-Revolutionary Era," *New England Quarterly* 3 (1930): 431. In the early nineteenth century, a Boston or Salem dwelling might have as much as one tenth of its "effects" originating in China, and Philadelphia would not have fallen too far short of that figure. Jonathan Goldstein, *Philadelphia and the China Trade, 1682–1846: Commercial, Cultural, and Attitudinal Effects* (University Park: Pennsylvania State University Press, 1978), 6. In Charleston, South Carolina, Chinese export porcelain is one of the most commonly found ceramics at archeological sites, accounting for 24 percent of all ceramics uncovered. The majority of these are shards of the blue and white inexpensive dinner and tea wares. Robert A. Leath, "'After the Chinese Taste': Chinese Export Porcelain and Chinoiserie Design in Eighteenth-Century Charleston," *Historical Archaeology* 33, no. 3 (fall 1999): 50.

4. In 1815, Charles Tyng, a sailor with the *Cordelia*, explained the order used by the crew to load a cargo in Canton: "The first part of the cargo was boxes of china tea sets, dinner sets &c. These were placed in the bottom of the ship, being much heavier than the rest of the cargo. They answered for ballast. Then came the tea of various kinds." Charles Tyng, *Before the Wind: The Memoir of an American Sea Captain, 1808–1833,* ed. Susan Fels (New York: Viking Penguin, 1999), 36–37. Robert Copeland, *Spode's Willow Pattern and Other Designs after the Chinese* (New York: Rizzoli, 1980), 4; and David Quintner, *Willow! Solving the Mystery of Our Two-Hundred-Year Love Affair with the Willow Pattern* (Burnstown, Ontario: General Store Publishing House, 1997), 166.

5. C. Toogood Downing, *The Fan-qui in China, 1836–1837* (London: Henry Colburn, 1838), 2:98; Crosby Forbes, *Hills and Streams: Landscape Decoration on Chinese Export Blue and White Porcelain: A Loan Exhibition from the Collection of the China Trade Museum* (Washington, D.C.: International Exhibition Foundation, 1982), preface.

6. Crosby Forbes, preface.

7. Quintner, 168; and Ivor Noël Hume, *Pottery and Porcelain in Colonial Williamsburg's Archaeological Collections* (Williamsburg, Va.: Colonial Williamsburg, 1969), 40.

8. Warren Cox, *The Book of Pottery and Porcelain* (New York: L. Lee and Shepard; distributed by Crown, 1944), 611–12.

9. Crosby Forbes, preface.

10. Alice Morse Earle, *China Collecting in America* (New York: Scribner's Sons, 1892), 186–87, 191–93.

11. Whereas all Chinese ceramics were hand-painted, the British employed this mechanical technique. A design engraved on copper was printed onto a piece of tissue paper, which was then transferred onto the ceramic object. Crosby Forbes, preface; Davis, 119.

12. Copeland, 4.

13. Geoffrey Godden, "The Willow Pattern," *Antiques Collector* (June 1972): 148–50.

14. Copeland, 33.

15. It was a common practice both for potters to lend engravings to one another and for successful factories to purchase the master patterns belonging to potters who were selling their businesses. Copeland, 4.

16. As a sign of the increasing success of the British industry, Charles Tyng reported that in 1821 his ship used stones for ballast, whereas in 1815 the practice had been to use Chinese porcelain: "China ware was no longer shipped, the English ware having taken its place." Fels, 75.

17. Harry Barnard, *The Story of the Wedgwood Willow Pattern Plate* (Hanley, England: Catalogue Printers), 2–7. Josiah Wedgwood and Sons published this guide book to Wedgwood porcelain.

18. Ada Walker Camehl, *The Blue-China Book: Early American Scenes and History Pictured in the Pottery of the Time* (1916; reprint, New York: Dover, 1971), xxvii.

19. Cox, 768–69.

20. In this version of the story, the father, not the duke, finds the lovers on the island. Camehl, 287.

21. Longfellow composed "Kèramos" in 1877 and first published it in *Harper's*. *The Works of Henry Wadsworth Longfellow*, ed. Samuel Longfellow (Boston: Houghton, Mifflin, 1886), 3:231–32. Another American author, Nathaniel Hawthorne, viewed a porcelain "China tea-set" as strange but intriguing. In *The House of Seven Gables* (1851), he described it as "painted over with grotesque figures of man, bird, and beast, in as grotesque a landscape . . . a world of vivid brilliancy" ([Oxford: Oxford University Press, 1991], 76–77).

22. Quintner, 152.

23. Perhaps realizing that Americans preferred to think of the willow legend as of Chinese origin, the Buffalo China Company, the first American pottery company to produce willowware, misinformed potential customers in its 1905 catalog: "The legend illustrated by the Blue Willow ware decoration is centuries old. It originated in China and forms a love story so alive with human interest that it never grows old."

Quintner, 128. Similarly, Ada Walker Camehl wrote that what she believed was a Chinese story had inspired Thomas Minton to make the original willow pattern. Camehl, 287. Finally, Amy Carol Rand, in an article instructing women how to design table linen using the willow pattern, also wrote under the misconception that the pattern was Chinese in origin (*The Modern Priscilla* [July 1910], 4).

24. Earle, 181–82.

25. In Louisa May Alcott's *Eight Cousins; or, The Aunt-Hill* (1875), the protagonist, Rose, states that a Chinese man she meets "looked as if he had walked out of one of those rice paper landscapes on the wall" (Cleveland: World, 1948), 72.

26. Reverend E. Wentworth, "Celestial Women," *The Ladies' Repository* (August 1874), 136.

27. *The Diary of William Bentley, D.D., Pastor of the East Church, Salem, Massachusetts* (Salem: Essex Institute, 1905), 1:175; Margaret C. S. Christman, *Adventurous Pursuits: Americans and the China Trade* (Washington, D.C.: Smithsonian Institute Press, 1984), 113; and Haskell's album, doc. 7, Downs Collection, Winterthur Library; Hugh Brown, account book, 1844–45, Downs Collection, Winterthur Library.

28. Walter Barrett, *The Old Merchants of New York City* (New York: Carleton, 1863, 44.

29. Samuel Wells Williams, *The Middle Kingdom: : A Survey of the Geography, Government, Education, Social Life, Arts, Religion, &c., of the Chinese Empire and Its Inhabitants* (New York: Wiley and Putnam, 1848), 2:175.

30. For information on Tingqua, see *Chinese Repository* (May 1847), 209–10. In 1850, the *Frolic*, owned by Augustine Heard and Company, departed Canton for San Francisco with four cases of paintings from Tingqua's studio. The ship wrecked off the coast of California. Thomas Layton, *The Voyage of the "Frolic": New England Merchants in the Opium Trade* (Stanford: Stanford University Press, 1997), 134.

31. The French observer was named M. La Vollée. Quoted in Carl L. Crossman, *The Decorative Arts of the China Trade: Paintings, Furnishings, and Exotic Curiosities* (Woodbridge, Suffolk, England: Antique Collectors' Club, 1991), 200.

32. Downing, 98. See also John Warner, *Tingqua, Paintings from His Studio* (Hong Kong: Hong Kong Museum of Art, 1976), introduction.

33. Osmond Tiffany Jr., *The Canton Chinese; or, The American's Sojourn in the Celestial Empire* (Boston: James Monroe, 1849), 83–84.

34. The anonymous author of a book devoted to Chinese history made the following statement about the paintings' relationship to Western science: "Some native artists employed at Canton and Macao, by English naturalists, have delineated various specimens in botany and zoology scientifically" (*The People of China; or, A Summary of Chinese History* [Philadelphia: American Sunday-School Union, 1844], 164).

35. Tiffany, 83–85.

36. Two repositories for these fragile works are the Downs Collection at the Winterthur Library and the Asian Exports Department at the Peabody Essex Museum.

37. Collection 111 (14 boxes), Joseph Downs Collection of Manuscripts and Printed Ephemera, Winterthur Library.

38. *Chinese Repository* (May 1847), 209–10.

39. For all thirteen stages, see Crossman, appendix G.

40. Crossman, 183–84.

41. The Asian Exports Department at the Peabody Essex Museum owns several of these display apparatuses.

42. Craig Clunas, *Chinese Export Watercolours* (London: Victoria and Albert Museum, 1984), 25–29.

43. Crossman, 184.

44. Tiffany, 85.

45. Brantz Mayer, "China and the Chinese," *Southern Quarterly Review* 12, no. 23 (July 1847): 6.

46. *Boston Atlas* (15 September 1845). Quotation is cited in Ronald J. Zboray and Mary Saracino Zboray, "Between 'Crockery-dom' and Barnum: Boston's Chinese Museum, 1845–47," *American Quarterly* 56, no. 2 (June 2004): 272.

47. Samuel G. Goodrich, *Manners and Customs of Nations* (Boston: G. C. Rand, Wm. J. Reynolds, 1844), 343.

48. *Peter Piper's Tales about China* (Albany: R. H. Pease, n.d.), 4. The book is located in the Free Library of Philadelphia, Rare Books Division. Neither the author nor the date of publication is given. However, that it is a part of the series Peter Piper's New Lithographic Toy Books probably places it in the 1840s or 1850s, when lithographic images began to appear in children's books.

49. L. C. Meyer, *Far Off; or, Asia Described* (London: Longmans, Green, 1900), 87.

50. The writer apparently took the Mandarin's whip from the willow legend to be a fishing pole. *Punch's Guide to the Chinese Collection* (London: Punch Office, 1844).

51. Carter H. Harrison, *A Race with the Sun; or, A Sixteen Months' Tour from Chicago around the World* (New York: G. P. Putnam's Sons, 1889), 130.

52. "Information for Travelers Landing at Hong Kong," pamphlet (published by Thomas Cook and Son, n.d.), New York Public Library, Travel Pamphlets, BEI n.c. 1–4.

53. Jean-Baptiste Du Halde, Jean-Baptiste Grosier, George Staunton, and Sir John Barrow all wrote books on China that were published in this period.

54. William W. Wood, *Sketches of China: With Illustrations from Original Drawings* (Philadelphia: Carey and Lea, 1830), vi–vii.

55. According to Orville A. Roorbach, who compiled a record of every book published in the United States between 1820 and 1861, twelve editions of *Arabian Nights* appeared in this period. Roorbach, ed., *Bibliotheca Americana: Catalogue of American Publications, Including Reprints and Original Works, from 1820 to [January 1861]*, 4 vols. (New York: Peter Smith, 1939). Other editions were widely available before 1820, the first year covered by Roorbach. For instance, the Rare Books Division at the Free Library of Philadelphia owns five separate American editions of the book published before 1820, with the earliest dating back to 1794. The Free Library also owns several British editions that were probably sold in the United States. See also Holly Edwards, *Noble Dreams, Wicked Pleasures: Orientalism in America, 1870–1930* (Princeton: Princeton University Press, 2000), 170.

56. *Tales from the Arabian Nights' Entertainments, as Related by a Mother for the Amusement of Her Children* (New York: Edward Walker, 1848).

57. *The Autobiography of Andrew Carnegie*, ed. John C. Van Dyke (1920; reprint, Boston: Northeastern University Press, 1986), 25.

58. The tale begins with the following lines: "In the capital of one of the largest and richest provinces in the kingdom of China, there lived a tailor, whose name was Mustapha. . . . His son whom he called Aladdin, had been brought up in a very careless and idle manner." *Aladdin; or, The Wonderful Lamp* (London: Hardy, 1789), 1. Another well-known tale, "The Princess of China," is also set in China.

59. *The Arabian Nights*, trans. Edward Forster (London: W. Savage, 1810), 1:x. In the early nineteenth century, when the American publishing industry was in its infancy, the bookselling market was dominated by English publishers and distributors. This edition was published in England but was probably also sold in the United States.

60. Caroline Howard King, *When I Lived in Salem, 1822–1866* (Brattleboro, Vt.: Stephen Daye Press, 1937), 28–30; and Walter Muir Whitehill, *The East India Marine Society and the Peabody Museum of Salem: A Sesquicentennial History* (Salem, Mass.: Peabody Museum, 1949), 45–46.

61. George C. D. Odel, *Annals of the New York Stage* (New York: Columbia University Press, 1931).

62. T. Comer, *Favorite Melodies from the Grand Chinese Spectacle of Aladdin or the Wonderful Lamp; as Produced at the Boston Museum* (Boston: Prentiss and Clark, 1847). The book can be found in the Library of Congress, Performing Arts Reading Room.

63. John M. Keating, *With General Grant in the East* (Philadelphia: Lippincott, 1879), 188.

64. Earle, 193.

65. Francis L. Hawks, *Narrative of the Expedition of an American Squadron to the China Seas and Japan, Performed in the Years 1852, 1853, and 1854, under the Command of Commodore M.C. Perry, United States Navy* (Washington, D.C.: A. O. P. Nicholson, printer, 1856), 135.

66. William Heine, *With Perry to Japan: A Memoir*, trans. and ed. Frederic Trautman (Honolulu: University of Hawaii Press, 1990), 6.

67. Dorothy Hawes, "To the Farthest Gulf: Outline of the Old China Trade," *Essex Institute Historical Collections* 77 (April 1941): 120. Hawes does not cite the source for this first impression of Canton.

68. Tiffany, 40.

69. Tyng ascended rapidly through the ranks, becoming a captain, ship owner, and merchant. Though he possessed talent, his rise was aided by his family connections. He was related to James, Thomas, and Samuel Perkins, who were prominent merchants in the China trade. Tyng, *Before the Wind*, xiii–xiv, 14, 28–29.

70. Joan Kerr Facey Thill, "A Delawarean in the Celestial Empire: John Richardson Latimer and the China Trade" (master's thesis, University of Delaware, 1973), 51.

71. "English and Chinese," *Illustrated News* (21 May 1853), 322.

72. It was the positive view of the approach to Canton, not the negative one, that tended to filter into children's books, as is evident in the following passage from *Peter Parley's Tales about Asia*: "By and by we began to approach Canton. The banks of the river were beautifully cultivated; the plains, the slopes, and the very hills which hung over the water, were covered with many kinds of fruit, grain, and vegetable. The whole landscape . . . seemed like one extensive garden. . . . At first it all appeared to me a dream. The houses . . . were unlike any I had seen before. . . . The fashion of the boats was strange; the dress, complexion, and features of the people were all new." [Samuel G. Goodrich], *Peter Parley's Tales about Asia* (Philadelphia: Desilver Jr. and Thomas, 1833), 21–22.

73. *The Journals of Major Samuel Shaw, the First American Consul at Canton*, ed. Josiah Quincy (Taipei: Ch'eng-wen, 1968), 167–68, 178–179.

74. Davis, 243.

75. Thill, 34. Benajah Ticknor, *The Voyage of the Peacock: A Journal*, ed. Nan Powell Hodges (Ann Arbor: University of Michigan Press, 1991), 178.

76. Thill, 34–35.

77. Mayer, "China and the Chinese," 15.

78. Tiffany, 85, 90.

79. Tyng expected that the shopkeepers would become annoyed by his frequent visits, apparently because he was just a boy and unlikely to make a purchase. He was pleasantly surprised by their kindness; they would "take things down to show me" and even give him small knickknacks free of charge (*Before the Wind*, 34).

80. B. L. Ball, *Rambles in Eastern Asia, Including China and Manila, during Several Years' Residence* (Boston: James French, 1855), 121.

81. Maggie Keswick, *The Chinese Garden: History, Art, and Architecture* (New York: Rizzoli, 1978), 14–15.

82. Elma Loines, ed., *The China Trade Post-Bag of the Seth Low Family of Salem and New York* (Manchester, Maine: Falmouth Publishing House, 1953), 6.

83. Manhop later failed as a merchant and was exiled to the frontier region in the northwest of China. Mayer, "China and the Chinese," 18–19.

84. Brantz Mayer, *A Nation in a Nutshell* (1839), 24. The book is located in the Library of Congress, Department of Rare Books..

85. Forster, *Arabian Nights*, trans. Forster, 3:21.

86. Tiffany, 271.

87. Tiffany, 70–71, 166–67.

88. Bayard Taylor, *A Visit to India, China, and Japan, in the Year 1853* (New York: G. P. Putnam, 1859), 330.

89. Davis, 243.

90. Wood, 92–94; Jane Gaston Mahler, "Huguenots Adventuring in the Orient: Two Manigaults in China," *Transactions of the Huguenot Society of South Carolina* 76 (1971): 12; *Journals of Major Samuel Shaw*, 179; William C. Hunter, 40; and Lawrence Waters Jenkins, *Bryant Parrott Tilden of Salem, at a Chinese Dinner Party* (Princeton: Princeton University Press, 1944), 17, 23.

91. Walter Bole, "A Day in Canton," Appletons' Journal of Popular Literature, Science, and Art (23 July 1865), 108.

92. Francis E. Clark, *Our Journey around the World* (Hartford, Conn.: A. D. Worthington, 1894), 172. Clark was president of the United Society of the Christian Endeavor.

93. Clark, 164–65.

94. See the advertisement placed in *Cook's Tours*, a sightseeing guide published by Thomas Cook and Son: "The oldest Guides to the City of Canton are the AH CUM FAMILY who, for three generations since 1858, have conducted nearly all the Principal Visitors with perfect safety through the mazelike labyrinth of that most curious but fascinating City" (New York Public Library, Travel Pamphlets, B.E.I. n.c. 1–4). The guidebook is undated but probably appeared just after the turn of the century. Carter Harrison, who had just finished serving four terms as mayor of Chicago, embarked on a trip around the world. In Canton, he received a tour from Ah Cum. Harrison, 117–29. Also in 1894, George Raum, an American tourist, secured the services of the Cantonese tour guide (George Raum, *A Tour around the World* [New York: William S. Gottsberger, 1895], 368–72).

95. Even today, guides at a Chinese garden in Shanghai, reputed to have been in existence since the sixteenth century, make the same claim to tourists. Quintner, 126.

96. Julia B. Curtis, *Chinese Porcelains of the Seventeenth Century: Landscapes, Scholars' Motifs, and Narratives* (New York: China Institute Gallery, 1995), 20; and Osvald Sirén, *Gardens of China* (New York: Ronald Press, 1949), 3.

97. Lew Chew, a Chinese American businessman in New York, recounted a memory from his childhood in China in the mid-nineteenth century: "I worked on my father's farm till I was about sixteen years of age, when a man of our tribe came back from America and took ground as large as four city blocks and made a paradise of it. He put a large stone wall around and led some streams through and built a palace and summer house and about twenty other structures, with beautiful bridges over the streams and walks and roads. Trees and flowers, singing birds, water fowl and curious animals were within the walls. . . . The man had gone away from our village a poor boy. Now he returned with unlimited wealth, which he had obtained in the country of the American wizards." Hamilton Holt, *The Life Stories of Undistinguished Americans* (New York: Routledge, 1990), 183. This interview was originally published as "The Biography of a Chinaman" in the *Independent* (19 February 1903).

98. Sirén, 4, 10–14, 32–36, 42.

99. Keswick, 91, 101.

# 3. PURSUING THE CHINA EFFECT

## A Country Described Through Marketing

Every time the American trader William Wood returned to Philadelphia from China in the 1820s, he experienced "considerable annoyance at the multitude of questions," many of them "absurd," from the legions of "curious catechists." He found that a "romantic illusion" had enveloped China in the American mind and, much to his frustration, that people had decided to pester him to find out more about the wonderful yet mysterious country. To answer pre-emptively future barrages of questions, Wood wrote and illustrated *Sketches of China* (1830), which provided the uninitiated with a thorough but readable introduction to the country and its inhabitants. But Wood hoped his book would accomplish more than merely provide curious readers with a primer on Chinese civilization. He believed the American public's estimation of China was far too high, an overvaluation that he, like Houckgeest before him, attributed to the exceedingly positive accounts reported by Catholic missionaries centuries earlier. Wood claimed that his book delivered at last the hard truth on China, shattering once and for all the "romantic illusion."[1]

Although Wood was correct in identifying a "romantic illusion," he probably overestimated the role played by the Catholic missionaries in causing it. In fact, right beneath his nose, a contemporary source of positive images was operating that dwarfed the Catholic missionaries in mythmaking power: his own trade. Wood possessed many talents, but business acumen was not among them. He was famously unsuccessful as a merchant in the employ of Russell and Company, a large American trading firm.[2] Perhaps for this reason, he appears to have overlooked the important influence of his more prosperous peers who sold Chinese goods in the United States—tea, silks, porcelain, fans, lacquered furniture. Aggressive advertising campaigns designed to accentuate the intrinsic "Chineseness" of these products were employed by American merchants in an effort to move product off the shelves. With this strategy, merchants were able to entice consumers, promising them the opportunity to participate in an exotic Chinese experience and thereby escape the monotony of their daily lives.

In this chapter, I examine the marketing techniques employed by merchants occupied in two different areas of the China trade. First, Nathaniel and Frederick Carne, discussed briefly in the previous chapter, invented a novel advertising scheme—one perhaps better characterized as a promotional stunt—that involved the exhibition of an actual woman from China to open up an entirely new market for Chinese goods: the sale of non-necessities to middle-class customers. Second, tea merchants quietly released a steady stream of Chinese images into the marketplace to stimulate the consumption of their product. In both cases, the merchants not surprisingly constructed China and Chinese people in a way Americans would find appealing: The Chinese landscape was always enchantingly picturesque and Chinese people were always delightfully exotic. The advertisements were almost never mean-spirited, although the cost of that was that it had the effect of covering up some of the very real problems facing China, such as poverty, famine, and opium addiction.[3]

## THE CHINESE LADY

In 1830, Harriet Low, the niece of the China trader William Henry Low, strolled through the narrow streets of the foreign factories of Canton, in defiance of a Qing law forbidding the presence of Western women in China. Not surprisingly, she attracted quite a crowd of curious Chinese onlookers, most of whom had never before seen a Caucasian woman. In her journal, she commented on their behavior: "I think the Chinese are much more civil than either American or English people would have been if a Chinawoman with little feet had appeared in our streets, dressed in the costume of her country. Why, she would be mobbed and hooted at immediately!"[4] Four years later (and about fifteen years before the first Chinese gold prospectors reached California), Low's prediction was tested as a Chinese woman did appear in New York, and anyone willing to pay the price of admission could see her "little feet." Unlike other human beings put on display in antebellum America, the "Chinese Lady," as she was called, was not brought to the United States by a Barnumesque showman. Her story is interwoven in the larger tapestry of the commodity trade between the United States and China.[5]

Soon after the *Howard* returned to New York harbor from Canton in 1832, Nathaniel and Frederick Carne, the vessel's owners, placed the cargo of Chinese goods up for auction. The event was commonplace enough, but the Carne brothers were not China traders in the usual sense; in fact, the *Howard* represented one of their first forays into this market. They had previously specialized in imports from France, luxury goods intended for upper-class American consumers. However, a change in the economic climate had prompted the Carnes to toss their stake into the China trade. Before the Jacksonian era, the market for Chinese goods had only two tiers: luxury goods (along with fine teas) for wealthy Americans, and low grades of porcelain and cheaper teas for everyone else. However, starting in the 1830s, there began to emerge in the United States a middle class that possessed some disposable income, and efforts were made to coax its members into spending much of it.

Alert to this change in the economic landscape, the Carnes were among the first to detect the possibility for a third tier in the market for Chinese goods: fancy but affordable items for emerging middle-class consumers. As promising as this situation might have seemed, the brothers knew they could convert this untapped potential into profits only if two crucial assumptions proved correct. First, they assumed that middle-class Americans possessed a latent desire for non-necessities or fancy goods, a desire that would eventually conquer their deeply entrenched frugality and distaste for ostentation—so long as the new imports could be made affordable. Second, the Carnes assumed that, instead of importing expensive versions from France, as they had previously done, they could contract Chinese artisans to produce the fancy goods and thereby keep the prices low. Acting on the premise that the Chinese possessed a genius for imitation, the brothers sent samples of French luxury items to Canton and paid Chinese craftsmen to attempt replicas.[6] Satisfied with the results, they hired the Chinese to manufacture the same items in bulk. It was while working with the Chinese that the Carnes apparently also became enamored with genuine articles of Chinese finery. Convinced of the commercial potential of the latter, they had both kinds of goods shipped to New York.[7]

Since the auction catalog for the cargo of the *Howard* survives, we can view a list of the exact items the Carnes imported to New York. Absent from the catalog are many of the standard items that had come to characterize the China trade. One sees neither exquisite luxury items for the wealthy—such as fine porcelain, silver, and jade—nor the inexpensive ceramic wares used by lower-income American families. Instead, the catalog lists an assortment of goods that, though affordable, one would classify as fancy non-necessities: pongee handkerchiefs, crape shawls, colored window blinds, fireworks, silk boxes, lac-quered backgammon boards, ivory chessmen, snuff boxes, feather dusters, col-ored paper, walking canes, lacquered furniture, baskets, and a variety of fans.[8] With products such as these, the Carne brothers endeavored to fill the new niche in the consumer market.

Though one cannot say for certain how the cargo of the *Howard* fared in the marketplace, we do know that the arrival in 1834 of a similarly laden vessel, the *Thomas Dickinson*, coincided with an economic slump. As a result, the Carne brothers were unable to collect a high return on their investment. In addition to the sorts of commodities brought in on the *Howard*, the Carnes were now also importing silks and watercolor paintings by Chinese artists. According to Wal-ter Barrett, a clerk who later wrote a book about New York's merchants, the Chinese silk weavers had imitated European varieties "not only to perfection" but had actually "improved on the patterns." As for the paintings, Barrett re-ported that they came bound in silk albums, each containing about twelve pic-tures, and covered a wide array of Chinese subjects. The Carnes had invested a total of twelve dollars for one hundred of these albums and then sold each at auction for a single dollar, and so they were able to turn a "snug profit" on wa-tercolors despite their disappointment with the cargo as a whole.[9]

Undeterred by the market downturn and buoyed by the success of Chinese watercolors, the Carnes brothers became determined not to experience with their next cargo, to be conveyed by the *Washington*, a repeat of the *Thomas Dickinson's* troubles. Toward this end, they developed a novel marketing strat-egy which would both attract attention to their goods and lend them an exotic aura that consumers would find appealing. Although the Carnes probably hoped only to tempt consumers enough so that they would loosen their purse strings and go shopping, their promotional stunt ended up creating a sensation in New York.

When the *Washington* sailed into New York harbor on October 17, 1834, it immediately generated excitement in the city. The cargo included some tea and the expected assortment of fancy non-necessities that had become the Carnes' stock and trade.[10] But what made this ship's arrival extraordinary were the un-usual circumstances surrounding one of the passengers, who received mention in an announcement printed in the *New-York Daily Advertiser*:

> The ship Washington, Capt. Obear, has brought out a beautiful Chinese Lady, called *Juila Foochee ching-chang king*, daughter of *Hong wang-tzang tzee king*. As she will see all who are disposed to pay twenty five cents. She will no doubt have many admirers.[11]

A similar announcement in the New York Sun added that the father was "a distinguished citizen" of China who was "residing in the suburbs of Canton," a detail that, whether or not it was true, placed her among China's elite.[12] A short article in the New-York Commercial Advertiser printed her name as "Miss Ching-Chang-foo" and provided a detailed description of the practice of footbinding, which caused a Chinese woman "to twaddle about all her life."[13] The new arrival from China had yet to appear before the public, but already the press was beginning to circle around her.

From the time of the Washington's arrival, the Carne brothers required only three weeks to secure an exhibition hall (No. 8 Park Place); ornament it with appropriate objects, furnishings, and wall hangings; and have the Chinese Lady ready to entertain visitors. During this period, odd stories and rumors involving the Chinese Lady appeared in the newspapers. For example, the New York Journal of Commerce recounted what transpired when the Chinese Lady encountered a person sewing with her left hand. Having "never before seen a left-handed person," she gazed for some time "to comprehend the mystery" and then "burst into an immediate fit of laughter." Apparently the Chinese Lady aroused such curiosity that editors deemed newsworthy even the most trivial incident.[14] Other newspapers, however, printed stories that were more sensational in content, with one even claiming that the Chinese Lady had been reported missing. According to the Commercial Advertiser, guns fired during a political rally had frightened her into running away. In the same issue, the paper reported the rumor that she had been removed to Boston, presumably by the Carne brothers.[15] Such rumors evidently lacked validity, however, as preparations were well underway for the first day of her exhibition.

On November 6, when the first of many lengthy advertisements began to appear in city newspapers, two changes were apparent. In addition to doubling the price of admission to fifty cents, the Carnes had also requested that the Chinese Lady drop her longer Chinese name and adopt instead the moniker Afong Moy. The advertisements also offered the first physical description of her. She was nineteen years of age, four feet ten inches in height, "dressed in her national costume," and her feet were "but four inches in length," the result of her having worn "iron shoes" throughout her childhood. Starting on November 10, advertisements announced, the general public would be able to see Afong Moy from the hours of 10 a.m. to 2 p.m., and then again from 5 until 9.[16]

When that day arrived, the doors to No. 8 Park Place opened, allowing in a crowd of curious ticket holders. Included in this group was a reporter dispatched by the Commercial Advertiser to cover the unique event. He provided an account of his experience in a rather lengthy article that, when it appeared several days later, stood out in a newspaper that ordinarily dispensed the news in small capsules of pithy text. At ten o'clock, he wrote, Afong Moy emerged from her quarters and discovered that "a number of ladies and gentlemen were already occupying her drawing rooms." The reporter described Moy as a "princess" who "resembles a healthy, bouncing girl of 14." Her complexion was "tinged with copper" but "sufficiently transparent" to reveal that "roses are blooming" beneath her skin. In addition, she wore a costume befitting a lady "of her rank" and had evidently spent four to five hours at her toilette. Though he found her overall appearance prepossessing, her "little feet" provided by far "the most novel and interesting feature of her appearance."

The reporter then proceeded to offer a detailed account of the various activities undertaken by Afong Moy that were intended to show off this most remarkable physical feature. At first, her performance consisted of little more than sitting on a "throne of rich and costly materials" and displaying her feet by elevating them on a cushion before the intrigued spectators. As women in the audience approached her to take a closer look, the seated Moy would bow her head approvingly and smile. However, when males made similar advances towards her feet, she was less accommodating. "We saw on her brow," the reporter observed, "a frown of indignant rebuke." One "professional gentleman" in the audience, perhaps a doctor, harbored a deep desire to examine "the anatomical distortions of the foot." However, since the removal of the Chinese Lady's shoes apparently was not a part of the show and the rules of civility forbade this individual from even uttering his special request, his wishes went unmet.

Though Afong Moy did not speak English, visitors could communicate with her because she was joined in the room by her interpreter, a Chinese man named Atung. Audience members undoubtedly wondered about her life in China, the practice of footbinding, her long voyage to America, and her impressions of New York, and so it was questions along those lines that Atung most likely fielded and translated into the Cantonese dialect for Moy. In addition, Atung issued commands for Moy to follow. Every few minutes, he would speak a few words to her, after which she would rise from her chair and hobble with difficulty two or three times across the room before returning to her seat. A few more moments would pass, and Atung would repeat the same command. The sight of a woman so "disabled in her physical structure" inspired the reporter to pen a small diatribe against the "cruel process to which she has been subjected." Chinese women lived in "vassalage to the lords of the other sex," he wrote, who "tortured and deformed" their bodies and simultaneously kept their minds "in a state of ignorance." The reporter expressed his sincerest hopes that missionaries bringing the gospel into China could effect the emancipation of the country's female population.

This burst of indignant outrage aside, the reporter was, on the whole, pleased and intrigued by the novel spectacle he had witnessed. He concluded his article by writing that he did not need to write any more to "induce our citizens to attend." As it was, Afong Moy was already "receiving more calls every day, than any other young lady of our acquaintance," and the reporter doubted that the public's curiosity would be sated during her sojourn in the city.[17] Despite his endorsement, not all New Yorkers flocked to see the Chinese Lady. Some viewed the public display of a woman, regardless of her country of origin, as a case of blatant exploitation. The *New-York Mirror* published an editorial explaining why the magazine had elected not to cover the Chinese Lady in its pages: "We have not been to see Miss Afong Moy, the Chinese lady with the little feet; nor do we intend to perform that universal ceremony, unless we should find the notoriety which the non-performance must occasion inconveniently burdensome. . . . The lovely creatures were made for anything but to be stared at, for half a dollar a head."[18] That this editor bothered to print his justification for *not attending* the exhibition suggests it succeeded in sparking a tremendous amount of public interest.[19]

Indeed, for most Americans, the chance to see a Chinese woman with bound feet was too novel an experience to pass up. One can best understand the rarity she posed by recognizing that even foreigners residing in China around this time seldom set their eyes upon a Chinese woman from the upper class. "A Chinese lady I have never seen," wrote John Latimer, an American trader living in Canton. "They never walk, indeed I believe they cannot owing to the barbarous custom of confining the feet while young." Latimer added that a Chinese friend had promised him a pair of shoes, 3_ inches long, once worn by that man's wife.[20] Brantz Mayer, a travel writer who visited Canton in 1827, described the "well-born lady" in China as "a hot-house plant, grown under glass and watched as carefully as the choicest bud"; her "paleness" was a symptom of her "concealment" and "seclusion." At the time of writing, Mayer had successfully secured a pair of the greatly sought-after tiny shoes.[21] And according to Osmond Tiffany, foreigners' intense fascination with respect to this Chinese custom eventually reached the awareness of Chinese shopkeepers. Eager to profit from this curiosity, some of them began to sell clay models of "contracted feet, painted flesh color and set into shoes of the same size as those actually worn."[22] And so, quite ironically, while New Yorkers had access to a genuine Chinese lady with bound feet, Americans living in Canton settled for shoes placed on sculpted imitations formed from clay.

While the Carnes certainly profited off Afong Moy through ticket sales, the real gains were to be had elsewhere. The Carnes' entry into the China trade coincided with a fashion trend that favored articles of clothing or household objects decorated in the chinois fashion—Western in origin but modeled in a style perceived as Chinese. However, despite this fashion, most Americans were not in the habit of purchasing fancy items in stores; being both parsimonious and adept at household arts and crafts, they preferred to buy inexpensive items that they could embellish with ornaments themselves. In 1831, Godey's *Lady's Book*, a popular magazine that both reflected existing fads and initiated new ones, taught women how to decorate plain objects "in the Chinese style":

> A variety of articles, such as work-boxes and baskets, screens, and small ornamental tables, may be procured at the fancy shops, made of a beautiful white wood, quite plain, for the purpose of being ornamented, by ladies, in the Chinese style. The subjects generally represented are Chinese figures and landscapes . . . or grotesque ornaments. Patterns on paper . . . are also supplied at the same places.[23]

The article went on to explain how one could use tracing paper to transfer a desired pattern onto an object.

The Downs Collection at Winterthur Library owns a design book from this same period that had once belonged to an "H. Wrightson." Wrightson, who was probably a young woman, possessed an interest in the same Chinese styles that Godey's *Lady's Book* recommended. However, instead of purchasing "patterns on paper" in a shop, Wrightson drew Chinese scenes in her own hand and transferred them onto fabrics, wallets, screens, pouches, or boxes. Her design book is a valuable artifact not only because it provides evidence for the popularity of the Chinese style in this period but also because the sketches reveal the image of China lodged in the imagination of a young women (fig. 3.1). Though her drawings are understandably somewhat amateur, one can see that the pastoral ideal found on porcelain animates her Chinese scenes; she drew landscapes that were filled with flowers, butterflies, streams, fishermen, and Chinese architecture. It was as if she were attempting a close-up of the willow pattern in order to explore the figures, architecture, and vegetation it depicted only from afar.[24]

Wrightson was precisely the kind of person the Carnes brothers hoped to entice with their fancy Chinese imports. They gambled that she would put down her pen, her tracing paper, and her needle and thread and instead open her purse. Of course, their hopes hinged on an American middle class that would actually go against deeply ingrained mores of frugality to purchase non-necessities from China, most of which served a purely decorative purpose. It was in this area that the Carnes probably hoped Afong Moy would play a crucial role. They believed her public display would stimulate consumer desire in the early stage of this commercial experiment. She could help create a vogue for the exact commodities the Carnes were attempting to introduce into the marketplace.

Toward this end, Moy appeared not in a sterile environment but rather before an elaborate backdrop, as the advertisement states: "At the same place are also to be seen various objects of Chinese curiosity, in themselves well worthy of the attention of the curious."[25] As a surviving lithographic print indicates (fig.

3.2), she was snugly ensconced in an opulent setting of fancy Chinese articles—lanterns, mirrors, curtains, wall hangings, paintings, vases, lacquer furniture, and ornamental boxes. These were exactly the sort of items that the Carnes were concurrently putting up for sale. In sum, although the brothers presented New York with a *text*, Afong Moy, that was ostensibly ethnographic in nature, their not so subtle *context* was strictly commercial. New Yorkers not only witnessed an upper-class Chinese woman and her supposed possessions, but they also discovered that they could transport this desirable oriental elegance into their own homes—if they were willing to pay the price.

## THE TEA TRADE

Louisa May Alcott, best known as the author *Little Women*, also wrote *Eight Cousins* (1875), a novel set in New England, the heart of the China trade. The main character, Rose, has an uncle Alec who is a merchant in the trade. In one telling moment, Rose sums up succinctly all that she knows about China: "No one explained anything to us, so all I remember is that tea . . . come[s] from there, and the women have little bits of feet."[26] Thus far, we have examined how Afong Moy and her diminutive feet were used to sell Chinese goods to the emerging middle class. It remains to be seen how the importers and retailers of tea used images of China to sell their product.

Robert Waln, a former supercargo in Canton, commented in the 1820s that in the United States tea had joined the list of "necessities," achieving an "importance almost equivalent to that of bread." Nearly all families, "however humble their situation," enjoyed "this exhilarating beverage."[27] For Americans of all classes, tea had become a fixture in everyday life. And perhaps more than any other import, Americans came to associate tea with its country of origin—in this case, China. In 1850, several classes of New York public-school children, mostly between the ages of nine and thirteen, were asked to write their responses to a series of questions related to China. When asked what they knew about China, 27 of 34 students included tea in their answer. In another classroom, children were asked to write down what they knew about tea and coffee; here, all 19 associated tea with China. And when a third group was asked to describe China, 9 of 14 remarked that China was famous for tea.[28]

How did such a strong mental linkage between tea and China develop? One could point to several sources, but certainly the aggressive marketing campaigns launched by American tea sellers taught consumers to make this association. In the nineteenth century, advertisements for tea were ubiquitous, and they appeared in large numbers for a good reason: Taken collectively, they formed the tea merchants' response to two serious crises that threatened the industry.

First, even though tea had become a staple in nearly every American home, the tea market was seldom stable; instead, it earned a reputation as being competitive, highly speculative, impossible to forecast, and susceptible to dramatic fluctuations.[29] A change in any number of conditions could precipitate a lower market price than expected and, therefore, a loss of profits for those involved. For example, in 1790, American traders imported more than 2 million pounds of tea, when consumer demand hovered only around 1 million pounds. When the market went bust, all the merchants in the trade, desperate to unload their cargoes, flooded the newspapers with advertisements announcing the sale of fresh tea "just received."[30] A similar glut in 1807 caused tea prices to drop through the floor; varieties of tea that had cost 63 cents per pound in Canton sold for 55 cents in the United States.[31] And in 1826, a foolish maneuver by a single merchant brought spectacular losses for all who traded in this commodity. Thomas Smith attempted to take advantage of a U.S. government regulation that allowed importers to delay paying duties on tea for as long as eighteen months. He unwisely took all of the money he owed U.S. Customs and invested it in tea, which he promptly released on the market all at once. The market quickly became saturated, and prices plummeted. As the result of this bold but ill-advised scheme, numerous traders incurred heavy losses, and Smith himself went bankrupt.[32] Merchants came to view advertising as the answer; by stimulating demand when supply surged, it could help them cope with the vicissitudes of their trade.

Second, opium trafficking exerted indirect but constant pressure on merchants to sell more tea. For European and American merchants, the problem with the China trade had always been that, while their own countrymen demonstrated a strong demand for Chinese goods, Chinese consumers showed only a mild desire to purchase Western products and manufactures. This disparity compelled Western traders to purchase Chinese goods with silver, which resulted in a net flow of silver out of Europe and the United States and into the Chinese economy.[33] Looking to offset the trade imbalance and stem the flow of silver, the English began, in the late eighteenth century, to cultivate opium in India for sale on the Chinese market. In the decades that followed, the nefarious trade grew steadily until, by 1832, Chinese addicts were annually consuming 23,570 chests of opium brought by "country traders" licensed by the East India Company. The introduction of this narcotic effected a reversal in the flow of silver such that, instead of enjoying a net gain, China began to hemorrhage the precious metal.[34]

Some American merchants also conducted the morally reprehensible trade. Yet they discovered to their chagrin that opium failed to provide the economic panacea for which they had been looking. By leveling off the trade imbalance, it solved the most immediate problem, but at the same time it created a disastrous long-term problem. As American mills and factories became more efficient and productive by the middle of the nineteenth century, traders increasingly entertained high hopes of one day selling surplus American manufactures in China. But now that the Chinese were spending their silver on opium, they possessed nothing with which they could purchase other imports. According to the American trader Robert Bennet Forbes, the sale of opium ultimately placed undue stress on the tea trade. "It appears to us," he wrote, "that we must materially increase the consumption of tea . . . in this country [the United States], before we can expect to enlarge materially our trade to China." Forbes believed that, if Americans would only drink more tea, the Chinese could sell more of it and thereby generate "more ready cash" with which to purchase American "manufactured goods."[35]

Confronting a challenging economic environment, American merchants responded by aggressively marketing tea to consumers. And almost without exception, their advertising involved deployment of attractive images of China. Such a tactic may seem obvious today, but tea merchants and shopkeepers in the nineteenth century certainly had alternatives. For example, they might have demonstrated to consumers the salutary effects of drinking tea. Although Americans consumed tea in large quantities, no one knew for sure whether it would improve health or harm it. In fact, the effect of tea drinking appears to have been a contentious issue. On the positive side of the argument, the China trader Gideon Nye wrote a treatise in which noted its benefits. Tea drove off drowsiness, cleansed the body of impurities, promoted digestion, stimulated the renal glands, and curbed the intemperate individual's craving for alcohol.[36] Likewise, the Pekin Tea Company celebrated the virtues of tea in its advertising by calling attention to the exemplary health and vigor of the Chinese people. The *Guide to Tea Drinking*, a pamphlet printed and distributed by the company, pointed out that the beneficial properties of tea "may be seen alike in the admitted superiority of the Chinese in personal strength and capacity of enduring fatigue over the people of western climes." In addition, the Chinese had somehow avoided the ravages of influenza and cholera despite their large population. In the pamphlet, their mysterious resistance to disease was attributed to voluminous tea consumption: Some Chinese imbibed as many as one hundred cups of tea every day! The guidebook even went so far as to credit tea with producing the "politeness" and "manners" of the Chinese people.[37]

On the negative side, dissenters insisted that tea could pose a health risk, especially if consumed in large quantities. As if on a moral crusade, William Alcott, a physician and reformer, compiled as much evidence as he could find to argue against the widespread consumption of tea. In his book *Tea and Coffee*

(1839), he cited the laboratory experiments of a "Dr. Burdell" from New York who administered highly concentrated doses of the beverage to animals. Burdell found that a single drop of the potent liquid was enough to kill a yellow bird within a minute, and eight drops fed to a rabbit eventually yielded the same grim result: "In ten minutes it was dead. During the first three or four minutes, it was highly excited—exhilarated—it then lay down upon its side, moaning, as if suffering much pain, until it died. Its muscles were fixed, as in a spasmodic state." To Alcott, Burdell's findings could not have been more conclusive: "Now can any one receive these statements, and not find himself compelled to place tea on the same footing with other poisons?"[38]

Given the lack of consensus on this issue, tea companies might have channeled their advertising dollars into the effort to convince consumers of the positive effects to be enjoyed from tea drinking. That the vast majority opted instead to promote their product using images of China strongly suggests that their awareness that China, being distant, mysterious, idyllic, and exotic, occupied a special place in the American imagination. As such, it was the perfect destination for an escapist fantasy. Just as the Carne brothers understood that Afong Moy could stimulate consumption by starting a fad for things Chinese, so too did tea merchants realize that sales of their product would increase if Americans could be taught to perceive the daily tea-drinking ritual as a delightfully exotic Chinese experience.

To achieve this end, the merchants used advertising to disseminate a carefully constructed version of China designed to accelerate sales. As the goal was to encourage escapist fantasies, it was necessary that certain aspects of China be highlighted while others be suppressed entirely. Banished from the tea merchant's China was anything that might disturb the consumer or discourage flights of fancy—famine, blight, rebellion, xenophobia, poverty, opium addiction. In place of these arose a timeless and picturesque vision of the country that was free of turmoil: In a sylvan setting of pagoda-topped hills and charming tea fields, silk-clad merchants sip tea and direct the armies of happy workers as the latter blithely go about their business of preparing tea for export. In the place of reliable information, this sanitized and romanticized version of China acquired a high degree of credibility among Americans.

## PRINTED ADVERTISEMENTS

Before the advent of lithography in the 1830s, merchants relied primarily on metal print ornaments to replicate and disseminate a given image. Although the resulting black-and-white pictures were quite simple, even crude, by later standards, the print ornament nevertheless armed the merchant with a potent advertising tool, allowing him to use a picture at a time when visual images were scarce. In 1796, Binny and Ronaldson began producing metal ornaments in Philadelphia, and in 1809 the company issued the first American specimen book of print ornament types. Shortly thereafter, several foundries entered the business and produced specimen books of their own.[39] These trade catalogs offered anyone in need of a picture thousands of print ornaments from which to choose. The most common ornaments included farm animals, the American eagle, the Bible, a steamboat, a globe, George Washington, a ship at sea, a runaway slave with stick and bundle, the signs of the zodiac, and a mourner weeping beside a tomb. Ornaments designed specifically for tea merchants were also common, appearing in every specimen book.

Tea merchants who used print ornaments were operating under a single, fundamental principle: In a world dominated by the printed word, a picture would draw attention. Their print ornaments often depicted a crate of tea, a Chinese man, or a combination of the two; for further effect, some ornaments also included a background portrayal of a Chinese landscape complete with a pagoda. According to the missionary Samuel Wells Williams, pagodas were "so peculiar to China, that any views of that country are hardly complete without them."[40] A few ornaments depicted a trader selling the tea right on the wharf, with the tall ship that had presumably transported the tea stateside looming in the background (fig. 3.3).[41]

Newspapers provided one effective location for a picture printed with an ornament. Ranken's Tea Warehouse, for example, used an ornament that not only included nearly all of the usual elements but also provided a blank space for the company's name. The lavishly attired Chinese tea merchant in the picture directed the observer's attention to this convenient message board (fig. 3.4). Companies found for their ornaments other applications as well, such as on the company letterhead, on order forms for tea, and in advertisements placed in city directories (fig. 3.5). In short, the ornaments would have been ubiquitous as well as arresting. In an era dominated by text, these uncomplicated pictures proved to be an effective advertising tool for tea merchants.

With the advent of lithography in the 1840s, printed advertisements grew more sophisticated. Now a tea provider could either commission an artist to execute an attractive picture or adapt an existing painting by a Cantonese artist; next, he would use the lithographic technique to churn out hundreds or thousands of replicas. Merchants found lithography a particularly effective way to enhance the appearance of trade cards. Among the most common and potent advertising forms of the nineteenth century, the trade card combined an eye-catching picture with the name and address of a business. People enjoyed the pictures and so would pass the cards around to friends and even collect them for display at home.

Joseph Stiner and Co. of New York distributed a card that shows Chinese laborers loading tea crates onto the junks before an idyllic backdrop (fig. 3.6).[42] This sort of scene was quite common; a similar one was used by a Chinese immigrant who sold tea in the United States. Oong Ar-Showe of Boston offered a "View of Canton" in his trade card. In the foreground of the picture, laborers load tea crates onto a Chinese junk, the sail of which provides a convenient space for the company's name (fig. 3.7). In the background, pagodas embellish Canton's appealing cityscape.[43]

In printed advertising, the Great American Tea Company stood out as a particularly inventive company. In 1859, George Hartford took over his brother's tea business, which had consisted of driving a cart around what is now midtown Manhattan, peddling tea door to door. Hartford had the inspired idea to purchase an entire cargo of tea and sell it to people right on the dock for a modest markup. He succeeded for both an economic and a psychological reason. By eliminating middlemen, he could charge a price that was one third what the tea retailers were asking. Also, Hartford realized that, while standing on the wharf, surrounded by stacks of tea crates and tall ships, customers appreciated the *process* that brought tea all the way from the tea districts of China to American harbors. Purchasing tea straight off a ship appealed to consumers because this act connected them to the land that fascinated them.[44]

When Hartford moved his business off of the wharf and into a chain of stores, he held fast to this important principle: The pleasure involved in buying tea could be greatly enhanced if the customer could feel connected to China. Hartford employed several forms of advertising, but nearly all involved Chinese themes. His company issued several trade cards, including one that featured a Chinese laborer rushing several crates of tea to waiting vessels and using a wheelbarrow equipped with a sail (fig. 3.8). In the minds of Americans, wheelbarrows propelled by wind power had been a symbol of Chinese ingenuity since the late eighteenth century; Houckgeest had registered his astonishment on witnessing a fleet of these amazing devices.[45] On another card that was cut in the shape of a tea cup, a colorful Chinese tea merchant with flowing robes and a triangular hat points to the name of the company (fig. 3.9).[46]

Even more impressively, Great American published a monthly newspaper distributed free of charge at the company's several stores. If a rare surviving edition of the *Advocate* (June 1867) offers any indication, then the newspaper typically included tea prices, remarks on tea, poems about tea, and positive articles about Chinese people and their customs. Indeed, to promote tea by shining a flattering light on China appears to have been the paper's central function.

Thus, while sipping a cup of Great American tea, one could simultaneously learn about the beverage and its country of origin.[47]

Great American also used lithography to print posters that it displayed in its several tea stores, gave away free of charge, or posted in various locations around New York. One poster in particular consolidated into a single view all the different stages of the tea-production process: from the harvesting of tea in the fertile fields, to the packing of tea in crates inside the mammoth tea hong (warehouse and packing center), to the loading of the boats that would transport the tea crates to a waiting American vessel (fig. 3.10). Interestingly, this intriguing picture was not created by Great American; rather, the company adapted an already existing watercolor by the Chinese painter Tingqua (fig. 2.5). By comparing the lithographic advertisement with the original watercolor, one can see that, though Great American left the original largely unchanged, it did superimpose its slogans onto available blank spaces. And, for a final touch, the company inserted into the background the single most indispensable feature of the Chinese landscape—a pagoda.

The poster succeeded by doing more than just showing the grandeur of the tea industry. It involved the viewer. Through the tripartite division of space—the background of the print, the foreground, and the viewer's own surroundings—it adroitly brought the viewer into the tea-production process. In the background, visible through the gaping aperture, the viewer can see the pastoral paradise where the tea is grown, harvested, and ferried to the colossal tea hong. In the foreground, Chinese laborers pack the tea in crates, weigh it, and prepare it for shipping. The immediate surroundings of the viewer constitute the third space. While examining the print inside of a Great American store, the viewer may have initially felt oceans apart from the wonderful Chinese scene that had captured his attention. If so, the advertisement would bridge that gap with the following claim: "THE GREAT AMERICAN TEA COMPANY Sell ALL their Teas in Original Packages." From these words, the viewer learned that the tea crates he has observed in all Great American outlets were the same crates shown in the poster. And so, if he chose to shop at Great American, the tea he purchased could connect him to that bucolic, pagoda-decorated landscape that beckoned to him through the massive doors of the great tea hong.

The poster was effective also because Tingqua's depiction of the tea process brilliantly fused realism with subtle hints of idealism that were almost impossible to detect. In fact, by comparing the painting with the traveler Osmond Tiffany's firsthand account of his visit to a tea hong, one can see that the print was ostensibly faithful to reality in every detail:

> The hongs front upon the river, stretching back into the suburbs. Fancy a building twelve hundred feet long by . . . forty feet broad, and in some portions of it fifty feet

high. . . . These hongs are of one story, in some places open to the sky, and so long that at the end of one of them the human form diminishes, and we see beings engaged in occupation, and we hear no noise, for they steal along like shadows . . . through the high door beyond, we see the lively river and chop boat waiting, ready for the cargo.

The stacks of crates that Tingqua included in his watercolor were also common sights; Tiffany described one tea hong as "crammed almost to suffocation, with big square chests . . . piled up to the ceiling."[48] One encounters difficulty finding any inaccuracy in the painting (except for the obvious fact that tea fields and tea hongs were never located in close proximity to one another). The people are lifelike, all of the different jobs are represented, and the tea fields as well as the architecture of the various structures appear realistic.

Despite this apparent fidelity to the real-life China, Tingqua subtly injected idealism into his work. The Cantonese watercolorist produced paintings solely for foreign consumption; as a result, he tended to take into consideration what he understood to be Western desires.[49] Although he paid attention to the details in reproducing individual elements of his subject, he simultaneously cast a romantic glow over it. Banished from the scene were the grueling realities—sweat, disputes, injuries, low wages, poverty, and harsh working conditions—faced by the laborers working in one of the world's largest industries. Hard work is represented in the painting, but it hardly looks like the backbreaking toil it must have been. Traders who spent years in China knew better. The American trader John Murray Forbes offered a bleak assessment of the laborer's struggle for existence; China is a country, he wrote, "where the hardest labor of strong men barely earns food and clothes enough to sustain life."[50]

Also absent is the latent animosity that many of China's working class harbored toward foreigners. Robert Forbes (John Murray's father) recounted an instance from 1830 in which he and his party were beset by "a collection of very rough coolies . . . armed with bamboos and brickbats." A "general mêlée" ensued that left one American trader "streaming with blood from head to foot."[51] Such attacks were apparently so common that when Benjamin Ticknor, a U.S. naval surgeon, visited Canton in 1831, he hoped for and fully expected one to occur: "I was disappointed in not meeting with rough treatment from the Chinese; for I had been frequently told that foreigners rarely escaped abusive treatment."[52] But in the poster, the Chinese conduct their myriad tasks under agreeable conditions in a sylvan setting replete with verdant fields, delightful boats and sampans, quaint cottages, a pagoda, a river, hills, and clouds. As a result, viewers received an overall impression that tea was brought to market by contented workers in a Far Eastern agrarian utopia, and they judged this depiction to be true to life.

This Great American poster was not alone in subtly distorting reality. Nearly all the images discussed here, from the simple print ornaments to the more-sophisticated trade cards, romanticized their subjects to a degree. The Chinese laborers never seem disgruntled, fatigued, or exploited in any way. On the contrary, they come across as acquiescent, willing, even sprightly in performing their tasks. Instead of actual people, they become benevolent tea elves who live solely to cultivate this single crop and prepare it for export to the West. Were the beverage to go out of style, these laborers would quickly vanish into thin air, as if they had never existed. Although the advertisements could not be fairly characterized as pernicious, they did have the effect of transforming a living, breathing people into abstract symbols for the commodity they produced. And they covered up some of the real problems plaguing China, such as poverty, famine, rebellions, and opium trafficking. Nonetheless, as the aforementioned written responses of the New York schoolchildren demonstrate, China and Chinese people had become synonymous with tea.

## TEA-STORE DISPLAYS

Great American's lithographic poster succeeded because it involved the viewer, using tea to connect him to a distant and exotic land. The company employed the same strategy when designing its stores, taking care to employ Chinese motifs. The fronts and interiors were painted in Chinese vermilion flaked with gold. And since no Chinese setting could be complete without a pagoda, facsimiles of the distinctive Chinese tower were installed around cashier cages. In this way, by transforming the otherwise dull chore of purchasing tea into an exotic Oriental experience, the company hoped to entice customers to enter the store. Shopping at Great American became the next best thing to buying tea in China itself.[53]

Great American was not the first company to embellish its stores with Chinese elements. By the 1840s, it had become common practice among tea retailers to attract customers with elaborate interiors and storefront displays. Since some proprietors featured their store façades in printed advertisements that have survived, we can examine the arrangements they used. From the lithographic advertisements of J. C. Jenkins and Company and the Pekin Tea Company (figs. 3.11 and 3.12), we can recognize the display value of two types of objects: crates and statues.

Originally, Chinese crates had served only the practical purpose of providing merchants with a suitable container in which to transport tea. Tea arrived in

American stores in Chinese crates only because merchants believed that the process of unpacking tea and repackaging it in new containers would damage the fragile leaves. However, though originally implemented to ensure quality, this practice of shipping tea in the original Chinese crates presented merchants with an unanticipated advantage. From observing their customers, tea merchants realized the tremendous appeal of stacks of authentic Chinese crates on the tea-store floor. People seemed to harbor a curious fascination for these simple wooden boxes.

In response, tea merchants often wrote to their agents, captains, and supercargoes in Canton, insisting both that the tea remain in its original Chinese crates, chests, or boxes and that these be attractive. In 1799, Ebeneezer Townsend, supercargo of the Neptune, confirmed in his journal that the "fine teas are exported in the same chests that they are brought from the country in."[54] In 1815, Thomas Butler in New York issued the following instructions to William Law, his supercargo in Canton: "A great part of the tea . . . I wish you to procure in the smallest & handsomest packages, as well as whole chests."[55] Similarly, in 1819, associates of Russell and Company expressed this same desire in requesting that Samuel Russell, stationed in Canton, obtain teas of "good passable quality in handsome Chests or boxes."[56] And in 1832, Thomas Perkins, writing from Boston, issued Captain Dumaresq in Canton the following directive: "You will have all the . . . chests of your cargo kept in their original packages or in chests in which they were brought from the country, not unpacked in Canton."[57]

After receiving their cargoes of tea, companies back in the United States like J. C. Jenkins and Pekin Tea would display the original tea crates, as the lithographs show. What was it about Chinese tea crates that made them so intriguing to the public? Consumers enjoyed knowing that actual Chinese people had picked the tea and packed the crates; the crates made the tea seemed more authentically Chinese. It was for this reason that Great American advertised its tea as sold in "original packages," and Redding and Company of Boston assured customers that "a Native Chinaman superintends the packing" of all of the company's tea.[58] Customers regarded a tea crate as a genuine artifact from China, something that provided them with a material link to a distant and enchanting land. (Any merchant who removed the teas from their original containers severed this vital link; in doing so, he diminished the pleasure customers could derive from the shopping experience.)

Moreover, the physical appearance of the crates also attracted the eyes of customers. Constructed out of a cheap, unfinished wood and possessing little intrinsic value, most tea crates have long since disappeared. However, by examining the few that remain, we can see that they were not mere boxes with six blank sides. On the contrary, they often carried colorful emblems or pictures that symbolized their country of origin. Some crates had Chinese characters that, in China, had served the practical purpose of identifying the kind of tea as well as the supplier (fig. 3.13). But when the context changed, so too did the function of the characters. Once the crates were on display in the United States, where Americans found Chinese calligraphy indecipherable but interesting nevertheless, these once meaningful characters became exotic hieroglyphs that signified China itself.

If Chinese characters were not exotic enough, some tea retailers doctored tea crates intended for display, artificially heightening their "Chineseness." They accomplished this by pasting attractive picture labels onto the sides of the crates. One retailer papered a display crate with lithographic reproductions of export watercolors originally executed by Chinese painters in Canton (fig. 3.14). Since each side presented a different stage of the tea-production process, the curious customer needed only to rotate the crate to understand how tea was planted, picked, prepared, and packed for export.[59]

Another retailer went further. Onto genuine Chinese tea crates, he affixed ersatz Chinese scenes depicting the lifestyle of a wealthy Cantonese merchant. In one view, the latter is sipping tea in his ornate robes before a background of hills, birds, tropical trees, and a pagoda (fig. 3.15); in another view, which is set in his garden, his adoring wife hands him a blossom. These labels are intended to appear Chinese, but we know they are spurious because bogus Chinese calligraphy adorns the gold border that frames the scene. Although resembling written Chinese, the characters are completely nonsensical to anyone who can read the language. Clearly, retailers believed that picturesque crates could draw potential customers into the store.

With tea crates on display, Americans took notice. Evidence suggests that people studied tea crates, seeing them as legitimate conveyors of ethnographical and topographical information. Brantz Mayer wrote that the simple tea crate was, astonishingly, one of the objects through which "this *enlightened* age has been . . . making its opinion of the Chinese nation!"[60] In D. P. Kidder's children's book *The Chinese; or, Conversations on the Country and People of China* (1846), a character acknowledges that he inspects tea chests: "When I see Chinese figures on tea-chests, they have almost always fans or umbrellas in their hands; and then there are sure to be two or three temples at no great distance." The "temples" to which he refers are almost certainly pagodas.[61] Another children's book, *Peter Piper's Tales about China*, instructed young readers to examine tea chests for accurate information on China. "You may form a good idea of the manner in which the Chinese dress upon ordinary occasions," the author advised, "by noticing the figures which they delineate upon their . . . tea-chests."[62] The narrator in *Uncle Oliver's Books for Children* described the crates as "all marked over with strange looking characters" that are as comprehensible to the Chinese as "A, B, C" are to "our people." "If you have never seen one of these boxes," he advised young readers, "if you ask Mr. Smith to let you look at one, the next time you go to his store, he will show you all about it."[63] Clearly, Americans regarded tea crates as artifacts of an exotic nation whose image-bearing sides left indelible images in their minds.

Along with crates, statues also captured the attention of potential customers who passed by a tea store. Like the wooden Indian once positioned outside to-bacco stores, the Chinese statue provided the public with an attractive and eas-ily recognizable symbol for tea. Though once a common feature in American commercial districts, nearly all statues have vanished over time. Fortunately, a surviving pair owned by the Henry Ford Museum allows us to see how they looked (fig. 3.16).

According to the lithographic print of J. C. Jenkins and Company, the statue belonging to this company depicted a laborer in his characteristic posi-tion: carrying two chests of tea by balancing a bamboo pole across his shoul-ders. In the print, the Lincolnesque gentleman wearing the stovepipe hat strikes a pose of fascination; from his example, anyone viewing the print knew that the statue was an attraction worth seeing. The Pekin Tea Company ap-pears to have included several statues, at least five, in its display (a tall one perched outside the second floor of the building and four smaller ones that seem to peer out the windows). In contrast to J. C. Jenkins's tea laborer, these statues represented Chinese from the upper crust, with their flowing garments indicating their higher status. In this way, they probably resembled the statues owned by the Henry Ford Museum. Like the print of J. C. Jenkins, this litho-graph also includes fascinated pedestrians who are attracted to the store by the displays.

For another tea distributor, statues played a major role in its aggressive adver-tising campaign. Redding and Company of Boston promoted its statues as spectacles that were worthy of the public's interest and that the competition could not match. People might come to see the statues and, once inside the store they would, the company hoped, also purchase tea. To increase public awareness of the attraction, Redding and Company issued a trade card that car-ried a picture of one of the statues (fig. 3.17) and provided the following infor-mation about it:

> The above engraving is by Hammatt Billings, Esq., and is taken from a statue of a Chinaman, of half life size, modeled by Ball Hughes, Esq., *from an original done in China*. Duplicates of this statue are to be seen at the Branch Tea Stores of RED-DING & CO., at No. 78 Hanover Street, and No. 43 Beach Street. . . . These are COLORED; but the first copy, in STONE, may be seen at the Principal Tea Store, No. 198 Washington Street. The object of these statues is to adorn and desig-nate these well-known Tea Depots, and at the same time to protect the public from

imposition in cases where the style of Redding & Co.'s Stores, and their Signs, are used. [Emphasis added.][64]

Just as Great American modified a watercolor by Tingqua for its posters, so too did Redding and Company replicate an original Chinese statue to suit its marketing needs. It apparently purchased the prototype from a Chinese sculptor and then had copies made for display in its several stores. In addition, the company also claimed that, by providing consumers with a fail-safe method for identifying the genuine stores, its prominently displayed statues protected the public from being deceived by imitators. Regardless of whether impostors actually existed, the company probably did feature the statues in its advertising to help consumers distinguish Redding and Company from the competition.[65]

## HUMAN DISPLAYS IN TEA STORES

However, as the number of these statues increased, their usefulness in helping one tea shop stand out from the competition declined. The more shops that could boast of a statue, the less special or remarkable each statue became. Realizing that statues alone did not suffice, Redding and Company in the 1840s actually brought over from Canton "a Native Chinaman" named Achowe and gave him the responsibility of overseeing the packing of all teas. Of course, the presence of a living, breathing native of China enhanced the pleasurable illusion that shopping for tea was an exotic experience—the next best thing to an actual trip to China. For this reason, the company made Achowe very visible; an advertisement placed in the *Boston Post* announced that he "will be happy to have his friends call on him."[66]

Although Redding and Company probably hired Achowe as a marketing ploy, he did at least have real experience working in China's tea industry (if we are to believe the advertisement) and did perform necessary services for the company. And since very few Chinese people lived in the United States in the 1840s, Redding and Company's competitors must have regarded the hiring of a Cantonese man as a marketing coup not unlike the Carne brothers' exhibition of Afong Moy in 1834. But over the course of the next quarter century, the ripples from a large-scale demographic shift would alter the face of tea advertising forever.

In the 1850s, Chinese immigrants began to arrive on the West Coast in large numbers, seeking either gold or opportunities for gainful employment.

Some later migrated to eastern cities, and by 1870 New York possessed a size-able population of Chinese people seeking work. Any tea-store proprietor who was observant quickly realized that, for a small amount of money, he could hire a Chinese man not to supervise the packing of tea, as Achowe had done, but rather to do little more than stand in front of the entrance in an exotic costume. Such an individual was paid solely to pose; he was a human statue.

In 1870, Mark Twain published in the *Galaxy* a letter sent to him by a cor-respondent who had observed this new phenomenon:

> As I passed along by one of those monster American tea stores in New York, I found a Chinaman sitting before it acting in the capacity of a sign. Everybody that passed by gave him a steady stare as long as their heads would twist over their shoulders without dislocating their necks, and a large group stopped to stare deliberately.[67]

Though the pedestrians' reaction indicates that the owner's strategy was having the desired effect, Twain's correspondent took umbrage at the exploi-tation of a fellow human being for mere commercial purposes: "Is it not a shame that we who prate so much about civilization and humanity are con-tent to degrade a fellow-being to such an office as this?" Although he cen-sured the passing crowds for their shameful displays of curiosity, his detailed description of the human statue indicates that he too had taken a good long look: "Men calling themselves the superior race, the race of culture and of gentle blood, scanned his quaint Chinese hat, with peaked roof and ball on top; his long queue dangling down his back; his short silken blouse, curiously frogged and figured . . . and his clumsy, blunt-toed shoes with thick cork soles."

Interestingly, the correspondent also described the Chinese man's attire as "outlandish" as well as "dilapidated, and awkwardly put on," descriptors that suggest the outfit was not only strange and exotic in the minds of pedestrians but was unnatural for the wearer himself. Furthermore, at the end of the letter, where the Chinese man is quoted, he actually gripes that his employer required that he purchase the garments himself ("the bloody furrin clothes that's so ex-pinsive"). From these two points, we can establish that the Chinese man was not wearing his usual clothes but instead had on some kind of costume. His costume is important because it tells us that, in the mind of his employer, his being Chinese was not enough in the same sense that often a tea crate's origin in China was not enough—ersatz Chinese labels had to be affixed. For if the man's race had been all that mattered, the owner would have allowed him to pose in his ordinary clothes.

Instead, the job required that the Chinese man don a costume so that he could appear as *a specific kind of Chinese man.* More than just a flesh-and-blood human being posing as a wooden statue, he was a genuine Chinese man impersonating the generic tea "Chinaman"— the nationally recognized symbol for tea in the United States. After decades of print ornaments, trade cards, lithographs, and statues, the generic tea Chinaman had become so ingrained in the American consciousness that tea merchants believed they needed to perpetuate this image in order to sell their product.

After Twain's correspondent finished scolding the store's owner for wrongful exploitation and the onlookers for insensitive gawking, he showcased his own powers of sympathy to demonstrate that he was above the crowd. Through the use of his imagination, he attempted to enter the Chinese man's thoughts as the latter supposedly dreamed about his homeland. The correspondent's intentions may have been noble, but his reverie reveals to what extent an idyllic vision of China was lodged in his mind:

> In my heart I pitied the friendless Mongol. I wondered what was passing behind his sad face, and what distant scene his vacant eye was dreaming of. Were his thoughts with his heart, ten thousand miles away . . . among the rice-fields and the plumy palms of China? under the shadows of remembered mountain-peaks, or in groves of blooming shrubs and strange forest trees unknown to climes like ours? . . . A cruel fate it is, I said, that is befallen this bronzed wanderer.

Oblivious to the rebellions, droughts, and various economic considerations that spurred many Chinese to seek new lives in America, the correspondent carried an idealized construction of China in his head. Convinced that no Chinese citizen would ever voluntarily leave this pastoral Asian paradise, the correspondent assumed that "cruel fate" must have somehow hurled the lonely "wanderer" onto the streets of New York. China, after all, was a place for Westerners to escape to, not for Chinese to escape from.

Certain of his logic, the correspondent approached the Chinese man, tapped him on the shoulder, and urged him to "cheer up" because help was on the way: "Americans are always ready to help the unfortunate. Money shall be raised—you shall go back to China." When he next inquired about the wages received for this demeaning work, the Chinese man's response delivered a rude awakening: "four dollars a week . . . but it's aisy." Discovering that the Chinese man cared little about his own exploitation, the correspondent decided to wash his hands of the entire affair: "The exile remains at his post. The New York tea merchants who need picturesque signs are not likely to run out of Chinamen."[68]

# THE END OF THE ROMANTIC ERA

The New York tea merchants did not face a shortage of "Chinamen" because, by 1870, the diaspora that would bring tens of thousands of people from the southern provinces of China to American shores was well underway. One could argue that the presence of Chinese immigrants benefited tea merchants by providing them with a new advertising gimmick, but what is more likely is that they rued the day that Chinese people began immigrating to the United States. Whereas the Carnes in 1834 could publicize Afong Moy and in the 1840s a mere statue could draw a crowd, by 1870 the sighting of a Chinese person in New York would not have been uncommon. This new demographic shift threatened the efficacy of the tea industry's most basic marketing strategy: Sell more tea by encouraging consumers to associate the beverage with a distant land populated by an exotic people. After all, how could the tactic continue to be effective if the Chinese were visible on American streets and lacking in exotic costumes?

The tea store to which Twain's correspondent referred coped with the problem by masking it. By hiring this human being to stand in a place once occupied by a statue, the tea merchant was essentially paying a genuine Chinese American to impersonate Americans' imagined conception of a Chinese man in China. In other words, an individual who actually represented a new transnational Chinese identity posed here as an anachronism; the bewildering and ever changing present dissembled as the static and romantic past.

More than either the transition from clipper ship to steamship or the forced opening of China by the Western powers, the arrival of Chinese immigrants brought about the end of the romantic era of the China trade. Twain's correspondent was not the first to comment on the sight of a Chinese man in the streets of New York. Fifteen years earlier, the presence of a Chinese man had so astonished a magazine contributor that he felt compelled to convey the significance of the event in verse:

> Sits he by the dusty footway through the torrid day.
> Alas! What brought thee hither, poor native of Cathay?
> And thine olive, moveless features, transfixed as in a dream,
> Mid the crowd of busy faces like wooden features seem.
>
> When our curious childhood marvelled at figures quaintly wrought
> On the ancient heir-loom China—ah! me! We never thought
> E'er to see their breathing image beside us on the path;
> And what strange, discordant background the curious picture hath!

*Not the tall Pagoda's summit, not the tea trees, stunted train,*
*Not the pointed roofs of Pekin, not the flat, unvaried plain,*
*But the world's great heart pants round thee, a rushing progress sweeps*
*Thy vague, unwoken being along its sounding deeps.*[69]

Having been introduced to China through commodities ("When our curious childhood marvelled at . . . the ancient heir-loom China"), the poet had grown accustomed to seeing Chinese figures set before idyllic backgrounds of pagodas, tea trees, and pointed roofs. Since he had conceived of Chinese people only in the context of the imagined landscape of Cathay, the sight of a Chinese man sitting before the cityscape of New York seemed "discordant" to him.

However, unlike Twain's correspondent, the poet understood the economic forces that might have propelled this individual to the New World: "How the wild Sierra gleameth, with gold in every cleft." With the promise of riches acting like a magnet, the Chinese man had embarked for California to seek his fortune and had somehow ended up in New York. Interestingly, the poet reacted to the novel sight not with passive resignation but with anxiety. He fervently desired that the Chinese man return to China and, in an effort to tempt the latter to depart, he invoked the image of China as an agrarian utopia. "Speed thee home!" he exclaimed, because "thy rice-fields still are pleasant, and the Tea Tree scents the air, / And the Central Flowery Kingdom doth still its beauty wear."

The urgency in the poet's tone initially strikes the reader as perplexing, but his desire to effect the departure of the Chinese man had nothing to do with racial prejudice. On the contrary, he assured the latter that, if he agreed to return home to China, the two countries would continue to enjoy frequent contact with one another through trade:

*And us you lose not ever—we will be there anon—*
*Shall our sea-birds dip their pinions below thy walls, Canton?*
*We, the vanguard of the nations, we poise our wings for flight,*
*And we'll rest within thy shadow, oh! Starry Eastern night!*

In these stanzas lies the crux of the poet's mysterious and profound discontent. He interpreted the Chinese man as a harbinger of change whose presence in New York meant the end of an era. In the recent past, Americans had been the ones to traverse oceans in their mighty sailing vessels ("sea-birds") in search of wonderful Chinese goods that could be found only in Canton. Motion was strictly the provenance of Western nations, of whom the Americans could boast the highest proficiency: "We, the vanguard of the nations, we poise our wings for flight."

In stark contrast, the Chinese remained distant, passive, mysterious, exotic, and, most of all, immobile. A Chinese port provided a destination for others but never served as a point of departure for the Chinese themselves.[70] And so the presence of a Chinese man in New York threatened this status quo. For if the Chinese boarded ships and crossed the Pacific Ocean to pan for gold, how could Americans maintain their monopoly on this glamorized conception of themselves as a vigorous, rugged, hearty, seeking people who possessed a restless energy, an indomitable spirit, a willingness to take risks, and a thirst for adventure? In this way, the images of China that emerged out of the tea trade were necessary to sustain Americans' own idealized self-portrait.

The immigration of Chinese brought about no substantial material changes in the China trade in that American vessels continued to transport goods to the United States, as they had been doing since 1784. However, the romantic era of the trade effectively came to a close, because the romance had always existed not in the flow of commodities but in the American mind or, more specifically, in this self-congratulatory fiction based on the comparison of the two national identities involved: The Chinese were a wonderfully exotic faraway people, and Americans were a courageous seafaring folk. These opposite identities were mutually dependent. Neither could exist without being in juxtaposition to the other. The presence of the Chinese man in the New World contradicted half of the idea, and, in doing so, precipitated the collapse of the whole construction. Although the poet probably did not realize the significance of his poem at the time, what he had composed was the epitaph for the romantic era of the China trade.

# CONCLUSION

In the late eighteenth and early nineteenth centuries, the China trade flooded the American imagination with idealized images of Chinese landscapes and people. Traders could have pointed out the multiple inaccuracies inherent in the images and thereby disabused their countrymen of their false notions of China, but for a variety of reasons they declined to do so. Instead, they allowed the images to pass through to their customers unchallenged, sometimes going so far as to develop and disseminate images of their own. As a result, the images were ubiquitous and therefore inescapable, reaching Americans through porcelain, watercolors, newspapers, trade cards, and tea stores. In the absence of accurate and accessible information on China, Americans exercised a sort of license to use the images creatively to construct China as they wished it could be. They did just that and, as a result, the enchanting kingdom of Cathay arose out of their collective imaginations.

As has been explained, Chinese immigration in the latter half of the century would eventually deliver a decisive and fatal blow to this "romantic illusion." However, decades before that demographic development had begun, one American who had lived in China took it upon himself to dismantle this pleasurable but erroneous view of China by supplying Americans with factual information. Ironically, this individual was none other than a merchant.

## NOTES

1. William Wood, *Sketches of China* (Philadelphia: Carey and Lea, 1830), vi–vii, xi.

2. W. C. Hunter, *The Fan Kwei at Canton before Treaty Days, 1825–1844* (London: Kegan Paul, 1882; reprint, Taipei: Ch'eng-wen, 1965), 113.

3. In finding the image of China disseminated by American traders to be overwhelmingly positive, this chapter represents a departure from the conclusions drawn by Stuart Creighton Miller. Miller made extensive use of the journals and diaries of China traders to support his claim that these men contributed to a generally negative view of the Chinese people. Yet Miller placed too much importance on personal writings that reached only a limited readership, if they were published at all. He overlooked a far more influential venue at which merchants transmitted images to millions of people: the marketplace. In this locus of commercial activity, Americans were bombarded with positive images of China. And so, regardless of the opinions merchants may have held privately, they contributed heavily to the proliferation of images that were generally favorable, albeit unrealistic. See Stuart Creighton Miller, "The American Trader's Image, 1785–1840," chapter in *The Unwelcome Immigrant: The American Image of the Chinese, 1785–1882* (Berkeley: University of California Press, 1969).

4. Elma Loines, ed., *The China Trade Post-Bag of the Seth Low Family of Salem and New York* (Manchester, Maine: Falmouth Publishing House, 1953), 126. Evidently, the Chinese took this prohibition of Western women very seriously. One supercargo was advised by his superiors: "Should there be any females on board, they must be landed . . . at Macao, for to carry a woman into China would produce your ruin!!!!!!!!" Sea Journal of supercargo of ship Confederacy (1804), fol. 153, Downs Collection, Winterthur Library.

5. While conducting research for her dissertation, Nancy Ellen Davis first came across the arrival of Afong Moy in a merchant ship. Nancy Ellen Davis, "The American China Trade, 1784–1844: Products for the Middle Class" (Ph.D. diss., George Washington University, 1987), 57–60.

6. Osmond Tiffany commented on this stereotype: "Some people, who know less about the Chinese than they profess to, say that they are not an inventive, but merely

an imitative race. What nation have they imitated? Are they not the originators of al-most every art they possess? Are they not adepts in some arts, that no other nation can attempt?" Osmond Tiffany Jr., *The Canton Chinese; or, The American's Sojourn in the Celestial Empire* (Boston: James Monroe, 1849), 86.

7. Walter Barrett, *The Old Merchants of New York City* (New York: Carleton, 1863, 40.

8. Mills, Brothers, and Co. (New York), *Catalogue of Canton Fans, Grass Cloths, and Fancy Goods Now Landing from the Ship "Howard," from Canton . . . June 5th, 1832*, auction catalog (reprint, Boston: Childs Gallery, 1968).

9. Barrett, 44–45.

10. See advertisements for "fresh teas" and "200 cases China silk goods" from the ship *Washington* in the *New York Evening Post* (17 and 23 October 1834).

11. *New-York Daily Advertiser* (20 October 1834).

12. *New York Sun* (18 and 19 October 1834).

13. *New-York Commercial Advertiser* (18 October 1834). The writer of this article noted that he learned about footbinding by examining the model of a Chinese wom-an's foot on display at the museum of the East India Marine Society in Salem, Mas-sachusetts (now the Peabody Essex Museum).

14. *New York Journal of Commerce* (25 October 1834).

15. Both rumors were printed in the *New-York Commercial Advertiser* (28 October 1834). As for the gunfire, this pro-Whig newspaper reported on all the activities of the rival Democratic Party during the congressional elections of 1834.

16. See advertisements placed in the *New-York Daily Advertiser,* the *New York Sun,* the *New-York Commercial Advertiser,* and the *New York Evening Post* starting on No-vember 6 and running through most of the month. We cannot be certain of Moy's age, as an undated broadside owned by the Library Company of Philadelphia lists her as seventeen years old, not nineteen.

17. *New-York Commercial Advertiser* (15 November 1834).

18. *New-York Mirror* (6 December 1834).

19. New York's other amusements at this time included the following: a thrower of Oriental daggers; Major Stevens who, being "the smallest man now living," appears to have been a precursor to General Tom Thumb; Major Jack Downing, "the cele-brated monkey"; and two boa constrictors, an anaconda, "Gallipago turtles of great size," and a flamingo. See "Amusements," *New York Evening Post* (22 October 1834).

20. Joan Kerr Facey Thill, "A Delawarean in the Celestial Empire: John Richard-son Latimer and the China Trade" (master's thesis, University of Delaware, 1973), 42.

21. Brantz Mayer, "China and the Chinese," *Southern Quarterly Review* 12, no. 23 (July 1847): 22–23. According to Osmond Tiffany, clay models of "contracted feet, painted flesh color and set into shoes of the same size as those actually worn," were sold in Canton to foreigners. Tiffany, 51.

22. Tiffany, 51.

23. "Chinese Painting," *Lady's Book* (April 1831), 177.

24. H. Wrightson, Design Book, doc. 528, Downs Collection, Winterthur Library.

25. Davis, 58.

26. Louisa May Alcott, *Eight Cousins; or, The Aunt-Hill* (Cleveland: World, 1948), 74.

27. Waln passed several months in Canton in 1819 and 1820. As supercargo, he served as a proxy for the ship's owner by keeping the books and handling the buying and selling in Canton. Margaret C. S. Christman, *Adventurous Pursuits: Americans and the China Trade* (Washington, D.C.: Smithsonian Institute Press, 1984), 25–26. According to statistics, Americans consumed 10 to 20 million pounds of tea annually from 1820 to 1850 (Gideon Nye, *Tea: And the Tea Trade* [New York: Geo. W. Wood, 1850], 23–24).

28. Beekman Papers, manuscripts, box 25, folder 2, New-York Historical Society. Stuart Creighton Miller cited this source in *The Unwelcome Immigrant*, 11.

29. *The Grocer's Companion and Merchant's Hand-Book* (Boston: New England Grocer Office, 1883), 154.

30. Carl Seaburg and Stanley Patterson, *Merchant Prince of Boston, Colonel T. H. Perkins, 1764–1854* (Cambridge, Harvard University Press, 1971), 56.

31. Ibid., 179.

32. Conrad Edick Wright, "Merchants and Mandarins: New York and the Early China Trade," in *New York and the China Trade*, ed. David Sanctuary Howard, (New York: New-York Historical Society, 1984), 30.

33. According to Charles Tyng, in 1815 the *Cordelia* used silver specie to purchase a cargo of tea. Charles Tyng, *Before the Wind: The Memoir of an American Sea Captain, 1808–1833*, ed. Susan Fels (New York: Viking Penguin, 1999), 16.

34. The standard chest contained 130 to 160 pounds of opium. Instead of involving itself directly in the opium trade, the East India Company sold licenses to Western merchants called "country traders," who then transported the narcotic from India to China. Jonathan D. Spence, *The Search for Modern China* (New York: Norton, 1990), 128–32.

35. Forbes believed that the best scenario, and one he did not believe would come to pass, was the abolition of the opium trade. Robert Bennet Forbes, *Remarks on China and the China Trade* (Boston: Samuel N. Dickinson, 1844), 24–25, 55–56.

36. Nye, 12, 40, 53.

37. *Guide to Tea Drinking* (New York: Pekin Tea Company, 1845), 6, 25, 28. Prints Room, New-York Historical Society,.

38. William Alcott was the cousin of Bronson Alcott, who was noteworthy for being a Transcendentalist, an education reformer, the founder of a utopian community, and the father of Louisa May Alcott. William Alcott, *Tea and Coffee* (Boston: George W. Light, 1839), 55–56.

39. Clarence P. Hornung and Fridolph Johnson, *Two Hundred Years of American Graphic Art: A Retrospective Survey of the Printing Arts and Advertising since the Colonial Period* (New York: George Braziller, 1976), 37.

40. See the account of Williams's lecture on China in Philadelphia. *Dollar Newspaper* (24 February 1847).

41. The print ornaments described here originate in the following specimen books, all of which can be found in the Rare Books division at Winterthur Library. L. John-

son, *Specimen of Printing Types and Ornaments Cast by L. Johnson* (Philadelphia, 1844), ornaments 61, 62, 84, 734, 1077; Hobart and Robbins (established 1824), *New England Type and Stereotype Foundery* (Boston, circa 1850), 86, 401, 595; Paul Howland, *Specimen Book of Printing Types* (New Bedford, 1884), 620; Farmer, Little, and Company, *The Later Specimens and Reduced Price List of Printing Types* (New York, 1879), 515; John T. White, *Specimen of Modern Printing Types at the Foundry of John T. White* (New York, 1839), 526, 575, 590; Alexander Robb, *Specimen of Printing-Types and Ornaments Cast by Alexander Robb* (Philadelphia, 1846), 61, 62, 84, 154; Greele and Willis, *Specimen of Printing Types and Metal Ornaments, Cast at the New England Type Foundry by Greele and Willis* (Boston, 1831), 32, 157, 279; A. S. Gilchrist, *Book of Specimens of Printing Types, Cuts, Ornaments, &c., Cast at the Knickerbocker Type Foundry of A. S. Gilchrist* (Albany, 1857), 93; James Connor and Sons, *Specimens of Printing Types and Ornaments, Cast by James Connor and Sons* (New York, 1855), 107, 323, 820, 1184, 1467, 1859; MacKellar, Smiths and Jordan, *Print Types, Borders, Ornaments and All Things Needful for Newspaper and Job Printing Offices Made by MacKellar, Smiths and Jordan* (Philadelphia, 1880), 2735; L. T. Wells, *Specimens from the Cincinnati Type Foundry* (Cincinnati, 1852), 314, 398.

42. Two archives possess excellent collections of trade cards related to tea: Back.the Warshaw Collection of Business Americana (Archive Center, National Museum of American History, Behring Center, Smithsonian Institution) and the Downs Collection (Winterthur Library).

43. Oong Ar-Showe left China in 1850 and immigrated to South Boston, where he operated a highly profitable tea-and-coffee store at 21 Union Street. In 1853, he married a woman named Louisa Hentz who, in 1854, bore him a son, William. That same year, the father and son were baptized together, with the father adopting the name Charles. In 1860, Charles Ar-Showe became a naturalized U.S. citizen. With his business success, Ar-Showe soon rose to become a highly visible figure in the city's social and political affairs. And in 1876, he regaled the city with a huge display of fireworks, paid for entirely by himself, to celebrate the Centennial. After his wife died in 1878, he gave her the largest funeral in the history of Maplewood, Massachusetts. In 1878, when Ar-Showe decided to return to China to live out his final years, a local newspaper praised his generosity, and a small delegation of important people escorted him to New York, his port of departure. Doris Chu, *Chinese in Massachusetts: Their Experiences and Contributions* (Boston: Chinese Culture Institute, 1987), 34.

44. Victor Margolin, Ira Brichta, and Vivian Brichta, *The Promise and the Product: Two Hundred Years of American Advertising Posters* (New York: Macmillan, 1979), 27; William Walsh, *The Rise and Decline of the Great Atlantic & Pacific Tea Company* (Secaucus, N.J.: Lyle Stuart, 1986), 17–21.

45. Numerous early travelers in China mentioned the device. Benjamin Franklin knew of it, and Charles Willson Peale's museum in Philadelphia possessed one. Owen Aldridge, *The Dragon and the Eagle: The Presence of China in the American Enlightenment* (Detroit: Wayne State University Press, 1993), 81–82, 166–67.

46. Both trade cards can be found in the Prints Department at the New-York Historical Society.

47. Warshaw Collection of Business Americana, Archive Center, National Museum of American History, Behring Center, Smithsonian Institution.

48. Tiffany, 112, 115.

49. Craig Clunas, *Chinese Export Watercolours* (London: Victoria and Albert Museum, 1984), 25–29.

50. *Letters and Recollections of John Murray Forbes*, ed. Sarah Forbes Hughes (New York: Arno Press, 1981), 79–80.

51. After the Opium War, antiforeign mobs and riots occasionally broke out in the streets of Canton. Robert Bennet Forbes, *Personal Reminiscences* (Boston: Little, Brown, 1882), 376–77.

52. *The Voyage of the Peacock: A Journal by Benjamin Ticknor, Naval Surgeon*, ed. Nan Hodges (Ann Arbor: University of Michigan Press, 1991), 178.

53. *Penrose Scull, From Peddlers to Merchant Princes: A History of Selling in America* (Chicago: Follett, 1967), 159–63.

54. Thomas R. Trowbridge, ed., "The Diary of Mr. Ebeneezer Townsend, Jr.," *Papers of the New Haven Historical Society* (New Haven, 1888), 4:94–95.

55. Microfilm (mic. 107), Downs Collection, Winterthur Library.

56. See Russell and Co. Papers, box 2, Manuscript Division, Library of Congress. Quoted in Christman, 110.

57. Philip Dumaresq, Letter book, 1831–1840 (doc. 753), Downs Collection, Winterthur Library.

58. Advertisement for Redding and Company, in Coolidge and Wiley, *The Boston Almanac for the Year 1850* (Boston: B. B. Mussey, 1850), 184.

59. For a complete series of twelve views, see Carl Crossman, *The Decorative Arts of the China Trade: Paintings, Furnishings, and Exotic Curiosities* (Woodbridge, Suffolk, England: Antique Collectors' Club, 1991), 440–41.

60. Brantz Mayer, *A Nation in a Nutshell*, pamphlet, Department of Rare Books, Library of Congress (Philadelphia: Brown, Bicking, and Guilbert, 1841), 26.

61. D. P. Kidder, ed. *The Chinese; or, Conversations on the Country and People of China*, Department of Rare Books, Library of Congress (New York: G. Lane and C. B. Tippett, 1846), 13.

62. *Peter Piper's Tales about China* (Albany, N.Y.: R. H. Pease, n.d.), 4.

63. *People and Customs in Different Countries.* Uncle Oliver's Books for Children (Auburn, N.Y.: Oliphant and Skinner, 1837).

64. Warshaw Collection of Business Americana, Archive Center, National Museum of American History, Behring Center, Smithsonian Institution.

65. With no evidence to the contrary, we can only take this claim at face value. However, the invention of fictitious imitators has long been known as an effective advertising strategy. Quite simply, if consumers believe a particular brand has inspired imitations, they are apt to regard the original as of high quality.

66. *Boston Post* (17 November 1847). See also Coolidge and Wiley, *The Boston Almanac for the Year 1850* (Boston: B. B. Mussey, 1850), 184.

67. Letter to Mark Twain, "John Chinaman in New York," Galaxy (September 1870), 426. Although I refer to the author as "Twain's correspondent," the colorful

language and the sophisticated social commentary suggest the letter might have been composed by Twain himself.

68. Twain, 426.

69. The poet is listed as "F.M." "On a Chinaman in Broadway," *United States Review* (May 1855).

70. A writer for *Poulson's American Daily Advertiser*, a business-oriented newspaper published in Philadelphia, explained the difference between the people of China and America, attributing it to the difference between their forms of government: "Compare the timid slave [of China] creeping through shallows in his clumsy junk, with the American Seaman; 'among the tumbling mountains of ice, of the arctic circle, penetrating to the antipodes, and engaged under the frozen serpent of the south. Yet we know he has not been squeezed into this hardy form, or inhaled this daring spirit; from the constraints of a watchful and suspicious government.'" (21 January 1820).

## 4. CHINA IN MINIATURE

### Nathan Dunn's Chinese Museum

Tantalized by stories of huge fortunes acquired in a short time, Nathan Dunn of Philadelphia sailed to Canton in 1818 to eliminate a rather substantial debt he had amassed after several failed business ventures. In 1822, he was still relatively new to the China trade, but by then he had legitimate grounds for optimism. His fledgling trading enterprise had performed well, he had adjusted to life in the foreign factories, and he had forged a valuable friendship and alliance with Tingqua, a Hong merchant (a different person from the artist described in chapter 2). Yet Dunn knew better than to become complacent, because the China trade was prone to dramatic shifts without warning. He knew that an unforeseen disaster—a storm at sea, an attack by Chinese pirates on a cargo-bearing vessel, a sudden market fluctuation—could rise up and instantly erase his profits, hurling him back into the state of severe debt from which he had only recently emerged.

Late one evening in early November, sometime after midnight, a fire broke out in Canton, just a short distance from the foreign factories. As gusty winds blew through the rows of houses, the fire spread easily and soon rose to the level of a full-scale conflagration. The foreign community, observing that it was rapidly moving toward their factories, pleaded with the Chinese to raze a line of buildings in and so stop the fire from advancing. But their calls for containment were ignored. Chinese property owners reasoned that the fire was still some distance away. Why should an individual voluntarily sacrifice his own home or business for a threat that might never materialize? With no measures being taken to obstruct its path, the fire continued to spread, and foreigners resigned themselves to salvaging what they could before it destroyed their lodgings, offices, and warehouses.

Soon pandemonium broke out, as foreign and Chinese merchants made frantic attempts to transport their storehouses of goods onto ships anchored in the harbor. Adding to the mayhem, a torrential current of Cantonese citizens streamed out of the burning city to the water's edge, holding their belongings. Amid the hysteria, Nathan Dunn was unable to find any Chinese laborers willing to move the contents of his warehouse—holdings valued at the substantial sum of $150,000—to a safe location. And so, as the fire began to encroach on the foreign factories, Dunn stood helplessly in the street, watching the brilliant red glow in the night sky. For the second time in his life, he faced the specter of utter financial ruin.

As the flames began to lick against the sides of structures close to Dunn's warehouse, Tingqua recognized his friend's dire situation and came to his aid by quickly dispatching about eighty of his own men along with a fleet of small boats. To Dunn's amazement, the men proceeded to load crate after crate of his goods onto the boats, rendering them safe from the fire. Remarkably, while Tingqua's men were busy saving Dunn's livelihood, the Hong merchant's own factory was severely damaged in the blaze. Yet Tingqua conducted business on a scale that dwarfed that of Nathan Dunn. But he knew that, whereas his deep monetary reserves allowed him to absorb the occasional pecuniary setback, the fire would have proved devastating for his friend. Tingqua had simply selected the only course that would permit both men to continue to seek prosperity. "All this is now gone by," Dunn wrote a decade later, "and I shall ever remember with gratitude to him."[1]

Like many Americans in the China trade, Dunn went on to make his fortune. Unlike the others, though, he transcended commerce, converting his experience in China into something of educational value. While in Canton, he diverted a portion of his newly acquired wealth to the formation of the world's largest Chinese collection. After returning to Philadelphia, he installed it in a museum and opened the doors to the public. From his personal experiences in China, his overall impression of the Chinese was quite favorable, and so Dunn used his exhibit to construct the Chinese as a people worthy of Americans' admiration.

However, other factors besides warm feelings played a role in shaping the exhibit. Like Houckgeest, Dunn was animated by what we may call an ideology of Enlightenment science, which instilled in him a will to understand China comprehensively and categorically. He aspired to assemble a collection that was all-inclusive, covering the natural as well as the human world throughout China's vast territory, not just in Canton. Blocking this ambition, however, was the Qing ordinance that restricted all Westerners to the foreign factories. Since the law precluded Dunn from undertaking the collecting himself, he appealed to his Chinese friends for assistance. Obliging his request, they helped him secure a team of agents who fanned out across the provinces for collection purposes. And so, although an American conceived of this grandiose project and set the general guidelines for its assembly, it was the Chinese who ultimately decided what went into the collection and what was left out.

In the end, Dunn's ambition yielded a museum that was encyclopedic to the point where he could state, "It is China in miniature."[2] Many of the visitors arrived possessing only scant knowledge of China; for them, a simple piece of willowware would have been sufficient to inspire dreams of Cathay. On entering the salon, they confronted a staggering number of artifacts, pictures, statues, and natural-history specimens all arranged systematically by a man who intended to challenge Americans' groundless oriental fantasies with authentic Chinese objects.

## THE GAMBLE

Nathan Dunn was born in 1782 to a farming family in Salem County, New Jersey. His father died shortly after his birth, and his widowed mother remarried and became a well-known Quaker minister. In his father's will it was stipulated that he learn a trade, but Dunn instead moved to Philadelphia in 1802 and entered the business community, becoming an apprentice to a merchant. In 1805, Dunn and a partner launched their own business, and that same year the Monthly Meeting of Friends in Philadelphia received him as a member.[3] However, over the course of the next decade, Dunn slowly slid into a quagmire of debt.[4] Although the details are not clear, the Monthly Meeting disowned Dunn in 1816 on the grounds that he had become "embarrassed in his affairs and unable to meet his engagements" and, more specifically, that he had "assigned his effects so as to secure some of his creditors in preference to others." While the dismissal must have been hard for Dunn to accept, the Monthly Meeting did offer a chance for future redemption: "We testify that we no longer acknowledge him a member of our religious society; yet we desire that he may experience a qualification to be rightly restored."[5] Heavily in debt and expelled from the Quaker society, Nathan Dunn by the age of 34 had reached bottom.

Looking for both a fresh start and a way to pay off his creditors, he decided in 1818 to enter the risky yet potentially lucrative world of the China trade.[6] His decision was far from uncommon, as many men mired in financial difficulty resorted to this burgeoning trade. Since a single voyage might earn a return of 400 to 500 percent, a fortunate merchant could accumulate wealth in a short time.[7] Yet, being in arrears, Dunn lacked the capital to secure a ship, purchase a cargo, and hire a captain and crew. For these he turned to his friend John Field, who had some past experience in the China trade. Field was also one of Dunn's creditors, and apparently the failed businessman owed Field a substantial sum. "I proposed this voyage to him," Dunn wrote, "and though he at the time had no intention to make another voyage to China, he finally acquiesced on the condition that the commissions accruing on the shipment should be applied in part to liquidate a debt I owed him." Apparently, Field believed that financing his friend provided the only means whereby he might one day see his loans repaid. "This was all right," Dunn wrote of Field's terms. "I was willing to pay as much as I could of the debt of my previous misfortune." The two men became partners, and Dunn began a career that would take him to China (fig. 4.1).[8]

While Field remained in Philadelphia to oversee the domestic side of the business, Dunn embarked for Canton in the spring of 1818 in a vessel aptly named the Hope. Dunn acted as the ship's supercargo, which meant that he was responsible for keeping the books and handling all transactions—both the sale of American goods to Chinese merchants and the subsequent purchase of Chinese commodities intended for the American market. On arriving in Canton, Dunn saw on his first day most of what he would ever see of China, as the strictly enforced Qing ordinance confined him to the foreign factories (fig. 4.2). Dunn and the other foreign traders lived, ate, slept, and conducted business in a space measuring just 400 yards in length and 300 in width—about one twenty-fifth of a square mile.[9] When Dunn's curious niece wrote to him asking for a description of China, Dunn could not oblige her request, stating that "the limits prescribed to foreigners are through the jealousies of the officers of the Government, very much confined."[10]

While a trader's movement was severely restricted, his life in the foreign factories was not always dull. Besides tending to business, he found plenty that was amusing just by walking into the public square between the factories and the waterfront. David Abeel, an American missionary whose residence in Canton coincided with Dunn's, described the sights and sounds in vivid detail. "As the morning opens upon this scene," he wrote, "silence retires and the ears of the stranger are assailed by a new and peculiar combination of sounds." This "inharmonious concert" was composed of the "harsh, drawling tones" of human voices, the "cries of confined dogs and cats," the "screams of roughly handled poultry," and the "notes of feathered songsters."

As the day progresses, the area rapidly becomes alive with "multitudes of natives," who congregate daily "to transact business, gratify curiosity, or murder time." Indeed, Abeel found many interesting people to observe: Chinese gamblers engaged in games of chance, itinerant barbers setting up shop for the day, "quacks" hawking remedies for all sorts of maladies, "idlers" who would gather in large crowds around jugglers and storytellers, and merchants out peddling meat, fish, vegetables, fruits, drugs, and manufactures. In addition, many Chinese would come from far away just to observe the strange outsiders for whom they harbored an "insatiable curiosity." According to Abeel, a foreigner who appears on his veranda or enters the square immediately becomes the object of prolonged stares. The Chinese turn to look, he wrote, and then freeze in a fixed position, "approaching to statues," and "continue to stare as though riveted by a magic spell."[11]

If Dunn were to extend his gaze past the square and into the water, new sights would unfold within his field of vision: the "water population." In Canton harbor, one could find an entire civilization that lived on boats, with many people passing their entire lives without touching land. According to Abeel, these people enjoyed "every convenience of land as well as water." In addition to "edibles," one could find barbers, theatrical productions, shrines for worship, and "flower boats"—floating brothels that elicited Abeel's outrage.[12] In sum, wherever Nathan Dunn chose to look, he was sure to find some interesting activity.

Despite these distractions, Dunn remained focused on his primary task, which was to build a successful business that would allow him to pay off his crippling debts and clear his name in the Quaker Monthly Meeting. As for the nature of this business, advertisements placed by John Field and Nathan Dunn in Philadelphia newspapers indicate that they imported mostly the usual Chinese commodities: crates of tea, nankeens (a durable yellow cloth), and silken goods.[13] However, although the American side of the trade was fairly standard, on the Chinese side Dunn was able to make one key innovation that would eventually place him on a trajectory toward economic prosperity.

The problem with the China trade had always been that, while Western consumers demonstrated a strong demand for Chinese goods, the Chinese showed only tepid interest in Western products. Hoping to bring balance to the trade, merchants were always hunting for goods that appealed to Chinese tastes. During his first sojourn in Canton, Dunn identified in the Chinese market a niche that traders had yet to exploit. "I soon found when in Canton that there was an opening for the introduction of the different kinds of British goods," Dunn recalled, "and that by procuring them . . . better calculated for the Chinese wants . . . a fair profit could be realized" (emphasis added). In other words, if suppliers in England could tailor their manufactures specifically "to suit the

Chinese taste," the Chinese would respond by increasing their demand. Dunn's next move was to sail for England, where he promptly lined up several British manufacturers, including James Brown and Company of Leeds, who commenced filling his unique order.[14]

Writing to his brother and sister from Liverpool in November 1821, Dunn informed them that he was heading back to China soon and that "I may be detained a little in Canton."[15] Unbeknownst to him at that time, that "little" stay in Canton would swell to over eight years as, starting in May 1822, his unique trading strategy would keep him exclusively in the Chinese port. In essence, he established what amounted to a triangular trade. American ships would convey American goods to England, where the cargoes would be promptly sold with the profits going toward the purchase of these specialized English manufactures, altered so as to appeal to Chinese consumers. The ships would then continue on to Canton, where Dunn had permanently stationed himself. When the ships docked in Canton harbor, Dunn would sell their British cargoes and then proceed to load their compartments with Chinese goods meant for the American market.[16]

Dunn's uninterrupted residence in Canton was a key component of this strategy. From this post, he could watch the fluctuations of the Chinese market and, when prices dropped, buy up Chinese goods and warehouse them until his ships arrived. The permanent residence also allowed him to forge alliances with the Hong merchants. As any American trader was well aware, Hong merchants were indispensable to any foreigner who wanted to succeed in the China trade before the Opium War. Some Hong merchants used their positions to become fabulously wealthy, but the responsibility of handling China's entire foreign trade also carried formidable risks. If after a series of failures a Hong merchant were to accumulate a debt so severe that he could not recover, the Qing government would banish him to the frozen north of Tartary (Manchuria). That two unfortunate merchants had experienced this sad fate in Dunn's time prompted another American trader, Robert Bennet Forbes, to write, "We wish no greater punishment to our worst enemy than that he might be made a 'Hong merchant.'"[17]

Always wary of this possible outcome, Hong merchants had to handle their business transactions in a careful, shrewd, and calculating manner. Likewise, American traders had to be circumspect in their dealings with them. To the captains, supercargoes, or younger merchants in their employ, experienced traders wrote admonitory letters filled with advice regarding the selection of the right Hong merchant to handle a cargo. These correspondences usually contained thorough character sketches of each of the twelve or so men, and they offered valuable information as to which ones could be trusted, which ones were devious, and which ones were financially unsteady.[18]

Dunn established especially strong ties with two Hong merchants, the more prominent of whom was Houqua. In 1819, Charles Tyng, an American sailor, described Houqua as "magnificently dressed in silks and satins of various rich colours." "He was an old man," Tyng continued, "I think near seventy, not bad looking, with rather a long mustache, all the rest of face and head nicely shaved, excepting the queue."[19] To this physical description, Robert Forbes added a caricature of Houqua's intellectual and personal qualities. "He had a most comprehensive mind, and united the qualities of an enterprising merchant and sagacious politician," Forbes wrote. "He was always a warm friend to the Americans, and through them was supposed to have carried on a considerable trade."[20]

In a business rife with deception and bribery, Houqua secured the lion's share of the trade by maintaining a lofty reputation among foreigners as the most trustworthy and reliable of all the Hong merchants.[21] But his probity came at a cost, as he charged foreigners dearly for the right to trade through him. By 1834, Houqua had amassed such a vast fortune that his net worth was estimated at $52 million—making him perhaps the wealthiest commoner alive in the world.[22] As Forbes stated, Houqua possessed a special fondness for Americans and frequently held soirées for his American friends at his estate, known for its magnificent gardens.[23] With limitless wealth and connections, Houqua was in a position to provide Dunn with invaluable assistance both in commerce and in his later attempt to collect artifacts.

Besides the illustrious Houqua, Dunn also enjoyed good relations with a lesser-known Hong merchant, Tingqua, who handled Dunn's ships when they entered the harbor and was relatively new to his position when Dunn arrived in China. On two separate occasions he acted to save Dunn's career. Of course, the more dramatic of these incidents took place when the massive fire of 1822 threatened to destroy Dunn's business. Tingqua's timely decision to send manpower over to Dunn's warehouse prevented Dunn from sustaining a huge financial loss that would have sent him spiraling back into debt. On another occasion, Tingqua risked his own economic future in order to protect Dunn from a colossal enemy intent on destroying his nascent enterprise.

In fact, it was Dunn's triangular trading scheme that placed Tingqua's business in a precarious position. Though clearly an impressive display of Yankee ingenuity and entrepreneurial skill, Dunn's scheme depended heavily on forays into England. Since Dunn was somewhat audaciously treading on the territory of the British East India Company, his activity soon provoked the ire of the economic giant. "But here the East India Company's jealousy was awake," Dunn wrote, as "they were not to be interfered with by an American coming to China direct from England with British Goods." Since Tingqua had been securing Dunn's ships, the company employed a strategy of incentives and threats to convince the Hong merchant to sever ties with the troublesome American.

The company first called Tingqua into its offices to make him an offer. "Now you are a new house just beginning business," a company representative stated, and "we will aid you if you comply with our wishes." The company promised to channel $200,000 of its annual business to Tingqua if he would agree to cease handling "Mr. Dunn's ship," for "she has our kind of goods." After Tingqua walked out of the office, refusing to make any kind of agreement, the company called on him later that day to issue an ultimatum: "If you secure this ship we will withdraw our business from you." Even in the face of such pressure, Tingqua remained obstinate: "I will secure Mr. Dunn's ship, and you may if you please take away your business." Tingqua remained loyal to Dunn despite the great risk to his own commercial enterprise, and Dunn never forgot his friend's sacrifice. He knew that, had it not been for this friendship, he would not have amassed the fortune that made his Chinese collection possible.[24]

## AN IDEA GERMINATES

Nathan Dunn's experience in China was far from typical. "I was to be found at my post through all the seasons," he wrote. "This I thought I ought to do, both to take advantage of the market in selling the goods, and in purchasing silks, teas, &., when no other persons were in the market. I never visited Macao until a short time before I embarked for Europe in 1831."[25] That visit to Macao, which took place in June 1830, was noted in the journal of a young woman named Harriet Low, the niece of an American China trader who was residing there because Qing law strictly forbade the presence of Western women in Canton (a law she broke on one occasion). "After breakfast received . . . from Canton . . . a splendid comb, brought by friend Dunn, who has not seen a lady for eight years!" she wrote. "He has come down [to Macao] to do his countrywomen the honor of being the first ladies he has called on in China."[26] From the amazement registered in Low's tone, we can surmise that Dunn's avoidance of Macao was somewhat extraordinary. Indeed, most traders passed the hot summer months in the Portuguese-controlled city, which had become something of a resort town for foreigners who were ill, craving entertainment, or in need of female companionship. Macao, its recreational opportunities, and its cosmopolitan society were a part of the typical trader's China experience, but not a part of Nathan Dunn's.[27]

Why did Dunn remain aloof from the expatriate society in Macao for so many years when other traders partook of it regularly? The most obvious answer relates to Dunn's past failures; he had suffered profound humiliation after both earlier misadventures in business and his subsequent expulsion from Monthly Meeting. Quite possibly, his decision to stay in Canton was motivated by a personal desire to achieve redemption by recovering his losses, paying off debts, and regaining his good name.

Yet one other possibility exists. Dunn chose to remain a bachelor throughout his life. And, as will be discussed below, Dunn faced sodomy charges in Philadelphia in 1841, a decade after his return from China. Though he was acquitted of any crime, the episode opens up the possibility that he was gay.[28] If so, his sexual orientation would help to explain why he elected to eschew the sensual pleasures of Macao to remain in Canton's male-dominated society of Chinese and foreign merchants. It also would help illuminate Dunn's strong affinity for and understanding of Chinese people, which far exceeded that felt by most merchants. Since Dunn was never able to see any part of China other than Canton, his Chinese experience was more interpersonal than it was geographic. In other words, he confronted China not through travel but through interactions with Chinese people. Though his close relationship with Tingqua might have been based purely on friendship, it might also have contained a sexual component. If so, we can begin to see how Dunn, by experiencing intimacy with a Chinese individual, was able to surmount racial, cultural, and linguistic barriers and see the true humanity of the Asian "other." In short, through a sexual relationship, Dunn may have acquired for Chinese people a love and understanding that other traders were never able to experience. These positive feelings would later find expression in his museum.

Still, the monotony of eight uninterrupted years inside a small contained space did test Dunn's endurance. At some undetermined point in the 1820s, Dunn began to collect Chinese things as a diversion from the daily tedium. His original plan, which was quite modest, entailed only the formation of "a cabinet sufficient to fill a small apartment." It was meant both "for his own pleasure and that of his friends." And so in the early stages he was gathering items "not with any view to its general publicity." However, what began as a mere hobby quickly gathered momentum as Dunn proved unable to quench his ardor for collecting. As the Chinese collection grew, his "passion for accumulation" grew at a commensurate rate such that "every year his plan expanded wider and wider."[29] Consumed with collecting fever, the scope of the project soon swelled to colossal proportions. Dunn was not alone in his ambition. Like his predecessor Houckgeest, he was attempting to assemble an all-inclusive Chinese collection.

Other parties interested in collecting soon discovered that success depended on more than just deep pockets and a desire to shop. Anyone desiring a collection that was representative of the entire nation faced the problem of access. The Qing government simply would not grant to any foreigner the permission to rove throughout the interior of China and hunt for artifacts. For this reason, the attempts made by each of the major contenders, all large companies or institutions, inevitably ended in disappointment. Even the East India Company—with its army of agents, the backing of the British government, and deep monetary reserves—tried to build a grand collection but failed.[30] According to one report, its entire Chinese holdings amounted to only about one tenth of what Dunn would ultimately acquire. The Dutch East India Company also made an attempt, but Dunn's collection would dwarf this one as well. Finally, the members of the East India Marine Society hoped to include a substantial Chinese component in their museum in Salem, Massachusetts. They, however, netted only objects of a "souvenir" nature and blamed the failure on "wealthy mandarins" who, themselves connoisseurs of Chinese things, disdained to part with anything unique or of value.[31]

Why was a solitary American trader able to succeed where large institutions found their efforts thwarted? Benjamin Silliman, a professor of chemistry and natural history at Yale, posed this question to Dunn during a tour of Dunn's museum. He learned that Dunn achieved his goal in part because he had those "wealthy mandarins" working for him. They appreciated the way that he, unlike most agents of the East India Company, had learned to respect the "ingenuity" and the "intelligence" of the Chinese and to treat "all classes" well.[32]

More important, at a time when few American traders openly objected to the opium trade, and some confessed to deriving one half their income from it,[33] Dunn held firm to the position that the trade was morally unjust, and he led the opposition to it in Canton.[34] "Opium is a poison," he wrote, "destructive alike of the health and morals of those who use it habitually, and, therefore, the traffic in it . . . is nothing less than making merchandise of the bodies and souls of men."[35] Brantz Mayer, who met Dunn during a trip to Canton in 1827, observed the positive effect of Dunn's stance in the Chinese community. "Instead of dealing in OPIUM . . . and thus aiding (as too many Americans have done) in fixing on the Chinese all the curses which flow from the habitual use of that intoxicating drug," Mayer wrote, Dunn received "presents . . . of valuable curiosities . . . *from the natives*" who sought to show their "thankfulness for the virtue which induced him to abstain from assisting in the ruin of thousands of their countrymen."[36] Dunn, in short, cared about the health and well-being of the Chinese people whereas many other traders did not.

Dunn's stance on the pernicious drug eventually reached the attention not only of local officials but also of the Chinese government in Peking and, finally, of the emperor himself.[37] As a result, Dunn was able to ingratiate himself with China's elite. According to Silliman, he frequently entertained "the most distinguished officers of the Government" at his "house and table." After winning their "esteem and confidence," he "soon discovered that it was in his power to obtain favors not usually granted to strangers." Of course, the two Hong

merchants, Tingqua and Houqua, who were already in Dunn's camp, also possessed the power and connections to provide him with invaluable assistance.[38]

These powerful Chinese men transformed a seemingly impossible objective
into a reality by providing Dunn with the means to circumnavigate the Qing
restrictions on foreigners. In addition to giving him rare and valuable objects,
they helped him hire Chinese agents willing to travel to other regions purely for
collection purposes.[39] A guidebook to Philadelphia would later highlight this
penetration of the interior and present it as Dunn's greatest triumph: "When it
is considered, that most of the CURIOSITIES of the Chinese Empire, are entirely beyond the reach, of even those who have visited her cities . . . the intelligent public will be able to appreciate the value" of the collection.[40] Likewise,
the *Philadelphia Saturday Courier* credited Dunn's "Chinese friends and
agents" for the artifacts "brought from the interior of China, where foreigners
rarely if ever penetrate."[41]

That newspaper also noted the efforts of "a young Philadelphia naturalist,
Mr. W. W. Wood," whom Dunn befriended in Canton probably because the
two shared the same contempt for the opium trade and the British East India
Company.[42] Like Dunn, William Wood had ventured to China to get rich, and
in the 1820s he found himself clerking for the American firm of Russell and
Company. Unlike Dunn, Wood lacked business acumen and never achieved
any success that can be measured in dollars. He was, however, a true romantic,
and his years roving across Asia proved to be anything but uneventful. The son
of a famous actor, he possessed a deep reservoir of artistic talent. Another
American residing in Canton aptly described Wood: "He abounded in wit, was
well read, and of no fixed purpose." Known as a clever poet, Wood would com-
pose parodies of famous poems and base them on life in Canton.[43] Also a
skilled draughtsman and caricaturist, he offered art lessons in the foreign community and even wrote and illustrated his own book, *Sketches of China*, published in 1830.[44]

Wood also founded and edited the first English-language newspaper in
China, *The Canton Register*, which he printed himself on a borrowed hand-
press. In his editorials, he frequently inveighed against the East India Company,
sparking controversy in the foreign community and prompting a rival editor to
challenge him to a duel. Wood protected his honor when the challenger not
only failed to show but actually fled the country.[45] Ever the romantic, Wood fell
in love with Harriet Low and made frequent visits to Macao, ostensibly to give
her drawing lessons. When he secretly asked for her hand in marriage, she, enthralled by this brilliant and energetic figure, readily accepted. Unfortunately,
her uncle discovered the engagement and objected to his niece marrying a
"penniless adventurer." Wedding plans were canceled, and Wood spent the rest
of his life as a bachelor. Years later, perhaps while he was managing a coffee and

sugar plantation in Jala Jala, he would introduce photography to the Philippines, and some sources credit him with doing the same in China.[46] It was this side of William Wood, that of the romantic adventurer, that Dunn would find so useful.

## COLLECTION METHODOLOGY

Anyone looking to capture the essence of a culture through the collection of artifacts must make choices as to what to include and what to omit. To guide the decision making, the collector formulates a methodology into which he incorporates his personal sense of what is important. For example, the naturalist hunts for specimens of plant and animal life; the ethnologist searches for artifacts that can illuminate human cultures; and the art connoisseur seeks the finest works of painters and sculptors. Dunn, however, resisted the imposition of any such limits on the scope of his collecting. According to Silliman, he eventually "conceived the idea of transporting to his native shores everything that was characteristic or rare . . . no matter how costly that might be" (emphasis in original).[47] Instead of specializing in one particular area, the collection would encompass all things in both the human and the natural realm in China.

This all-inclusive methodology, far from making Dunn an anomaly in his own time, was actually consistent with the ideas that he frequently confronted in his young adulthood in Philadelphia. In the first two decades of the nineteenth century, Philadelphia stood as the intellectual capital of America. Thanks to its people and institutions, Dunn's formative years were awash in the spirit of the Enlightenment. It was a period shaped by Linnaeus, the great Swedish botanist. Through his system of classification he attempted to impose coherence and order onto the confusion of the natural world. Having studied this work, amateur naturalists would scour the New World for plant and animal specimens that could be given a Latin name and assigned their proper place in the Great Chain of Being.[48] In Philadelphia, one could find Charles Willson Peale, who aspired to stuff, mount, and display in his museum all the links of the Great Chain, from the lowest plant forms to the highest form of Homo sapiens. Since no one epitomized the latter better than Benjamin Franklin, Peale hoped to apply his skills as a taxidermist to the great founding father, who apparently would have agreed to the arrangement. Franklin, however, died two years before the museum was formed.[49]

Also in Philadelphia, John Bartram tended an elaborate botanical garden composed of as many types of plants as he or anyone could find; it was a microcosm of

North American botany. Alexander Wilson, a precursor to John James Audubon, sought to create a pictorial record of all the birds of North America. And George Catlin, who was a near contemporary of Nathan Dunn and received his artistic training in Philadelphia, hoped to do the same for some Native American tribes.[50] And of course Houckgeest contributed in his own way to this ambitious scientific community by creating the prototype for a Chinese museum, one that, through pictures and objects, essayed to cover all aspects of Chinese life. In sum, these naturalists, ethnographers, museum proprietors, and painters all composed epic works suffused with the belief that humankind could catalog the entire universe—or at least some corner of it.[51]

However, though the principles of the Enlightenment provided the intellectual underpinnings for these scientific forays into both the natural world and non-Western cultures, the activities of the individuals behind them soon veered into romanticism. Although possessing the impulse to classify all new phenomena and to assign them their proper place in the Great Chain of Being, explorers, artists, and men of science encountered a world burgeoning with a variety that resisted any attempts at classification. The endless heterogeneity of cultures and of biological life overwhelmed the Great Chain and ultimately exploded its rigid hierarchies. For this reason, these individuals were really transitional figures between the Enlightenment and the Romantic Age. They headed out into the unknown world and returned with artifacts, specimens, descriptions, and paintings that appealed to the romantic imagination. Instead of the orderly and predictable mechanistic universe of the Enlightenment, here was a world that was vast, colorful, enchanting, infinitely diverse, sublime, and full of wonder.[52]

Nathan Dunn's formative years were steeped in the ideas and discoveries of these seekers. He adopted both their curiosity for the outside world and their methods for comprehending it. For this reason, he did not invent a new system for understanding China; rather, he simply embraced the preexisting methods and applied them to China's human culture and natural history. After observing both Dunn's final exhibit in Philadelphia and his collecting activities in Canton, Brantz Mayer could easily discern the influence of Enlightenment science. Dunn, he wrote, had succeeded in *enclosing a whole people in glass cases*. . . . He classified the people as we classify the collections of naturalists. Their habits, their crafts;—their follies, their amusements;—their manners, costumes, dwellings, and implements of war or husbandry" (emphasis in original).[53]

Opting not to confine his efforts to the human realm, Dunn covered the flora and fauna of China as well. To amass a sizeable natural-history section for his collection, Dunn employed the skills and ingenuity of William Wood, granting the latter carte blanche to spend whatever sum was necessary to procure the finest zoological, botanical, and mineralogical specimens. Wood was well aware of the similar ambitions of the rival East India Company, and he must have relished this opportunity to assist the American David in his duel with the British Goliath. Here was a chance to help one man triumph over the largest and farthest-reaching commercial institution the world had ever known.

Of course, to Wood's great vexation, he too was confined to Canton. "The empire abounds with subjects of the greatest interest to naturalists," he wrote, "and it is to be regretted that the obstacles opposed to research by the Chinese government, render our knowledge of the subject so limited and imperfect." Making the best of the situation, Wood employed a scheme that depended heavily on the Chinese to supply the bulk of the natural-history section. Through "industry, money, flattery," "kindness," and "subterfuge," he was able to convince a team of Chinese agents to undertake field work.

These men were willing, but Wood feared that their work would not meet his standards. Convinced of the virtues of the Linnaean system, he judged the field of natural history in China to be both flawed and lacking in scientific rigor. "The ideas entertained by Chinese writers on the subject of animals are vague and imperfect, fable and absurdity being mingled in the strangest manner with truth and good sense," he wrote. "They possess no systematic arrangement of animated beings, and commit the most glaring errors in classification." To make sure that the agents followed correct procedures, Wood devoted considerable time and energy to their training in the proper handling of the specimens. After acquiring these skills, they fanned out, traveling "by land and water," in search of birds, fish, reptiles, insects, shells, animals, plants, and rocks. On returning to Canton, many were able to present "new and interesting animals" to a pleased William Wood.[54]

Wood supplemented their findings both by collecting specimens of fish on the China coast and by making accurate drawings of them. In addition, he sometimes secured interesting species in unlikely ways. For instance, since Chinese exhibitioners would often capture wild animals for their portable zoos, Wood would attend their shows and, at the conclusion, offer to buy the animals from the owner. In this fashion, he acquired both a boa constrictor and a wildcat.[55] Even after Dunn returned to the United States, Wood continued this collection service by shipping specimens to Philadelphia at a tremendous cost. Fortunately, only the moths and butterflies, it was said, suffered over the course of these transcontinental passages. In the end, the natural-history collection earned the approval of some of America's top scientists, including Silliman, who praised Wood's thoroughness: "Mr. Wood was indefatigable for many months in completing the herpetology of China; the conchology is fully represented," and there are "some remarkably fine carbonates of copper, both nodular and radiated."[56] The exertions of Wood and his Chinese agents helped stock an exhibit that, quite impressively, could stimulate the minds of naturalists in their special fields.

## BUILDING THE CHINESE MUSEUM
## IN PHILADELPHIA

In 1831, Dunn made preparations to depart Canton for good. That he was apprehensive about his return was evident in his response to a friend who had inquired about his apparent depression: "I am . . . returning to Philadelphia so changed in appearance that none will remember me, and certainly I shall know but a few when I land."[57] According to Harriet Low, Dunn received a warm and festive send-off from the community in Canton: "Mr. Dunn took passage in the *Canning* for England, after having been feasted, toasted, and cheered to his heart's content. He has the good wishes and good will of all who have ever known him in Canton."[58] Although heavily in debt when he first left Philadelphia more than twelve years earlier, Dunn was now returning home one of the city's wealthiest citizens.[59] One of his first actions following his return was to invite all his creditors to a sumptuous banquet, where he placed under each plate a check for the amount of his debt plus interest in full.[60]

Despite his triumphant return, Dunn was not content. To the botanist John H. Reeves he sent a letter in which he complained that he did not like "the manner of living" in Philadelphia, that he was "freezing to death," and that "the help is no help at all." Dunn clearly missed the warm climate of southern China as well as the servants he employed there.[61] Perhaps in an effort to transplant aspects of his life in China in his new American setting, he commissioned an architect to design for him a mansion in the Chinese style. In 1832, at the corner of High Street and Bartram Avenue in Mount Holly, Dunn began to build his "Chinese Cottage" just as, 35 years before, Houckgeest had constructed "China's Retreat."[62] Up to this point, Dunn's life as a China trader had yet to diverge from the standard pattern outlined by the travel writer Osmond Tiffany. "Men who had landed [in Canton] with scarce a dollar," he observed, "by enterprise, industry, and patience have in a few years been enabled to carry home sufficient [wealth] to enable them to live in luxury all the rest of their lives, to build palaces, and astonish their old friends . . . with . . . curiosities."[63]

Yet unlike Houckgeest and others, Dunn did not long for the detached life of the eccentric millionaire who passed his remaining years showing off his possessions to friends. On the contrary, he wanted to integrate himself into American life and sought civic responsibility commensurate to his newly acquired wealth and stature. According to J. S. Buckingham, a traveler from England, Dunn was "rich enough to need no further addition to his fortune, and ambitious enough to desire that his labors should enjoy their deserved reputation in his native city."[64] Though he returned home to a nation caught up in the market and social revolutions of Jacksonian America, Dunn continued to harbor ideals about the gentleman's role in society, ideals that had been shaped by the mores of an earlier era. In the classical republican tradition, he believed that, after spending a number of years pursuing financial success, one could become a virtuous gentleman only by withdrawing from the business sphere and devoting one's time and energies to the public welfare, whether that involved entering politics, engaging in scientific pursuits, or assisting in worthy philanthropic causes.

In this respect, Dunn followed the example of Benjamin Franklin, who, after amassing sufficient wealth as a printer, retired at the age of forty-two. Of course, during these years of "retirement," Franklin entered a period of tremendous activity in which he served as a statesman, advanced scientific knowledge, made several remarkable inventions, and formed institutions for the public good.[65] Dunn's impact on America's political and intellectual life could not match Franklin's, but on retiring from the China trade he did aspire to the same ideals. He joined the American Philosophical Society and the Academy of Natural Sciences and became manager of the Philadelphia House of Refuge. Perhaps to redeem himself in the eyes of the Quaker community, Dunn bailed out the foundering Haverford College, a Quaker institution, with a timely gift of $20,000.[66]

Most important, the Philadelphia Museum Company, formerly the museum of Charles Willson Peale, appointed Dunn to its board of directors in 1836. There Dunn joined a distinguished group that included John Kintzing Kane, the father of Elisha Kent Kane, who would later make a name for himself as an Arctic explorer.[67] In 1786, Charles Willson Peale had founded his museum on the concept of "rational entertainment." He designed his exhibits so that they would amuse patrons while simultaneously offering them instruction about the world. However, his son Rubens Peale assumed managerial responsibility after 1810, and competition from various other attractions such as panoramas, small circuses, and theatrical troops forced the son to compromise some of his father's ideals in order that the museum would survive. When Rubens quietly removed the museum's more prosaic exhibits and replaced them with curiosities, the museum founded on the principle of "rational entertainment" was beginning to shift away from the "rational" and toward pure "entertainment."[68] It was slowly transforming into what Neil Harris described as the typical antebellum museum: "indiscriminate assemblages" in which "paintings and sculpture" existed alongside of "mummies, mastodon bones," "stuffed animals," and other assorted oddities.[69]

The museum was undergoing hard times financially as well, and George Escol Sellers, Charles Willson Peale's grandson, believed it could stand to benefit from the invigorating influence of an entirely novel exhibit. Sellers conceived of a revamped Philadelphia Museum, to be housed in a brand-new building, in which Peale's exhibits and the Chinese collection of Nathan Dunn would coexist under one roof. Dunn agreed to the proposition and immediately backed the project with the necessary capital. He then moved to secure the plot of land, at the corner of Ninth and George Streets, that Sellers thought a propitious location for the new edifice. On January 20, 1836, the purchase was made from funds from two sources: a loan of $32,000, from the Bank of the United States, and another, from Dunn himself, amounting to $20,000. In exchange for Dunn's large initial payment, the Philadelphia Museum agreed not to charge him rent for a period of ten years. When construction was complete, Peale's Museum moved into the upper floor, and on the lower floor Dunn began to install his collection. On July 4, 1838, Peale's Museum opened in its new building with due fanfare.[70]

Dunn was not ready. He along with Titian Peale and a team of artists were working furiously in the hope that they could complete the installation of the Chinese exhibit by the end of the year.[71] The job proved to be difficult because Dunn's collection methodology had generated an exhibit of such enormous proportions that it exceeded the available space. China, it seemed, possessed a vast diversity that surpassed the holding capability of a museum. Unable to display everything at once, Dunn resigned himself to the disappointing conclusion that he would have to keep many items in storage and introduce them into the exhibit on a rotating basis.[72] He encountered the same problem in writing the *Descriptive Catalogue*, a booklet of 120 pages that would provide visitors with a guided tour. "A very large number [of exhibited items] have been omitted in the catalogue," he wrote, "as, if all had been introduced, it would have swelled the pamphlet to an unconventional size."[73] Despite these problems, Dunn and the others continued to work at a feverish pace. "The Chinese collection requires all my time," he wrote to his sister in November 1838. "I find without great exertions it cannot be opened by Christmas."[74]

## "A PANORAMIC PAGEANT OF ORIENTAL LIFE"

On the evening of December 22, Dunn held a large reception for distinguished citizens of Philadelphia to introduce his exhibit, which now bore the title "Ten Thousand Chinese Things." A group of well over one hundred invited guests, composed of "artists, merchants, mechanics, editors, literati, military and naval officers, and a goodly representation from all the learned professions," sipped a beverage made by adding sugar and cream to a juice extracted from a Chinese plant. Dunn also served a variety of tea that was so rare and of such high quality that the Chinese refused to export it. Among those in attendance was E. C. Wines, a former principal in a Philadelphia school and personal friend of Nathan Dunn. Wines described Dunn as glowing with gratification on this night as he beheld "his labours so happily terminated, and the long cherished object of his ambition crowned with so brilliant a success."[75] A journalist granted early access to the exhibit predicted that "the wonders of China" would "absorb the conversation of all, even of the busy politician and the solitary book worm." Up to now a "sealed book," China was now revealed by the museum to be "the most extraordinary nation on the earth."[76]

The next day visitors paid twenty-five cents for admission (money which went to charity), and entered the spacious saloon that measured 163 feet in length, 70 in breadth, and 35 in height.[77] Twenty-two square pillars, each adorned with paintings, supported the ceiling. According to E. C. Wines, the initial sensory overload triggered a sense of wonder in the guests:

> Here, as if touched by the wand of an enchanter, we are compelled to pause. . . . . The view is imposing in the highest degree. But it is so unlike anything we are accustomed to behold, that we are at a loss for descriptive epithets. . . . Brilliant, splendid, gorgeous, magnificent, superb—all these adjectives are liberally used by visitors.[78]

Guests were initially struck by the ten-foot, multicolored Chinese lanterns that hung from the ceiling as well as by the two enormous rectangular screens facing each other at either end of the hall. Each measured fifty feet in length and was divided into compartments that offered detailed depictions of Chinese flowers as well as panoramic views of landscapes, seascapes, and river scenes.[79] They also encountered three colossal gilded idols that presided majestically over the saloon, a representation of the Buddha in his past, present, and the future manifestations (fig. 4.3). These were recreations of originals that had caught Dunn's attention during a visit to a Buddhist shrine on Honam island, across the Pearl River from the foreign factories.[80]

Waiting to greet the guests was Nathan Dunn himself. Sidney George Fisher of Philadelphia visited the museum and noted that "Mr. Dunn was in the room himself and explained to us the nature and uses of many things."[81] In this effort, Dunn was assisted by a young Chinese man, whose job was to circulate throughout the museum and help guests understand the various displays. Of course, since most of them had never before met someone from China, the exhibitor doubled as a de facto exhibit. "What increases the interest of the scene," wrote one reporter, "is a young Chinese, in full costume, who walks about the Hall, explaining things to the visitors in bad English, and with a most amiable manner that shows he is gratified in being useful." Since no other account mentions the young man, he probably did not stay with the museum for a very long time.[82]

Even without the young Chinese man, Dunn's museum did not lack a human presence. No fewer than fifty life-size clay statues populated the salon, representing all strata of Chinese society: mandarins, priests, mourners dressed in white, tragedians, itinerant barbers, shoemakers, smiths, shopkeepers and their customers, boatmen, beggars, merchants, soldiers, and many others. J. S. Buckingham was impressed by how closely the statues and their settings approximated life:

> They are all actual figures, as large as life, moulded in clay, with a resemblance to life . . . greater than that of the finest wax-work figures. They are placed in the most natural and appropriate attitudes imaginable. They have all actual dresses of the exact kind worn by the several classes they represent and are surrounded by those several auxiliaries and accompaniments which belong to their respective dwellings or occupations, and have a reality about them, which comes the nearest to actual life of anything I have ever seen.[83]

Instead of placing rigid statues before a blank backdrop, Dunn employed dioramas. By posing the figures, providing them with the appropriate props, and situating them before colorful backgrounds, he was able to show the characteristic actions of the Chinese as well as the environments in which they lived and worked. He probably learned this exhibition technique from Peale's Museum, whose innovation it was.[84]

In the case of the scholar and his student, viewers could observe not just their respective garments but also the deferential pose struck by the student. In another case, they could see three literati discuss arcane matters while servants tended to their needs (fig. 4.4). And in Dunn's reproduction of a silk shop, visitors could watch the customer as he scrutinized the silk fabric while the shopkeeper made quick calculations on an abacus. In the most impressive of these dioramas, two sedan-chair bearers carry a Chinese gentleman down a full-scale reproduction of a Cantonese street (fig. 4.5). Surrounded by statues, one guest felt he had traveled to China and found time mysteriously standing still: "The visitor must feel as if he were examining a country, where the breath of life and the noise of instruments had suddenly ceased, and every object animate and inanimate had been left unchanged."[85] Brantz Mayer called the combined effect of all these statues and backgrounds "a panoramic pageant of Oriental life," so eerily accurate that "we almost expect to hear them speak and see them move."[86]

That each statue was unique augmented the realism of the museum. Unlike mannequins, which are only as interesting as the garments placed on them, the Chinese statues each bore the exact likeness of some actual Chinese personage. Driven to provide Americans with an accurate portrayal of China, Dunn had spent three years supervising their production, employing sculptors who used a special technique to model the clay figures from the fifty "living subjects" he had selected. And to add a final touch of realism, his sculptors embellished the statues with real human hair. The effect was such that visitors to the museum who had previously sojourned in Canton could actually recognize specific people they had seen there.[87] Dunn's statues have not survived, but the Rhode Island Historical Society possesses a statue that was brought from Canton at around the same time and that may be of the same variety (fig. 4.6).[88]

After visitors recovered from the overall effect achieved by the museum's interior, they next delved into the particulars contained in the fifty-three glass cases, each covered by a facsimile of a Chinese roof. In the cases were furniture; models of bridges, canals, pagodas, and boats; an actual boat; musical instruments; weapons; jewelry; varieties of porcelain and porcelain vases, some being six feet tall; lacquer-work; agricultural tools; a coffin; bamboo pillows; seventeen concentric ivory balls carved from a single block of ivory; spectacles with frames made of tortoise shells and lenses composed of rock; coins; a stuffed Chinese buffalo sent by William Wood; a thirteen-foot boa constrictor coiled around a wild cat of China (described above); and more than three hundred prints and paintings depicting almost every aspect of Chinese life. It was, wrote E. C. Wines, enough to "astonish" those who had previously seen only export wares.[89]

## LEARNING THROUGH OBJECTS

According to Brantz Mayer, Americans based their mental picture of China on "a tea chest" or "a China plate."[90] Clearly, Dunn saw his museum's primary mission as being didactic. Guests might enter either wholly ignorant with regard to China or possessing only fanciful images derived from porcelain, tea advertisements, or the *Arabian Nights*, but it was imperative that they not exit so same poorly informed. To effect this beneficial transformation, Dunn employed several strategies, one of which a newspaper reporter attempted to explain:

Books describe and even give engravings; but the thing described is much more forcibly impressed on the mind when we see it; we learn geography by travelling and
when a giraffe is presented to the eye, the perfect impression remains. So it is with
other matters. We are not far wrong in saying that Mr. Dunn's collection . . . at once
transports us to China. . . . [E]ven [Dunn's] highly coloured pictures would probably
fail with many [guests], if they were not conjoined with the greatest portion of the
very things they were meant to illustrate.[91]

Dunn and his visitors subscribed to what historian Steven Conn has called
an "object-based epistemology."[92] That is, they believed that displays of objects
could most forcefully convey ethnographic information. Objects were also
deemed more trustworthy than words or pictures, both of which were merely
representations of something real—not the real thing itself. Any verbal description or artist's sketch necessarily had to pass through the subjectivity of the observer, an intermediate stage during which errors or exaggerations could seep
into the presentation, tainting its accuracy. In contrast, Dunn's museum eliminated this stage of distortion by placing the authentic objects themselves before
the interested party, creating a sense of immediacy and therefore the feeling
that one had been transported to China.[93]

However, the presence of objects in a room did not in itself guarantee the
successful transmission of knowledge. Many museums in Dunn's era, though
rich in tangible things, either failed at their attempts to teach or did not bother
to try. J. S. Buckingham was so charmed by Dunn's museum that he returned to
it on numerous occasions, but he withheld his praise when commenting on
American museums as a whole:

In America . . . Museums are almost always the property of some private individual,
who gets together a mass of everything that is likely to be thought curious—good,
bad, and indifferent—the worthless generally prevailing over the valuable. The collections are then huddled together, without order or arrangement . . . and there is
generally a noisy band of musicians, and a juggler . . . to attract visitors . . . ; and
mere amusement, and that of the lightest and most uninstructive kind, is the only
object sought in visiting them.[94]

Though entertaining, such eclectic assemblages of curious oddities, lacking
in theme and organization, possessed very little educational value.

The one other institution in America that had a sizeable Chinese collection,
the East India Marine Society of Salem, was marred by flaws of the kind delineated by Buckingham. From merchants who sailed "all over the world," the
Society received a "flood of objects, good, bad, and indifferent," which included
many things from "China, India, Zanzibar, the East Indies and the Oceanic

Islands." Instead of classifying these objects by nation of origin, the curators indiscriminately jumbled them all together, creating an oriental hodgepodge out of which even the ambitious visitor would have been hard-pressed to extract information on China. In 1830, when the curators decided to check their inventory, they found not only that rust and moths were destroying numerous artifacts but also that the museum lacked an organizational scheme. However, instead of erecting partitions between the various Asian countries, they elected to group the objects by function. They placed all cooking utensils together and did the same for hats and weapons. Buckingham found the museum worth visiting but observed how few people were inside.[95]

Such museums failed to instruct because they extricated artifacts from their natural setting and placed them in exhibition halls. Once the integral parts of a human culture or natural environment, the objects became mere oddities in the eyes of visitors, devoid of didactic value. Dunn sought to remedy this situation by restoring the lost context, at least as much as was possible. The dioramas provided a colorful backdrop and gave guests a sense for how a tool was used or a body ornament worn. In addition, he hoped, visitors would purchase and consult his *Descriptive Catalogue* while they inspected the exhibits. This booklet was designed to enrich the overall museum experience by covering the macro as well as the micro: It attempted to explicate Chinese culture as a whole while also offering background information on many of the specific items on display.

But the *Catalogue* also addressed another of Dunn's pressing concerns. He was aware that many visitors would enter the exhibition hall only to find themselves visually overwhelmed. He seems to have worried about the aimless guest, that individual who would wander about in desultory manner, constantly amazed yet never really subjecting the exhibits to serious study. Such a person was easily capable of spending hours in the exhibit without registering any detectable increase in knowledge. What's worse, instead of discarding the willowware vision of China, this person might simply use the visually spectacular exhibit to inject color and detail into the bare blue-and-white outlines. In short, even after visiting the museum, a visitor might continue to conflate China with Cathay

The *Catalogue* was Dunn's attempt to exercise control over a guest's visit. Acting as a museum guide, it imposed structure onto the experience by directing the visitor's movement through the entire exhibit: "The visitor is requested to commence with the screen at the entrance, and then, turning to the left, to take the cases in the order in which they are numbered." Labeling cases with roman numerals and individual items with arabic numerals, Dunn established a specific sequence that visitors were encouraged to follow. And, as they moved through the exhibits, they could glance down at the Catalogue to gather further information about any object they found striking:

Case XIII . . . 214. Splendid cameo, presented to Mr. Dunn by Houqua, the Hong merchant. This cameo is of extraordinary size. It represents an extended landscape, including earth and sky, and embracing various rural scenes and objects.

So that Chinese characters would not mystify visitors, the *Catalogue* offered translations of anything in Chinese, such as the Chinese proverbs written vertically on the numerous wall hangings that adorned the salon. By equipping visitors with readily accessible information, Dunn hoped to obviate the usual vacuous utterances that could plague any exhibition of a foreign culture—that the objects were merely "strange," "bizarre," and "curious."

If Brantz Mayer's shifting perceptions of Dunn's museum followed a sequence shared by others, then Dunn succeeded in his didactic mission. Initially, Mayer couched his impressions purely in the terms of magic and fantasy: "The spectator seems placed in a world of enchantment—the scene is so unreal and fairylike." Though bewitched at first, he eventually shook off the trance and proceeded to use the exhibits to learn about China: "Never have I derived more instruction in the brief space of a few hours—never have I experienced more pleasure in the pursuit of knowledge—never has my imagination been more excited—never my mind more interested."[96] Initially entranced by the idea of escaping to a "world of enchantment," Mayer did, however, eventually use the museum for its intended purpose—"the pursuit of knowledge."

Indeed, Dunn's *Catalogue* did convey knowledge to visitors; however, knowledge is distinct from truth or fact. Instead, it is an understanding of a subject (here China) that is charged by ideological or personal circumstances. It was by viewing China through the ideological lens of Enlightenment science during his long residence there that Dunn acquired most of the knowledge presented in the *Catalogue*. Fittingly, it resembles in form Thomas Jefferson's *Notes on the State of Virginia*, perhaps the quintessential document that describes a region from the perspective of the American Enlightenment. Like Jefferson's *Notes*, Dunn's *Catalogue* comprehended its subject by breaking it down into categories, which included government, the arts (literature, theater, music), religion (Daoism, Buddhism, and elements of Confucianism), education, natural history, military ("the army is little better than a rabble rout, mere men of straw"), population, women (it explains the practice of footbinding), marriage (a man could divorce a woman for her garrulity), funerals, costumes, festivals, sports and pastimes, vocations, diet, agriculture, manufactures, inventions (most notably, gunpowder, magnetic needles, and a printing press), transportation, architecture (including models of summer homes, pagodas, bridges, and the Great Wall), trade, justice and the penal system (including *lingchy*, the punishment for treason, that involved cutting the offender into ten thousand pieces).

But Enlightenment science could not account for all of the knowledge contained in the *Catalogue*. In fact, Dunn acquired his strangest notion when he applied to the Chinese people a pseudoscientific theory, one related to phrenology, which had not been in circulation when he had first embarked for China in 1818. Phrenology was founded on the belief that the human mind was not unitary but rather consisted of separate organs, thirty-seven in number, each of which determined a trait, ability, or proclivity toward a certain virtue or vice. Since practitioners claimed to know the exact location of each organ, they believed they could understand an individual by reading and then interpreting the contours of the head.[97] Though now discredited, phrenology in the late 1830s was growing not only in popularity but also in acceptance by experts, as many respected men of science joined its legions of converts in believing that it held the key to understanding human nature. In fact, John Davies, who has written on the phrenology movement in America, judged the brief span of years from 1838 to 1840 to be the high-water mark.[98]

Being the intellectual capital of the country, Philadelphia attracted many prominent phrenologists who were extremely successful at convincing even the most educated and respected citizens of the scientific validity of their discipline. For this reason, phrenology and other fad sciences were an integral part of the cultural matrix in which the Chinese Museum was situated. In fact, Dunn undoubtedly knew several phrenologists personally. When the museum opened, Orson Fowler, who would become America's greatest popularizer of phrenology, was giving lectures and head examinations just a few blocks away. And in even greater proximity, George Combe of Scotland, the world's foremost phrenologist following the death of Joseph Spurzheim, was delivering a series of lectures in Peale's museum and drawing audiences of five hundred people. Dunn's exhibits occupied the same building, and Combe enjoyed a pleasurable tour of the Chinese Museum.[99]

Also in Philadelphia, one could find Samuel George Morton, who was a professor of anatomy at the Pennsylvania College, the author of *Crania Americana* (1839), and the owner of the country's largest collection of skulls. Morton's most fundamental belief was that the human skull held the key to unlocking the intellectual capability of the various races of humanity. To measure the cranial capacity of each, he collected skulls from all over the world. His laboratory research involved inverting a skull, pouring white-pepper seed into its cavity, and recording how much it could hold. Missionaries in Canton, aware of his work, sent him several Chinese specimens, including the skull of a pirate and that of a criminal who had been hanged. Though not a phrenologist by definition, Morton recognized that his theories had much in common with those espoused by phrenologists, and hence his decision to include in *Crania Americana* a lengthy essay on phrenology by George Combe.[100] Dunn probably saw both Combe and Morton on a regular basis, since all three were active members in both the Academy of Natural Sciences and the American Philosophical Society. Morton's masterwork, *Crania Americana*, rested on Dunn's bookshelf.[101]

Dunn had formed his own views of the Chinese while residing in Canton, but after returning home to Philadelphia he allowed these new theories to influence, ex post facto, observations he had already made concerning the race. In fact, we can attribute to these theories one of the rare negative assessments of the Chinese included in the *Catalogue*—a bizarre blanket statement regarding the impact of a despotic government on the anatomies of its citizens. With these new ideas percolating in his mind, Dunn revisited the subject of Chinese racial characteristics by inspecting the clay heads of his own statues. He detected "a remarkable sameness of feature and expression running through the whole collection" and, in a dangerous extrapolation, went beyond his small sample of Cantonese people to ascribe these same "general characteristics" to "the whole empire." Despite the great variation in "soil and climate" in the regions of China, he argued that a single set of physical traits prevailed: high cheekbones, black eyes, flat noses, and a yellow complexion. To explain this phenomenon, Dunn made recourse to the new pseudosciences. The subjects of a despotic regime like China, he asserted, are "all reduced to the same level, urged by the same wants, engaged in the same pursuits, actuated by the same passions." Therefore, "through a long succession of ages," they "necessarily assimilate, both mentally and physically." In other words, when rulers compel their subjects to think alike, over time this inner homogeneity manifests itself on the human exterior; all faces begin to look alike[102]

One might be tempted to dismiss Dunn's fascination with pseudoscientific theories on the grounds that, for him, it represented merely an aberration, a single ill-advised turn into an intellectual dead end made by an individual who otherwise demonstrated all the attributes of a respectable amateur scientist. However, such an assessment fails to do justice to the situation. In Dunn's mind, these theories were not separate from and unconnected to the other scientific methods of his day; rather, they existed as the logical extension of the latter and carried the same prestige. Dunn's experimentation with these spurious theories, though yielding the most outlandish idea contained in the *Catalogue*, did emanate out of a desire to understand the world, the same desire that was also the inspiration for legitimate scientific inquiry.[103]

Excepting this single instance, Dunn used the *Catalogue* to cast China in a positive light. Being a citizen of a republic that measured its age in decades, Dunn was fascinated by the amazing endurance of Chinese civilization over the centuries, a longevity he attributed to two effective strategies. First, since the "ambitious" who are thwarted in their aspirations "generally overturn governments," the Chinese designed their examination system to encourage these men to expend their energies constructively through official channels. No man in China "inherits office," regardless of his bloodline; instead, men are placed in positions of power solely through the examination system and on merit alone. In this way, the talented and ambitious are led to assist in the governing of China instead of to "the dreadful alternative of revolutionizing the country."

Second, Dunn pointed to a complex set of duties and responsibilities that dictated an individual's relationships with his family, society, and the government. This "doctrine of responsibility," as Dunn called Confucianism, enjoyed universal acceptance because it was effectively inculcated at an early age: "The sentiments held to be appropriate to man in society, are imbibed with the milk of infancy, and iterated and reiterated through the whole of subsequent life." In this regard, the Chinese "set us an example worthy of imitation" because, whereas we speak only of "Our rights," the Chinese focus on *our duty* (emphasis in original). Here, Dunn appears to show concern for a potential problem in American society, one that Alexis de Tocqueville observed in 1830 — that is, the need for a counterweight to offset rampant individualism.[104] Unlike in the United States, in China one could count on state-sanctioned Confucianism to hold the destructive selfish impulses of individuals in check. The early and constant education on "personal and political duties" functioned as a kind of social glue, Dunn wrote, lending cohesion for the whole nation. The result was "a country enjoying . . . a perpetuity of national existence unequalled in the world's history."[105]

The *Catalogue* also contains Dunn's appreciation of Chinese industry. "Whoever attentively examines the immense collection of Chinese curiosities," Dunn claimed, "will need no further proof of the ingenuity of the Chinese in arts and manufactures" and in the "several branches of labour, both agricultural and mechanical." As the United States was then in an early stage of industrialization, Dunn could appreciate the "various contrivances," many being "simple, ingenious, and efficient," through which the Chinese were able to "force nature to become their handmaid."[106] He found an attentive audience in Benjamin Silliman, who saw the exhibits of "rakes, hoes, axes, shovels" and other implements to be particularly eye-opening. Whereas Silliman had been taught to believe that an American tool offered the only way to accomplish a given task, the museum showed him that a completely different tool of Chinese origin was just as good for the purpose. A given "operation," he wrote, "is equally well executed by another of totally different figure." In addition, Silliman noted a "thousand things" that proved that many of our "common usages" were derived from devices in China, a country that "we are accustomed to believe" is "centuries behind us." Among these, he found especially amusing a Chinese mousetrap, of a design patented in America, "that has been used in

China for ages." In short, the exhibit proved to him that his preconceptions regarding China were wrong.[107]

In favorably describing Chinese civilization as accomplished, durable, complex, and even innovative, Dunn was merely conveying his own true assessment to readers of the *Descriptive Catalogue*. Yet he also had a rhetorical strategy, as readers discovered when, on reaching the end of booklet, they met with his views on the opium trade. Even for a reader who had agreed with Dunn's overall appraisal of the Chinese up to this point, outrage was the only suitable reaction to this dark side of the Chinese economy. It was true, Dunn wrote, that through the sale of opium the British had accomplished their objective in that a trade imbalance that had previously favored China had now reversed course: He estimated that $20 million flowed annually out of China and into the English economy. But what were the moral ramifications of this apparently effective economic strategy? "Yet if the sum were ten times as great as it is," Dunn wrote, "it could not affect the question in its moral bearings. Opium is a poison, destructive alike of the health and morals of those who use it habitually, and, therefore, the traffic in it . . . is nothing less than making merchandise of the bodies and souls of men." In short, as silver bullion moved from the East to the West, filling English treasuries with wealth, morality flowed in the opposite direction, leaving England morally bankrupt.

Though much of the culpability deservedly rested on English shoulders, Dunn was quite familiar with the trading practices of his own countrymen after living for eight uninterrupted years with them in the foreign factories. "But it is not England alone that is to blame in this matter," he wrote. "Most of our own merchants in Canton are guilty in the same way, and to an equal extent." In mentioning American involvement, Dunn hoped he could raise the ire of ordinary citizens. And to augment their outrage further, he explained the relationship between opium and the Protestant missions. Dunn was raised a Quaker and Quakers usually did not proselytize and certainly did not have any presence in China. Yet he knew that America was in the throes of an evangelical movement (now called the Second Great Awakening) and that the majority of the visitors to his museum were Protestants who supported the foreign missions. Acutely aware of this audience, he explained exactly why missionaries were encountering so much resistance in China. The "grasping avarice" of opium traders, he wrote, undermines the moral and spiritual message of the missionaries and "sets at naught every Christian obligation before the very eyes of the people whom it sought to convert!" The Chinese would never choose to convert to Christianity as long as the most visible emissaries from a Christian nation, the merchants, continued to inflict a blight on their society.[108]

With Dunn's emphasis on education, the museum soon acquired such an excellent reputation that people from other cities and towns began forming travel parties solely for the purpose of paying it a visit.[109] But just because the museum was, by mid-nineteenth-century standards, well-equipped to educate does not mean that it did. After all, education depends as much on the receptivity of the student as it does on the capability of the instructor. Also, the museum's popularity did not mean that visitors swallowed whole Dunn's generally positive views of China. They might have processed the exhibits in their own preconceived frameworks, or they might have eschewed intellectual engagement altogether despite the structured nature of the kind of visit advised in the *Descriptive Catalogue*. What do the jottings of visitors say about the reception of the museum?

## RESPONSES TO THE EXHIBIT

After returning from China, Nathan Dunn maintained a strong curiosity about distant lands, filling his shelves with travel narratives and histories of other nations.[110] In this sense, his interests mirrored those of his countrymen who were showing a penchant for seeking out the facts about foreign places. Carl Bode, in his work on popular culture, isolated "restlessness," "a thirst for new experience and knowledge," and a "desire to explore" as common American traits in the antebellum era. However, since most Americans were bound to their farms, places of business, or families, only a small number of people could actually act on these yearnings. The rest simply enjoyed what appeared to be the next best thing—the "vicarious experience" one could obtain by reading about the journeys of others. This appetite generated a "vogue for travel literature."[111]

But was reading truly the next best thing? In assessing the contribution of Dunn's exhibit, one writer identified three modes of vicarious experience and ranked them in ascending order: reading travel narratives, seeing two-dimensional panoramas, and walking through the three-dimensional experience exemplified by Dunn's creation.[112] Dunn's all-inclusive collection methodology had yielded an exhibit composed of realistic statues positioned in dioramas, a plethora of paintings, and a prodigious number of authentic Chinese objects. In the minds of visitors, all of these combined to simulate an actual tour of China, and they voiced the near-unanimous opinion that a feeling of virtual travel made the museum experience remarkable. We will "long remember our last Saturday evening's excursion to Canton," wrote a reporter for the *Public Ledger*.[113] "Mr. Dunn's collection," agreed the *Saturday Courier*, "at once transports us to China."[114] Another journalist expressed awe of a quasireligious nature at the illusion of travel: "You can hardly realize that you have not been transported by some superhuman power to the opposite side of the globe" because the many marvelous sights "combine to produce a most bewildering effect upon the startled gaze of the beholder as he enters, and it is long before he can realize that he is in the city of Penn."[115]

Some guests theorized that the exhibit had ushered in not only the next great stage in the evolution of tourism but also the final stage. For, quite ironically, just as the United States was entering into its transportation revolution, Dunn's *virtual travel* had, or so it was thought, forever rendered *actual travel* obsolete. E. C. Wines chimed in on the theme of stationary sightseeing, proclaiming that one no longer had to "subject one's self to the hazards and privations of a six months' voyage on distant and dangerous seas, to enjoy a peep at the Celestial Empire."[116] Another writer suggested that, by removing travel from the equation, Dunn had democratized the international experience. Although the new "locomotive facilities" afford some with the opportunity to travel, many "cannot avail themselves of these facilities" owing to financial considerations. But they "may yet obtain the most minute knowledge of distant countries" thanks to this concept of "presenting exact resemblances" of a country. Whereas the railroad can "annihilate distance," the Chinese Museum "may be said to approximate places."[117]

The exhibit, then, raised an intriguing question: If one possessed the means to construct an exact replica of a place, was a journey to the actual place still worth the trouble? J. S. Buckingham believed that, for most people, it was not. The Chinese Museum, he wrote, "comes the nearest to actually traveling in the country, and communicating personally with the people, of anything that has yet been devised." Moreover, the exhibit inspired Buckingham to envision a futuristic London that would be complete with exhibits from all nations and that would follow Dunn's model. So that "the tour of the globe might thus be made" at home, he proposed that the British government part with one million sterling to acquire such hypothetical collections.[118]

Brantz Mayer adopted this same theme in his description of the Chinese Museum, claiming that Dunn had placed China "within the reach of the remotest inquiring inhabitant of our Union." "China re-existed in America," he wrote, "as by necromancy." Since Mayer had visited China in 1827, he felt qualified to vouch for the strong resemblance between Dunn's fabricated China and the real place: "The verisimilitude is perfect and seems to be the prestige of magic."[119] As these references to "magic" and "necromancy" suggest, the experience of seeing China in the United States was akin to the occult.

Mayer also went so far as to state that "a man may learn more of China . . . in a single visit to Mr. Dunn's Collection, than could be acquired in a month's reading, or even in a voyage to Canton."[120] A guidebook for Philadelphia echoed this sentiment, declaring that "every one who takes pleasure in accurate knowledge, will here find, in a few hours, that which cannot be procured, from reading, views from engravings, or even an *actual visit to China*" (emphasis in original).[121] Similarly, J. S. Buckingham wrote that one could learn more about China in the museum than by "a month's hard reading on the subject."[122] And in what was clearly a common refrain, Joseph Sturge, another traveler from England, agreed that "by spending a few hours in his museum, with the aid of the descriptive catalogue, one may learn more of the Chinese than by laborious perusal of all the works upon them that have ever been written."[123]

While these claims that the museum surpassed both books about China and actual experience in China may seem like hyperbole, we must recall that foreigners at this time had access to only a small strip of riverfront land outside Canton. Just prior to the opening of the Chinese Museum, an American named T. C. Downing published *The Fan-Qui in China in 1836–7*, a book about his journey to China. In a review of it, the writer voiced a complaint that applied to all books on China: "Mr. Downing seems to have had no other scope for observation than that which is furnished by the usual passage from Macao to Canton." The reviewer added that any "glimpses" from other parts of the empire, were they to become available, would be "greedily digested."[124] Since Dunn's museum actually provided the greatly anticipated "glimpses" of the country beyond Canton, one can easily understand the excitement it aroused.

## THE EXHIBIT IN ENGLAND

J. S. Buckingham, in urging Dunn to move the collection to London, noted how poorly understood it was in the United States. Americans, he insisted, lacked the proper "temperament" to comprehend the collection; they were inhibited by a "coldness and indifference" to the acquisition of knowledge. It was within their ability to comment only that this object was "neat" while that one was "pretty" and to guess the total value of the collection and the profits reaped by the owner.[125] Buckingham would have his wish, but the evidence does not support the charge of "indifference" he leveled against Americans. In nearly three years in Philadelphia, hundreds of thousands came to visit the Chinese Museum, and Dunn sold 50,000 copies of the *Descriptive Catalogue*.[126] By comparison, in London an enlarged and partially illustrated version of the *Catalogue* sold only 20,000 copies over a longer span of time.[127]

The chain of events that resulted in the move to London began in November 1841. On the morning of November 6, a warrant was issued in Philadelphia for the arrest of Nathan Dunn on charges that he had committed "assault and battery, with an intent to commit an unnatural crime." His accuser, a man named Lewis V. Curry, offered testimony that the "alleged transaction between the parties" took place in the pit of the Walnut Street Theatre. Nathan Dunn, apparently fearful of prison and the embarrassment of a public trial, agreed to pay his accuser $1,000 if the latter would drop all charges.

Although this resolution appeared to end the matter, the city magistrate, not certain that justice had been served by the hasty settlement, revisited the case for further examination. He deemed the alleged crime to be "far too gross for a recital" but identified at least two major problems with Curry's testimony. First, in "so populous a city as Philadelphia," Curry's failure to produce a second witness was problematic. Second, his credibility suffered a serious blow when he at first identified the perpetrator as Nathan Dunn, "not the proprietor of the Chinese Museum, but some other Nathan Dunn," before ultimately accusing the owner of the Chinese collection. In the end, the magistrate sided with Dunn: "To justify the binding over of a citizen of honest character on such accusations, the evidence should be unimpeachable." It was not, and Dunn was summarily discharged. Curry, on the other hand, did not fare as well; the magistrate indicted him with extortion.[128]

Dunn does not refer to this episode in any of his existing letters, but he may have believed that it had sullied his reputation to the point where he could not remain in Philadelphia. Whatever its impact, he had an economic reason for departing. In 1841, the financial ineptitude of the Philadelphia Museum Company reached his attention, and he promptly ordered a full investigation. The findings revealed that the company and the bank had never finalized the purchase of the land on which the museum stood. In addition, the new building had cost nearly $60,000 more than the contracted figure of $80,000. And so, not only was the magnificent new edifice resting on property to which the company had no title, but the company was mired in substantial debt. Dunn had had enough, and later that year he struck the decisive blow. He would follow Buckingham's advice by moving the collection to London.[129]

If Dunn was repelled by these two incidents, he was equally attracted by the unique benefits afforded by London. According to the London Illustrated News, "many influential scientific and learned persons" had been urging Dunn to show his collection in England. Indeed, the exhibit could draw a different kind of visitor in the British capital, it being larger and far more cosmopolitan than Philadelphia.[130] And more important, London provided a superior location for a man intent on effecting a specific kind of political change. With England and China now at war, Dunn hoped that, by demonstrating the beauty of Chinese civilization to English subjects and dignitaries, he could alter British policy in some way beneficial to the Chinese. If the indignant reaction of Joseph Sturge, an Englishman, offered any indication, Dunn had every reason to be confident. Sturge's experience in the museum prompted a diatribe against his own country's "cruel and unjust war" against a "highly cultivated and unoffending people." Like the slave trade, opium trafficking was "hateful in the sight of God and man" and needed to be "suppressed."[131]

Perhaps sensing his exhibit's political potential, Dunn declined the generous offer of Louis Philippe, the iing of France, to purchase the collection for $100,000.[132] Instead, he had all four tons of it loaded onto the packet ship *Hendrick Hudson*, and, in December 1841, he set sail for London.[133] The Chinese Collection had left Philadelphia for good, but it had not failed to make an indelible impression. "By the power of mneumonic association," wrote Brantz Mayer, "I feel that after having seen the Chinese Collection—if I either think or speak of any part of the room . . . the whole salon will rise at once to my view—and I shall seem to survey, as in a mental panorama, all that is worthy or wonderful in the Chinese Empire."[134]

When Dunn settled in London in 1842, the English had just scored a decisive victory over the Chinese, had taken Hong Kong as part of their spoils, and were aglow with a chauvinistic euphoria. They also hungered for information on China, as no public exhibitions were available to satiate their curiosity. As recently as 1838, Londoners could have attended the nightly unfurling of a panorama of Chinese scenery (based on an original by a Chinese artist) painted by Robert Burford. Promoters claimed that the panorama could "equal what the most brilliant fancy, or glowing imagination, could have conceived of this extraordinary people," but it actually supplied only a view of the foreign factories.[135] With almost no competition, Dunn could capitalize on the new popular interest in China and educate the public about the nation over which England now exerted a greater influence.[136] He moved his collection into a building at Hyde Park Corner that was specially constructed for its use. For a public that had only recently expressed tremendous enthusiasm for George Catlin's Indian Gallery in the Egyptian Hall, Dunn's Chinese Museum promised a similar pleasure.[137]

Following English protocol, Dunn gave private tours to important personages before opening the museum to the general public: first to the queen, then to the nobility, and finally to the "men of literature and science."[138] Queen Victoria, in fact, contacted Dunn and "expressed her gracious intention of honoring the exhibition with her presence." At the scheduled hour, Dunn escorted Victoria and Prince Albert through the exhibit, with Dunn presenting the contents of each case to his royal guests. That the queen had studied up on China before the visit was evident in her ability to describe a given article's function without the aid of Dunn's explanation. The queen arrived at a quarter to four and did not leave until half past five.[139] As for Dunn, he felt honored by her patronage and even saved the glove he had worn that day.[140]

When the museum opened to the general public, large placards posted all over the city whetted the public's appetite, and omnibuses made runs from all sections of London.[141] From the street, visitors first entered through a two-story pagoda with green roofs edged with vermilion, and next they walked beneath a grand sign written in gilded Chinese characters that read, "Ten Thousand Chinese Things." They then passed into the main exhibition hall, which was 240 feet long, 50 feet wide, and dominated by the three imposing statues of Buddha.[142] At some point in the collection's stay in London, the museum employed actual Chinese people with whom visitors could converse. Two children, A. Sheng and A. Yow, made a living at the exhibition after the death of their English sponsor, a sea captain.[143]

Dunn had hoped the Chinese Museum would influence British policy, and in this regard he was probably disappointed. He tried to arrange an exclusive showing for both houses of Parliament by soliciting the aid of the duke of Wellington, who had made a previous visit. The duke, unfortunately, proved unhelpful. A special showing was unnecessary, he politely replied to Dunn, since any parliamentary member whom the museum might influence would undoubtedly make plans to visit on his own time.[144] Although the Chinese Museum failed to alter policy, it did at least show the victors of the Opium War the face of the vanquished. Many reporters expressed a heightened appreciation for Chinese culture; a columnist for *John Bull* wrote that "many of our preconceived notions were scattered to the winds by it."[145]

The exhibit captured London's interest for nearly half a decade, netting $50,000 a year.[146] One publication hailed it as "more amusing, interesting, and instructive than any we have ever had in the British Metropolis."[147] When the duke de Montpensier, the son of the king of France, visited England in 1844, he chose to see only one museum during his stay—the Chinese Museum.[148] As testimony to its popularity, James Robertson Planché, the playwright, composed Drama at Home, a theatrical production that spoofed Dunn's Chinese exhibits along with the other attractions of London—Catlin's Indians, Madame Tussaud's wax figures, and P. T. Barnum's prized midget, General Tom Thumb. The main character, Puff, describes the Chinese Collection in terms of virtual travel: "If only to see China is your care, / You needn't stir a step—you have it *there*"(emphasis in original).[149]

By the time the London audience at last tired of the Chinese Museum in 1846, their fascination had outlived even the owner. Nathan Dunn died in Vevey, Switzerland, on September 29, 1844.[150] Under the guidance of the curator, Dunn's longtime friend William B. Langdon, the exhibit began a tour of the provinces.[151]

# CONCLUSION

Interestingly, some visitors expressed their sincere opinion that Dunn's Chinese Museum would be the first as well as the last of its kind to ever grace an American city. It was "formed by a happy combination of circumstances," wrote a reporter, "that may not, and probably will not, ever occur to an American again."[152] Even if someone could muster a comparable effort, many questioned the need for a new Chinese exhibit. The Chinese, they reasoned, demonstrated so much pride and satisfaction in their cultural attainments that they would not ever see the need to make alterations. And since China would never change, another exhibition of its culture could only be redundant. Holding this view, Brantz Mayer conferred symbolic significance onto the three Buddhist idols, asserting that the Chinese Museum possessed "permanent value" because it represented the "PAST—the PRESENT and the FUTURE of the nation." The Chinese were, he concluded, *a petrified people* (emphasis in original).[153]

After Dunn removed the collection to England, the effects of the Opium War were already starting to consign Mayer's predictions to obsolescence. In 1843, Nathan Dunn watched from his home in London as one ship after another set sail for Canton. British merchants and missionaries, no longer convinced that change in China was impossible, were heading there with newfound vigor. In Dunn's opinion, their hope for finding China more open to British manufactures and evangelism was ill-founded. In a chilling prophecy, he augured failure for merchants and missionaries alike. The former dreamed of reaping a "golden harvest" from greater access to China's markets in the wake of the war, but they would find only "straw," as the opium trade was "draining that country of all the precious metals." If the trade were not stopped, "in ten or fifteen years more China will [be] a poor country," unable to purchase foreign goods. And as for the missionaries then "going out in great numbers," Dunn predicted that they would confront a populace that associated their efforts to proselytize with the sins of the avaricious merchants. Missionaries would ultimately face the hard truth, he predicted, that "opium and the Bible cannot enter China together."[154]

Still, everyone agreed that the increased foreign presence in China would force China to change. One British reporter who wrote a piece on the museum, forgoing the standard rhapsodizing on the wonders of virtual travel, opted for something more elegiac in tone. "It is singular enough," he wrote rather dolefully, "that to Mr. Catlin and Mr. Dunn . . . we are indebted for the most valuable assemblages of modern times: the one rescuing the memory and memorials of the Red Indians from oblivion; the other portraying China as it was five years ago, but, most probably, as it will never be again—for the European has entered its sanctuaries, and, the privacy of the Chinese once violated, they must become more assimilated to us in all things."[155]

China was indeed opening up to the world. Just a few years after Mayer's pronouncements regarding the permanence of Dunn's museum, the idea for a similar museum was already churning in the mind of America's great showman. P. T. Barnum, residing in London in 1844 to promote his latest sensation, General Tom Thumb, witnessed firsthand the attractive power of Dunn's Chinese Museum. According to one newspaper, he even reached an agreement with Dunn to purchase the Chinese collection.[156] This report turned out to be inaccurate (Barnum may have spoken with Dunn but the collection never changed hands), but Barnum would later acquire a different Chinese collection, which he displayed in New York.[157] And just two months after the Dunn's death, word reached the United States that a second Chinese museum, one larger than his, was "about to be attempted by a gentleman in this country." John Peters, an attaché on Caleb Cushing's diplomatic mission to China, was in the process of assembling his own mammoth Chinese collection.[158] His story will be told in chapter 7.

## NOTES

1. The events surrounding the fire of 1822 also impressed on Dunn a favorable view of China's poorer citizens. For in the midst of all the chaos, an elderly Chinese gentleman walked away with about ten bags of silver belonging to Dunn, each worth $1,000. As well as being poor, the man had a large family, and he could easily have kept the small fortune without getting caught. However, in an act of honesty that, according to Dunn, "says something for the poor people of China," he returned the bags of silver to the pleasantly astonished owner. *Isaac Jones, Richard Oakford, and Samuel T. Jones vs. Nathan Dunn, Defendant, February 1832,* (Philadelphia: Brown, Bicking, and Guilbert, printers, 1835; the only known account of this legal case is owned by the Library Company of Philadelphia), 34–35; and Joan Kerr Facey Thill, "A Delawarean in the Celestial Empire: John Richardson Latimer and the China Trade" (master's thesis, University of Delaware, 1973), 40.

2. Nathan Dunn, *"Ten Thousand Things Chinese": A Descriptive Catalogue of the Chinese Collection in Philadelphia* (Philadelphia, 1839), 3.

3. Philadelphia Directories. Nelson B. Gaskill Papers, Historical Society of Pennsylvania.

4. Jean Gordon Lee, *Philadelphians and the China Trade, 1784–1844* (Philadelphia: Philadelphia Museum of Art, 1984), 14. Arthur Hummel, "Nathan Dunn," *Quaker History* 59, no. 1 (1970): 34–38.

5. Testimony against Nathan Dunn, 28 November 28–5 December 1816, Minutes from the Monthly Meeting of Friends of Philadelphia, Gaskill Papers.

6. Hummel, 34–38.

7. John Curtis Perry, *Facing West: Americans and the Opening of the Pacific* (Westport, Conn.: Praeger, 1994), 41. John Murray Forbes and John Cushing in just a few years each made enough money to retire and invest their substantial profits in American industry. Yen-p'ing Hao, "Chinese Teas to America—A Synopsis," *America's China Trade in Historical Perspective: The Chinese and American Performance*, ed. Ernest R. May and John King Fairbank (Cambridge: Committee on American–East Asian Relations of the Department of History in collaboration with the Council on East Asian Studies, Harvard University; distributed by Harvard University Press, 1986), 29–30. The trader Benjamin Shreve of Salem listed his priorities in life: "approving conscience . . . irreproachable character, good health, a good wife, and plenty of money!" Carl Crossman, *The China Trade: Export Paintings, Furniture, Silver, and Other Objects* (Princeton, N.J.: Pyne Press, 1972), 7.

8. *Isaac Jones, Richard Oakford, and Samuel T. Jones vs. Nathan Dunn*, 33.

9. Tyler Dennett, *Americans in Eastern Asia: A Critical Study of the Policy of the United States with Reference to China, Japan, and Korea in the Nineteenth century* (New York: Macmillan, 1922), 49; and Foster Rhea Dulles, *The Old China Trade* (Boston and New York: Houghton Mifflin, 1930), 18–19.

10. Nathan Dunn, letter, 13 April 1824, Quaker Collection, Haverford College.

11. David Abeel, *Journal of a Residence in China, and the Neighboring Countries* (New York: Leavitt, Lord, 1834), 77–85.

12. Ibid.

13. *Poulson's American Daily Advertiser* (3 January and 16 February 1820).

14. *Isaac Jones, Richard Oakford, and Samuel T. Jones vs. Nathan Dunn*, 33–34.

15. Nathan Dunn, letter, 19 November 1821, the Quaker Collection, Haverford College.

16. *Isaac Jones, Richard Oakford, and Samuel T. Jones vs. Nathan Dunn*, 33–34.

17. The two banished merchants were Man-hop and Pac-qua. William Wood, *Sketches of China* (Philadelphia: Carey and Lea, 1830), 221–22, 227–28. Robert Bennet Forbes, *Remarks on China and the China Trade* (Boston: Samuel N. Dickinson, 1844), 14.

18. See Henry Hollinsworth to John Latimer, letter, 6 May 1815, Latimer Family Papers (col. 235). A similar list appears in the papers of William Bell (mic. 107) and in the 1804 "Sea Journal" of the anonymous supercargo of the ship Confederacy (Downs Collection, Winterthur Library).

19. Charles Tyng, *Before the Wind: The Memoir of an American Sea Captain, 1808–1833*, ed. Susan Fels (New York: Viking Penguin, 1999), 67.

20. Forbes, 14. Since Houqua could not speak English very well and Dunn knew only a few words of Cantonese, the two undoubtedly communicated using Pidgin English. Pidgin English was a hybrid language that involved the insertion of English, Indian, and Portuguese words into Chinese sentence patterns. One could learn this simple language quickly, and business interactions between Western and Chinese traders depended on it.

21. Dennett, 59.

22. Perry, 29. Elma Loines, ed., *The China Trade Post-Bag of the Seth Low Family of Salem and New York* (Manchester, Maine: Falmouth Publishing House, 1953), 300–1.

23. Loines, 6. Houqua also used his American friends to invest in the stock market for him. Patrick Conner, *George Chinnery, 1774–1852: Artist of India and the China Coast* (Woodbridge, Suffolk, England: Antique Collectors' Club, 1993), 172. As well, Houqua was fascinated by what he had heard of American railroads. After his death in 1843, his family invested some of his wealth in this booming industry. Yen-p'ing Hao, 30.

24. *Isaac Jones, Richard Oakford, and Samuel T. Jones vs. Nathan Dunn*, 33–34. William Wood, a friend of Dunn's, explained the economic situation and England's retaliatory measures: "The extensive importation of British goods in American vessels had been materially detrimental to the Company's trade in China, and, as they found it impracticable to prevent the exportation from England by Americans, they resolved to thwart them, by using their influence to affect their sales in Canton." William Wood, *Sketches of China*, 64.

25. *Isaac Jones, Richard Oakford, and Samuel T. Jones vs. Nathan Dunn*, 37.

26. Harriet Low, journal entry, 22 June 1830, in *China Trade Post-Pag*, ed. Loines, 127.

27. Dennett, 46–49.

28. "*Commonwealth v. Nathan Dunn*," *Reports of Some of the Criminal Cases on Primary Hearing, before Richard Vaux, Recorder of the City of Philadelphia: Together with Some Remarks on the Writ of Habeas Corpus and Forms of Proceeding in Criminal Cases* (Philadelphia: T. and J. W. Johnson, 1846), 4–12.

29. For Dunn's collecting, see Brantz Mayer, *A Nation in a Nutshell*, pamphlet, Department of Rare Books, Library of Congress (Philadelphia: Brown, Bicking, and Guilbert, 1841); E. C. Wines, *A Peep at China in Mr. Dunn's Chinese Collection* (Philadelphia: Ashmead, 1839), 10; and J. S. Buckingham, *The Eastern and Western States of America* (London: Fisher, Son, 1842), 2:44.

30. Benjamin Silliman, "Mr. Dunn's Chinese Collection," *American Journal of Science and Arts* (January 1839): 392–93; and *Public Ledger* (28 December 1838). Also see Dunn's obituary in that same newspaper (24 October 1844).

31. Walter Muir Whitehill, *The East India Marine Society and the Peabody Museum of Salem: A Sesquicentennial History* (Salem, Mass.: Peabody Museum, 1949), 37–38.

32. Benjamin Silliman, *Mr. Dunn's Chinese Collection in Philadelphia*, pamphlet, Department of Rare Books, Library of Congress (Philadelphia: Brown, Bicking, and Guilbert, 1841).

33. Lee, 14–15; Jonathan Goldstein, *Philadelphia and the China Trade, 1682–1846: Commercial, Cultural, and Attitudinal Effects* (University Park: Pennsylvania State University Press, 1978), 51–53; Loines, 7, 298. Perry, 41.

34. Conner, 227.

35. Dunn, *Descriptive Catalogue*, 119.

36. Mayer, *A Nation in a Nutshell*.

37. Wines, *A Peep at China*, 10–11.

38. Silliman, *Mr. Dunn's Chinese Collection.*

39. Buckingham, 2:44.

40. Daniel Bowen, *A History of Philadelphia . . . Designed as a Guide to Citizens and Strangers* (Philadelphia: Daniel Owen, 1839), 85–86.

41. "Chinese Collection," *Philadelphia Saturday Courier* (22 December 1838).

42. Goldstein, 51.

43. One such poem is reprinted in W. C. Hunter, *The Fan Kwei at Canton before Treaty Days, 1825–1844* (London: Kegan Paul, 1882; reprint, Taipei: Ch'eng-wen, 1965), 109.

44. William Wood, *Sketches of China* (Philadelphia: Carey and Lea, 1830).

45. For an account of the duel, see Harriet Low, journal entry, 30 April 1832, in *China Trade Post-Bag*, ed. Loines, 151.

46. H. H. King, ed., and Prescott Clarke, *A Research Guide to China-Coast Newspapers, 1822–1911* (Cambridge: Harvard East Asian Research Center, 1965), 15–17, 160. Wood's exact role in the introduction of photography to China is uncertain, and other figures deserve attention. George West, an artist and photographer attached to Caleb Cushing's mission to China in 1844, is discussed in a later chapter. And Eliphalet Brown, the daguerrotypist who accompanied Commodore Perry to Japan in 1854, helped Hong Kong become an important center of early photography. William H. Goetzmann, *New Lands, New Men: America and the Second Great Age of Discovery* (New York: Penguin, 1986), 347–48.

47. Silliman, "Mr. Dunn's Chinese Collection," *American Journal of Science and Arts* (January 1839): 393.

48. Joseph Kastner, *A Species of Eternity* (New York: Knopf, 1977), xii–xiv, 3–5.

49. Peale was organizing his museum in 1792, two years after Franklin's death. Charles Coleman Sellers, *Mr. Peale's Museum: Charles Willson Peale and the First Popular Museum of Natural Science and Art* (New York: Norton, 1980), 60.

50. William H. Goetzmann and William N. Goetzmann, *The West of the Imagination* (New York: Norton, 1986), 15–35.

51. The individual who summed up this age and whom many of these Philadelphians lionized most was Alexander von Humboldt, the great Prussian explorer. William H. Goetzmann, *New Lands, New Men*, 59.

52. William H. Goetzmann, *New Lands, New Men*, 2–3, 59–60.

53. Mayer, "China and the Chinese," *Southern Quarterly Review* (July 1847), 6–7.

54. William Wood, *Sketches of China*, 243.

55. After stuffing the wildcat, Wood was able to sell the skinless body back to the showman, who used it to concoct "a panacea, an elixir of life" meant "to prolong the life of his father." William Wood, *Sketches of China*, 197

56. Silliman, "Mr. Dunn's Chinese Collection," *American Journal of Science and Arts* (January 1839): 398–99.

57. Hummel, 34–38.

58. Harriet Low, journal entry, 25 January 1831, in *China Trade Post-Bag*, ed. Loines, 135.

59. According to Bowen's 1839 guide to Philadelphia, Dunn was one of the city's "most wealthy and respectable citizens." Bowen, 82.

60. Sellers, *Mr. Peale's Museum*, 273.

61. John Reeves's son to Harriet Low, letter, received by Low on 18 August 1832, Gaskill Papers.

62. Hummel, 34–38.

63. Osmond Tiffany Jr., *The Canton Chinese; or, The American's Sojourn in the Celestial Empire* (Boston: James Monroe, 1849), 213. Tiffany traveled to China in 1844.

64. Buckingham, 44.

65. Gordon S. Wood, *The Radicalism of the American Revolution* (New York: Knopf, 1992), 38, 85–86, 104. See also *The Autobiography of Benjamin Franklin: A Genetic Text*, ed. J. A. Leo Lemay and P. M. Zall (Knoxville: University of Tennessee Press, 1981).

66. Lee, 16.

67. Sellers, *Mr. Peale's Museum*, 271.

68. Sellers, *Mr. Peale's Museum*, 15, 19, 60, 215; Neil Harris, *Humbug: the Art of P. T. Barnum* (Boston: Little, Brown, 1973), 35; and Edward Alexander, *Museum Masters: Their Museums and Their Influence* (Nashville, Tenn.: American Association for State and Local History, 1983), 5.

69. Harris, 78–79.

70. Sellers, *Mr. Peale's Museum*, 273–75, 280. See "Chinese Museum, Account of Financing of Philadelphia Museum's Building," *Philadelphia Saturday Courier* (7 July 1838), Society Collection (1838), Historical Society of Pennsylavia.

71. Sellers, *Mr. Peale's Museum*, 34–35, 92, 280. According to the *Philadelphia Saturday Courier*, "A great number of artists have been at work for three months in getting it ready, and really the labor performed in that period has been surprising" (22 December 1838).

72. Wines, *A Peep at China*, 12.

73. Dunn, *Descriptive Catalogue*, 92.

74. Nathan Dunn to Rhoda Osborn (his sister), letter, 23 November 1838, Quaker Collection, Haverford College.

75. Wines, *A Peep at China*, 10, 15; *Public Ledger* (28 December 1838).

76. "Chinese Collection," *Philadelphia Saturday Courier* (22 December 1838).

77. Sellers, *Mr. Peale's Museum*, 294–95.

78. Wines, *A Peep at China*, 15.

79. *Chinese Repository* (November 1843), 567–58. Since Nathan Dunn's friends and acquaintances back in Canton were intrigued by his museum, he sent the Repository a packet of press clippings, which it then used as the nucleus of an article.

80. Both David Abeel and William Wood described the same shrine. Abeel, 88–89. William Wood, *Sketches of China*, 87.

81. *A Philadelphia Perspective: The Diary of Sidney George Fisher Covering the Years 1834–1871*, ed. Nicholas B. Wainwright (Philadelphia: Historical Society of Pennsylvania, 1967), 65–66.

82. *Public Ledger* (28 December 1838).

83. Buckingham, 2:46–47. Buckingham probably appreciated Dunn's anti-opium stance, having himself brought before Parliament, on 13 June 1833, an invective on the demoralizing tendency of opium. Forbes, 51.

84. Charles Coleman Sellers, "Peale's Museum and 'The New Museum Idea,'" *Proceedings of the American Philosophical Society* 124, no. 1 (February 1980), 25–27.

85. *Chinese Repository* (March 1840), 583–84.

86. Mayer, "China and the Chinese," 6–7; Mayer, *A Nation in a Nutshell.*

87. Silliman, "Mr. Dunn's Chinese Collection," *American Journal of Science and Arts* (January 1839): 394; and Crossman, 205.

88. In 1833, Isaac Bull sent this statue of a male, along with a statue of a female, from Canton to his uncle Edward Carrington, the former U.S. consul to China. Rhode Island Historical Society.

89. Wines, *A Peep at China*, 80–81.

90. Mayer, *A Nation in a Nutshell.*

91. "Chinese Collection," *Philadelphia Saturday Courier* (22 December 1838). The reporter chose the giraffe as his example because, in the closing months of 1838, Philadelphia was awaiting with great anticipation the arrival of a giraffe from Africa via New York—it was the first time a representative from this species had been exhibited in the United States (*Philadelphia Saturday Courier* [15 September 1838]). By the opening of Dunn's museum, the giraffe had arrived (*Public Ledger* [25 December 1838]).

92. Steven Conn, *Museums and American Intellectual Life, 1876–1926* (Chicago: University of Chicago Press, 1998), 4. E. C. Wines, a former school principal, surely approved of Dunn's use of objects. In a treatise (published the same year that the museum opened) on popular education, Wines stressed the instructive value of objects. E. C. Wines, *Hints on a System of Popular Education* (Philadelphia: Hogan and Thompson, 1838), 218–22.

93. Brantz Mayer, in trying to assess Dunn's contribution to society, pointed to the same educational philosophy: "It is somewhat difficult to assign to Mr. Dunn, precisely the rank which he is to assume among great and good men of the day; but, if he is to be considered as teaching instead of by book, and tame literary description, by palpable, tangible, and magnificent illustration not of pictures only, but of the people themselves. . . . Mr. Dunn should receive all the honor and station they can give him." Mayer, *A Nation in a Nutshell.*

94. Buckingham, 1:539.

95. The Society also made little attempt to render their museum accessible to the public. In fact, in the 1830s, in an effort to keep "strangers" out of the museum, the Society passed a motion to limit visitors to those personally introduced by a member. Although the Society later revoked this resolution, that it even considered such measures suggests that its commitment to educate Americans was limited. Whitehill, 17–31, 37–38, 45–51.

96. Mayer, *A Nation in a Nutshell.*

97. After the museum had moved to London, one guest performed a cursory Phrenological examination on the statue of a hairless mandarin official, which "being bald . . . presents a fair mark all over to the . . . phrenologist." The inspector claimed to be "struck by the smallness and meagreness of the cranium." "Wang Tang Jin Wuh," *Fraser's Magazine* (February, 1843). For a brief discussion of Phrenology in the United States, see David S. Reynolds, *Walt Whitman's America: A Cultural Biography* (New York: Vintage Books, 1996), 246. For a more extensive analysis, see John B. Davies, *Phrenology: Fad and Science: A Nineteenth-Century American Crusade* (New Haven: Yale University Press, 1955).

98. Davies, 21–22.

99. Advertisements for the lectures and services of George Combe and Orson Fowler can be found in the *Public Ledger* (28 December 1838). For mention of the attendance for Combe's lectures, see Davies, 21. For George Combe's description of his visit to the museum, see his *Notes on the United States of North America, during a Phrenological Visit in 1838–39–40* (Philadelphia: Carey and Hart, 1841), 1:307.

100. William Stanton, *The Leopard's Spots: Scientific Attitudes toward Race in America, 1815–1859* (Chicago: University of Chicago Press, 1960), 31–32. Samuel George Morton, *Crania Americana; or, A Comparative View of the Skulls of Various Aboriginal Nations* (Philadelphia: J. Dobson, 1839), 44–45. *Catalogue of Skulls of Man, and the Inferior Animals in the Collection of Samuel George Morton, M.D.* (Philadelphia: Turner and Fisher, 1840). See skulls numbered 3, 56, 94, 426, and 427.

101. For a listing of all books Dunn owned at the time of his death, see "A Plain Copy of the Inventory and Appraisement of Nathan Dunn, Dec'd," Gaskill Papers.

102. For Dunn's theory, see his *Descriptive Catalogue*, 33–34.

103. For the respect accorded to phrenology by the scientific community, see Davies, x–xi.

104. Alexis de Tocqueville, *Democracy in America*, trans. and ed. Harvey C. Mansfield and Delba Winthrop (Chicago: University of Chicago Press, 2000), 485–92. The original work was published in France in two volumes, 1835 and 1840.

105. Dunn, *Descriptive Catalogue*, 7, 13, 97, 100.

106. Ibid., 30–33, 105.

107. Benjamin Silliman, *Mr. Dunn's Chinese Collection in Philadelphia*.

108. Dunn, *Descriptive Catalogue*, 118–20.

109. Bowen, 86.

110. "A Plain Copy of the Inventory and Appraisement of Nathan Dunn, Dec'd," Gaskill Papers.

111. Carl Bode, *The Anatomy of American Popular Culture, 1840–1861* (Berkeley: University of California Press, 1959), 223.

112. *Chinese Repository* (March 1840), 583–84. A panorama of China displayed in New York is covered in chapter 7.

113. *Public Ledger* (28 December 1838).

114. "Chinese Collection," *Philadelphia Saturday Courier* (22 December 1838).

115. "Curiosities in Philadelphia," *The Farmers' Cabinet* (15 August 1840).

116. Wines, *A Peep at China*, 13.

117. *Chinese Repository* (March 1840), 581–82.

118. Buckingham, 2:56, 72.

119. Mayer, *A Nation in a Nutshell*; Mayer, "China and the Chinese," 6–7.

120. Mayer, *A Nation in a Nutshell*.

121. Bowen, 86.

122. Buckingham, 2:55.

123. Joseph Sturge, *A Visit to the United States in 1841* (London: Hamilton, Adams, 1842), 62.

124. Review of *The Fan-Qui in China in 1836–7* by C. Toogood Downing, *The Museum of Foreign Literature, Science, and Art* (October 1838), 177–78.

125. Buckingham, 2:43.

126. *London Illustrated News* (6 August 1842), 204–5. The figure of 50,000 is also mentioned in William Langdon, *"Ten Thousand Chinese Things": A Descriptive Catalogue of the Chinese Collection, Now Exhibiting at St. George's Place, Hyde Park Corner, London* (London, 1842), 1.

127. Lee, 17.

128. *Commonwealth v. Nathan Dunn*, 4–12.

129. Sellers, *Mr. Peale's Museum*, 290–91.

130. *London Illustrated News* (6 August 1842), 204–5.

131. Sturge, 68. Buckingham reacted similarly: "It is impossible that a visitor can walk through the Museum . . . without feeling indignant at the avarice and arrogance displayed in the conduct of those who pretend to be their superiors." Buckingham, 71.

132. Buckingham, 2:44.

133. *Niles National Register* (4 December 1841), 224.

134. Mayer, *A Nation in a Nutshell*.

135. The panorama, entitled "Description of a View of Canton, the River Tigress, and the Surrounding Country," opened in 1838. The program of sixteen pages includes a foldout miniature of the painting. New York Public Library.

136. Richard D. Altick, *The Shows of London* (Cambridge: Harvard University Press, Belknap Press, 1978), 292–93.

137. Ibid., 292, 297–81.

138. *London Times* (23 June 1842).

139. *Chinese Repository* (November 1843), 562.

140. Newspaper clippings, Gaskill Papers.

141. *Chinese Repository* (November 1843), 576–77. Omnibuses are noted in the London Times (13 November 1843).

142. Interestingly, Charles Dickens was living in London and writing *A Christmas Carol* while Nathan Dunn's museum was open to the public. Though purely a matter of speculation, the three idols representing the past, present, and future could conceivably have provided the inspiration for the three ghosts that famously visited Ebeneezer Scrooge on Christmas Eve.

143. Lee, 18. *London Times* (26 October 1846).

144. Duke of Wellington to Nathan Dunn, letter, 26 September 1842, Gaskill Papers; and William T. Alderson, ed., *Mermaids, Mummies, and Mastodons: The Emergence of the American Museum* (Washington, D.C.: American Association of Museums, 1992), 55.

145. *Chinese Repository* (November 1843), 568–69.

146. Sellers, *Mr. Peale's Museum*, 294–95.

147. *Art Union* (December 1842), 283.

148. *London Times* (17 October 1844).

149. "Drama at Home," *The Extravaganzas of J. R. Planché, Esq.*, ed. T. F. Dillon Crocker and Stephen Tucker (London: Samuel French, 1879), 2:288–95. Raymund Fitzsimons, *Barnum in London* (New York: St. Martin's Press, 1970), 100–2.

150. Laurel Hill Cemetery Company to Nelson Gaskill, letter, 19 July 1944, Gaskill Papers.

151. *London Times* (26 October 1846).

152. "Chinese Collection," *Philadelphia Saturday Courier* (22 December 1838).

153. Mayer, *A Nation in a Nutshell*.

154. Nathan Dunn to Hannah C. Dixey (his niece), letter, 3 March 1843, Quaker Collection, Haverford College.

155. *Art Union* (December 1842), 283.

156. Chinese Museum," *Pittsfield Sun* (11 September 1845).

157. In London, Barnum was always very cognizant of the other exhibits. Fitzsimons, 26.

158. *Niles National Register* (23 November 1844), 192.

# 5. A FLOATING ETHNOLOGY

## The Strange Voyage of the Chinesejunk *Keying*

If the Cantonese crew members on board the Chinese junk *Keying* felt cooped up, they had good reason. Since departing Hong Kong in December 1846 and sailing all the way to New York via the Cape of Good Hope, they had worked, eaten, and slept on this 160-foot-long boat. When they initially signed on, the British captain had assured them that the junk was headed only as far as the island of Java. And after they discovered the deception, he exercised brute force to keep them with the craft. But whereas the surrounding ocean and a coercive captain had once kept them from leaving the junk, now crowds of New Yorkers did. As one of the top attractions of the summer, the *Keying* drew droves of curious people who were eager to board it and meet the crew. For the latter, these visitors could be exhausting as well as annoying—especially the children who repeatedly tugged on their dangling queues.

Tired of being an exhibit, several members of the crew decided to stretch their legs and see the sights of Gotham. On August 2, 1847, they disembarked and headed into the city. Of course, being Chinese in a predominantly white city, they were unable to blend into the crowds and so continued to be an exhibit even while taking time off. The crew members eventually arrived at the exhibition space of Afong Moy, the Chinese Lady. Originally brought to New York by China traders as part of an ingenious marketing ploy, Moy had long since become a fixture in the city's diverse landscape of popular amusements.

Now, in a most peculiar encounter, she found herself face to face with the latest Chinese act. According to the *New York Herald*, the existence of the Chinese lady "astonished" the crew members, who had previously believed that "they were the only 'natives' in the country." In its usual playful style, the newspaper expressed the opinion that the crew should behave "in a sociable way" by inviting "their fair countrywoman" to their junk to "talk over old times."[1]

Of course, we can never know what words the two parties actually exchanged during this meeting. However, at least symbolically, the encounter occurred at an important juncture, where the end of one era was rubbing up against the beginning of another. To most who saw her, Afong Moy stood for a China that was remote and mysterious, effectively sealed off from the curious gaze of foreigners. Indeed, the heyday of her exhibition took place before the Opium War (1839–42), when foreigners were prohibited from penetrating China's interior. In addition, her alleged status as a lady from the upper crust further enhanced this aura of mystery because Chinese men of affluence were known to sequester their wives and daughters from the public. Since these ladies seldom ventured onto the streets, even Americans who lived in China could not claim to have ever witnessed a Chinese lady. And so the exhibition of Afong Moy proved irresistible to Americans, because it seemed to grant them access to a doubly forbidden sight: Afong Moy was a woman secluded from society inside a country sealed off from the world.

If Moy symbolized a closed China, the *Keying* signified China's openness in the wake of the Opium War. During that conflict, England's naval superiority forced China to accede to demands for greater access to Chinese markets. In the ensuing Treaty of Nanjing (1842), China conceded to England the right to trade in four ports in addition to Canton: Ningbo, Shanghai, Xiamen, and Fuzhou. Indeed, the *Keying* seemed to reflect this new power arrangement, for here was a Chinese crew manning a Chinese vessel that was owned and commanded by a British captain. Even the junk's name carried symbolic importance in that it was named for Qiying (*Keying*), the internationally famous Chinese statesman responsible for negotiating the Treaty of Nanjing.

For many Americans, the reconfiguration of China's relationship to England triggered a concomitant repositioning of their own attitudes toward China. When Afong Moy first appeared in New York in 1834, most people were too enamored with China's elegant mystery to make disparaging remarks. Here visitors appear not to have preached to her, mocked her customs and appearance, or harshly criticized her country of origin. Although some disapproved of footbinding, most people mainly passed their allotted time in her company relishing the cultural difference that she represented and admiring the silky world of Oriental luxury in which she was snuggly ensconced.

But by the time the *Keying* arrived, China had already fallen several notches in the estimation of most Americans. Many, though, instead of merely devaluing Chinese civilization in the wake of the Opium War, increasingly spoke of China with an air of condescension and mockery. In fact, a new and unflattering construction of the Chinese emerged in this period, the entire purpose of which was to generate laughter. First, Chinese males became effeminate fops, who dressed in motley silk costumes and sported ridiculously long fingernails. Second, the Chinese enjoyed a diet that consisted of rats, mice, dogs, and cats. Third, they were heathens who worshipped strange deities and regularly bowed down before gaudy idols. Fourth, their officials were pompous buffoons who proudly adhered to their own customs and beliefs despite unmistakable evidence the rest of the world had passed them by. And finally, they were opium addicts who were comically pathetic in their inability to resist the poppy and the pipe. Like Cathay, this construction of China and the Chinese was more grounded in fantasy than in fact. Unlike its picturesque predecessor, though, it lacked innocence and charm. It was a cruel Cathay.

In sum, the people whom Dunn had admired had now become a race of clowns who entertained the rest of the world with their ludicrous appearance, their absurd arrogance, and their grotesque habits. The perceptive British captain quickly sensed this shift in the public's view of China. And thinking of his junk more as a business venture than as an educational tool, he applied a profit-centered calculus to all decisions regarding the exhibition of *Keying*. In the end, he chose to reinforce the patronizing views of his customers in order to reap the financial rewards.


## FROM CHINA TO NEW YORK


With the onset of the Opium War in 1839, interest in China surged in the United States, and it would remain at a high level well into the 1850s. In playhouses in the major eastern cities, a spate of new theatrical productions appeared that were designed to capitalize on the collective turn of Americans to the Far East. The scripts of these plays have not survived, but their titles offer testimony to the fascination Americans held for China: *Yankees in China; or, A Union of the Flags* (1840), *The Enchanted Chinese; or, A Fete at Pekin* (1841), *Bohea-Man's Gal* (1845), *Celestial Empire; or, The Yankee in China* (1846), *Mose in China* (1849), *Female Guard; or, Bloomers in China* (1851), *The Lamplighter of the Pagoda; or, The Chinaman's Revenge* (1854).[2] In addition, the Ravel family, a theatrical troupe from France, arrived in 1852 to perform *Kim-Ka!*, a pantomime about a French balloonist who descends on China and ends up marrying the emperor's daughter.[3] White Europeans and Americans almost certainly wrote, produced, and acted in all of the above productions, but there was at least one Chinese genuine stage act during this period: The Tong Hook Theatrical Troupe of Shanghai treated people in San Francisco and New York to authentic Chinese opera in 1852 and 1853.[4]

The most intriguing China-centered event, however, took place not on a stage but on the deck of a sailing craft. Aware that one could make money by feeding the current fascination with China, an anonymous American conceived of the idea of somehow acquiring a Chinese junk, manning it with a Chinese crew, and loading its lower compartment with curiosities and then sailing for the United States. In 1846, this individual apparently went so far as either to build a junk based on models of the real thing or to purchase one.[5] If he chose the latter course, the transaction would not have been extremely difficult. In 1842, junks that for centuries had monopolized the transport of goods and passengers along the China coast began to face competition from European vessels. The latter, being better armed and faster than the pirate ships that menaced the area, forced many of the junks out of business.[6] And so an individual with financial means could probably convince a junk owner easily enough to quit the coastal shipping business and sell his vessel.

After going so far as to purchase the *Keying*, the American for unknown reasons abandoned the entire scheme later in 1846 and sold it for $75,000 to Charles Kellett, a British captain who had recently surveyed the Chinese coast in order to create charts that could facilitate navigation.[7] Intending to sail the junk to London for exhibition purposes, Kellett proceeded to stock it with Chinese objects, creating in effect a floating museum. He also hired twenty European sailors and selected a man named Revett to be his chief mate, since the latter seemed to posses the desired trait of loyalty.

Most important, he secured a Chinese crew of about forty men by offering to pay them eight dollars for each month of service. Although they would perform various duties on the vessel, Kellett mainly intended them to be a part of the show once the *Keying* arrived in London. In finding these men, he did not have to look hard, since junk hands, who were already poor, desperately needed work now that European competition had left many junks idle.[8] To add color and prestige to the *Keying*, Kellett signed on a low-ranking mandarin, Hesing (fig. 5.1), as well as a Chinese artist, Sam-sing. Chinese law forbade any junk to leave Chinese waters, but Kellett bribed the right officials and set sail for Hong Kong, now a British possession.

At this point, sources conflict as to whether the Chinese crew understood the true nature of the voyage. In Kellett's own version of the story, contained in a later letter to Queen Victoria, the crew knew all along that the ultimate destination was London. While Kellett admitted that he never informed the Chinese crew members of this information personally, he claimed they must have known because, for several weeks prior to departure, the junk was harbored in Hong Kong, where the entire English-speaking community was aware of the nature of the voyage. The Chinese did not speak English, but Kellett claimed that they came into frequent contact with his bilingual Chinese stewards who would have apprised them of the junk's true purpose. The Chinese understood the itinerary, Kellett insisted, and had not objected.[9]

However, in the much more likely version, Kellett comes across as a duplicitous man willing to say anything to ensure the success of his moneymaking venture. Suspecting that the Chinese would not voluntarily sail to London, Kellett deliberately told them the falsehood that the junk was on a simple trading mission and bound only as far as the island of Java. Although the vessel itself would be continuing on to another port after Java, he assured the Chinese that they were not obligated to proceed any further. The actual contract, while containing nothing about Java (that much was imparted to the crew orally), did stipulate that the sailors were required to work for Kellett for eight months. At the expiration of that period, any sailor who chose to leave the junk became free to do so, and Kellett was obligated to arrange for his passage to Canton and defray the cost. Believing themselves to be embarking on an eight-month journey that would take them only as far as Java, the Chinese willingly signed their contracts. The junk departed Hong Kong on December 6, 1846.[10]

It was at Java that the Chinese crew members first realized that Kellett had not been entirely truthful about his intentions. After the *Keying* reached the island in late January, a Malaysian boat came out to meet the junk in the harbor. Oblivious to their whereabouts, the Chinese crew members were astonished to learn that they were in Java. How was it possible, they asked themselves, that in less than two months they had already arrived at a destination they were supposed to have needed eight months to reach? And equally troubling, why was it that their captain had neglected to apprise them of their true location? Their astonishment soon darkened to fear when, without warning, the junk began to leave the harbor. As Java shrank on the horizon, the Chinese looked out on the vast expanses of water before them, feeling grave uncertainty about what lay ahead. They now understood the nature of their predicament: They were in the power of untrustworthy men who did not have their best interests in mind.

After departing Java in late January, the *Keying* entered the Indian Ocean, which would require approximately two months to cross. It was here that the junk received the first major test of its seaworthiness, a test that temporarily shifted attention away from simmering conflict. On March 22, the junk began to sail right into a massive squall. The Chinese watched as lightning illuminated the nighttime sky and winds and waves battered the vessel. Although designed only for short trading missions up and down rivers and along China's coast, the junk succeeded in weathering the storm and eventually passed into calmer waters. On March 30, the craft successfully rounded the southern tip of Africa at the Cape of Good Hope and headed into the Atlantic Ocean.

Kellett next guided the *Keying* to the island of St. Helena, a small British possession off the western coast of Africa, and arrived there on April 17. The junk remained there six days, during which time Kellett replenished stores of provisions, had repairs made to the damages wrought by the storm, and allowed local visitors to see the junk, meet the crew, and inspect the many Chinese objects below deck. Throngs of curious people boarded the vessel, and Kellett presumably charged admission. The *Keying*'s stay in St. Helena would not remain peaceful for long.

An atmosphere of fear and distrust had hung over the junk ever since its departure from Java, but it was here, in St. Helena, that tensions rose to the surface. Many of the Chinese started to grow restive. The more unruly they became, the more Kellett feared they would imperil his ambitious business venture. To add to the captain's worries, some members of the European crew were also becoming disgruntled. Fearing a mutiny, Kellett began to treat the Chinese sailors as coolies rather than as what they truly were—free men temporarily in his hire.[11] He instructed the men who remained loyal to him to force the Chinese to work and beat them into submission, using ropes as whips. Chief Mate Revett was apparently the most brutal in coercing labor. Next, at Kellett's request, the island's police magistrate boarded the vessel and, wielding a gun, threatened to shoot the crew members if their insubordination continued. As the junk departed St. Helena, one Chinese sailor, hoping to escape the lash and perhaps preferring death to captivity, jumped overboard. He was caught and taken back onto the junk. As the *Keying* sailed out into the Atlantic Ocean, it was a segregated vessel. On one end, Kellett and his faithful sat with pistols, ever vigilant of any activity going on at the other end, which was occupied by the Chinese.

As the journey proceeded, problems continued to mount for Kellett. In addition to the lingering threat of mutiny, provisions were running low again. Reluctantly, he abandoned the idea of sailing directly to London and headed to the port of New York instead.[12] Although Kellett must have been disappointed, the revised itinerary did afford certain financial benefits. Americans, he knew, would come in droves to see an authentic Chinese junk and crew and, most important of all, they would bring their wallets. Kellett decided to exhibit the *Keying* for several months on the East Coast of the United States before departing for London, where he planned to arrive well before the commencement of the Crystal Palace Exposition of 1851.[13]

## EARLY RECEPTION IN NEW YORK

When the *Keying* arrived in New York harbor on July 9, 1847, it became an immediate spectacle. Before Kellett allowed guests onboard, steamboats headed to Staten Island and filled with thousands of passengers passed near the junk, "such was the anxiety of the people to catch a glimpse of the strange 'craft.'"[14] Unaware of the greed, mendacity, and violence that had brought the *Keying* to their city, New Yorkers turned out in large numbers to inspect this picturesque vessel (figs. 5.2 and 5.3). Walt Whitman, who was interested in the great diversity of human experience, of course went out to see it.[15] To many Americans, it seemed like an emissary from an enchanted land, the China of their imaginations. Brewster Maverick, a young boy living in the city, saw the junk in precisely this context. Chronically ill, he typically used his diary to track his various ailments or record the mundane happenings of each passing day. However, starting with the entry for July 10, his tone abruptly changed as he reported the arrival of the *Keying*.

For an imaginative child, the Chinese junk could not have been more magical or mysterious. Maverick would even ascend to a lofty perch and peer at it through a spyglass. Moored side by side with New York's tall merchant vessels, the Chinese junk seemed wonderfully out of place, and Maverick and others must have enjoyed juxtaposing the drab and quotidian world of commerce with this colorful envoy from Cathay. Of course, any contrast between enchantment and business was merely an illusion because money was clearly the driving force that had propelled the *Keying* to America. In fact, Kellett was able to profit from Brewster Maverick's curiosity; the young boy purchased a ticket and, after returning home, elatedly reported to his diary that he "Shook hands with Chinese."[16]

The junk provided Maverick with a temporary escape from his own life, allowing him to pass a couple of pleasurable hours inside a floating Chinese world. Indeed, according to the *Herald*, it was the *Keying*'s ability to elicit this sensation of virtual travel in visitors that made it a remarkable attraction:

> We question if one of ten thousand of our readers will ever visit China. . . . They are not aware, perhaps, that they have an opportunity now of learning as much as they could do by taking a trip to the Celestial Empire. Yet it is a fact. By visiting the junk now in our harbor, they can see every thing of interest appertaining to that people. They will be on board of a ship constructed by Chinese shipwrights—they will be in the presence of Chinese idols—they can converse with Chinamen—in fine, they can see all that they could see in the great city of Pekin or Canton . . . an opportunity they never had before, and, in all probability, never will have again.[17]

Much like the earlier press coverage devoted to Dunn's museum, the *Herald* also stressed the educational value of the junk, asserting that "one hour's stay on board of her will give a better insight into Chinese manners and customs than can be learned in a library of books."[18] As indicated above, the junk did carry a small museum below deck; the collection included musical instruments, scrolls, idols, toys, lanterns, shoes, costumes, paintings, and porcelain (fig. 5.4).[19] And clearly some visitors did treat a visit to the junk as an educational opportunity. A man named A. C. Van Epps, for instance, accosted Sam-sing to inquire about silk production in China. He left quite pleased, stating that the artist was "entirely familiar with the production of silk in his native country."[20]

Like Van Epps, Orson Squire Fowler also saw the junk as a tremendous opportunity to learn about the Chinese. Yet he fervently believed that the *Keying* could supply a specific kind of knowledge that one could not find in "a library of books." Fowler was America's most famous phrenologist and, as such, he thought he could best comprehend the Chinese character by feeling and measuring the contours of a Chinese head. As far as he was concerned, the skull—more than books, museums, or even a visit to China—was what could yield accurate ethnographic information. "The architecture and implements of this ship are well worth seeing," he tellingly wrote, "but the MEN in attendance far more so."[21]

The new "science" of phrenology (discussed in the previous chapter) had been founded by Franz Joseph Gall in Vienna in the late eighteenth century and popularized by his protégé, Joseph Spurzheim, throughout the Western world. After introducing it in England, Spurzheim traveled to New York in 1832, where many prominent Americans greeted him with open arms. He probably would have enjoyed success in the United States had he not fallen ill and died just as his American tour was getting underway. The job of spreading phrenology through the United States ultimately devolved to his disciple, George Combe. After arriving in 1838, Combe commenced a tour of major cities that included Philadelphia, where he visited Dunn's Chinese Museum and almost certainly met with Fowler. His lectures were well attended, but it was mainly to upper-class Americans and intellectuals that Combe appealed.[22]

The popularization of phrenology was well served by the evangelical fervor and entrepreneurial instincts of Orson Fowler. Unlike his European colleagues, Fowler added almost nothing of theoretical value to the field. Instead, his genius was in understanding how to convert esoteric European theories into a comprehensible set of principles with practical applications for ordinary men and women. He parlayed this single insight into an entire industry. Through his efforts, phrenology achieved mass appeal and exerted a pervasive influence over antebellum American culture. In Manhattan, with the assistance of his brother and sister, Lorenzo and Charlotte, he opened the Phrenological Cabinet and filled it with skulls, skeletons, and busts to attract visitors. Although a visit to the Cabinet was free, little else was: Fowler offered character readings for a fee, churned out a monthly magazine, The American Phrenological Journal, published a small library of self-help books, and sold phrenological kits complete with lecture notes, charts, busts, and skulls—all that the aspiring traveling practitioner needed to launch his own head-reading business.[23]

While Fowler peddled easy answers to life's impossible questions, he was not a deceitful charlatan exploiting the hopes and ignorance of his customers through the sale of a spurious product. His belief in the validity of phrenology's claims was sincere, and he sought out opportunities to use his expertise to describe the nature of the different races of humankind with whom Americans were increasingly coming into contact in this seafaring age. He had previously conducted skull readings of Chang and Eng, the Siamese Twins, and in 1848, in the pages of his magazine, he enthusiastically announced the donation by a sea captain of a set of authentic Chinese skulls.[24]

With the arrival of the Keying, Fowler relished this chance to examine the heads of living Chinese and report his findings:

> The interest taken by the Editor in specimens of humanity from the other side of the globe, amounts almost to a passion. The reason is this: They exhibit human nature in phases differing materially from those usually seen, and these diversified aspects of the MAN are peculiarly interesting and instructive to close students to this last and greatest work of God. Hence, words can but poorly poutray [sic] the pleasure and instruction I experienced in visiting the CHINESE JUNK and its occupants.

Before touching a single head, Fowler noted the Chinese custom of sitting on haunches instead of on chairs, a practice that he viewed as simian in nature: it "evinces a state of civilization quite inferior to our own," he wrote, and bordered on "monkeyism." But the judging of mannerisms was not his forte, and Fowler quickly moved on to his area of expertise. Observing the numerous paintings that adorned the interior of the junk, he selected Sam-sing as his first subject and applied his fingers to the painter's cranium. Although noting that the overall size of the brain was small, Fowler reported mostly positive traits. The "cerebral organization," for example, was quite strong and superior to that found in the other Chinese heads he inspected that same day.[25]

Of course, not everyone placed their faith in the kind of analysis Fowler was performing. Indeed, as popular as phrenology was, it attracted its share of detractors. One vocal critic was Caleb Cushing, a congressman from Massachusetts who had led the U.S. diplomatic mission to China in 1843 (discussed in chapter 7). In 1839, Cushing wrote a lengthy article in which he denounced phrenology as "one of the delusions of science" and systematically debunked its claims. Just as astrologers drew "maps of the heavens" in order to link the cosmos to the "future fortunes of men," so too did phrenologists "with their maps of the brain" attempt to predict behavior. According to Cushing, phrenology originated in the hubris of humankind. It "perverted desire of men" to "lift the veil in which nature covers so many of her operations" and gain "authority over the mysterious and unknown" against the will of the supreme deity. In other words, phrenologists were inspired by the desire to know the world, the same desire that motivated the more respectable men of science but, instead of seeking knowledge along the legitimate channels of painstaking scientific research, they looked to the occult for instant explanations to creation's most vexing mysteries.[26]

## CHINA DOWNGRADED

While Fowler's methods were grounded in theories now discredited, he clearly did understand the *Keying* as a locus for instruction, though not of the conventional sort. However, many other visitors viewed the junk mostly as an opportunity to mock the Chinese in a playful but condescending manner. Given this behavior, the reception of the junk in New York stands in stark contrast to that given to Dunn's museum nine years earlier. Of course, one can account for some of the differences by drawing a distinction between the entertainment scene in Philadelphia and that in New York. After all, the citizens of the latter, conditioned by P. T. Barnum to view all popular exhibitions with irreverence, might have been predisposed to see an exhibit like the *Keying* in this manner. However, other evidence suggests that the times had changed and that a new attitude toward China, far from being a New York phenomenon, pervaded the entire nation in the 1840s.

When the American missionary Samuel Wells Williams returned to the United States in 1845, he noticed a change in the air. When Williams first departed for China in 1833, he left from a country that, although lacking in information about China, was still enchanted by it. The accounts of Jesuit missionaries, the fabulous tales of the *Arabian Nights*, and the idyllic images on commodities all worked in concord to instill in the national consciousness the idea that China was different, intriguing, and wonderful. On returning stateside, he was astonished to observe that it had suffered a precipitous decline in the public's opinion. A people who had been the object of admiration had, in the interim, become the target of ridicule. China was now "the object of a laugh or the subject of a pun." In particular, Williams was bothered by a derogatory poem that, to his annoyance, people seemed fond of repeating in his presence:

*Mandarins with yellow buttons, handing you conserves of snails;*
*Smart young men about Canton in Nankeen tights and peacocks' tails.*
*With many rare and dreadful dainties, kitten cutlets, puppy pies;*
*Birds nest soup which (so convenient!) every bush around supplies.*[27]

The demeaning verses, Williams believed, epitomized this disturbing new attitude toward China. Americans now laughed at the Chinese for being comically foppish and effeminate in appearance and for adhering to a diet that was bizarre and "grotesque." Williams was not alone in observing the stark transformation of American views. In 1849, Osmond Tiffany, who had recently returned from China and now observed and decried what Williams did, the rampant mockery of Chinese people: "Their manners, their habits, language, dress, and sentiments, have all been made the butt of witless ridicule too long."[28]

Neither Williams nor Tiffany indicate how or when this tone of condescension first infected the public discourse, but certainly reaction to the Opium War played a decisive role. For many Americans, China's humiliating defeat cast the vanquished nation in a new light.[29] But other nations had lost wars without becoming the objects of derision. Why was China different? In 1842, Thomas Smyth, a Presbyterian minister in Charleston, South Carolina, explained why China suddenly elicited chuckles rather than respect. "We are very unwilling to believe that a whole people exist only to be laughed at," he wrote, "yet how is it, that the greatest nation upon earth, in point of numbers, is the only one which history exhibits in an aspect purely ludicrous?" Smyth had never visited China and was not an authority on it. His nonexpert status lends to his testimony a certain force, qualifying him to articulate, in a way that Samuel Wells Williams could not, the popular thinking on China.[30]

In Smyth's view, China demonstrated an excessive affinity for highfalutin pomp, ridiculous ceremonies, and gratuitous formalities, all of which served only to provoke laughter since they were conducted with an air of high seriousness. "Their most solemn acts of government, of legislation, of negotiation, and of war," he wrote "are comic, and, in many cases, farcical. It is impossible to read them without a smile." That the "Chinaman" proceeded with all of this "grave buffoonery" utterly "unconscious of his own absurdity" only added to the humor. In addition, Smyth faulted the Chinese for being haughty, supercilious, and self-superior in refusing to entertain the notion that the rest of the world could think or make anything of value. "In every national and individual act," Smyth observed, "they seem to say, We are the people and wisdom shall die with us." Considering themselves to be the "centre of the universe," the Chinese deigned to allow "the savage English and Americans" to leave their "howling wilderness" and "clamour at Canton for tea." This same cultural arrogance loomed behind the kowtow, a strictly enforced ritual of Chinese protocol that required foreign emissaries to fall to their knees and hands before the emperor.[31]

By themselves, this excessive pride and fondness for pageantry were not cause for ridicule. But to many, the ease with which British gunboats dispatched the Chinese navy during the Opium War was eye-opening. The war delivered a revelation tantamount to Dorothy's as she appears before the Wizard inside the Emerald City of Oz. After the stentorian voice and pyrotechnical display of the Wizard cow Dorothy and her friends, they shudder in fear before his terrifying image. When Toto pulls down a nearby curtain, however, Dorothy finds herself staring not at an awe-inspiring power but an ordinary man operating a special-effects mechanism. Similarly, in Smyth's view, the British victory tore down China's grandiose façade, exposing China's true weakness for all the world to see. And yet, despite the overwhelming evidence of their own impotence and futility, the Chinese failed to adopt even a measure of humility and instead persisted in believing the illusion of their own power. "Every junk that puts out from the coast is to destroy the British fleet," Smyth wrote, "and when it fails, they are as confident as ever that the next will be successful."[32]

To illustrate the sudden and dramatic shift in public attitudes toward China, Smyth asked his readers to participate in a small experiment. Allow your "imagination," he said, to "conjure up" before you "some familiar form from the Chinese Museum" of Nathan Dunn. Although the exhibits had inspired respect for China before the war, Smyth assured readers that, under the present circumstances, "they will find it much more difficult to keep their countenances"— that is, to refrain from either smirking or laughing outright. In sum, Americans still looked on China as an object of fascination; however, for many the majestic front had crumbled just like China's coastal forts when faced with barrages of British cannon fire.[33]

## THE BARNUMIZATION OF CHINA

Unlike visitors to Dunn's museum, those who boarded the *Keying* treated it like an exhibit in P. T. Barnum's American Museum. They enjoyed the junk for its amusement value and scrutinized it to determine whether it truly was what it purported to be, a craft that had sailed all the way from China. In fact, according to a widely spread rumor, the *Keying* was not of Chinese origin at all but rather another hoax perpetrated by the master of humbug himself. According to this story, Barnum had secretly ordered the construction of a Chinese-looking craft on Long Island and then arranged for it to sail triumphantly into New York harbor as if it had come all the way from China. Although factually groundless, the rumor linking the *Keying* to Barnum did carry a symbolic truth. Unlike Dunn and more like Barnum, Captain Kellett concerned himself less with informing visitors and more with reaping the financial rewards of entertaining them. And unlike Dunn's audience, many of the *Keying*'s visitors construed the junk less as an organ for instruction and more as a spectacle. In short, the Chinese junk ushered in a new stage in the exhibition of Chinese culture in America—the Barnumization of China. Ironically, the great showman had not played a role in the process.[34]

Interestingly, although the Chinese junk became an object of ridicule, it did possess all the components for a genuine educational exhibition. The vessel was authentic; the collection of artifacts, if properly explained, could have provided an object lesson in Chinese customs, handicrafts, and daily life; Hesing, the mandarin, was studying English and so could have explained aspects of Chinese culture; and Sam-sing, the artist, could have provided demonstrations of Chinese painting.[35] But on arriving, Captain Kellett lent his acutely sensitive ear to the prejudices and cravings of the New York public. And like Samuel Wells Williams, he noted the change in the American view of China, and he realized that a floating version of Dunn's museum was not in his economic interests. He opted instead to assemble his components into an event that appealed to the basest desires of New Yorkers so as to reap the financial rewards.

This rather cynical view of Kellett's motives is based on the coverage of the *Keying* in James Gordon Bennett's *New York Herald*. Almost daily, the paper fed its readers brief news items that depicted the Chinese as a comically absurd people who blindly adhered to bizarre and grotesque customs. Although these stories are ostensibly attributed to some anonymous journalist rather than Kellett, one has good reason to believe that the British captain wrote most of the content himself. First, almost every issue of the *Herald* carried a story even though it is highly unlikely that every day the paper assigned a reporter to report the latest events on the junk. Since reporters were not this expendable, the daily news items must have come from another source. Second, in exchange for the purchases of advertising space, some New York newspapers, including the *Herald*, often permitted entertainers to promote their events in the paper with tantalizing news items composed in their own hand. Through this mutually beneficial quid pro quo, advertisements could dissemble as legitimate news in the paper. Indeed, P. T. Barnum may have been the first to develop this symbiotic relationship with the press; he knew that people were more likely to visit an attraction if they viewed it as a sensation that was constantly generating news.[36]

Typically, the writer for the *Herald* (most likely Kellett) would inject false but amusing material into a news story that may have had a factual component, creating a news item that was an unreliable hybrid of fact and fiction. Stereotypes mingled with the truth to the extent that, from any given story, we cannot determine precisely what happened. For example, the paper reported that two Chinese crew members were seen admiring an American woman—that is, until they spied her feet. They "suddenly turned away, shaking their heads."[37] Whereas this story could provoke a chuckle because all Americans (especially after Afong Moy's prolonged exhibition) were familiar with the Chinese custom of footbinding, another depended on the reader's familiarity with images of Chinese people disseminated through advertising for tea: "We saw one of our Chinese friends in Broadway on Saturday last—under one arm a small tea chest, a pair of Chinese sandals on his feet, his long hair done up in a flowing pigtail hanging behind him."[38] A third story toyed with the stereotype that the Chinese rigidly adhered to their own customs: "The Chinamen of the Junk are rapidly adopting the manners and customs of our citizens. They use knives and forks at their meals instead of chopsticks, but they are very awkward with them. They smoke cigars from morning till night."[39] The Chinese were known for stubbornly resisting change, and readers could enjoy laughing at crew members' clumsy attempt to adopt Western customs.

The paper also inserted opium smoking into as many news items as it could. These stories playfully depicted it as something funny—yet another colorful habit that made the Chinese amusing. For instance, one story described the collective dreams of the Chinese crew during an opium-induced sleep: "In the dreams of opium land, they had fancied that they were still in the land of Mandarins and Hanging Gardens, and that they were being attacked by the ferocious outside barbarians, and reduced to powder as fine as their best gunpowder tea. Happily, however, they found that it was only a dream."[40] In addition to making light of the Opium War, the story also purported that the Chinese were addicts. Were the crew members addicted to opium? If we look only at the *Herald*, it is impossible to know for sure, as the paper demonstrated a penchant for mixing hard facts with absurd fantasies. For example, on August 31, it reported that Hesing, the mandarin, "cannot give up his opium, which he indulges in to excess."[41] Yet this statement contradicted a news item printed just three days earlier: "If you want to see opium smoking, visit the junk. All except the mandarin indulge."[42]

The truth appears to be somewhere in the middle. Samuel Wells Williams, who spoke Cantonese and visited the junk in August, discovered that one of the Chinese was smoking opium. That crew member, according to Williams, had not brought the drug from China but rather had obtained it from a shop in New York. Interestingly, Williams registered his surprise not at the opium usage itself (he had, after all, lived in China and witnessed its effects) but rather at the failure of Kellett to take measures to stop it. Here it is important to note that Williams was under no delusions regarding the morality of Captain Kellett; by this time, the missionary had already registered his disapproval of the deception perpetrated by the latter. Williams simply reasoned that Kellett was an unscrupulous businessman who, as such, might have been expected to better protect his investment from dissipation and even premature death: "I had supposed that the English captain who had deceived the men to get them here would not suffer them to destroy themselves." Employing this logic, the missionary guessed that Kellett had probably tried to restrain the Chinese opium user but had failed because the Chinese "will of course do what they please with their own money."[43]

But Williams was wrong. What he failed to take into consideration was the potential role opium played in Kellett's profit-centered calculus. Kellett had apparently realized that he could enhance the junk's appeal, and thus sell more tickets, if the Chinese would behave in accordance with popular stereotypes. And so, far from discouraging the opium usage, Kellett chose instead to exploit it for gain. He turned a tragic habit into an attraction that New Yorkers could learn about in the pages of the *Herald*. Although the ravages of opium on Chinese society was a serious issue that merited the American public's attention, Kellett's presentation encouraged audiences to do little more than laugh at the addicts. Whereas Nathan Dunn had, through his museum, crusaded against the opium trade and placed the burden of moral culpability squarely on the shoulders of Europeans and Americans who trafficked in the drug, Kellett opted instead to de-problematize the issue by de-historicizing it. In his presentation both on the junk itself and then in the pages of the *Herald,* the British traders utterly vanish from sight, leaving behind for public scrutiny only the Chinese and their vice. The implied message was that opium addiction was the logical extension of the dissolute Chinese character and that it provided yet another clear example that this race was not fit for the modern world.[44]

While at least one member of the Chinese crew probably did smoke opium, sometimes the true behavior of the Chinese did not, much to Kellett's disappointment, conveniently conform to the popular stereotypes. In such cases, the captain simply coaxed, cajoled, or fooled the Chinese into going through the motions before audiences. Indeed, for visitors, part of the entertainment onboard the junk ultimately came from watching Chinese crew members participate in farcical tableaux vivantes that presented a grotesque versions of Chinese customs. For example, the *Herald* explained that meals onboard the junk were of interest to spectators because one could enjoy watching the Chinese eat with chopsticks. To add a sensational element to the spectacle, the *Herald* claimed rodents were on the menu: "The Chinese . . . dispose of their mice and rats quicker than we do of our meals." At mealtimes, curious spectators undoubt-edly gathered around the Chinese crew members, convinced that rats were be-ing consumed. The Chinese crew members did not eat rats and were probably oblivious to the *Herald*'s assertion that they did; in this way, they were the un-witting participants in performances meant to demean their own culture.[45]

In addition to opium smoking and rat eating, strange pagan ceremonies also intrigued visitors, and Kellett was more than willing to gratify them with staged demonstrations of Chinese idol worship. "The citizens of New York will have an opportunity today of witnessing Chinese idol worship," the *Herald* an-nounced, "with all its concomitants of kneeling, sacrificing, and offering of gifts." To maximize attendance, the paper warned that an "opportunity like this, will, in all probability, never be again presented to our citizens."[46] After the ceremonies were completed, the paper declared them "the most amusing and interesting spectacle we ever beheld," and then immediately announced, quite conveniently, that Captain Kellett has "induced the natives . . . to repeat them."[47] Interestingly, during the long voyage from China, the Chinese crew members had practiced their religion until their captain had pressured them to desist; at that time, Kellett had probably viewed idol worship as an offensive heathen practice that needed to be eradicated from the culture. Yet once in New York, he awoke to the moneymaking potential of such exercises in "idol worship" and reversed course—now enthusiastically organizing the very cere-monies he had earlier sought to suppress.[48]

## A SCUFFLE, AN ARREST, AND A DATE IN COURT

In August 1847, the Chinese had grown tired of performing burlesque versions of their own customs and rituals. They also knew that they were contractually obligated to remain with Kellett for a period of only eight months, which had now expired. In an attempt to secure greater control over their lives, a group of Chinese decided to seek out Kellett to discuss both their return passage to Can-ton and lingering financial matters. Since the junk continued to rake in profits, Kellett of course had no intention of living up to his end of the agreement. When the group tried to confront him, Kellett therefore promptly took evasive measures. The Chinese followed him into one room of the junk, only to dis-cover that he had already slipped out through another door. Unable to accost the elusive captain, they next approached Chief Mate Revett to present their complaints. When he also deliberately sought to avoid them, the Chinese tried to constrain him physically, and an altercation ensued. Kellett quickly alerted the police, who boarded the junk, arrested seven Chinese, and incarcerated them on the charge of assault.[49]

The *Herald*, locked into a mode of reporting wherein facts were mingled with stereotypes, at first reported an erroneous version of the incident. According to the story, Kellett had merely attempted to pay the Chinese their salaries when, "under the effects of opium," they "turned their combined force against the captain." Though preposterous, this version of events might have seemed plausible to readers who had for weeks been reading reports about the debauched Chinese crew's addiction to opium.[50] If Kellett had been using the *Herald* to generate publicity for his attraction, however, at this juncture he had begun to lose control. For now that the events swirling around the *Keying* were headed to court, the newspaper could no longer print Kellett's version as legitimate news and instead assigned a court reporter to handle coverage. The intervention of the Chinese crew had the effect not only of disrupting Kellett's storytelling ability but also of putting forward a competing version of the Chinese character: Rather than being passive and tractable opium smokers who were the comical representatives of a failing race, they became active fighters who rebelled against wrongful treatment and abuses of power.

As court proceedings commenced, the Chinese were officially charged with having assaulted Chief Mate Revett. As for their defense, they were quite fortunate in that they received legal representation from W. Daniel Lord, a prominent New York attorney, who apparently took the case as pro bono work. Of course, to present the defense's side of the story, Lord hoped to rely on two sources: the spoken testimony of the detained Chinese crew members, who spoke Cantonese, and the contracts they had signed in Hong Kong, which were written in Chinese. This posed an immediate problem for the court, since no ordinary citizen of New York—indeed, very few people on earth—understood both Chinese and English well. Fortunately, two such people were residing in New York at the time.

One was Samuel Wells Williams, the missionary enjoying a temporary residence in the city. Williams possessed the conviction that the Chinese crew had been wronged, and he was eager to help the court resolve the matter in a manner favorable to them. "I hope these men will . . . find their way back to their native land soon, for they consider themselves to have been very badly used," Williams wrote. "The Chinese are easy people to get along with when they feel pretty sure of honorable treatment."[51] Williams could speak and write Chinese fairly well, and so he would be able to provide the court with reasonably good English translations of both the written contracts and the verbal complaints of the crew. To aid him in this endeavor, he enlisted the aid of his friend, Lin-King-Chew, a Chinese Christian living in New York. Williams held Lin in high regard for "his beauty, his vanity, his linguistic powers, &his respect for the fair." He also admired Lin's courage for handling his extreme minority status in the city. "He seems to manage for himself bravely in going about the city," Williams noted, "and contrives to make himself understood among people, as well as attract no small share of attention."[52]

On September 3, 1847, Williams and Lin entered a courtroom that the former described as "crowded with spectators." The judge began by preparing the Chinese for the worst, informing them that the court might very well order them back to the junk. They responded with an outpouring of heartfelt emotions. After the proceedings were underway, Kellett's strategy became clear. He hoped to put blinders on the court by keeping it focused on the physical scuffle between himself and the Chinese, all the while keeping it ignorant of the long string of abuses that had begun back in China. Toward this end, both Kellett and Revett, on taking the stand, tried to avoid offering any testimony that did not relate directly to the recent squabble. They were thwarted in this effort, however, by Daniel Lord. According to Williams, the lawyer's cross-examinations "made them enter into details respecting the whole treatment," not just those pertaining to recent events in New York. More damaging still, Lord "pulled their testimony to shreds" and even "made them contradict themselves."

With the credibility of Kellett and Revett in shambles, the court was prepared to hear the other side of the story. Here Lord's arguments, the translations of Williams and Lin, and the testimony of the Chinese crew all combined to effect a full disclosure of Kellett's egregious behavior: the lies he told the Chinese to convince them to sign onto the junk's voyage, the brutal treatment he inflicted on them once at sea, and his refusal to honor his contractual obligation to pay for their return trip to China.[53] In the end, the court discharged the Chinese, issued Kellett a stern reprimand, and ordered him to abide by the contract. Any member of the Chinese crew, if he so desired, was now free to return to China at Kellett's expense.[54]

Out of a group of forty Chinese crew members, twenty-six elected to return to Canton. Yet the matter was not completely resolved, since Kellett insisted on contesting the ruling. In the meantime, he refused to part with the large sum required to convey twenty-six men to China, offering only to give them twenty dollars in addition to their wages. Since he had refused to follow the court's order, his junk was temporarily seized by the United States marshal of the New York district. According to Williams, Kellett and the junk's non-Chinese sailors were not able to garner any sympathy from the public as they awaited a final verdict. They were all "low-looking people," Williams wrote, "who treated the men [Chinese] most barbarously." "If they lose soundly for their refusal to do what is right, nobody will sympathize with them, in as much as it is generally believed that the receipts have been over $20,000, and that the number of visitors has exceeded a hundred thousand."[55]

As the twenty-six crew members awaited the final resolution of their case, they stayed in the New York Sailor's Home and were looked after by Lin and several American missionaries who had taken an interest in their predicament. Samuel Wells Williams worried that, if the matter did not resolve itself soon, the onset of winter could prove difficult for these men from Southern China who lacked winter clothes. To pass their time, the Chinese worked on making a wooden model of a Chinese junk.

When at last the court ordered Kellett to pay for the return trips, the twenty-six Chinese crew members were elated by the prospect of finally heading home. They first visited Lord to present him with the model junk as a token of their appreciation. Next they went to Williams, to express their gratitude to him as well. He gave them a tour of his home and explained the various objects in his possession. Close to the day of their departure, he offered speculation as to whether this group of poor and uneducated junk hands had learned anything from their strange but remarkable journey to the West: "Most of them are so ignorant that they will not, I fear, derive much benefit from their visit to this country, though they will appreciate the kindness which has been shown them in securing their return home." On October 6, 1847, the Chinese embarked for Canton on board the Candace.[56]

Unfortunately, Kellett's treachery in New York may not have ended at this point. Almost immediately following the departure of the Candace, Lin was arrested, charged with stealing camera parts, and imprisoned. Aghast by the imprisonment of his friend, Williams suspected foul play. Kellett, he believed, was working behind the scenes to publicly humiliate Lin. Angered by Lin's interference with the Chinese crew, Kellett had arranged, purely out of vindictiveness, for a friend to make false charges. The plaintiff was thus little more than "the tool of the captain of the junk." The charges apparently had their desired effect. Although Lin proclaimed his innocence and was bailed out the following day, the newspapers provided coverage of his travails. Afraid that "everybody will point at him as a thief," he decided to stay home and wait for the story to blow over.[57]

## FROM NEW YORK TO BOSTON TO LONDON

As for Captain Kellett, he headed north to Boston with his junk, the English sailors in his employ, and the remainder of his Chinese crew, which numbered about fourteen. Despite the relatively short distance involved, the trip required more than two months because Kellett made frequent stops at the various coastal towns of New England. The junk met with genuine interest in some towns but with only a tepid reception in others. In Newport, for example, it did "not appear to have excited too much curiosity, and the number of visitors is said to be small." Similarly, another town reported that it "does not appear to excite much attention."[58]

As the junk at last made its approach to Boston by sailing up the Charles River, an unforeseen problem at the Warren Drawbridge extended Kellett's recent run of bad luck. Whereas the drawbridge spanned a distance of exactly 30 feet, the junk's width measured 30 feet, 4 inches. With a mere 4 inches preventing its passage, the "strange and clumsy specimen of marine architecture," as one newspaper called it, floated helplessly beside the bridge. At this point, Kellett descried a disturbing new development that was every showman's worst fear. Crowds of several thousand people began gathering on the riverbanks for the purpose of watching the helpless Chinese junk free of charge. Seeing his potential for profits dwindle with each passing hour, he took the junk to the Boston side of the river, established this location as the permanent venue, and began to sell tickets.[59]

The junk received visitors in the Boston area for about three months before Kellett decided to set sail for London. On February 17, 1848, the wealthy China trader Robert Bennet Forbes, generously hitched the junk to his steamship and towed it sixty miles out to sea.[60] After arriving in London, Kellett, eager to vent his frustrations with America, wrote a letter to Queen Victoria, blaming the United States for all his problems. Greatly "incensed" that this "wonder of wonders" was British and not American property, the Americans, Kellett claimed, had endeavored to sabotage the entire venture. Kellett went on to accuse Samuel Wells Williams on this count, although he did not single out Williams by name. American missionaries, Kellett claimed, "were employed to disseminate malevolent ideas among the Chinese," including the preposterous lie that "they could never survive the severity of the North American winter," all in an effort to convince them to abandon the junk.

In Kellett's account, the missionaries were even behind the court case in which the Chinese falsely claimed to have been misled in Hong Kong. The junk's crew, he wrote, had known all along that England was to be the final destination. It is hardly surprising that Kellett would suspect Williams of plotting against him. After all, had Kellett not seen this man onboard the junk conversing with the Chinese in their own tongue? And had not Williams reappeared in court to translate for the Chinese crew? Regardless of whether Kellett believed his own tale of missionary skullduggery, his next charge was pure slander. In an amazingly brazen indictment, he claimed American missionaries had distributed opium among the Chinese! With this letter to Queen Victoria,

Kellett probably hoped to arouse the sympathy of the English public and gener-ate free publicity for his spectacle.[61]

In London, Kellett had to contend with Nathan Dunn, even though Dunn had been dead for four years and the magnificent collection had left the British capital in 1846 to tour the provinces.[62] The Chinese Museum and its proprietor had left such a positive imprint in the memories of Londoners that any succes-sor would inevitably find his attraction drawn into a comparison. This posed a real problem for Kellett, as surely he knew he would lose in such a contest. Dunn's collection exceeded in size and quality what was carried by his junk; and although the junk's Chinese crew was a major selling point, Dunn had also found authentic Chinese people willing to circulate through the museum in London. Yet Kellett was not one to take defeat easily, and in the visitor's guide to the *Keying* we can see his shrewd handling of the specter of Dunn:

> Not very long since, there was exhibited, near Hyde Park, a most interesting and valuable collection of Chinese curiosities. These, however, were things which could be put into packing cases, and transported, with comparative facility, from one part of the world to another: the difficulty of bringing them to England depended more upon the proprietors' means than upon anything else. Not so with the acquisition of the Junk: the money was the least part of the matter.[63]

Quite cleverly, Kellett deflected attention away from the contents of the two attractions and toward their respective narratives. This was a brilliant move be-cause it allowed Kellett to transform all of the accidents and mishaps he had encountered inside of China, on the high seas, or in America into positive at-tributes. The same incidents that once had vexed him now contributed to an amazing tale of adventure, danger, and, ultimately, triumph.

In the visitor's guide, Kellett provided readers with an epic account of the junk's exodus from China and its subsequent voyages to the United States and London. Casting himself as the hero, he portrayed himself as a man of "skill, perseverance and courage," qualities that enabled him to execute the "daring scheme" of sailing a Chinese junk to the Western world. Kellett's narrative cov-ered his covert purchase of the junk in China, the bribery that allowed him to circumvent Chinese surveillance, the storms encountered at sea, and the threat of mutiny posed by the Chinese crew. Kellett and his men clearly faced many "obstacles," but they "persevered," and in the end "success crowned their ef-forts." In contrast, the story behind the formation of the Chinese Museum, summed up as wealthy man first buys and then ships Chinese objects, seemed prosaic in comparison.[64] Regardless of how successful he was in his efforts to minimize Dunn's achievement, Kellett could not have been pleased when, after its tour of the provinces, Dunn's collection returned to London in 1851, in time to capitalize on the crowds of people flowing into the city to experience the Crystal Palace. Adding to Kellett's worries, a new attraction had joined forces with Dunn's collection—a beautiful Chinese lady and her entire retinue.[65] This group was sure to provoke more curiosity than the *Keying*'s small contingent of Chinese sailors.[66]

Still, the junk appears to have enjoyed considerable success in London for at least a short while. The playwright James Robertson Planché, who had earlier spoofed Dunn's Chinese collection, included the *Keying* in a comic play.[67] The junk also aroused the curiosity of Charles Dickens, who found it enchanting and thought-provoking. The Chinese junk, he wrote, possessed the magical power to make the ugliness of the city vanish: "In half a score of minutes, the tiles and chimney-pots, backs of squalid houses, frowsy pieces of waste ground, narrow courts and streets, swamps, ditches, masts of ships, gardens of duckweed. . . . whirl away in a flying dream, and nothing is left but China." Using the *Arabian Nights* as his frame of reference, Dickens ascribed to the Chinese sailors a belief in magical charms: "As Aladdin's palace was transported hither and thither by the rubbing of a lamp, so the crew of Chinamen . . . devoutly believed that their good ship would turn up, quite safe, at the desired port, if they only tied red rags enough upon the mast." For Dickens, the visit to the junk prompted a meditation on his own culture. He wondered whether the British, though supposedly an enlightened people of "progress," also engaged in their own forms of superstitions that, though cloaked in the respectability of Christianity, were actually comparable to the red rags of Chinese sailors.[68]

# CONCLUSION

That New England newspapers did not devote much attention to the Chinese junk suggests it did not enjoy as much popularity there as it had in New York. If true, several factors could explain this lukewarm reception. In addition to the debacle at the bridge, the defections of most of the Chinese crew members greatly diminished the exoticism of the vessel. Whereas New Yorkers saw a Chinese junk manned by a Chinese crew, Bostonians met with an enigmatic floating chimera—a predominately white crew guiding a Chinese craft. But perhaps most important, in New York the Chinese junk provided the city with its first major Chinese spectacle (if we do not count Afong Moy). Boston, however, in 1847 had only recently enjoyed a splendid Chinese museum that possessed a

vast and rich collection of artifacts (chapter 7). The assortment of oddities below the deck of the junk must have seemed paltry in comparison.

## NOTES

1. *New York Herald* (3 August 1847). The meeting was somewhat fortuitous, for, had
the crew members waited a few more weeks, Moy would have departed for Boston.
*New York Herald* (3 September 1847). The *Herald* advised parents to instruct their
children not to play with the queues (19 August 1847).

2. Bohea is a kind of Chinese tea. Walter J. Meserve, *Heralds of Promise: The
Drama of the American People during the Age of Jackson, 1829–1849* (New York:
Greenwood Press, 1986), 90, 93, 156, 170; and Arthur Herman Wilson, *A History of the
Philadelphia Theatre, 1835–1855* (Philadelphia: University of Pennsylvania Press, 1935),
554, 559, 572, 575, 618, 670.

3. Dave Williams, ed., *The Chinese Other, 1850–1912: An Anthology of Plays* (Lanham, Md.: University Press of America, 1997), 1.

4. *Alta California* (20 October 1852). Ronald Riddle, "The Cantonese Opera: A
Chapter in Chinese-American History," in Chinese Historical Society of America,
*The Life, Influence, and the Role of the Chinese in the United States, 1776–1960: Pro-
ceedings, Papers of the National Conference Held at the University of San Francisco,
July 10, 11, 12, 1975* (San Francisco: Chinese Historical Society of America, 1976),
41–42. According to John Kuo Wei Tchen, who chronicled the financial difficulties of
the troupe, corrupt business managers cheated the performers out of their money before abandoning them, leaving them stranded and penniless. John Kuo Wei Tchen,
*New York before Chinatown: Orientalism and the Shaping of American Culture,
1776–1882* (Baltimore: Johns Hopkins University Press, 1999), 63–71.

5. "Novel Speculation," *The Farmers' Cabinet* (11 February 1847). "The Chinese
Junk," *The Farmer's Cabinet* (26 August 1847).

6. Linda Cooke Johnson, *Shanghai: From Market Town to Treaty Port, 1074–1858*
(Stanford: Stanford University Press, 1995), 273–75; Frederic Wakeman, *Strangers at
the Gate: Social Disorder in South China, 1839–1861* (Berkeley: University of California Press, 1966), 100–1.

7. *Chinese Repository* (February 1847), 84–86.

8. *Boston Daily Advertiser* (2 November 1847). According to Samuel Wells Williams and Henrietta Shuck, the first female missionary to China, the men who
worked on junks typically came from the lower economic classes. In fact, missionaries at one time believed that the discontent of junk men might render them open to
a new religion. Henrietta Shuck, *Scenes in China; or, Sketches of the Country, Religion, and Customs of the Chinese* (Philadelphia: American Baptist Publication Society, 1853),130; and Frederick Wells Williams, *The Life and Letters of Samuel Wells*

*Williams, LL.D., Missionary, Diplomatist, Sinologue* (New York: G. P. Putnam's Sons, 1889), 80.

9. For a description of the American's original plan, see the *Boston Daily Advertiser* (2 November 1847). For the price of the junk, see the *Niles National Register* (7 August 1847). Kellett's letter, which first appeared in the *London Morning Chronicle*, is reprinted in Holden's *Dollar Magazine* (April 1848), 252.

10. *The Chinese Repository* (December 1846), 624.

11. In the nineteenth century, coolie labor occupied a middle ground between slavery and indentured servitude. Although a coolie, unlike a slave, was not owned and did receive wages, he did not enter voluntarily into his often lengthy term of manual labor but was instead coerced or deceived into doing so.

12. Kellett did not explain why New York was easier to reach than London, but the direction of oceanic currents probably factored into his decision making.

13. Most of the account of the *Keying's* journey uses information compiled from two sources. First, Samuel Wells Williams, the missionary who served as interpreter for the Chinese crew members during their court hearing, described Kellett's deception and brutality in his private correspondence. See his letter to Sarah Walworth, 4 September 1847, box 1, series 1, Samuel Wells Williams Family Papers, Manuscript Collections, Yale University Library. Hereafter, this collection will be cited as SW-WFP. Second, the catalog for the junk's engagement in London provided further background and relevant dates. *A Description of the Royal Chinese Junk, "Keying"* (London: J. Such, 1848), 6–9. Other helpful sources include *New York Herald* (4 September 1847); and "The Chinese Junk, 'Keying,'" *Illustrated London News* (1 April 1848). For accounts by historians, see John Kuo Wei Tchen, *New York before Chinatown* (Baltimore: Johns Hopkins University Press, 1999), 64–68; and Arthur Bonner, *Alas! What Brought Thee Hither? The Chinese in New York, 1800–1950* (Madison, N.J.: Farleigh Dickinson University Press, 1997), 2–3.

14. "The Chinese Junk *Keying*," *Pittsfield Herald* (22 July 1847). This article originally appeared in the *New York Herald*.

15. Paul Zweig, *Walt Whitman: The Making of the Poet* (New York: Basic Books, 1984), 58–59.

16. Brewster Maverick Pocket Diary, entries for 10, 12, 15, and 16 July 1847. New-York Historical Society, Manuscript Division.

17. *New York Herald* (10 August 1847).

18. *New York Herald* (21 July 1847).

19. The catalog, *A Description of the Royal Chinese Junk, "Keying,"* contains a list of the items displayed.

20. A. C. Van Epps, "Silk and the Silk Culture," *De Bow's Commercial Review of the South and West* (April 1848), 332.

21. Orson Fowler, "The Chinese Junk," *American Phrenological Journal* 9 (1847): 328.

22. John Davies, *Phrenology: Fad and Science: A Nineteenth-Century Crusade* (New Haven: Yale University Press, 1955), 3–21.

23. *The American Phrenological Journal* eventually achieved a circulation of 50,000. Davies, 33–62.

24. Orson Fowler, "The Phrenological Character of Chan and Eng, the Siamese Twins, with a Likeness," *American Phrenological Journal* 8 (1846), 316–17. "Chinese Skulls," *American Phrenological Journal* 10 (1848), 260.

25. "I examined carefully the head of their ship's painter, many specimens of whose art decorated the main cabin. It was twenty-one inches around Individuality and Philoprogenitiveness. It was high at the crown. Firmness, Approbativeness, and Veneration predominated, and Adhesiveness and Parental Love were amply developed, as were Perceptiveness and Language; yet Causality was small, and the brain, as a whole, considerably under size, though the temperament was excellent. Constructiveness and Imitation were large, and Ideality was full. Individuality, Eventuality, Form, Size, Locality, Order, and Color were also large, and the cerebral organization quite superior to that of the rest of the crew." Orson Fowler, "The Chinese Junk," *American Phrenological Journal* 9 (1847): 328.

26. Caleb Cushing, "Delusions of Science," *National Magazine and Republican* (March,1839), 245, 254.

27. Frederick Wells Williams, 144–46. Samuel Wells Williams, *The Middle Kingdom: A Survey of the Geography, Government, Education, Social Life, Arts, Religion, &.,* of the Chinese Empire and Its Inhabitants* (New York: Wiley and Putnam, 1848), 1:xiii–xvi. This poem apparently enjoyed a wide circulation. A Dr. Scott (whose first name is not given) cited it in his "Lecture on the Chinese Empire," delivered in New Orleans before the Mechanic's Institute, 26 January 1854. New York Public Library. The poem is also quoted in an adventure novel set in China. Harry W. French, *Our Boys in China: The Thrilling Story of Two Young Americans, Scott and Paul Clayton Wrecked in the China Sea, on Their Return from India, with Their Strange Adventures in China* (New York: Charles Dillingham, 1883), 45.

28. Osmond Tiffany Jr., *The Canton Chinese; or, The American's Sojourn in the Celestial Empire* (Boston: James Munroe, 1849), 266.

29. According to Stuart Creighton Miller, China received national attention for the first time during the Opium War because the conflict coincided with the rise of the penny press. And since these widely read newspapers portrayed China's military efforts as futile and its leadership as pompous, many Americans grew to be more critical of Chinese culture. *The Unwelcome Immigrant: The American Image of the Chinese, 1785–1882* (Berkeley: University of California Press, 1969), 83–84.

30. Smyth wrote his detailed description of current views toward China to set up an analogy with the Episcopal Church. He likened the pomp and ceremony of that denomination to the Chinese empire. Thomas Smyth, "The Prelactical Doctrine of Apostolical Succession Examined," *Princeton Review* (January 1842), 139–41.

31. Smyth, 139–41.

32. Ibid..

33. Ibid.

34. The rumor regarding Barnum apparently traveled north to Boston, where the *Boston Herald* publisheded it before it was refuted by two other papers, the *Boston Courier* (25 November 1847) and the *Boston Daily Advertiser* (2 November 1847).

35. Hesing's English ability is noted in the London catalog *A Description of the Royal Chinese Junk, "Keying,"* 10.

36. Barnum enjoyed this relationship with several newspapers. A. H. Saxon, *P. T. Barnum: The Legend and the Man* (New York: Columbia University Press, 1989), 74–75. Frederic Hudson, the *Herald's* managing editor, viewed the advertisement as a form of news and the advertiser as a kind of reporter since he provided "a picture of the metropolis" (Hudson, *Journalism in the United States, from 1690 to 1872* [New York: Harper and Brothers, 1872], 286).

37. *New York Herald* (18 August 1847).

38. *New York Herald* (17 August 1847).

39. *New York Herald* (31 August 1847).

40. *New York Herald* (24 July 1847).

41. *New York Herald* (31 August 1847).

42. *New York Herald* (28 August 1847).

43. Samuel Wells Williams to Sarah Walworth, letter, 19 August 1847, box 1, series 1, SWWFP.

44. Though the opium smoking observed by Williams was possibly a performance, it was far more likely to have been genuine for two reasons. First, Williams had seen opium smoking first hand in China and was less apt to be fooled by an insincere show. Second, he spoke Cantonese and, therefore, could speak with the Chinese crew members to ascertain the truth.

45. *New York Herald* (11 August 1847).

46. *New York Herald* (28 July 1847).

47. *New York Herald* (4 August 1847).

48. *A Description of the Royal Chinese Junk, "Keying,"* 6.

49. *New York Herald* (4 September 1847)

50. *New York Herald* (31 August 1847).

51. Samuel Wells Williams to Sarah Walworth, letter, 31 August 1847, box 1, series 1, SWWFP.

52. Samuel Wells Williams to Sarah Walworth, letter, 4 September 1847, box 1, series 1, SWWFP.

53. Samuel Wells Williams to Sarah Walworth, letter, 4 September 1847, box 1, series 1, SWWFP.

54. *New York Herald* (4 September 1847).

55. Samuel Wells Williams to Sarah Walworth, letter, 13 September 1847, box 1, series 1, SWWFP. "Chinese Junk," *Farmers' Cabinet* (7 October 1847).

56. Samuel Wells Williams to Sarah Walworth, letters, 29 September and 6 October 1847, box 1, series 1, SWWFP. "Sailing of the Chinese Sailors, Belonging to the Cochin China Junk," *The American Magazine* (13 November 1847), 726–27.

57. Samuel Wells Williams to Sarah Walworth, letters, 11 October and 18 October 1847, box 1, series 1, SWWFP.

58. *Boston Daily Advertiser* (13, 17, and 18 November 1847); *Boston Courier* (30 October and 1 November 1847); *Farmers' Cabinet* (4 November 1847).

59. *Boston Daily Advertiser* (23 November 1847); *Boston Courier* (23 November 1847); *Boston Post* (23 November 1847).

60. *A Description of the Royal Chinese Junk, "Keying,"* 7.

61. Kellett's letter, which first appeared in the *London Morning Chronicle*, is copied in Holden's *Dollar Magazine* (April 1848), 252.

62. Nathan Dunn's collection commenced its tour of the provinces in the autumn of 1846. "The Chinese Collection," *London Times* (26 October 1846).

63. *A Description of the Royal Chinese Junk, "Keying,"* 5.

64. Ibid., 6–10.

65. *Illustrated London News* (10 May 1851). P. T. Barnum, *Struggles and Triumphs; or, Forty Years' Recollections* (Hartford: J. B. Burr, 1870), 366. *London Times* (26 October 1846).

66. Hesing apparently enjoyed the opening ceremony at the Crystal Palace. According to one correspondent's report, Hesing stood with other foreign dignitaries during the event. As the choir performed the Hallelujah Chorus from Handel's *Messiah*, the mandarin became suddenly overcome with emotion. He made his way through the "ambassadors, courtiers, and all the distinguished circle which surrounded the throne" and, on reaching the queen, "saluted" her. His gesture was "most graciously acknowledged." "Hon. Mr. Plunkett's Letters from Europe," *Piitsfield Sun* (22 May 1851).

67. Part of the drama takes place on the junk. The captain, who is Chinese, not British, sails the junk into a giant sea serpent that he has mistaken for an island. "The King of the Peacocks," *The Extravaganzas of J. R. Planché, Esq.*, ed. T. F. Dillon Crocker and Stephen Tucker (London: Samuel French, 1879), 3:263–308.

68. John Forster, *The Life of Charles Dickens* (London: Cecil Palmer, 1928), 487–89. The practice of tying red rags to parts of the boat is explained in the visitor's guide, which Dickens appears to have read. *A Description of the Royal Chinese Junk, "Keying,"* 6.

# 6. GOD'S CHINA

## *The Middle Kingdom* of Samuel Wells Williams

As Samuel Wells Williams watched the story of the *Keying* unfold, he reflected on its meaning in a letter to his fiancée. To the American missionary, the treachery of Captain Kellett, the travails of the Chinese crew, and the derisive laughter of visitors to the junk did not, when taken together, comprise an isolated incident that he could easily dismiss. Instead, the Chinese junk, he wrote, was "a specimen of the treatment the people of heathen lands receive at the hands of Christians." By the late 1840s, Williams had grown frustrated with the mocking, callous, and unsympathetic attitudes adopted by many of his fellow Christians in their treatment of the Chinese. By using the word *specimen*, he meant that the *Keying* was a floating microcosm: The abuses on board this single craft reflected in miniature the disturbing new trends in the relations of Christians with "heathen lands."[1]

The American missionary could make such a connection between the local and the global because he had witnessed many of these abuses firsthand, both on the junk and in China. Far from being an anomaly, the behavior of Captain Kellett, which oscillated between deception and violence, only mirrored the actions of the merchants and government officials who represented Christian nations in China. These men were all too willing to sacrifice the well-being of the Chinese by surreptitiously smuggling opium into the country and then resorting to outright force when the Chinese mounted resistance. Similarly, the mockery to which ticketholders subjected the *Keying*'s Chinese crew was perfectly consistent with a more widespread feeling among Americans that the Chinese, as a race, were hopelessly pathetic. To Williams's great vexation, ordinary Americans now saw fit both to "ridicule the idea of evangelizing" the Chinese and to "laugh at all the efforts to teach them." In sum, the Christian people whom Williams had always assumed would treat the Chinese with caring and compassion had become, if not outright adversaries, hindrances to God's divine plan to spread Christianity throughout China.[2]

And since Williams viewed his own life as existing in perfect alignment with the will of God, he took these disturbing developments quite personally and decided to act. While the specific grievances of the *Keying*'s Chinese crew would find resolution in the courthouse, for the larger problem of Christian ignorance and insensitivity no solution that simple existed. To cure this more pervasive ill infecting American society, Williams would need to attack the source. With this realization, he redirected his substantial intellectual energy into a new project. Instead of convincing the Chinese to accept Christ, he would turn 180 degrees and preach to a new audience: Americans. Williams took it upon himself to teach his Christian countrymen about the richness, the complexity, the flaws, and yet—what was most important—the overall worthiness of Chinese civilization. He would explain the ways of China to Americans.

## THE EARLY YEARS

Samuel Wells Williams was born in 1812 in Utica, New York, to what would become a very large family of fourteen children. He enjoyed few close friendships outside of his own family but did forge a lifelong bond with his neighbor and schoolmate, James Dwight Dana.[3] After Samuel completed high school, where he had shown considerable academic promise, he dreamed about continuing his education at the college level and about following Dana to Yale. The two young men hoped to study natural history under Benjamin Silliman, the top geologist in the country. Unfortunately, Samuel's father had other plans. William Williams owned and operated one of the largest printing houses in western New York, and he fully expected to pass on the family business to his first son. He refused to pay for a Yale education, choosing instead to make Samuel his apprentice. To Samuel, the disappointment was profound. He would later regret that he had not insisted more vigorously on attending Yale even if it had meant paying his own way by finding a job in New Haven.[4]

Although he would not join Dana at Yale, Samuel Wells Williams did continue his formal education. After he had spent several months working with his father, it became abundantly clear to both father and son that Samuel, although he might one day become an able printer, possessed absolutely no business sense. Williams simply would not be able to succeed in a career in printing. And after Samuel's mother died in 1831, William Williams relented and agreed to fund several additional years of education for his son. By way of the recently completed Erie Canal, Williams traveled to Troy, New York, and enrolled at the Rensselaer Institute.

The Rensselaer Institute had been founded in 1824 to encourage the application of science to practical affairs.[5] When Williams arrived there, what he found was a school that was still in an inchoate state: Only six students were then enrolled, and the school could not even provide him with a bed to sleep in. After assessing his prospects in Troy, Williams wrote to Dana in New Haven: "To tell you the truth, James, I never, never experienced such a disappointment, such an utter failure of expectations, in my life."[6] And so, while James Dana had successfully moved to the center of America's intellectual world at Yale, the equally talented Williams remained on the periphery.

Despite this inauspicious beginning, Williams grew to enjoy the curriculum at the Rensselaer Institute, which placed heavy emphasis on natural history. Through his study of botany, entomology, zoology, and mineralogy, Williams learned how to collect, classify, and sketch natural specimens.[7] These experiences in studying the natural world apparently instilled in him a reverence for the Creator. In a letter to his father, Williams wrote enthusiastically about the revelations he had received from his astronomy class, describing the sun, stars, nebulae, the Milky Way, and the vastness of the universe. "Yet the goodness and infinite wisdom of the Creator," he continued, "is as much shown in the formation and habits of the water-spider as in these suns, the size of which we cannot conceive." To Williams, the goal of science was to discern God's blueprints for the universe, and, with this noble purpose in mind, the young student decided on his career. He would become a naturalist.[8]

While Samuel was pursuing his coursework, his father learned that the fledgling Protestant mission in Canton was in dire need of a qualified individual to operate its printing office. William Williams immediately suggested his oldest son, apparently without consulting him. The father's act may seem rash, but this notion that one or more of the Williams boys would spend their lives engaged in missionary work had come up before. Sophia Williams, Samuel's mother, had been an active church member after experiencing a religious awakening following the difficult birth of Samuel. One Sunday in 1831, she had found herself in church and without any money as the collection plate began to circulate through the congregation. In a move that proved fateful, she placed a slip of paper into the plate that read, "I give two of my sons." Though she died later that year, her words were not forgotten.[9]

When Samuel learned that he had been volunteered for the position in China, he immersed himself in a single night of intense meditation and prayer. After emerging the following morning, he somewhat reluctantly agreed to go. Quite possibly, the recent passing of his mother played a role in his decision. If so, the fact of her death probably influenced him less than the manner in which she had died. Describing her final moments to Dana, he wrote, "Had you, dear James, been near her dying couch . . . you would have thought that death, judgment, and eternity were realities, that religion was not a thing of convenience."[10] While Williams accepted the post in China, he did, however, harbor one serious reservation. "So deeply has the love of the works of God . . . got imbued into me," he wrote his father, "that I fear, if I went [to China], any object of natural history would interest me more than anything else."[11] Williams feared that his passion for natural history would distract him and divert his attention away from his responsibilities as a missionary printer. However, as will be shown, Williams eventually found a way to synthesize his love for science with his religious obligations.

## THE CHINA MISSION

Williams was not naturally predisposed to a deeply religious life. In fact, he wrote of deriving no pleasure from religion as a youth and of accepting Christ into his heart only after being subjected to heavy "maternal suasion."[12] Yet once Williams had committed himself to God and Christ, Protestant Christianity proceeded to reconfigure his worldview, just as natural history had before. The mind of Samuel Wells Williams became papered with a vast cosmography, with Earth hanging precariously midway between Heaven and Hell. Believing that both God and Satan vied for influence over the human world, Williams in China developed an overarching objective that could not have been more grand in scale: to evict the devil from the Chinese empire and open the hearts of a full quarter of humanity to Christ. To him, China became a vast battleground on which warring supernatural forces were poised to collide.

On October 25, 1833, Samuel Wells Williams stepped off the *Morrison* and into the foreign factories outside Canton. He moved into the American factory, where he lived without paying rent in the quarters of D. W. Olyphant, an American merchant who possessed a strong passion for missions.[13] At that time, the Protestant mission, though charged with the ambitious task of transforming

China into a Christian stronghold, consisted of only two men, Elijah Bridgman and Robert Morrison. And to date they had secured but two Chinese converts.[14] Clearly, much work remained to be done.

While intent on accomplishing this work, Williams quickly discovered that the environment was not ideal for missionary work. First, the missionaries constituted a small minority in what was otherwise a colony of merchants, most of whom had a very different objective. "Collected from all parts of the world," Williams wrote, the merchants were animated by "the single desire to make money." To his dismay, Williams discovered that the avarice of these "wicked men" increased the difficulty of his job, in that the merchants were so visible. The Chinese regarded their behavior as reflective of the values to be found in Christian nations. And in Williams's view, the merchants were tragically unfit to represent Christ. Through their greed and immoral dealings, they were "constantly giving the lie to all the teachings of the gospel." As a result, many Chinese who might otherwise have been swayed by the missionaries' efforts were confused by these "unscrupulous" ambassadors whose actions diverged from the core tenets of Christianity. In fact, Williams went as far as to accuse the merchants of being "active guerilla parties of the evil one"; they abetted Satan in his nefarious scheme to subvert "the holy commands of God's law."[15]

Along with the merchants, the Qing government also threatened to thwart the ambitions of the missionaries as it erected obstacles of both a physical and a psychological nature. With respect to the former, Williams discovered, as Nathan Dunn had before him, that he was barred from venturing beyond the narrow perimeter of the foreign factories. Obviously, this limitation on his mobility severely curtailed his missionary activities. As for psychological obstacles, the Qing government had also built barriers designed to block meaningful communication between foreigners and Chinese. The most important of such barriers concerned language: the subjects of China were forbidden to teach foreigners Chinese.

But this restriction would not prevent Williams from continuing to consider language the key to the success of the Protestant mission. If he and his fellow missionaries could not speak to the people of China and could not print religious tracts in Chinese, the Christian cause there was obviously hopeless. To learn Chinese, Williams undertook a clandestine Chinese-language project, hiring teachers who took him on as a student only at tremendous personal risk. One teacher brought shoes to every lesson so that, should Chinese officials abruptly intrude on a lesson, "he could pretend he was a Chinese manufacturer of foreign shoes." Dr. Morrison's instructor resorted to more-drastic measures. He carried poison to each session, believing a quick death preferable to the torture that would result from the discovery of his illegal activity.[16]

In addition to tutorials, Williams launched an ambitious program of private study. For an average of five to six hours a day, he adhered to a strict regimen that required him to write Chinese characters over and over again, in meticulous and methodical fashion.[17] To add an element of practical experience, he sought out conversations with ordinary Chinese during walks which he took on an average of twice each day. Arising each morning half an hour before sunrise, Williams typically would stroll out into the public square to enjoy the cool morning air and chat with the Chinese vendors preparing to sell vegetables. After dark, he would venture out again in search of similar conversations. He found that the Chinese would react to him with varying degrees of cooperation; while some called him a "teacher" or a "gentleman," others spurned him as a "foreign devil."[18]

As Williams placed language study at the top of his list of priorities, other ambitions necessarily suffered. Regrettably, one pursuit that received a demotion was natural history. "I have latterly paid but little attention to natural science," he wrote his brother in 1835, "having concluded to wait until I have acquired sufficient knowledge of the Chinese language. It is now the chief end of my desires &of my life to promote the cause of Christ among this people." Williams regarded natural history as a worthy intellectual pursuit, but he also understood it as a decidedly personal ambition. And he knew that, to be a missionary, one needed to adhere to God's divine plan even if that meant subordinating one's own interests. While deemphasizing natural history, Williams did not abandon it completely, however. In fact, in a letter to his brother, he wrote excitedly about the three hundred species of fish he had examined. Amidst this exuberance, though, one senses the concomitant pang of guilt of one who might have felt he was shirking his religious responsibilities. In the same letter, he admitted almost apologetically, "I cannot keep my fingers off these pretty flowers &curious bugs." The implication was that he should.[19]

Along with language study, Williams devoted much of his time to the publication of the *Chinese Repository*. The *Repository*, established in 1832, was a monthly periodical devoted to the dissemination of knowledge in the foreign community. Although the *Repository* was published by the Protestant mission, much of its readership consisted of traders, and so it carried articles on both religious and secular matters. Along with his responsibilities as the *Repository's* printer, Williams also contributed content to its pages. Throughout the periodical's twenty-year run, only Elijah Bridgman authored a comparable number of articles.

But unlike Bridgman, who had honed his expository skills at two prestigious institutions, Amherst College and Andover Theological Seminary, Williams possessed training only as a naturalist.[20] Deeming himself inadequately prepared for a job that entailed so much writing, Williams, in letters he penned home, wrote of feeling acutely "my own incompetence."[21] In an attempt to compensate for the gap in his education, he obtained copies of the works of Charles Lamb, the great English essayist, and tried to imitate Lamb's prose. When Bridgman read the awkward result—articles about Canton written in a ludicrous high style—he could not contain his laughter.[22] The good-natured eruptions of a friend must have embarrassed the self-conscious Williams, who nonetheless worked hard to improve his writing. He gradually learned to write within his abilities and eventually developed a prose style that was clear and straightforward if lacking in literary flourish.

In writing for the *Repository*, Williams faced the same temptation that confronted all Westerners writing about China. He could have easily portrayed the Chinese as peculiar and their customs as different from those in the United States and, in this way, pass simplistic East-West comparisons off as legitimate ethnography. He resisted that temptation, however, choosing instead to hew to the periodical's mission: to disseminate the most-accurate information on China available.[23] Toward this end, he wrote more than one hundred major articles between 1833 and 1851.[24] Of course, the prominent storylines he covered during his tenure as writer, editor, and printer revolved around the twin issues of Christianity's advances in China and the trading privileges of Western nations (or lack thereof). But possessing a mind steeped in natural history, Williams was also able to depart from matters related solely to religion and commerce and to explore a diverse array of fields.

In the areas of geography and topography, he described China's provinces, the largest cities and towns of the empire, and the most prominent rivers and mountain ranges. In the area of natural history, he combined his own fieldwork around Canton with the best available published sources; he wrote articles on rocks and minerals, the tea plant, bamboo, lions, horses, bats, flying squirrels, cormorants, and bees and wasps. He reviewed books on China written by European and American authors. Most importantly, he used his articles to paint in piecemeal fashion a colorful portrait of Chinese life: diet, rice cultivation, festivals, the filial behavior of children, female education, dialects, pagoda-building, literature, theater, religion, mythology, and ancestor worship. Finally, Williams also served his readers in the foreign community by writing pieces that were directly related to their interests; he discussed Chinese imports and exports, the status of the Protestant mission, developments in the various internal rebellions threatening the empire, and the ascension of a new emperor to the throne. Of course, many of his topical pieces centered on opium: the smuggling by merchants, the problem of addiction in Chinese society, the response of Chinese officials, and the British military action.[25]

Williams's work with the *Repository* forced him to become an expert on China. For in order to write these articles, he had to observe the Chinese way of life, consult with Chinese people, employ his language skills to read Chinese literature, apply his training in natural history to the study of China's flora and fauna, and read all available Western sources on China. When taken together, the more than one hundred major articles that he wrote for this periodical, when combined with the thousands of others he edited, formed an unofficial first draft of his future masterwork—*The Middle Kingdom*.

Besides this experience with the *Repository*, one other ingredient was crucial to Williams's evolution as a writer. He needed to adopt a writer's eye for seeing the world. This transformation started to take place in 1836, his third year in China. "I have lately been accustomed to walk thro' the streets of Canton and Macao," he wrote to his brother, "with my mind half agog to see every new thing I could, just as if I was intending to write a letter or journal when I returned home." Of course, Williams had walked these streets hundreds of times in the past. However, while the sights had hardly changed at all, Williams was clearly evolving. He was acquiring a heightened awareness to his surroundings, and it allowed his vision to penetrate more deeply into sights he previously considered familiar, common, or mundane: "I never fail to see something unseen before." To his surprise, Williams also discovered that his level of curiosity was not typical. In fact, he expressed his disappointment with the sea captains with whom he frequently conversed. Although they had visited intriguing ports all over the world, most of them were "mentally stone blind" and could not relay any information to the inquisitive missionary. When presented with his queries, they would offer him the same excuse for their ignorance: "I had my ship to look after."[26]

Williams truly was far more curious and observant than most foreigners in China. Still, the descriptive writer inside of him occupied a subordinate position to the missionary; he could understand the sights he saw only by placing them in a Christian context. When he traveled by boat from Canton to Macao in 1835, he watched Chinese farmers harvest rice and later described the scene in a letter.

> We can see on both sides of the river . . . men, women, &children, engaged in the various occupations of thrashing, winnowing and gleaning. The weather is delightful, and all the population are now enjoying themselves as happily as they do at any season of the year. Even the beggars partake of the general rejoicing always attendant on gathering in the fruits of the earth. . . . The crop has been pretty good this fall. . . . There are near us two tall pagodas standing on two hills, which are picturesque and striking objects.

Williams's depiction of a happy harvest seems idyllic, but in the letter he goes on to tell a different story. Of course, the landscape was beautiful, the rice harvest was full, and the people were happy. However, while Williams appreciated all these attributes, he did not do so because they contributed to the well-being of the Chinese people. Rather, he valued them only as the "desirable qualities" that one looked for when selecting a site for a future missionary operation. "The day will come," he prophesied in the same letter, "when instead of pagodas, spires of churches will rise above the dull uniform town." In fact, without the Christian influence, the exuberant life he observed among the Chinese people only served the devil. For instance, during this trip, when a lusty boatmen shouted "indecent" things to the young female rice harvesters on the shore, Williams became greatly perturbed. "O the abominations of heathenism," he exclaimed. "May we live unspotted from the world, the flesh, &the devil."[27]

# PRIDE: INTERNAL AND EXTERNAL

Unfortunately for Williams, if Christianity was progressing at all in China, it was doing so only at a glacial pace. And so, after three years, Williams was frustrated. In a letter to his brother, he likened mission work in China to farming on rocky terrain. "We are apparently making but slow headway," he wrote. "Every step some stone must be rolled away, some weed plucked up. The fallow ground not being broken up, how can the seed be sown?"[28] When he tried to engage the Chinese in serious discussions about the miracles of the Savior, the ravages of opium smoking, or the sin of idolatry, they would show little interest, choosing instead to change the topic so as to "ask the price of your jacket" or "discuss the size of your nose."[29]

Such queries, besides being annoying, indicated to Williams that the Chinese were more concerned with superficial matters in this world than they were with weighty spiritual matters of the next. In his view, even their organized religion, which might have elevated their morality and shifted their attention to the afterlife, only served to reinforce their earthly concerns and materialistic values. Most of their "heathen worship," he observed, consisted of burning colored paper or lighting sticks of incense so as to succor the favor of spirits and deities and thereby ensure material prosperity. Thus, worship in China, far from helping people transcend human greed or lust, was merely an expression of the same. "The great god they worship is Mammon," Williams asserted, "and to him they burn daily incense both of soul &body."[30]

At the same time, one of Williams's most fascinating traits was his insistence on subjecting his own soul to the same scrutiny that the Chinese received. He earnestly believed that when one endeavored "to study human character," one "must begin at home" and "know something of what elements your own heart is made of, before you attempt much in scanning other people's."[31] While he faulted the Chinese for constructing an entire religious apparatus around false idols, he acknowledged that at least they were not hypocritical. After all, their outward forms of worship truly reflected the desires within their hearts. Williams was less sure about himself. Although he had devoted his life to the service of God, he admitted that, in the secret "niches" of his own heart, he would "daily &hourly offer incense to idols" like "pride" and "envy." "O Fred," he exclaimed to his brother in a moment of soulful anxiety, "how much more guilty too are you &I for this idolatry than the poor Chinese who only exhibit to all the same idolatry that I fear we keep to ourselves?"[32]

With Williams, the outward gaze toward China prompted an inward-looking examination of his own soul; the ethnographic and the introspective were inextricably linked. And as the years in China passed, the pride that he regarded as sinful continued to grow. He became increasingly aware that he possessed several attributes seldom concentrated in a single individual: amazing stamina and health, rare linguistic talent, a gift for writing, printing skills, and training as a naturalist. The man who had initially worried about his own "incompetence" increasingly grew concerned about the swelling of his own ego.

His pride concerned him so deeply because he understood it in a Christian framework. His own heart became a battlefield where Satan was attempting to turn him away from God by attacking him in his greatest area of vulnerability— self love. Indeed, of all possible sins, pride stood as the most dangerous, because it had the potential to corrupt everything he accomplished as a missionary. After all, missionary work entailed the humble subordination of one's own ambitions to those of God. If Williams's deeds in China were secretly aimed at winning glory for himself rather than for God, he might be carrying out God's will to all outward appearances and yet be losing his soul to Satan in the process. For this reason, Williams regarded pride as an oppressive force, and he longed to be delivered from it. One day in 1841 he left his quarters to take a stroll by himself. While walking, he posed a question to himself: "From what do you anticipate relief that will make heaven so desirable and happy a place?" In answer, he singled out "freedom from pride" as the one thing for which he yearned above all others. Pride was so "ingrained into me that I look upon entire deliverance from it as almost heaven itself."[33] Over the course of Williams's lengthy career as a missionary, pride would remain his greatest foe.

Interestingly, in the same letter, he imputed it to the Chinese as well.[34] And so Williams believed that he had something significant in common with the people he was trying to save. In both the microcosm of Williams's own heart and the macrocosm of China, Satan appeared to be employing the same strategy. Williams would necessarily have to combat pride on two separate battlefields.

He was not alone in ascribing cultural arrogance to the Chinese. Nearly all foreigners in China—merchants, government officials, and missionaries—regarded China's excessive pride as the root of most problems. In the opinion of merchants, it was what loomed behind the system of unequal treatment under which they chaffed. Foreigners could trade in only one port, Canton; they were required to transact all their business through the Hong merchants; they were compelled to abide by a long list of vexing rules or risk expulsion from the country; and when they registered complaints, these were often rudely dismissed by haughty mandarin officials. Foreign officials hoped to secure relief for the merchants, but they too experienced great difficulty in obtaining any concessions. Perhaps symbolic of the Chinese attitude toward the outside world, foreigners almost never received an audience with the emperor and, on the few occasions when these meetings did occur, the Chinese expected ambassadors to kowtow in his august presence.[35]

Williams readily added his voice to the growing chorus of complaints; he firmly believed that Chinese pride interfered with his missionary work. The Chinese were so smugly satisfied with the attainments of their own civilization as to render them impervious to new systems of thought, such as the one he was offering. "It was by no means pleasant," he wrote, "to live among people cherishing such self-conceited and supercilious notions regarding us."[36] In Williams's opinion, the arrogant Chinese needed to be humbled before they would become receptive to his message. But how could that ever come to pass? In the 1830s, Sino-foreign relations seemed to have settled into a state of stasis that worked to the disadvantage of foreigners. While merchants could grudgingly accept the present conditions because most were still able to turn a profit, missionaries could not make any headway in their godly work as long as the status quo persisted. This stagnation, were it to last for several decades, would force them to live their entire lives in vain. For an ambitious individual like Williams, the prospect of leading a life devoid of achievement was terrifying.

Clearly, a lot was at stake. But there was really very little Williams could do to shake up affairs in China. He and other missionaries longed for the intervention of an outside force—something powerful that could smash the prideful Chinese into humble submission and compel them to prostrate themselves before the Lord, just as they had forced others to kowtow in the presence of the emperor. In sum, on the grand theatrical stage that was China, Williams longed for a deus ex machina. And that is exactly what he got.

# THE BATTERING RAM OF GOD

"I am glad things in this region are coming to a crisis," Williams wrote to his brother in the summer of 1839, "for almost anything is better than the old dull way we were going on at a while ago, hampered and restrained beyond description." He went on to say that he was "quite confident" that God was in the process "answering the prayers of his people" and advancing "the great cause, whose progress must be onward."[37] Williams was referring to China's escalating conflict with England over the lucrative yet illegal opium trade. Williams despised the opium trade, largely because it ruined Chinese lives and taught the Chinese people to distrust all representatives from Christian nations—including men and women who sought to spread the Gospel. Even so, as the above letter indicates, Williams paradoxically favored a war waged to preserve it. And so when armed hostilities finally broke out in 1839, Williams's emotional reaction could best be described as disgusted exhilaration.[38]

To fully understand his peculiar reaction to the Sino-English conflict, we can return to his love of natural history. Williams believed that, if one studied the natural world, one could discern God's miraculous handiwork both in the largest of phenomena, such as a distant nebula, and in the smallest creatures, such as a water-spider. In other words, since God was omnipresent, one could detect his divine fingerprints everywhere. In this sense, the Lord did *not* move in mysterious ways, since human beings could comprehend His divine plan. To Williams, the world of human affairs was no different from the natural environment. Everything that happened—even wars—worked in some way to advance God's divine plan. But since the purposes of God in the realm of human events, like the processes of the natural world, were not immediately apparent, one could demystify them only by employing one's rational faculties. Williams attempted to do just that with the Opium War. Though ostensibly an abomination in the sight of God, the war on closer inspection revealed that His divine wisdom was dictating events.

Williams explained his understanding of events in a letter he wrote to his brother in November 1840, several months after the arrival of the English fleet in Chinese waters:

> I am happy . . . as God has made us so many assurances of his interest in the affairs of men, the expedition was no doubt sent here to advance his kingdom among the Chinese. . . . One of those lessons may be that they are weak by making them feel the tremendous power of foreign nations, &thus inspire them with a wholesome dread and fear of lightly trampling under foot those who come here. As a nation, this

people are inconceivably conceited &proud &cannon balls are a means of disabusing them of some of the supports of their traits of character. Punishment may in the
hand of God be made of great good service to this wicked people.[39]

In Williams's view, the proud Chinese needed to be humbled before they
would become receptive to the word of God. Although the English appeared to
be accomplishing exactly that, they were not heroes in Williams's estimation
because, after all, their war was a morally unjust one waged to protect the illicit
opium trade. Rather, in ways that were beyond the comprehension of the English themselves (yet perfectly clear to Williams), the mighty British fleet was
little more than an "entering wedge," a tool in the hands of God that He used to
pry open China. In essence, the war was an act of Providence, during which the
English military functioned unwittingly as the battering ram of God.[40]

Once the English had pummeled the Chinese into submission, the second
phase of what Williams's perceived as God's divine plan would go into effect.
With English cannons having leveled the "walls of separation," Williams wrote,
"we can go in &out" and "tell them [the Chinese] of Christ &his kingdom."[41]
This was how Williams sought to understand the large-scale events taking place
in his midst. On top of the greed, drug addiction, blood, misery, death, and
ruin, he placed the shimmering overlay of God's divine plan to open China,
and—almost magically—the seemingly foul war made perfect sense.


# HEADING HOME


Yet when the smoke from British cannon fire had cleared in 1842, Williams's
prospects in China had hardly improved. He learned that the vast changes that
were supposed to follow God's victory would not take place overnight. Feeling
frustrated, Williams parceled out some of the blame to his countrymen back
home who, inexplicably, were failing to seize this historic opportunity. Christians now knew that China had been forced open. To the missionary's great
vexation, however, they "are apparently no more ready . . . to take possession [of
China] than ever." Where were the legions of fresh missionaries and the new
sources of funding, both of which were supposed to arrive in the war's aftermath? Upon turning an ear to the United States, Williams heard only the deaf-
ening silence of apathy. He was "depressed."[42]

Adding to his melancholy was that Williams also felt oddly underused by
God. At precisely the juncture when he had expected God to give clarity to his
mission in China, he instead felt desultory, uncertain of purpose, and left adrift.

In God's cosmic chess match against Satan, Williams had happily volunteered to serve as a white pawn—a loyal, devoted, and selfless foot soldier committed to the cause. Understandably, God had relegated the eager white pawn to the side of the chessboard during the Opium War. But now that the great conflict had concluded, Williams fully expected to feel the hand of God putting him back into play. That nothing had happened left him feeling perplexed and perhaps abandoned. As Williams marked his ten-year anniversary in China, he had to wonder whether he was heaven's forgotten man.[43]

Contributing to his emotional discomfort were the deaths of a couple of fellow missionaries in China. "Two of our number have gone down to the tomb," he wrote to his brother in 1843, referring to Robert Morrison and Samuel Dyer, an English missionary in Singapore. Far more disconcerting than their deaths was the unclear or "vapory" meaning of their lives. Morrison had made a positive contribution in China, but Williams dolefully recognized that "it is not likely to be a lasting one, for succeeding events will efface the past, and the remembrances of his usefulness will in the public eye soon become mossy."[44] Though Williams maintained his trust in God, he nevertheless found it demoralizing to watch as, one by one, missionaries fell in the field without effecting noticeable change and without receiving appreciation, or even notice, from the Christian countries that had sent them.

Of course, behind his concern for Morrison and Dyer lurked a disturbing question: Would he share their fate? For the first time, Williams faced the possibility of passing his entire life in a faraway land without attaching his name to any lasting accomplishments and without receiving any recognition for his labors. Of course, since the work was supposed to be spiritually fulfilling by itself, a missionary was not expected to covet fame or recognition. But for Williams, who struggled mightily to control his pride, the bleak prospect of an anonymous life of futility was exceedingly difficult to accept.

Feeling jaded, he began to think seriously about returning home. More than ten years had passed since he had seen his family, his friends, and his hometown of Utica. "I feel sometimes a great desire to see you again," he wrote to his brother, "and replenish my heart with the social joys that are not here to be found." Yet since Williams had volunteered his entire life to the service of God, the mere contemplation of a furlough provoked deep questions. Was his "desire" for time away from the missionary field a fundamentally selfish impulse felt by one who had pledged a life of selfless "duty"? Williams believed that it was. Therefore, to keep the proposed furlough from being a selfish act, the directive to return home had to originate from God—not from personal reasons such as fatigue, frustration, or the need to see loved ones. This course of action was also problematic, however, since, as of late, God had been remarkably (and disturbingly) silent. And without God's guidance, Williams had become paralyzed, He felt utterly purposeless in China, and yet he also lacked a clear reason to depart for America: "I am sure that I have something here to do yet, for if otherwise it seems as if I should have found the opportunity for going."[45] In the end, all Williams could do is to stay put in China and simultaneously hold out his passport in the hope that God would ink it with His holy stamp and send the tired and frustrated missionary back home.

Fortunately, valid reasons swiftly presented themselves whereby Williams could justify a trip home as a part of God's plan to open China. The printing types he had been using to publish Christian tracts in Chinese had grown worn and antiquated. For the mission to succeed, new ones made of steel had to be manufactured in Europe. Furthermore, Williams would have to make the order himself because only he knew the exact specifications for this new type. Since it promised to be expensive, Williams would also need to raise money back in the United States.[46]

To this reason, Williams could add another, one of a tragic nature. While he had been away in Asia, his father's once prospering business had collapsed. To support his family, William Williams had become a farmer. Unfortunately, in a stagecoach accident, he sustained a severe injury to his head and it left his mental faculties permanently impaired.[47] And so, when the trader Gideon Nye offered to pay for Samuel Wells Williams's passage to New York in 1844, the missionary now possessed familial as well as godly reasons to depart China.[48] Heading home at last, he wrote to Peter Parker, the medical missionary stationed in Canton, to express his gratitude to the Lord: "I sail in the morning, 11 years &1 month from the day I landed in Canton, having received unnumbered mercies during that time."[49] He had not achieved as much as he had hoped, but now Williams had reason to depart China with a brightened outlook.


## A NEW MISSION IN AMERICA


Instead of returning by the most direct route, Williams made stops in Hong Kong, Singapore, Bombay, Egypt, Syria, Jerusalem, Malta, Rome, Paris, and London. After arriving in New York in October 1845, he wrote to his childhood friend James Dana, "Few of the Utica lads have wandered more than you &I."[50] Here Williams was not exaggerating, since Dana had served as a mineralogist on the United States Exploring Expedition (1838–42) commanded by Lieutenant Charles Wilkes.[51]

When Williams arrived home, he received a rude awakening. While living in China, he had sensed that something was not quite right with the attitudes of

Christians back home. Why, he wondered, had word of China's opening failed to inspire greater interest in and support for Protestant missions? His impressions at that time were vague, though, largely because his distance from the United States had muffled much of the anti-Chinese sentiment that was the cause of Americans' apathy. On returning to the United States, he confronted the ugly truth. As was explained in the previous chapter, Americans were now wont to mock, ridicule, and act superior to the Chinese in a manner that horrified the missionary.

Williams's disappointment was profound. We can best comprehend its depths when we recognize that Williams was comparing the unfortunate reality with the utopian dreams he had previously held. From his vantage point, the early 1840s must have seemed ripe for the consummation of his grandiose dream: the mass conversion of the Chinese people to Christianity. For at that time, he had been tantalized by the prospect of two major developments, one in China and the other in the United States, working in tandem to transform China into a Protestant nation. First, the Opium War had at last forced China to open her gates to foreign intercourse and influence. Second, the hundreds of revivals in the United States that comprised Second Great Awakening promised to rejuvenate Americans' interest in proselytizing nonbelievers in "heathen" lands.[52] In sum, for this rare moment in history, the forces of change appeared to be in perfect alignment: China was open to the West, and the United States had become a massive generator of zealous volunteers and generous donors.

When Williams finally returned home, however, he met only with disillusionment. These two major developments had in fact worked in synergy with one another, but they had done so toward an unanticipated and horrible result. The Opium War had convinced many Americans that China's seemingly impressive exterior was little more than an elaborate façade masking the nation's true ineptitude. What was worse, the Second Great Awakening had failed to instill in Americans a desire to convert the Chinese. It had instead produced a proud people who relished opportunities to feel self-superior by spurning the lowly Chinese "heathen" who had failed to embrace the Savior. In other words, Williams learned sadly that, after the Opium War, pride did not die, as he had hoped it would; rather, the war had merely transferred much of it from China to the United States.

The disturbing new attitude of Americans toward the Chinese appeared in the publications of Christian organizations. For example, in 1846, the Sunday-School Union of the Methodist Episcopal Church published *The Chinese or, Conversations on the Country and People of China*, a book designed to teach children about China. Ostensibly at least, its didactic purpose was meant to advance the cause of missions in China: "As a mission field it [China] is beginning to assume a high degree of importance. For this reason especially we desire to make the young in our Sabbath Schools well acquainted with its extent and its claims." Despite these superficially noble words, however, the book offers nothing that one would consider edifying. Instead, it portrays Chinese culture as stereotypically odd, grotesque, and backward. The book is centered around a dialogue between William and his Uncle Adam. Although William, a curious young boy, professes to know little about on China, his natural inclination is to like the Chinese after hearing great things about Nathan Dunn's Chinese Museum and enjoying the amusing pictures on tea chests. It is the job of the manipulative Uncle Adam to disabuse his nephew of these positive thoughts and replace them with cruel and inaccurate stereotypes.

In fact, Uncle Adam seems to favor the complete eradication of Chinese culture, to be followed by the introduction of superior Christian customs, principles, and beliefs. In a section devoted to the Chinese diet, Uncle Adam lists the foods consumed by the Chinese: dogs, rats, snakes, grasshoppers, snails, cats, grubs, worms, and birds' nests. The one food they lack but desperately need is "the bread of life," otherwise known as "the gospel of Jesus Christ." When William expresses a strong desire to see a display of Chinese fireworks, Uncle Adam delivers a devastatingly brutal reply: "And so should I, William; especially if, at the end of it, the Chinese had piled up in one high heap all the images they worship, and set fire to them." After William inquires about the city of "Pekin," Uncle Adam offers a mnemonic device to help his nephew understand the Chinese capital. He instructs him to simply remember "pigtails, pagodas, and porcelain." "What a number of P's!" William exclaims. "I shall be sure to remember the pigtails, pagodas, and porcelain of Pekin." In predictable fashion, Uncle Adam proceeds to highlight the chief difference between Pekin and New York. In the former, "the people bow down to idols," while in the latter, "the true and living God, the God of Abraham . . . is worshipped."

At one point in the book, readers encounter a chapter entitled "Odd Things in China," which delivers on its promise. Its sole purpose is to depict the Chinese as bizarre, well-deserving of laughter and disgust. Over the course of ten pages, the word *odd* and its derivatives (*oddest, oddity*) and synonyms (such as *strange*) are used thirty times. "They must be an odd people indeed," William declares at one point. "I wonder what odd thing you will tell me about next." Toward the end of the chapter, Uncle Adam quizzes his nephew to see if he can recite from memory all the "odd" things the Chinese do: "Let me now hear, William, how many you can remember of the odd things of which I have told you."

Even the Chinese Museum of Nathan Dunn was not immune to Uncle Adam's assault. Given its excellent reputation, young William has heard of its marvels and expresses his enthusiasm at the prospect of paying it a visit: "What a treat I should have at such an exhibition!" Uncle Adam agrees but offers one caveat—and it is a devastatingly damning one:

I have no doubt at all, that you would be very much entertained; but, in the midst of all the curious things in these collections, there is one thought which ought to be dwelled upon; it is this, that the figures, the carvings, the furniture, the lanterns, the porcelain, and the paintings . . . are the works of heathen men; of those who either bow down to images, or believe in falsehood. . . . Everyone, then, who visits a Chinese collection, should pray for the spread of the gospel in China. . . . There are hundreds who go to see Chinese collections who never think of these things; let us not be among the number. You would open your eyes wide at the sight of their golden or gilt idols, and very likely would think of the golden image that was set up by Nebuchadnezzar . . . in the province of Babylon.

By placing everything Chinese in a Christian framework, Uncle Adam succeeds in dispersing the aura of enchantment and enlightenment that had previously made China so enticing. And later in the book, a comment made by the boy indicates that Uncle Adam's strategy has worked: "I do not like the Chinese half so well, Uncle, as I did before."[53]

Samuel Wells Williams probably did not read this particular book, but he was nonetheless familiar with this kind of arrogant approach to missionary work and fervently objected to its underlying premise—that one could aid the Chinese by encouraging readers to regard them as silly, pathetic, and inferior. He knew that such a book would only undermine the very movement it purported to uplift because it portrayed the Chinese as a laughable race, utterly beyond hope, and obviously unworthy of a Christian's serious attention. Indeed, Williams far preferred Nathan Dunn's Chinese Museum, even though its agenda was not notably Christian. In fact, in the pages of the *Repository*, Williams and Elijah Bridgman had mostly lauded the museum and its proprietor, pronouncing Dunn "a true Friend of the Chinese."[54]

Williams's return home, then, prompted a sea change in his thinking. In the 1830s, he had identified the close-mindedness of the Chinese as the greatest obstacle preventing the advancement of God's will in China; in the 1840s, he came increasingly came to think that greatest obstacle was the close-mindedness of Americans. And since God had no British battleships at His disposal in the United States, Williams must have wondered what means He would use to blast away at the walls of American ignorance. It was at this juncture that Williams's furlough suddenly acquired vast significance: He realized that he must teach Americans the truth about the Chinese. With this epiphany, the former cloudiness that had hung over his missionary career dispersed and he saw his purpose with clarity. God had tapped the white pawn and shifted him back to the center of the cosmic chess match.

## CONVERTING AMERICANS THROUGH LECTURES

At first, Williams's chosen vehicle for accomplishing his objective was the lecture. He quickly worked up a series of lectures designed to provide his audiences with accurate and detailed knowledge of China. "I . . . hope that the information the people have received regarding China" he wrote of his efforts, "will not end in mere curiosity but produce more sympathy in behalf of the moral life of the nation."[55] Williams had already written numerous pieces for the *Chinese Repository,* and so his preparation of the lectures did not prove to be extraordinarily taxing. In fact, we can view the lectures as the second draft for the great work that was still to come.

Initially, Williams targeted the towns and cities not far from his family's home in Utica, but it was not long before word of his presentations spread. "Having heard that you are now delivering a course of Lectures in the City of Buffalo on China &the Chinese," a group of citizens from Rochester wrote to Williams, "&feeling a deep interest in that country &people &believing that the Lectures would be both interesting &profitable to our fellow citizens, we would respectfully request you to deliver the same courses in Rochester."[56] As Williams began to accept these invitations, his radius of influence lengthened. Soon what had started as a handful of regional engagements became an extensive tour of much of the Northeast.

In his travels, Williams expressed a strong preference for the western towns in New York, Pennsylvania, and Ohio over the large eastern commercial cities. In New York or Philadelphia, which were filled with popular amusements, Williams had trouble making an impression because "one new wave of interest washes with a single sweep upon and over the preceding one." Emblematic of this fact was that, when Williams delivered a series of lectures in Philadelphia, one newspaper did not even bother to get his name right, repeatedly referring to him as "Mr. Willard."[57] In contrast, in cities like Cleveland, Pittsburgh, or Buffalo, the citizens demonstrated an eagerness to hear a series of lengthy lectures that did not sensationalize their subject matter. In such places, Williams regularly drew over two hundred people. And to his pleasant surprise, he found that his audiences were able to maintain a high level of interest, even after he had spoken for two and a half hours! By the end of 1846, Williams had delivered more than one hundred lectures.[58]

During his stint as an itinerant lecturer, Williams also made a flattering discovery about himself: He knew more about China than anyone in the United States and perhaps as much as anyone in the entire Western world. He may have lacked strong institutional credentials, but his experiential credentials were unmatched. After all, who else had lived for over a decade in China; had learned much of the Chinese language; had observed and conversed regularly with Chinese people; had read the Chinese classics in literature, religion, statecraft, and philosophy; had studied China's natural-history and collected specimens; and had read nearly all European and American texts on the subject of China, old and new? In Canton and Macao, Williams's growing expertise had been camouflaged even to his own eyes. Since everyone in those cities knew something about China from firsthand experience, Williams's knowledge had not stood out in bas-relief. However, after removing himself to the American context, Williams realized that he was without parallel.

It was also during his furlough that Williams began to receive recognition for his knowledge. In addition to earning accolades for his lectures, he became an elected member of the American Ethnological Society. After reading a paper on China at a meeting held in the home of the president, Albert Gallatin, Gallatin acknowledged Williams's mastery of the subject. In addition, John Russell Bartlett, the secretary of the society, noted that Williams's reputation had reached Europe. The "eminent Sinologists of Europe," Bartlett wrote, now ranked Williams as "among the profoundest adepts" in Chinese "literature and philology."[59] The man who had never attended Yale, who could not be classified as a "man of letters," and who had made a clumsy attempt to imitate Charles Lamb was starting to receive recognition as a giant in his field. It was time to write a book.

## THE MIDDLE KINGDOM

Williams began writing *The Middle Kingdom* in New York in 1846, with the apartment of his brother, Henry Dwight Williams, serving as his temporary home and office. In writing this book, Williams was motivated by the same aspirations he had for his lectures.

> I am not mistaken as to some of the motives which induced me to undertake a book upon the Chinese, and one of them was to increase an interest among Christians in the welfare of that people, &show how well worth they were of all the evangelizing efforts that could be put forth to save them from disorganization as a government, depredation as a people thro' the effects of opium, and eternal ruin to their souls. Ignorance is a cause, an explanation, &a motive for indifference to a subject, and to remove this ignorance removes some of those reasons for inaction.[60]

This letter encapsulates Williams's overall view of the Chinese. Although he did not approve of Chinese civilization in its present state, he believed that its

glaring flaws in the areas of government, religion, and morality were manifestations not of biological inferiority but rather of the pernicious influences of
opium, inept government, and the devil. And yet, even with Satan locking the
entire nation in a stranglehold, the Chinese still managed to develop a stable
society that could boast of a rich intellectual tradition. If a book could teach
American readers about this civilization and eradicate crude stereotypes in the
process, the previously mocked Chinese would become a worthy but oppressed
people in desperate need of Christ's liberating power. A truly wonderful transformation could then take place: American people and dollars would flow into
the Protestant missions, which would then possess the means to save a quarter
of humanity. It was grandiose dream.

Fortunately for Williams, when he commenced writing his book, he was not
starting with a blank page. His articles for the *Repository* and his recent lectures
acted as drafts for the planned literary work.[61] Still, the task was an ambitious
one. After all, he intended to consolidate everything he knew about China into a
single work, without resorting to summaries and without omitting details. And
although such a prodigious undertaking merited single-minded attention, Williams could devote only a portion of his time and energy to his writing because
he needed to tend to other things. Not only did he continue to deliver lectures in
order to raise funds, but he also had begun to court a young woman.

In 1847, Henry Dwight Williams hosted a small gathering of friends, at
which his older brother was introduced to Sarah Walworth. The niece of a New
York chancellor, Sarah lived in Plattsburgh but spent her winters in Manhattan.
After just one meeting, Williams identified something in her character that he
liked. So when his lecture tour took him to Plattsburgh, he arranged to meet
with her again.[62] This second meeting apparently confirmed his initial impression; otherwise, he would not have dropped the following bombshell in his very
first letter to her:

> Brought together in the most casual manner, we have none but the slightest acquain-
> tance, though that has been quite enough to give me a very favorable estimate of
> your character, &to wish to make further acquaintance. . . . In a word, my chief ob-
> ject in proposing a correspondence is to learn whether you are disposed to engage in
> the good work of missions, and are willing to consider my proposal to accompany me
> [to China]. . . . I trust you will not be so much surprised at this, no doubt, unex-
> pected note, as not to consider it; and have hopes, too, you will not say me nay. . . . I
> lay my suit entirely in your hands.[63]

Wasting no time, Williams unveiled the big question regarding missions work
and the implied marriage. Apparently, the typical courtship, one that might unfold gradually over the course of several months or years, was not acceptable.

Why was Williams in such haste? The answer, quite simply, is that he knew his true calling was in missionary work, and he desired to return to the country he was already starting to miss. "I seldom hear from China now," he wrote to Peter Parker in 1846. "I long to return, and shall make arrangements to leave as soon as my book is published."[64] Indeed, just as he hoped to accelerate his romance, so too did he try to expedite the writing and publication of his book. While he did not place limits on its scope—he chose the all-inclusive model established by Nathan Dunn—he did place strict limits on his time. Not one to wait for the Muse, the indefatigable Williams worked at a feverish pace every day. "My book takes up much of my time," he wrote to Sarah in 1847, "but I hope 'twill advance the good of that great people of whom it treats, &induce some to take more interest in their welfare."[65]

Although the wooing of Sarah Walworth proceeded at a rapid pace, it was not without its tender moments. Somewhat comically, though, even these had to adhere to Williams's rushed schedule. For example, during one meeting, Williams surprised Sarah by kissing her without warning and then making a hasty exit. He subsequently explained his unexpected behavior in a letter: "Perhaps you thought I left you rather abruptly, stealing a kiss without your permission, &then running off, but I had used up about all the time. Forgive me the apparent rudeness."[66] Although Williams apologized for his aggressive (but probably appreciated) act, he indicates that it was motivated by the ever-ticking clock, calling him back to his lectures, his book, and China.

Indeed, since Williams spent most of this time either traveling to lecture venues or furiously writing his book in New York, it was mainly through letters that he had to convince Sarah to marry him and accept the missionary life. In the process, he had to reveal a large part of his private self—his deepest hopes, dreams, and anxieties. "You see," he explained to her, "I am the chief subject of my letters, the main argument of my writing. . . . Prevented from enjoying each other's society, we have need to become acquainted . . . to the degree that we can; and I lay open all my heart to you."[67] Thus, for the historian trying to understand the man who authored *The Middle Kingdom*, this correspondence provides us with a window into his innermost thoughts.[68]

In these private moments in which Williams exposed his soul, we see that his growing pride continued to torment him.

I have pride enough to supply a nation, and conceit mixed in with it; and pride, to my sorrow, mixes itself with even my religious duties, literary labors, social enjoyments, and daily conduct. I . . . am sure I have enough to destroy my soul for ever if the blood of Christ do not wash it all away. If one feature more than another appears desirable in the happiness of heaven, it is that I shall be totally free from pride.[69]

Williams divulged to Sarah the large extent that pride permeated and tainted most aspects of his life. While his outward behavior seemed to reflect only his devout service to God, Sarah learned the truth about his pride through confessional letters such as this one. He admitted that not even "religious duties" and "literary labors" (referring here to *The Middle Kingdom*) were free of contamination.

Given this revelation, one can only imagine the sorts of questions that may have flitted through Williams's mind as he labored over his masterpiece. Was *The Middle Kingdom* truly part of God's divine plan, as Williams told himself, or was it actually the self-aggrandizing work of young man who, barred by fate from proving himself at Yale, hungered for a chance to display his intellectual talents before the world? Although Williams was outwardly self-effacing, had he secretly luxuriated in the thrilling, self-affirming reality that a common boy from Utica had ascended to the rank of America's top Sinologist? And if so, was his role as God's humble and obedient servant just that—a theatrical role played by a man trying to mask the supreme act of hubris that was *The Middle Kingdom*? In producing a work intended to be the complete and final authority on China, was he, a mere mortal, audaciously questing for literary immortality? In sum, was his magnum opus written in the service of God or in the service of prideful ambition, which would necessarily make it the devil's work?

Williams clearly dreaded any confrontation with the terrible truth that the latter might be the case. In an attempt to convince himself otherwise—that the massive work was truly an expression of God's will—he reiterated this point again and again in his letters to Sarah. On August 10, 1847, he wrote that the "chief satisfaction" he derived from his literary effort was the knowledge that he was "advancing the great &good work of China: emancipation from sin &idolatry." He added that his work on the book was really no different from engaging in missionary work in China: "I feel that I am aiding in that work as honestly here as if I were in Canton, and hope the Master will honor it."[70] On August 23, he restated this basic point but then nonchalantly added that he might have reasons for writing the book that were unrelated to God: "Perhaps other motives have mixed with this in a large proportion." But to downplay the influence of these ungodly "other motives," he promptly reaffirmed his bedrock assertion that the book would be used by God "to the advancement of his design."[71]

On August 30, Williams professed his indifference to the public's reception of his work: "I have no very high expectations of making much noise with my book." He claimed to care only that God would find a way to steer it toward "advancing the work" in China.[72] On September 21, however, he admitted to caring about the verdict issued by readers, hoping that they would not be "disgusted with the subject through its bad treatment." Realizing he had here exposed his sensitive ego, he quickly moved to recover: "Whatever be the result of the effort, I think I can honestly say I have endeavored to do it for the good of China and the advancement of the great work of her regeneration."[73] Finally, on September 27, Williams asserted that he did not care at all "about the success" of the book; in fact, "all the good it does" ought to go directly "to the praise of the Author who gave me health and ability." Here, Williams elevated God as the true author of *The Middle Kingdom*, while diminishing his own role to that of the loyal scribe.[74] By professing the selfless nature of his act with such frequency and vigor, Williams revealed to Sarah how truly conflicted his soul really was.

## RELIGIOUS GOALS, SCIENTIFIC MEANS

Whether driven by personal ambition, love of God, or a combination of both, Samuel Wells Williams was prolific. As he continued to write, the manuscript continued to expand until it overflowed the confines of one volume and spilled into a second. "I find my manuscript stretches on like a long-standing account of lawyer's fees," he joked, "and I wish 'twere clipped."[75] Apparently, nothing was clipped. Williams possessed the grand ambition not just to write about China but, like Nathan Dunn and Houckgeest before him, to reproduce China. Consumed by a collecting mania, his predecessors had sought to accomplish this objective by amassing objects and pictures; Williams chose to accumulate words. The final work, completed in 1848, was comprehensive to the point of being encyclopedic. It filled two large volumes and stretched to a length just over twelve hundred pages.

The work was so long that Williams felt he owed it to his readers to justify the length in his preface. "If . . . the volumes seem too bulky for a general inquirer to undertake to peruse," he wrote, "let him remember the vastness of the Chinese Empire . . . and he will not, perhaps, deem them too large for the subject."[76] With these words, Williams equated his book with the country itself; since China was large, the book should be long as well. And if the book stood as a textual reproduction of the country, then the act of reading the book necessarily became tantamount to taking a tour of China. With this theme of virtual travel in mind, Williams arranged for an illustrator to draw a large Chinese gateway that, when situated both on the book's cover and its frontispiece, acted as a portal to a distant world (fig. 6.1). This gateway was complete with ornate dragons and Chinese characters that, when translated into English, tellingly stated: "Among Westerners there are wise people. Kind people love all people, strangers as well as relatives." With this inscription, Williams issued a challenge to his readers to open their minds and modify their view of China. In this sense, *The Middle Kingdom* was as much about American souls as it was about Chinese souls.

The similarity with Houckgeest and Dunn was not coincidental. Like theirs, Williams's mode of comprehending China was shaped by Enlightenment science. Of course, the overarching purpose of his book was religious—to advance the cause of Protestant missions in China through the dissemination of accurate information in America. Williams makes this point abundantly clear in his preface. "Respecting the origin, plan, and design of the present work, I may be allowed to express the humble hope that it will aid a little in advancing the cause of Christian civilization among the Chinese."[77] However, although religion provided the official impetus for the book, science offered a modus operandi. Williams gathered, arranged, and presented this information by following a scientific model. In this way, the religiously inspired *The Middle Kingdom* bears the distinct imprint of Rensselaer Institute.

To understand the role of science on Williams's mind, one need only scan the chapter titles and subheadings. Williams categorized all aspects of Chinese life just as a naturalist trained in the Linnaean system would classify species. He devoted the first four chapters to China's geography, covering the provinces, the colonies (Manchuria, Mongolia, and Tibet), and a general overview of the topographical features of the empire. He next moved on to China's natural history, covering mineralogy, botany, zoology, herpetology, ichthyology, and entomology. Shifting to the human sphere, he devoted two chapters to an explanation of the government, the legal system, the administration of the laws throughout the provinces, and the treatment of criminals. He also discussed at length both the education system and the examination system, which produced the scholar-officials who ran the government. Not surprisingly, one chapter describes the Chinese written language, a subject Williams knew as well as any living Westerner. The two chapters on Chinese literature explore the Five Classics and the Four Books, the significance of Confucius and Mencius, and novels (fiction), ballads, poetry, and works of history. Williams also studied the state of the arts and sciences: math, astronomy, military science, anatomy, astrology, music, and painting.

Indeed, almost no category was safe from Williams's exhaustive inquiry. He examined Chinese architecture, the manner of dress, and the diet. His study of Chinese social life offers depictions of ceremonies, festivals, marriage (including the custom of polygamy), naming practices, and various pastimes, such as gambling. In addition, Williams devoted space to Chinese commerce (complete with statistics of China's imports and exports), agriculture (including tea production), and the mechanical and industrial arts (metallurgy, glass, porcelain, lacquer, silk, and carvings in ivory). Not surprisingly, Chinese religion consumes an entire chapter, as does the role of Christian missions in China, past and present. The book also contains a thorough history of the Chinese empire, one that stretches from antiquity to the present, with the more recent history centering on China's intercourse with the outside world. Finally, *The Middle Kingdom* concludes with two full chapters that focus exclusively on the conflict with England and the opening of China.

By breaking down his vast subject into distinct categories, Williams followed a tradition begun by Houckgeest and continued by Dunn. He endeavored to make sense of China by imposing a rigid system of classification over its vastness and complexity. When all categories were filled, then and only then could he finally stop writing.

## THE MAGIC BULLET

In all areas of *The Middle Kingdom* that describe China's people, as opposed to its topography or wildlife, Williams walked a tightrope. He admitted as much in the text itself, with a statement that rendered his motives transparent: "We do not wish to depict the Chinese worse than they are, nor to dwell so much on their good qualities as to lead one to suppose they stand in no need of the Gospel."[78] In other words, the Chinese needed to come across as immoral and corrupt on the one hand and yet, on the other, as human and therefore redeemable. Toward the former aim, Williams formulated a critique of Chinese morals that was far harsher than anything that emerged out of Nathan Dunn's museum or even Captain Kellett's junk. He reported that the Chinese "are vile and polluted in a shocking degree" and that "their conversation is full of filthy expressions and their lives of impure acts." He went on to enumerate the myriad vices of which this people were guilty: "falsity," "mendacity," "thieving," "licentiousness," insufficient "hospitality," "female infanticide," and "cruelty towards prisoners."[79]

As unambiguously negative as these words appear, we do not, however, have an accurate understanding of Williams's construction of China if we examine them in isolation. In the following passage, he places his critique in the proper context:

> In summing up the moral traits of the Chinese character . . . we must necessarily compare it with that perfect standard given us from above; while also we should not forget that the teachings of that book are unknown. While their contrarieties indicate a different external civilization, a slight acquaintance with their morals proves their similarity to their fellowmen in the lineaments of a fallen nature. As among

other people, the lights and shadows of virtue and vice are blended in their character, and the degree of advancement they made while destitute of the great encouragements offered to perseverance in well-doing in the Bible, afford grounds for hoping that when they are taught out of that book, they will receive it as the rule of their conduct.[80]

When Williams refers to "the Chinese character" as immoral, he is not pronouncing the Chinese racially inferior to the people of Western nations. Rather, he is measuring the Chinese against "that perfect standard," by which he means the shining ideal of heavenly virtue contained in the Bible. In fact, far from highlighting racial difference, Williams emphasizes the innate sameness of the peoples of the earth. The "different external civilization" that the Chinese possess (and that had provoked so much mockery in the United States) is mainly superficial and masks a much deeper "similarity to their fellowmen."

Of course, the underlying "similarity" shared by different peoples was not something Williams chose to celebrate. It was instead the crux of the great problem to which he had devoted his entire life: humanity's fall from grace in the Garden of Eden and its subsequent need for holy redemption. He believed that Chinese vices flowed not out of innate biological inferiority but rather out of the "fallen nature" of their souls. Likewise, he attributed the Christian virtue that he found in Western nations to the people's exposure to the Word of God. But whereas citizens of Christian nations enjoyed opportunities to read the Bible, and many (but not all) had availed themselves of its wonderful truths, the Chinese had historically not been as fortunate. And so, Williams earnestly believed, if the Bible could penetrate China the people would turn to Christ en masse. When they did, the slough of sin, vice, and iniquity in which they currently wallowed would dry up and vanish. In sum, immorality in China was a pervasive ill for which there existed a magic bullet: the missionary movement.

## CONCLUSION

As Samuel Wells Williams sailed out of New York harbor in June 1848, he could look back on the achievements of his furlough with satisfaction. Most obviously, he was no longer alone. When he turned to his side, he was pleased to behold his young wife, Sarah Walworth Williams, standing beside him; they had been married in Plattsburgh on Thanksgiving Day the previous fall. In agreeing to wed Williams and adopt the life of a missionary, Sarah had clearly demonstrated great courage, as southern China was becoming less safe. After she had asked Williams about the threat of antiforeign violence, he tried to reassure her with the following assessment of their safety. "So far as the safety of the foreigners is concerned," he wrote, "there is little to fear; they [foreigners] are on the alert against any sudden rising, dwell close to the riverbanks, have steamers and boats lying off their factories to which they can repair at a moment's notice, and are so well armed that the Chinese . . . would be afraid to attack them."[81] Although one might question whether descriptions of evacuation plans and armament stockpiles would have the intended calming effect, Sarah still consented to accompany Williams to China.

Williams could also savor his massive achievement in completing the mammoth *The Middle Kingdom* in a period of about two years. While the task of writing it had been formidable enough, he had also encountered difficulty in locating a publisher; none wanted to gamble on an encyclopedic work that neither exoticized or sensationalized its subject. In fact, he succeeded in convincing Wiley and Putnam to accept his manuscript only after Gideon Nye, the wealthy China trader, promised to reimburse the publisher for any losses incurred from poor sales.[82] When *The Middle Kingdom* entered bookstores early in 1848, reviews were generally positive. Reverend Samuel Brown, a fellow missionary in China, read all the reviews in the New York newspapers and was able to make a favorable report to his friend: "I see it has been very highly lauded by the press in N. York."[83]

Yet Brown also understood the most obvious pitfall of a twelve-hundred-page book. "It is not everybody that will read such a work," he wrote. "Still fewer will pay $3 to procure it."[84] Indeed, many reviewers, while generally praising the content of *The Middle Kingdom*, predictably complained about the book's length and the author's lack of style. Williams "is far from being a finished or polished writer," wrote one, "nor has he sufficiently studied brevity, either by the compact adjustment of his materials or the omission of needless details."[85] Whereas Nathan Dunn's all-inclusive collecting had conferred a magical aura of virtual travel onto the Chinese museum, that same encyclopedic approach, when applied to writing, had produced two dauntingly weighty tomes that intimidated readers. Williams himself wondered if those who had purchased the book would "rather have their money returned than wade through so many pages."[86]

The somewhat deterrent effect of the book's size notwithstanding, on the whole the intellectual community embraced *The Middle Kingdom*, and almost immediately it became universally regarded as the definitive authority on China. For this singular achievement, Union College conferred on Williams an honorary degree (LL.D.) in 1848; it must have been a meaningful moment for a man who felt acutely his lack of institutional credentials.[87] While the cumbersome book was seldom read by the average reader, it did succeed in becoming the single most important reference work on China. For this reason, one can measure its influence less by its sales and more by the frequency with which it was cited in other works.

For example, on January 26, 1854, a Reverend Scott delivered a lecture on China at the Mechanic's Institute in New Orleans. He began his presentation by admitting his ignorance on the subject of China. To illustrate, he jokingly made reference to the only two Chinese words he knew: *tea* and *junk*. Despite his lack of knowledge, Scott demonstrated his full awareness of the condescending mockery that suffused Western attitudes toward the Chinese at the time. "No people on the globe have been more subjected to ridicule than the Chinese," he said. "They have been regarded as 'the apes of Europeans,' and their civilization such as it is, their arts, laws, and government considered as the burlesque of ours." Scott proceeded to review the standard list of cruel stereotypes and to repeat the derogatory poem that had earlier riled Williams: "Mandarins with yellow buttons, handing you conserves of snails; / Smart young men about Canton in nankeen tights and peacock's tails." However, after reviewing the usual insults, Scott did something interesting. He informed his audience that if they were expecting more of this sort of ridicule, they would leave disappointed. After invoking Samuel Wells Williams's *The Middle Kingdom*, he went on to deliver a lecture that owed almost all of its content to that masterful work.[88]

## NOTES

1. Samuel Wells Williams to Sarah Walworth, letter, 10 August 1847, box 1, series 1, Samuel Wells Williams Family Papers. Manuscript Collections, Yale University Library. Hereafter, this collection will be cited as SWWFP.

2. Samuel Wells Williams to Sarah Walworth, letter, 10 August 1847, box 1, series 1, SWWFP.

3. Frederick Wells Williams, *The Life and Letters of Samuel Wells Williams, LL.D. , Missionary, Diplomatist, Sinologue* (New York: G. P. Putnam's Sons, 1889), 20.

4. Ibid., 30–32.

5. Ibid.

6. Ibid., 34.

7. Samuel Wells Williams to James D. Dana, letter, 23 April 1832, box 1, series 1, SWWFP.

8. Frederick Wells Williams, 37–38. See also Jiang Qian, "Samuel Wells Williams and the Attitudes of U.S. Protestant Missionaries toward the Opium Trade and the Opening of China, 1830–1860" (master's thesis, University of Toledo, 1992), 4–5.

9. Samuel Wells Williams, "Autobiographical Sketch" (April 1878), box 13, series 2, SWWFP.

10. Frederick Wells Williams, 35.

11. Ibid., 39–40

12. Ibid., 27.

13. Andrew T. Kaiser, "S. Wells Williams: Early Protestant Missions in China" (master's thesis, Gordon-Conwell Theological Seminary, 1995), 33.

14. Samuel Wells Williams, "Autobiographical Sketch" (April 1878), box 13, series 2, SWWFP.

15. Samuel Wells Williams to Sarah Walworth, letter, 30 August 1847, box 1, series 1, SWWFP.

16. Frederick Wells Williams, 58–59.

17. Samuel Wells Williams to Peter Parker, letter, August 1839 (the letter does not contain a precise date), box 1, series 1, SWWFP. Approximately two of the hours were devoted to the study of Japanese. In 1836, Williams met three Japanese sailors in Macao whose vessel had been blown away from the Japanese coast by a storm. In 1837, in what was called the "Morrison Expedition," Williams and others failed in their attempt to repatriate the men (and establish contact with the Japanese). After their efforts were repulsed, however Williams employed them in his printing office and studied Japanese with them regularly. Frederick Wells Williams, 83, 93–100.

18. Frederick Wells Williams, 107–8.

19. Samuel Wells Williams to Frederick Williams, letter 15 May 1841, box 1, series 1, SWWFP.

20. *Michael C. Lazich, E. C. Bridgman (1801–1861), America's First Missionary to China* (Lewiston, N.Y.: Edwin Mellen Press, 2000), 13, 37.

21. Frederick Wells Williams, 66.

22. Ibid., 63.

23. Ibid., 62.

24. After the various treaties that followed in the wake of the Opium War, foreigners were free to live and work in several ports. Thus, by 1851, there was no longer a concentration of foreigners who were living in Canton and needed the *Chinese Repository*.

25. "List of Articles by S. Wells. Williams in the *Chinese Repository*," box 13, series 2, SWWFP.

26. Samuel Wells Williams to Frederick Williams, letter, 31 August 1836, box 1, series 1, SWWFP.

27. Samuel Wells Williams to Frederick Williams, letter, 17 December 1835, box 1, series 1, SWWFP.

28. Samuel Wells Williams to Frederick Williams, letter, 15 January 1836, box 1, series 1, SWWFP.

29. Samuel Wells Williams to Frederick Williams, letter, 29 July 1840, box 1, series 1, SWWFP.

30. Samuel Wells Williams to Frederick Williams, letter, 5 April 1840, box 1, series 1, SWWFP.

31. Samuel Wells Williams to Frederick Williams, letter, February 19, 1835, box 1, series 1, SWWFP.

32. Samuel Wells Williams to Frederick Williams, letter, 5 April 1840, box 1, series 1, SWWFP.

33. Samuel Wells Williams to Frederick Williams, letter, 29 September 1841, box 1, series 1, SWWFP.

34. Samuel Wells Williams to Frederick Williams, letter, 5 April 1840, box 1, series 1, SWWFP.

35. Jonathan D. Spence, *The Search for Modern China* (New York: Norton, 1990), 118, 122.

36. Frederick Wells Williams, 103–4.

37. Samuel Wells Williams to Frederick Williams, letter, 29 August 1839, box 1, series 1, SWWFP.

38. It is important to note that Williams was not warlike by nature and that he truly believed the Opium War was orchestrated by God. In fact, later in the 1840s, he expressed his strong objection to the U.S. war with Mexico. Samuel Wells Williams to Sarah Walworth, letter, 29 September 1847, box 1, series 1, SWWFP.

39. Samuel Wells Williams to Frederick Williams, letter, 30 November 1840, box 1, series 1, SWWFP.

40. Samuel Wells Williams to Frederick Williams, letter, 29 August 1839, box 1, series 1, SWWFP.

41. Samuel Wells Williams to Frederick Williams, letter, 29 August 1839, box 1, series 1, SWWFP.

42. Samuel Wells Williams to Frederick Williams, 29 May 1843, box 1, series 1, SWWFP.

43. Samuel Wells Williams to Frederick Williams, 15 June 1843, box 1, series 1, SWWFP.

44. Samuel Wells Williams to Frederick Williams, letter, 20 November 1843, box 1, series 1, SWWFP.

45. Ibid.

46. Before his death, Samuel Dyer engaged in making steel type for his Chinese press in Singapore. In fact, Williams had entertained hopes of adding Dyer's type to the older set he had been using in Macao. Unfortunately, on arriving in Singapore, Williams discovered that after Dyer's death much of the printing apparatus had been "dispersed" beyond the possibility of recovery. This disappointment increased the urgency of his need for new types, which he planned to have made in Germany. Frederick Wells Williams, 128–32.

47. William Williams died in 1850. Frederick Wells Williams, 129–30, 176.

48. Frederick Wells Williams, 131.

49. Samuel Wells Williams to Peter Parker, letter, 25 November 1844, box 1, series 1, SWWFP.

50. Samuel Wells Williams to James Dana, letter, 6 December 1845, box 1, series 1, SWWFP.

51. William H. Goetzmann, *New Lands, New Men: America and the Second Great Age of Discovery* (New York: Penguin, 1986), 273, 291–93.

52. In a letter to his brother, Williams commented optimistically on revivalism. Samuel Wells Williams to Frederick Williams, letter, 1 July 1841, box 1, series 1, SWWFP.

53. D. P. Kidder, ed., *The Chinese; or, Conversations on the Country and People of China Department of Rare Books, Library of Congress* (New York: G. Lane and C. B. Tippett, 1846), 5–6, 14–17, 34–39, 75–77, 80, 81–91, 101, 113, 136.

54. *Chinese Repository* (March 1840), 585, and (November 1843), 582.

55. Frederick Wells Williams, 147.

56. Citizens of Rochester to Samuel Wells Williams, letter, March 1846, box 1, series 1, SWWFP.

57. "Lecture on China," *Dollar Newspaper* (24 February and 10 March 1847).

58. Frederick Wells Williams, 147–48. Although preferring western New York and Ohio, Williams did not avoid the East Coast altogether. He offered lectures in New York, New Haven, and probably other cities as well. James Dana to Samuel Wells Williams, letter, 10 October 1846, box 1, series 1, SWWFP.

59. Frederick Wells Williams, 151. Samuel Wells Williams, "The Present Position of the Chinese Empire"; John Russell Bartlett, "The Progress of Ethnology"; and Albert Gallatin, "Introduction to 'Hale's Indians of North-west America and Vocabularies of North America,'" *Transactions of the American Ethnological Society* (New York: Bartlett and Welford, 1848), clxi, 148, 279.

60. Samuel Wells Williams to Sarah Walworth, letter, 23 August 1847, box 1, series 1, SWWFP.

61. Samuel Wells Williams, *The Middle Kingdom: A Survey of the Geography, Government, Education, Social Life, Arts, Religion, &., of the Chinese Empire and Its Inhabitants* (New York: Wiley and Putnam, 1848), 1:xiii–xiv. A perusal of the work's footnotes reveals that the *Chinese Repository* was one of the more frequently cited sources for information.

62. Frederick Wells Williams, 152.

63. Samuel Wells Williams to Sarah Walworth, letter, 29 May 1847, box 1, series 1, SWWFP.

64. Samuel Wells Williams to Peter Parker, letter, 19 May 1846, box 1, series 1, SWWFP.

65. Samuel Wells Williams to Sarah Walworth, 21 June 1847, box 1, series 1, SWWFP.

66. Samuel Wells Williams to Sarah Walworth, 10 August 1847, box 1, series 1, SWWFP.

67. Samuel Wells Williams to Sarah Walworth, letter, 23 August 1847, box 1, series 1, SWWFP.

68. To introduce Sarah to Chinese culture, Williams sent her Chinese literature translated into English and offered his personal assessment: "You will see that the Chinese have some imagination and fancy, though their novels are hardly equal to

Ivanhoe or Last of the Mohicans." Samuel Wells Williams to Sarah Walworth, letters, 13 and 19 August 1847, box 1, series 1, SWWFP.

69. Samuel Wells Williams to Sarah Walworth, letter, 23 August 1847, box 1, series 1, SWWFP.

70. Samuel Wells Williams to Sarah Walworth, letter, 10 August 1847, box 1, series 1, SWWFP.

71. Samuel Wells Williams to Sarah Walworth, letter, 23 August 1847, box 1, series 1, SWWFP.

72. Samuel Wells Williams to Sarah Walworth, letter, 30 August 1847, box 1, series 1, SWWFP.

73. Samuel Wells Williams to Sarah Walworth, letter, 21 September 1847, box 1, series 1, SWWFP.

74. Samuel Wells Williams to Sarah Walworth, letter, 27 September 1847, box 1, series 1, SWWFP.

75. Samuel Wells Williams to Sarah Walworth, letter, 11 November 1847, box 1, series 1, SWWFP.

76. Samuel Wells Williams, *The Middle Kingdom* (1848), 1:xiv.

77. Ibid., 1:xvi.

78. Ibid., 2:99.

79. Ibid., 2:95–99.

80. Ibid., 2:95.

81. Samuel Wells Williams to Sarah Walworth, letter, 29 September 1847, box 1, series 1, SWWFP.

82. Frederick Wells Williams, 163.

83. Samuel Brown to Samuel Wells Williams, letter, 10 February 1848, box 1, series 1, SWWFP.

84. Samuel Brown to Samuel Wells Williams, 10 February 1848, box 1, series 1, SWWFP (emphasis in original).

85. *North American Review* (October 1848), 269. Another reviewer agreed with the first that "the number and variety of his sources . . . are too abundantly exhibited" (United *States Magazine and Democratic Review* [April 1848], 319–20).

86. Frederick Wells Williams, 162–63.

87. Ibid., 162.

88. Rev. Dr. Scott, "Lecture on the Chinese Empire," delivered in New Orleans before the Mechanic's Institute, 26 January 1854. New York Public Library.

## 7. THE CULTURAL FRUITS OF DIPLOMACY

### A Chinese Museum and Panorama

On June 17, 1843, Caleb Cushing attended a dinner held at Faneuil Hall in Boston, the occasion being the dedication of a monument to be erected on Bunker Hill. The list of distinguished guests included the secretary of state, Daniel Webster, and the president of the United States, John Tyler. The president had recently tapped Cushing to lead a diplomatic mission to China with the following objectives: to meet with Chinese officials, to travel north to Peking to appear before the emperor, and to secure through negotiation a treaty comparable to what England had won through war. This treaty must grant the United States the right to conduct trade at the following four ports in addition to Canton: Ningbo, Shanghai, Xiamen, and Fuzhou. If Cushing were to fail here, England would possess an insurmountable advantage over the United States in the China trade.

As the evening wore on, the time came for Cushing to address the dinner guests. In a speech that combined humanitarian themes with bombast, he articulated what he believed was the overarching significance of the mission to China. Although civilization had originally flowed from the East to the West, the recent advances of the West had effected a reversal in the course, such that "knowledge is being rolled back from the West to the East." "We have become the teacher of our teachers," he said, and then turned to address President Tyler directly. "I go to China, sir, if I may so express myself, in behalf of civilization."

In his closing remarks, Cushing considered the purpose of the new monument, which was to commemorate the Battle of Bunker Hill, and speculated as to the significance of a second, hypothetical monument. It would commemorate not military activity, he said, but rather "the accumulating glory of peaceful arts" that have brought "civilized life."[1]

Cushing did not define either the "knowledge" that the West intended for China or the "peaceful arts" that had brought peace and prosperity to the United States, but in both cases he was almost certainly alluding to technology. In the 1840s, several important new technologies were reshaping American life: the telegraph, the daguerreotype, and the steam engine that powered trains and ships. Furthermore, in Cushing's home state of Massachusetts, the waterpowered looms of the new textile mills were producing cotton fabric with startling efficiency. With technology growing in importance in the United States, it not surprisingly occupied a central position in the Cushing Mission as well. First, the increasingly productive American factories sought foreign markets for their goods and now looked to Cushing to open up China for American commerce. Second, most American observers of the Opium War attributed the outcome to the large disparity in military technology separating British and Chinese forces. For this reason, American arms manufacturers and government officials alike believed that Cushing might encounter a country eager to revamp its military with assistance from the United States.

However, no one knew exactly what China would want from the Americans, if anything at all. Despite Cushing's rhetoric about America teaching China, his mission taught the Chinese surprisingly little about American culture. Yet the mission was not a total failure with regard to cultural understanding because, through the efforts of some of the young men attached to Cushing's legation, Americans learned new things about China. John R. Peters Jr., a brilliant young engineer, accompanied Cushing's mission in order to exhibit the finest fruits of American mechanical ingenuity before the Chinese. However, believing that his gifts of cultural explanation should flow in two directions, Peters also assembled a mammoth Chinese collection that he later exhibited in Boston, Philadelphia, and New York. One might expect that an engineer would measure any given civilization according to its mechanical prowess, but Peters defies our expectations. He did not judge the Chinese harshly for their lack of technological sophistication and, instead, surprises us with his open-mindedness. In China he confronted what he believed was a remarkable civilization and told Americans as much through his museum exhibits.

Joining Peters on the mission was George R. West, who served as the official artist. Instead of returning home at the conclusion of the mission, West took advantage of the new latitude given to foreigners in the wake of China's various international treaties. He traveled to the new treaty ports and their vicinities, sketching many places that Europeans and Americans had never before seen. On returning to the United States, he converted the hundreds of scenes in his sketchbook into a single colossal work—a panorama of China. Unlike Captain Kellett, Peters and West chose to dissent against the prevailing construction of China; the educational venues they created provided a counterweight to the mockery and raillery that infected the mainstream view. Through their efforts, a diplomatic mission founded on the condescending notion that China needed to change ended up, ironically, bolstering the opposite view: that China possessed a rich culture in its own right.

## PREPARATIONS

In the spring and summer of 1843, Caleb Cushing was inundated with letters. Although prominent political figures accounted for some of them, most came from people he did not know who wanted to ask him for a favor or make a request. A woman wrote to tell Cushing that a loved one had mysteriously disappeared in China. Would he attempt to locate this individual?[2] A Harvard student studying Chinese wrote to complain that the college library was woefully lacking in Chinese texts; Cushing ought to procure some, he asserted, so that he would no longer have to practice by reading "tea chests!"[3] The *New York Sun* wrote Cushing because the paper wanted to publish his letters from Asia.[4] The owner of a powder mill wrote because he had heard that Chinese gunpowder, unlike its counterpart in the United States, was not prone to accidental explosions; he urged Cushing to learn China's secret.[5] A scientist wrote because he needed information on winds and storms in China as well as accurate atmospheric data.[6] The department of natural history at the National Institute wrote to ask Cushing to secure Chinese plant specimens for its herbarium.[7] A phrenologist wrote offering to stock Cushing's traveling library "with all the materials which Phrenological writers have contributed to science with respect to the natural characteristics of the Chinese." A strong background in phrenology would aid the mission, he argued, because "you will not have to wait to learn their [the Chinese people's] peculiarities." This gentleman had obviously neglected to read Cushing's article from 1839 in which he denounced phrenology as a bogus science.[8]

Parents asking Cushing (and sometimes imploring him) to take their offspring to China accounted for many of the letters. A father wrote that his son was an excellent mechanic who would be of greater value to the mission than "a hundred politicians."[9] A mother asked Cushing to set up her daughter as the first female missionary in China, despite the young woman's "limited education."[10] Cushing sometimes read hard-luck cases, such as the poor fellow who had recently lost his wife and children and desperately wanted to escape his dreary life with a fresh start in China.[11] And a father inquired whether his son could be added to the mission as a private secretary. The lad was "in delicate health," but the father assured Cushing he was "not consumptive" and would most likely survive "a sea voyage." His chances for acceptance were not high.[12]

But the prospects of one group of young applicants were far more promising. Cushing received letters from young men possessing not just outstanding credentials but noteworthy pedigrees as well, and he was inclined to look favorably on them because he knew their fathers. He had already taken on Fletcher Webster, the son of Daniel Webster, to serve as secretary. In addition, John Kintzing Kane of Philadelphia, a judge in eastern Pennsylvania's district court and an acquaintance of Nathan Dunn, wrote to state the case for his son, Elisha Kent Kane, who had finished at the top of his class at the University of Pennsylvania medical school. Cushing appointed him to the mission as the official surgeon, a move that attained brilliance ex post facto when Kane went on to become an Arctic explorer and national hero in the 1850s.[13]

Cushing also received the following letter from John Peters Jr., a young civil engineer from New York, who outlined a bold proposal for both the mission and his role in it:

> I am desirous of being attached to the United States Embassy to the Empire of China, and respectfully solicit your approbation and appointment. The principal object of this request is to enable me to obtain the countenance and protection of the government in the enterprise of conveying, exhibiting and explaining models and specimens of American arts and productions under the auspices of the American Institute, and of obtaining whatever information may be practicable to acquire from the ancient nation for the benefit of our country. My profession is that of a Civil Engineer and mechanic; and I should hope under your direction and counsel to be useful to the national objects of your mission in promoting the great interests of Agriculture and the Arts under the patronage of the American Institute of this city.[14]

Peters believed the mission should effect a cultural exchange that would prove beneficial to both China and the United States. He proposed to demonstrate to the Chinese the virtues of various time- and labor-saving devices used in the United States; conversely, he aimed to discover tools and methods in China that might have practical utility for Americans. Fletcher Webster, who assisted Cushing in screening candidates, met with Peters in New York. "I did not give Mr. Peters much encouragement," he reported to Cushing after the meeting, "for it struck me that we have already machinery enough." While Peters seemed extraneous to the mission in Webster's view, he did add that the engineer appeared to be "a clever young man."[15]

What Webster did not realize was that powerful forces were already aligned behind Peters. Influential men and organizations backed his application, including Robert Morris, the mayor of New York. "John R. Peters," the mayor assured Cushing, "is a scientific and practical civil engineer and mechanic of strict moral worth and character, a son of our worthy citizen John R. Peters."[16] Indeed, one of Peters's most helpful advocates was his own father, who was a successful businessman in New York, a former member of the Common Council that oversaw the construction of the Erie Canal, and a personal friend of President John Tyler.[17] While Cushing was considering young men for his legation, the elder Peters sent a carriage to pick up Cushing in New York, and the two men cemented their friendship over—appropriately enough—cups of "China Tea."[18]

Most important, as the younger Peters's letter to Cushing indicates, the engineer was the choice of the American Institute of New York. T. B. Wakeman, who held a high-ranking position in that organization, wrote Cushing expressly to recommend Peters for the mission.[19] Founded in 1829, the American Institute was dedicated to the development and dissemination of technology in order to further the interests of American industry, agriculture, and commerce. The institution held annual fairs at which inventors congregated to display their new devices and to swap ideas with others engaged in similar pursuits. In fact, Samuel Morse had unveiled his telegraph at the institute just a few years before Cushing's mission.[20]

Advocates of the American Institute were incapable of modesty when it came to describing their beloved institution. Indeed, they conceived of a grand teleological framework in which the American Institute played a central role in bringing about the rapid ascension of the United States in the world. A writer for *Merchants Magazine and Commercial Review* used words that echoed those spoken by Cushing to commemorate the monument at Bunker Hill. In an article about the institute's annual fair, the author charted America's upward trajectory, from the period of colonization and then to the war for independence from Great Britain and finally to the present age, at which the importance of the military receded as the holy trinity of science, invention, and enterprise advanced. Development in these three areas, by increasing the efficiency and productivity of farms and factories, improved the quality of American life. "It can scarcely be denied," he asserted, "that this improvement has been, in great measure, advanced through the agency of the American Institute." The institute was successful, but the writer believed that it had yet to complete its great work: "We trust that they [the members of the institute] may go on and work out even greater benefits to the nation; that they may advance the public morals, elevate the national standard, and contribute to the real and solid glory of the Union."[21]

Similarly, a writer for *The American Review,* a Whig journal, credited the inventive spirit with driving America's rise to greatness. Though once "a vassal, kneeling at the feet of the Old World," the United States had "broken off the chain" and currently "stands up with a sublime aspect." "Her looms are sounding in a thousand villages" and "her streams are baptizing myriad wheels," and to these developments the nation owed much of her independence. Through industry and technology, the United States had effectively scripted "a second Declaration of Independence," which enabled it to become a free economic entity, not just a political one. As the embodiment of this inventive spirit, the American Institute took the vanguard position in a movement that many believed was transforming American life.[22] In sum, the institute's supporters held that, far from being sequestered from the mainstream of American life, the institute was an integral component of a divine mission to increase the nation's power, prosperity, and morality through technological innovation. This organization had tapped John Peters to become its lone crusader to China.

While it is clear that these authors allowed a certain amount of hyperbole to infuse their rhetoric, America truly was becoming a leader in technology. And while Cushing set as his primary objective the securing of a treaty, he was also aware that, beneath the surface of the mission, technology was a driving force. For those "looms sounding in a thousand villages" of New England were now producing cotton textiles with startling efficiency; as a result, the continued expansion of the American economy depended on Cushing's ability to secure new markets in China for American manufactured goods. Before Cushing's departure, Daniel Webster wrote to him to explain the vital importance of the four new treaty ports:

> These ports belong to some of the richest, most productive provinces of that empire, and are likely to become very important marts of commerce. A leading object of the Mission . . . is to secure the entry of American ships and cargoes into these ports on terms as favorable as those which are enjoyed by English merchants.

Although mostly optimistic, Webster did realize that wider access would bring scant economic rewards if the Chinese were to resist the introduction of machine-made goods.

In expressing his reservations to Cushing, he demonstrated the extent to which competing and contradictory constructions of China coexisted in his divided mind. On the one hand, he understood the Chinese to be "tenaciously attached" and "strongly wedded to their own usages." On the other, though, he perceived the race as "ingenious, acute, and inquisitive" and therefore capable of recognizing the value of new things.[23] Himself ambivalent, Webster implied that the success or failure of Cushing's mission hinged ultimately on the attitudes of the Chinese. Were they averse to change, as many said, or could they use their ingenuity to appreciate what was new?

Technology was also to the Cushing Mission also because it would arrive in China in the immediate wake of the Opium War. Most American observers of the war attributed the outcome of this conflict to the large discrepancy in military technology separating British and Chinese forces. The Tyler administration, assuming that the Chinese also understood their defeat in terms of technology, firmly believed that Cushing could achieve greater leverage in his negotiations if the Chinese were to perceive the United States as being in possession of the same technologies that had powered England's naval victory. Toward this end, the administration equipped Cushing with the *Missouri*, a state-of-the-art steamship. In a letter to Cushing, Tyler's friend John Peters (the father of the young engineer) explained the importance of the mighty vessel:

> You have now . . . the glorious opportunity of proceeding direct to China in the most complete and splendid steam ship in the world. . . . The President remarked to me the other day that he had thought of the importance of showing her to the Chinese. . . . They inform me that . . . they consider her superior to any British steamer. . . . But the most important consideration is that the Chinese government &people attribute the frightful power of the British to their use of steam power, &considering that the French are sending a formidable embassy . . . is it not infinitely important that you should arrive in the most imposing manner?[24]

With the *Missouri*, Cushing could arrive in grand style and awe the Chinese with an impressive show of America's military capability. Of course, Cushing need not mention to the Chinese that, at present, the *Missouri* was the lone ship of its kind in the U.S. Navy.

American shipbuilders and arms manufacturers also considered technology to be at the crux of the mission. They expected that Cushing would find a Chinese government eager to revamp its entire national defense and to do so using outside assistance. These arms suppliers flooded Cushing with letters asking him to pitch their products to the Chinese. One audacious shipbuilder asked Cushing to hand-deliver to the emperor the following letter in which he proposed to supply the Chinese navy with iron warships:

> Your Majesty will readily perceive the immense advantage to be derived from this invention, in enabling your seamen to cope with those of other nations who are farther advanced in naval tactics and architecture. It will be an overwhelming power in

your hands; putting in your possession instruments which will without doubt destroy the most powerful ships built, without endangering the safety of your crew.[25]

The ship builder offered to disassemble one such vessel and send it piece-meal to China along with a crew of workmen who, after reconstructing the craft, would demonstrate its awesome capabilities inside a giant water basin before the emperor. Cushing never did meet with the emperor, but he informed Chinese officials that he was willing to act as a liaison between the Chinese government and American arms manufacturers.[26]

Technology also provided the centerpiece of a scheme devised by a group of China traders but never implemented by Cushing. Since the U.S. government knew very little about China, Daniel Webster solicited advice from those who had experience working with the Chinese. The respondents included a consortium of prominent China traders from Boston and Salem, a group that included some of the richest men in America—Samuel Cabot, Robert B. Forbes, and Thomas Perkins. They advised Cushing to bring along models of steamboats, railroads, and cannons as well as "an Engineer who understands both Civil and warlike Engineering." Their proposal had little to do with boastfulness or chauvinism and everything to do with America's competition with England. "The Chinese . . . have a great fear of the encroachment by other foreign nations," the consortium wrote, "and if we could in a quiet way, without impinging upon the courtesies of Great Britain, contribute anything to their means of defense against further aggression, it would open the eyes of the emperor to the value of an alliance with us." In essence, the China traders conceived of a Sino-American alliance based on a transfer of technology: China would receive the ships and guns it needed to defend itself against British aggression and, in exchange, would look favorably on the Americans, presumably in matters of trade. The hypothetical alliance would improve the situations of the two countries involved while leaving Great Britain out in the cold.[27]

With technology playing a vital role on several fronts, Cushing's appointment of John Peters required little deliberation. The young man's engineering prowess made him a valuable asset to the mission. Moreover, his father's political connections, including a friendship with President Tyler, only made the decision that much easier. In the spring of 1843, Cushing formally offered the young man one of the highly coveted slots in his legation.

The position secured, Peters's grateful father provided Cushing with a character sketch of his son, describing him as humble and unassuming, almost to a fault. He "lacks confidence and the disposition to trumpet his own fame," the elder Peters wrote, "preferring to show his ability by his works." Peters, his father wrote, was more comfortable expressing himself through his mechanical creations than he was through spoken words. That said, his father continued, "he possesses indomitable enterprise and perseverance in pursuing his profession."[28] True to this characterization, the young Peters set about the task of preparing with a single-minded devotion his technological exhibits at the American Institute; as the date for departure drew near, he "occupied every hour to get his important models complete."[29]

While a system of political patronage had facilitated Peters's appointment, he was nonetheless an engineer of considerable skill who understood the workings of the most complex technologies of his day. He could assemble a steam engine, design a locomotive, construct a system of telegraphs, and install the gas works necessary to light a city. In fact, every model in his collection had been assembled with his own hands. And so that he might demonstrate the most recent innovations, he even secured permission from West Point and the largest American builder of steam-powered engines to use their patented technologies in his presentations. In sum, Peters was prepared to astound the Chinese with a marvelous technological display.[30]

## CUSHING AND PETERS IN CHINA

Although working at a feverish pace, Peters failed to complete his models before Cushing's departure and so could not accompany the envoy as he had hoped. Instead, he ended up sailing in a different ship, the *Bazaar*, that left for China at a later date.[31] After a five-month journey, Peters arrived in Canton in early April 1844, a little over a month after Cushing had steamed into Macao. Since events proceeded slowly at first and an opportunity to display his models would not arise for some time, Peters and the other members of the American legation spent most of their time waiting in the company of the local American missionaries, Peter Parker, Elijah Bridgman, and Samuel Wells Williams. During this stage, Peters assisted Cushing's mission mainly by carrying official dispatches to Chinese officials, errands which the mission's artist, George R. West, had handled prior to his arrival.[32]

Cushing and Webster passed the hours engaged in intensive language study, Cushing learning Manchu and the Webster learning Mandarin Chinese. Undertaken to help the two men make a positive impression on the Chinese, the lessons were fraught with peril for Webster's instructor.[33] Since the Qing government had yet to lift its ban on language instruction, Webster's Chinese tutor would at first teach the lessons only on the condition that the doors to the study remain locked. But even this precautionary measure was not sufficient to calm his frazzled nerves. After a few tutorials, he returned the money to Webster with the explanation that the stress had agitated him to such a degree that he had considered suicide.[34]

By precluding the creation of a pool of bilingual people, the Qing ban enlarged the role of missionaries in Sino-American negotiations. Indeed, without missionaries acting as linguistic intermediaries, China and the United States could not have enjoyed a dialogue. The missionaries, who had recognized that a proficiency in Chinese was sine qua non to their goal of spreading Christianity, were willing to disobey the Qing law and surreptitiously hire courageous Chinese instructors willing to offer them covert language programs. In this way, Williams, Bridgman, and Parker all learned Chinese, and the latter two handled most of the translating for the American mission.

To negotiate with the Americans, the emperor dispatched Qiying (the namesake of the junk Keying), who already possessed significant experience with foreigners, as he had previously handled the Treaty of Nanking. As his first move, Qiying sought to convince Cushing to abandon his request for a meeting with the emperor in Peking. Reluctant at first, Cushing agreed after Qiying assured him that doing so would substantially improve his chances for success in his other diplomatic objectives. With this matter settled, the two parties met in a temple inside the small town of Wanghia, just outside of Macao (fig. 7.1). Cushing, Webster, Parker, and Bridgman worked with their Chinese counterparts and eventually forged the terms and conditions of the Treaty of Wanghia (1844).

In addition to granting the United States essentially the same rights and privileges that the British had won by war, the treaty provided Americans with extraterritoriality. The relevant article stipulated that any case involving an American citizen accused of a crime in China was within the jurisdiction of American rather than Chinese courts. On this agreement, Cushing commented that "it was unwise to allow any control over the lives and property of American citizens in governments outside the limits of Christendom."[35] And perhaps reflective of the participation of Parker and Bridgman in the negotiations, the treaty also granted missionaries the right to build churches, hospitals, and cemeteries in the five ports now opened to Western intercourse.[36]

After the negotiations had closed, Cushing set his mind to other matters. Thinking of John Peters, he sent the following message to Qiying:

> Your excellency is doubtless aware that all the modern improvements in the arts of war &navigation are adopted and practiced in my country quite as thoroughly and extensively as in Europe. That if your government is desirous of books on . . . engineering, ship-building, steam engines, discipline of troops, or manufacture of arms, or any other subject whatever, I shall be happy to be the means of placing them in your hands. I also tender to you models for the construction of the instruments of

war as now used in Europe and America. Also the services of engineers skilled in these arts, to construct for your government ships, steamers, cannon, &arms of all sorts, either in China or in America as may be preferred.[37]

Qiying's letters to Cushing do not contain a response to this offer, and so we cannot determine when or if Peters presented his models in China. Before the ink had dried on the treaty, both parties became distracted by an unfortunate incident that tested the article of extraterritoriality. One evening, a mob of Chinese harassed a group of foreigners in Macao by pelting them with stones and brickbats. An American, feeling his life in danger, fired a shot that struck and killed a Chinese man named Lu Amun. Qiying believed that the American was responsible for the fatality, but Cushing convinced him as well as Macao's magistrates to allow an American tribunal to try the case. The court ruled in favor of the American, finding that he had fired his weapon in self-defense in what was a case of justifiable homicide.[38]

The tragic incident may have had the effect of pushing John Peters and his assignment to the bottom of both parties' agendas. While the evidence is inconclusive, Peters quite possibly never received an opportunity to demonstrate his models before an audience of Chinese officials. But even if Peters did have that chance, his exhibition certainly did not have the same effect on the Chinese as a similar exhibition would have on the Japanese a decade later. As a part of Commodore Perry's expedition, John Williams, the brother of Samuel Wells Williams, prepared the models of locomotives and telegraphs that ended up captivating high-ranking Japanese officials.[39] And though not the direct result of this particular technology show, Japan's Meiji Revolution included a sweeping modernization program that brought about an infusion of Western technology into Japanese culture.

Why did Peters fail to have any effect on China? Why was he not greeted enthusiastically by Chinese officials who, after the defeat to England, might have made an overhaul of the Chinese military a high priority? Contrary to American assumptions, the various groups of princes, officials, and literati that constituted the Chinese government did not achieve a consensus with regard to the meaning of the Opium War. In fact, according to historian James Polachek, not all factions within the government even conceded that the Chinese had lost the war at all. In the war's aftermath, a myth emerged that, in Guangdong Province, Chinese forces had dealt the British several defeats. Those who believed that was what happened attributed the Chinese success not to Qing imperial arms but rather to local militias led by scholar-officials. Since any kind of nationwide modernization movement would necessarily need to radiate from the center outward, this notion of a victory in the south prevented the Qing government from finding the consensus it needed to act.

Consequently, inertia rather than spirited reform characterized Qing policy in the ensuing two decades.[40]

Political forces beyond Peters's control rendered him ineffectual as a spokesman for American technology in China, but he would enjoy greater success teaching Americans about China. After Cushing departed Macao in August of 1844, Peters lingered for several months, during which time he set his mind to a new task with the same single-minded devotion that had characterized his earlier preparations at the American Institute. As his father informed Cushing, he was busy assembling "a more complete collection than Dunn's."[41] Like his precursor from Philadelphia, Peters could not achieve his goal without a substantial amount of help. Therefore, he enlisted "the aid of Chinese, and of the American Missionaries," two parties he had worked with extensively while fulfilling his responsibilities on the mission.[42]

Both groups were inclined to help because each believed that a museum that cast China in a positive light was certain to further their interests. Missionaries knew that Americans would contribute neither their money nor their time to evangelical efforts designed to uplift a people believed to be, in the word of Samuel Wells Williams, "unimproveable."[43] And the Chinese who assisted Peters undoubtedly knew that for the American public to be favorably predisposed toward the Chinese could only have a salutary effect. If Americans thought highly of China, they would be more apt to purchase Chinese commodities, and that would bolster a Chinese economy devastated by the ill effects of opium. Moreover, Americans would be less inclined to adopt a self-superior view that could potentially give rise to jingoism. In this way, the Chinese collection, though the brainchild of John Peters, would reflect the interests of China.

## THE CHINESE MUSEUM

While Peters was busy forming the collection, back in the United States his father made arrangements for its exhibition. In Manhattan, the elder Peters bought a plot on 539 Broadway and commenced building a structure large enough to house the collection. Since construction would not be completed by the time his son returned home, he also traveled to Boston and rented the Marlboro Chapel, a building on Washington Street, which would serve as the collection's temporary home. To ensure success for the grand opening, he invited Cushing not only to attend but "to present it [the collection] as a part of the fruits of your mission." The elder Peters knew that the mission to China enjoyed popularity in Cushing's native New England and that the diplomat's presence

was sure to lend prestige to and generate publicity for his son's cultural endeavor. When John Peters returned home on the *Bazaar* with what one magazine called "the largest collection of Chinese curiosities ever brought to this
country," he did not need to concern himself with either financial considerations or the need to find a physical structure large enough to accommodate
the sizeable collection. He could focus solely on the business of hanging pictures on walls and arranging objects in cases.[44]

When the museum opened in the autumn of 1845, China and Cushing's
mission were much discussed topics of conversation in Boston society. "Within
a few years past," John Peters wrote, "attention has been particularly directed
towards China" and "information is now eagerly sought after."[45] To meet this
demand for information, Fletcher Webster was in town in late October to deliver a series of lectures on China before heading to New York to do more of the
same. Cushing himself lectured on China at about the same time.[46] Both men
adopted a respectful tone in their remarks about the country. Cushing opened
by admitting that, on first landing in China, he found everything to be strange—
the clothing, the gongs, the ceremonies, the customs. However, if one were to
accept this "cursory view" and neglect to penetrate beneath the surface, "injustice will be done to a great and polished people."[47]

Webster also stressed the importance of moving beyond the simple and obvious perception that China was different. For example, he noted that, although
the costume of the Chinese "appears ridiculous to us," if "we examine the
weather we shall see that in that country ours is the inconsistent form of dress."
In short, the Chinese customs that Americans habitually labeled odd, strange,
or bizarre seemed that way only because they were viewed outside their proper
context. Both Cushing and Webster delivered lectures that were informative
rather than judgmental. In fact, Cushing obstinately refused to "pronounce
their morals of a higher or lower standard than those of Europe," because he
"did not believe it the province of a transient visitor to do so."[48]

John Peters's Chinese Museum also showed for China the same respect
shown by Cushing and Webster and by Nathan Dunn, who had died the previous autumn. Like those three men, Peters elevated the aim of instruction and
considered it his paramount objective. Toward that end, he subscribed to the
same object-based epistemology as did Dunn. Peters described his own era as a
"reading age" in which "books, periodicals and newspapers" have "multiplied"
to the point where "sight" becomes "necessary to make a lasting impression on
the mind." Along these lines, Peters quoted a Chinese maxim on the frontispiece of his catalog: "Words may deceive, but the eye cannot play the rogue."[49]

A reporter for the *Boston Daily Advertiser* picked up on Peters's philosophy,
referring to it as "EYE EDUCATION." Of all the "systems of education," he
wrote, the one that espouses the use of the "visual organ" to receive information

"is in many respects the best, because the actual imprint of the objects to be remembered . . . is made upon the brain." The power of visual evidence, he wrote, had led to a proliferation of pictures by artists in both books and panoramas. But, while these images leave the "eye pleased," the brain is "almost uninformed" because the accuracy of these pictures depends on an untrustworthy painter, "whose imagination probably, had so alienated him from truthfulness as to affect the work." By displaying the objects themselves and not just pictorial representations of them, Peters ensured that his museum met his day's criteria for accuracy.[50]

Peters's adherence to the same educational philosophy championed by Dunn yielded an exhibit that, not surprisingly, bore a strong visual resemblance to that of his predecessor. In addition to the cases of objects, Peters displayed about sixty life-size clay statues that he probably commissioned from the same sculptors Dunn had employed. Like Dunn, Peters went to great lengths to situate the figures in accurate reconstructions of their natural settings in China. In one diorama, the emperor Daoguang, seated on the dragon throne, is preparing to sign the Treaty of Wanghia, which Qiying has just presented to him. In another, a dissolute man of leisure reclines on a couch to inhale opium (the catalog explaining in detail how the drug is consumed). In a court scene, a judge metes out a sentence to a criminal as a guard stands by poised to inflict a punishment with a whip. In a classroom, a student recites his lessons before a stern teacher seated behind a desk. In a facsimile of the domicile of a well-to-do family, a lady plays with her children in a very life-like scene. And out in the countryside, a farmer ploughs his field with the help of a buffalo. In yet another diorama, a laborer in the tea industry carries two crates of tea. Most impressively, Peters apparently had an exact replica of a two-story shop built in Canton and then reassembled in his exhibition space.[51]

Although on first glance Peters's museum resembled Dunn's, a visitor fortunate enough to see both would have noticed one major omission from Peters's: natural history.[52] Peters did not possess Dunn's background in Enlightenment science and therefore did not feel compelled to gather natural specimens. His collection methodology, though extensive, encompassed only the human realm. One journalist who had seen both compared them as follows: "The exhibition is much more *practical* than that of Mr. Dunn. It has not so many objects of *vertu*, but the collection contains more things which show the real character of the people."[53]

Consistent with this emphasis on human society, Peters hired two Chinese men, T'sow Chaong and Le Kawhing, to become a permanent part of his museum. The former spoke English and therefore could field questions from the guests. The latter had worked as a music instructor in China and would sing and play Chinese instruments before audiences. According to Peters, Le Kawh-

ing had acquired an addiction to opium in China and had joined Peters because he hoped to break the habit by distancing himself from the purveyors of
the drug in China. (A Chinese man had circulated through Dunn's museum
too, but the paucity of newspaper stories that mention him suggests he graced
the exhibit for only a short while.[54])

Interestingly, the advertisements placed by Peters intimate his ambivalence
about the exhibition of these two Chinese men. Having lived in New York, he
probably knew from Afong Moy's success that the simple display of living Chinese people could provide a manager with a popular attraction. While Peters
certainly wanted to attract crowds to his museum, he also knew that the two
Chinese men could easily become a spectacle in their own right, capable either
of siphoning off the public's interest in the collection or of upstaging it altogether. Therefore, in his advertisements, Peters insisted on giving top billing to
the collection and devoting a smaller space to T'sow Chaong and Le Kawhing.
Although living Chinese possessed greater sensational value, the collection
possessed greater didactic value, and Peters apparently did not want to diminish
the importance of the collection.[55]

To further his museum's educational purpose, Peters followed Dunn's example by writing a descriptive catalog that bore the rather lengthy title *Miscellaneous Remarks upon the Government, History, Religions, Literature, Agriculture, Arts, Trades, Manners, and Customs of the Chinese.* While brimming with
information, the catalog is perhaps most remarkable for what is absent. As an
apostle for technology, Peters fervently believed that the mechanical inventions
now found in the West were truly remarkable, even revolutionary in their ability
to improve the quality of human life. Yet he did not allow the dearth of modern
technology in China to color his overall view of the country. Of course, he did
discuss China's mechanical devices in his *Miscellaneous Remarks* and was,
quite predictably, unimpressed by the antiquated pumps, waterwheels, and
mills he observed. These, he wrote, were "designed to direct [human] labour,
not to supercede it."[56] But, although many Americans in this optimistic age of
steam power would have viewed the low level of technology in China as symptomatic of a larger cultural failure, Peters insisted on keeping the issue compart-
mentalized, and he found much to admire elsewhere in Chinese civilization

In fact, as positive as Dunn's construction of China was, Peters quite possibly
promulgated one that was still more flattering. We can account for this by realizing that both men were reacting to a mainstream view they judged to be in
error. In 1838, Dunn had attempted to use his museum to dispel the myths and
fantasies that enveloped China in the American imagination. However, by 1845,
circumstances had drastically changed. While many Americans somewhat naively persisted in associating China with willowware, tea advertisements, and
the *Arabian Nights*, others now held the far more disturbing view that China

deserved to be mocked and ridiculed for its perceived backwardness. To combat this new adversary, Peters in his *Miscellaneous Remarks* adopted a stance that was more aggressively pro-China than even Dunn's had been.

Instead of dismissing, as had Dunn, the Chinese government as despotic, Peters argued that the "happy, contented, and industrious population is a pretty sure indication that the government is . . . well administered."[57] To support his argument, he allowed a Chinese voice to articulate China's greatest virtue:

> I felicitate myself that I was born in China; it constantly occurs to me, what if I had been born beyond the sea . . . where the cold freezes, or the heat scorches; where the people . . . are ignorant of the domestic relations. . . . I should not have been different from a beast. But how happily I have been born in China! I have a house to live in, have drink and food, and commodious furniture. . . . Truly the highest felicity is mine.[58]

The "domestic relations" to which the Chinese writer referred formed the basis of Confucianism, the social philosophy that, Peters and Dunn both agreed, held the country together.[59] Of course, as Peters praised China for its stability in the 1840s, he could not have known that the nation was about to enter a period of upheaval in which a series of internal rebellions would threaten to depose the Qing government—the Taiping Rebellion in the south (1850–64), the Nian Rebellion in the north (1853–68), and the Muslim Revolts in the northwest (1855–73). In the 1840s, China seemed to epitomize national harmony and unity.[60]

Most important, Peters engaged those like Thomas Smyth, the minister from Charleston discussed in chapter 6, who derided the Chinese for maintaining a pride in their own cultural preeminence despite incontrovertible evidence to the contrary provided by the Opium War. "The Chinese," Peters wrote, "have been ridiculed for assuming to be the only civilized nation in the world." He then proceeded to rebut China's critics first by insisting that the Chinese "are not to be judged by our standard" since they "live on the past, we on the future." In stating that the Chinese looked to the past, Peters did not mean to imply that the civilization was backward; rather, he was referring to the dearth of news about the outside world. He proceeded to attribute China's continued pride not to a pompous arrogance that was intrinsic to the culture itself but rather to the simple lack of information. Specifically, he cited advances in printing technology in the West that had only recently given the mass of Europeans and Americans access to worldly information. Ordinary Chinese, by contrast, lacked exposure to such news about developments outside of their own country. Consequently, Americans should not fault them for clinging to a self-image formed when China truly was "farther advanced in the arts of civilized life than any European nation." Even at the present, Peters added, the Chinese "are far in advance of the rest of Asia."[61]

Peters also challenged readers to view the behavior of Western nations from the Chinese vantage point. From there, he argued, China's refusal to pass the mantle of civilization to the West would no longer seem arrogant or ludicrous:

> Is it strange when they see the greatest European nation seize upon . . . India, and clandestinely flood their shores with a drug which destroys thousands . . . that they should look upon them as barbarians! Is it strange, when they saw the governments and merchants of foreign nations . . . perpetually quarrelling for the sake of gain, that they should look upon them all with suspicion . . . and call them . . . "foreign devils!"

Whereas Western standards for judging civilizations focused on wealth and military prowess, the Chinese emphasized morals. When measured against those criteria, the Europeans and Americans fared poorly in the Chinese mind, and justifiably so. In sum, Peters asked Americans to look in the mirror before casting aspersions at the Chinese.[62]


## RESPONSES TO THE MUSEUM


Peters presented a positive vision of China both through his exhibits and through the pages of his *Miscellaneous Remarks,* but ultimately the visitors decided for themselves how they would perceive China. It turns out that virtual travel played a major role in their experience, as it had in the case of Dunn's museum. One reporter wrote profusely about the opportunity to take a magical excursion to China.

> Who would not like to visit China, walk through the streets of its cities, penetrate the mansions of its inhabitants, partake of savory bird's nest soup . . . or quaff real souchong [tea], from real China ware, in the company with real Chinese? There are none who, if circumstances permitted, would not desire to see the many curious things which distinguish that curious people. To us, whose business, time or means, forbid so long a voyage, there is now offered a most desirable opportunity.[63]

Another reporter expressed his astonishment at the realism of the exhibit. It was "as if some enormous boring instrument had scooped up a whole piece of a Chinese city," he wrote, "and it had been dropped carefully within the walls of the old Marlborough Chapel."[64]

A reporter from the *Mercantile Journal* was also enchanted by the illusion of travel afforded by the museum. His approach to the Marlboro Chapel he described as a walk in the mud along Washington Street. Yet at the entrance, which was elaborately decorated in the Chinese style, the dreariness of the real world evaporated, and magic seemingly seized control of his experience. "I saw a sight which at first I could not understand. The entrance to . . . the Chapel seemed to have been metamorphosed by some of the genii of the lamp, who existed in Aladdin's time." After entering the museum, he became instantaneously overwhelmed as he beheld the interior for the first time. "We gazed in wonderment at the strangely gorgeous scene which suddenly presented itself to our astonished optics." Glowing lanterns, colorful paintings, dioramas, real Chinese people, and a giant dragon hovering majestically above the entire scene—all these marvelous spectacles captivated the reporter, temporarily convincing him that he had journeyed to China itself. Simply through the act of wishing, he had been "transported . . . by enchantment . . . to his desired destination in the twinkling of an eye." Indeed, his sense that magic had played a role prompted him to invoke a familiar story: "It seemed . . . as though we had set upon the wonderful blanket, of which we have all of us read in the *Arabian Nights*." Although the visitor clearly relished his escapist fantasy, he did eventually engage the exhibits at a serious level. And while he disliked Chinese music (it was not exactly the "music of the spheres"), he enjoyed learning about Chinese culture and history in an educational venue that "has not a parallel, I believe, in the world."[65]

A reporter for the *Boston Daily Advertiser* claimed to have astounded and befuddled his wife and children by returning home one day and announcing the impossible: "Yes—we have been to CHINA!" He recalled how in childhood he had "stared in wonder and admiration at the Willow patterned plates, which to our childish eyes were so marvellous"; now he had "realized the visions of our youth." To his family's utter bewilderment, he related how he had spent time "hob-knobbing with Keying [Qiying]," "taking snuff with Howkwa [Houqua]," strolling through the streets of Peking, listening to a Chinese musician (Le Kawhing) play his instruments, and kowtowing before the emperor as the latter signed the Treaty of Wanghia. "Yes," he proudly proclaimed, "I have been in China." At this point, his wife interjects, "are you mad? or drunk? You have never quitted Boston to my knowledge, and China is an outlandish place, far away, at least so Mr. Cushing and the newspapers tell us." To avoid incarceration in an insane asylum, the reporter divulges his secret: He has been to the Chinese Museum and promises to take his family the very next day for a "second trip" to China.[66]

This same reporter also revealed the disappointing impotence of Peters in shaping visitors' attitudes toward China. Though effusive in praising Peters's ability to re-create China in Boston, the engineer failed to alter substantially his views on China itself. After touring the exhibits, he persisted in echoing many of the sentiments expressed by Smyth. He depicted the Chinese as "odd looking human beings" who possessed quaint and ridiculous habits; the women followed the custom of "pinching their feet into perplexed shoes," and the men sported "pigtails" and grew their nails long. Furthermore, the arrogant Chinese, he wrote, possessed "the extreme impertinence to look down upon a free and independent people with contempt for our limited acquirements." Evidently, he either neglected to read Peters's *Miscellaneous Remarks* or read it but refused to part with his preconceived notions.[67]

Yet plenty of evidence suggests visitors looked to Peters to provide them with an educational experience. "The splendid collection of Mr. Peters," the *Dollar Newspaper* reported, "will give an inquiring mind more real ideas of the social and political state of that vast empire, than can be gathered from a library of books upon the subject."[68] Similarly, a children's book advised its young readers that at the Chinese Museum "the visitors could obtain a much better knowledge of many peculiarities of the Chinese, than from the readings of any books."[69] A reporter for the *Boston Daily Advertiser* praised Peters's *Miscellaneous Remarks* for being "drawn up so as to make the whole Exhibition intelligible." "Every thing in the museum," he continued, "is the work of Chinese hands, and the collection is so extensive and thorough, that a well-informed person will get a better insight from it of the details of Chinese life, than would be acquired by a common visit to a Chinese port."[70]

This statement may seem like groundless hyperbole, but it was lent some credibility by the journal of a navy midshipman who later visited China, in 1853. While serving on Commodore Perry's expedition to Japan, Yorke McCauley found himself docked temporarily at Hong Kong and decided to set off to explore the area. "We walked 'till [we] were as tired as it behooved us to get, trying to observe something new or remarkable, but found that more was to be learned by a visit to the Chinese Museum, I saw in Boston, than could be seen . . . in trudging about promiscuously in Hong Kong." Later in Canton, McCauley reiterated his point that "you can get as good ideas of China" by "visiting the Museums in the U.S. as you can by going to Canton."[71]

The museum remained in Boston for more than a year, attracting visitors from all classes and all age groups and taking in gate receipts that amounted to $28,000.[72] In 1847, Peters packed the collection onto the *Suffolk* and shipped it to Philadelphia, where it would occupy the same building vacated by Dunn six years earlier.[73] In early March 1847, the *Public Ledger* reported that, even though "sixty furniture car loads of curiosities" had arrived at the museum, more than half of the collection remained on the ship yet to be unloaded.[74] In Philadelphia, the museum coexisted with other attractions, such as the "Ohio Mammoth

Girl," an unfortunate twelve-year-old who weighed 330 pounds, and a man who could drink two gallons of water in one draught.[75]

Peters's true rival, however, was neither the Mammoth Girl nor the great imbiber but the lingering memory of Dunn's museum. But, from what we can glean from an article in the *Public Ledger*, it may have been that his following Dunn actually helped Peters. Instead of exhausting interest in China, Dunn's museum had stimulated the minds of Philadelphia's citizens and generated such a wellspring of positive feeling that many people were prepared to enjoy a second museum "of the same character." Even those who required novelty would have attended Peters's museum because, as it said in the paper, "it contains more articles than the former one, besides two natives of China, one of whom plays on several curious instruments and sings in Chinese style, which is altogether different from any other ever heard before."[76] With a museum that resembled Dunn's yet possessed a greater number of objects and two living Chinese, Peters provided an attraction that was at once new and familiar.

The museum also attracted those who were either unborn at the time of Dunn's museum or had been too young to enjoy it. In fact, Peters's museum forever altered the life of one precocious young boy who wandered through its doors. Though only about five years of age, William Elliot Griffis was as intellectually curious as many of the adults, and the exhibits made such a deep impression on him that more than sixty years later he recalled it as one of the formative experiences of his life:

> I visited many times the great Chinese Museum in my native city, Philadelphia. . . .
> There were life-sized groups of human figures, male and female, picturing all classes,
> from emperor and mandarins to cobbler and beggars, representations of shops and
> crafts, and a varied collection of genuine objects of use and beauty, intelligently se-
> lected and brought from the Middle Kingdom. Two Chinese gentlemen, in silk and
> nankeen dress and bamboo hats, explained things. Even then I longed to know more
> of what the Chinese thought and felt than of what they made, ate, bought, or sold.

While everything in the exhibit fascinated Griffis, he was most drawn to T'sow Chaong and Le Kawhing. For, although an object lesson in Chinese culture held some appeal, the young boy was really after a different kind of knowledge, one that no artifact could convey—"what the Chinese thought and felt." In the Chinese Museum, Griffis began a quest that would consume the rest of his life and would include a successful career as one of America's foremost Asian experts. He sought to understand the Chinese mind.[77]

After Philadelphia, John Peters moved the collection to New York and installed it in the brand-new building that his father had designed specifically to house it. When the museum opened on January 1, 1849, a little more than a year had passed since the departure of the Keying, and Peters hoped to change the tone of mockery that Captain Kellett had encouraged. However, toward this end, the collection alone would have to suffice, Peters apparently having lost the services of T'sow Chaong and Le Kawhing.[78] If accounts in the *Herald* offer any indication, New Yorkers drew a line of distinction between the junk and the museum, viewing the latter as a more sincere attempt to instruct. In an apparent slight to the Chinese junk, the paper claimed that the museum afforded New Yorkers "a better opportunity than ever before to become acquainted with the 'Celestial Empire.'" Choosing words that it had never used to describe the junk, the *Herald* called the museum a "highly intellectual and rational scene of amusement, eminently calculated to illustrate the manners and habits" of the Chinese. Kellett's junk had effected the Barnumization of Chinese culture, and Peters was intent on restoring China's respectability in the eyes of New Yorkers.[79]

## "HE IS AN ENTERPRISING FELLOW"

At some point in 1849, Peters became unable to manage the museum, perhaps owing to an illness. In late October 1849, an advertisement in the *Herald* exhorted "all those who never expect to see the Celestial Empire" to go visit the museum while they still had the chance. The museum closed its doors on November 5, 1849, with the final day's ticket receipts donated to a charity.[80] John Peters died some time between 1849 and 1853. In a transaction laced with irony, the collection was sold in early 1850 to P. T. Barnum (fig. 7.2).[81] Possessing no expertise on China, Barnum chose to buy the rights to Peters's *Miscellaneous Remarks* instead of writing his own catalog. Keeping the words of the late John Peters largely intact, Barnum (perhaps thinking of Dunn) renamed the booklet *Ten Thousand Things on China and the Chinese* and expunged from it any trace of the former owner.[82]

Peters's collection attracted Barnum for several reasons. First, he had probably wanted to operate a Chinese museum after witnessing Dunn's remarkable success in London. Second, in the early 1850s, Barnum was making a conscious effort to upgrade his public image. Not coincidentally, the purchase of the Chinese Museum coincided with the arrival of Barnum's most prestigious act: Jenny Lind, the famous "Swedish Nightingale." That Peters's museum enjoyed a strong reputation in New York only added to its luster as far as Barnum was concerned.[83]

Third, Barnum understood quite well Americans' romantic curiosity about the outside world in this age of exploration. To feed their hunger for information and stimulation, he had always organized his American Museum around a quasiscientific agenda. In the fields of ethnography and natural history, Barnum claimed to give his audiences access to the infinitely diverse and fascinating world. "He [Barnum] despatched [sic] agents to Europe, Asia, Africa, and the interior of our own continent," according to a section added to the end of the revised catalog, "for the purpose of securing any and every rarity to be obtained." As the result of this effort, "curiosities flowed in from every quarter." In this context, the acquisition of a Chinese collection made complete sense. It fit perfectly into Barnum's overarching ambition to present all that was "wonderful" about a world now opening up to the West.[84]

Fourth, that T'sow Chaong and Le Kawhing, who had worked in the museum in Boston and Philadelphia, did *not* make the move to New York with John Peters also enhanced the value of the collection in Barnum's mind, for the following reason. By the time Barnum had purchased the collection in 1850, it had received visitors for an entire year. Although the Chinese objects themselves were no longer novelties, New Yorkers had yet to experience the synergistic combination of a museum inhabited by living Chinese people. Thus, simply by hiring Chinese people, Barnum knew he could make the Chinese Museum novel *a second time*. And so, before reopening it under his own management, he secured the services of a "Chinese family" that included Pwan Yee Koo, whom he promptly dubbed the "Chinese Belle." With this addition, Barnum was able to arouse the curiosity of Ezra Beach, a young boy of thirteen. "I went to the Chinese museum," he wrote, because "I had never [seen] a chines [sic] and I thought them quite a sight." Beach described the Chinese as "a harmless set of people" who "wear their hair so long as to touch the ground" and sometimes "have little feet."[85]

That Beach recalled the Chinese people but not the Chinese objects does not come as a surprise. John Peters had worried that the presence of actual Chinese people could overshadow his collection, but Barnum had no such reservations about displays of live people. Under Barnum's stewardship, the Chinese collection became little more than a colorful backdrop for Pwan and her retinue. And to call attention to his latest attraction, he directed the full force of his substantial marketing abilities to generating publicity for the Chinese Belle.

In promoting the Chinese Belle, his first task was to cope with the lingering memory of the Chinese Lady, Afong Moy. In the shadow cast by Moy's recent appearances in New York, Pwan was hardly an original attraction. For this reason, Barnum needed to find a way to discredit Moy in order to increase the novelty of Pwan. Since the Chinese Lady's status as Chinese was beyond dispute and therefore unassailable, Barnum instead attacked her credentials as a lady, as a woman of wealth and status. In a small addendum to Peters's catalog, Barnum wrote that Pwan "is the first Chinese *lady* that has yet visited Christendom," as the "only other female ever known to have left the 'Central Flowery Nation'" was of "apocryphal reputation and position in her own country."[86] Interestingly, as recently as 1848, Afong Moy had shared an exhibition space with Tom Thumb, who was then still under contract with Barnum.[87] This unusual pairing leaves open the intriguing possibility that Moy had moved under the Barnum umbrella at some point in the 1840s. If so, by assailing Moy's credibility, Barnum was essentially cannibalizing his own exhibit, one that had served its purpose, to bestow vitality on a new one.[88]

Whether Barnum did or did not sacrifice the Chinese Lady to ensure the success of the Chinese Belle, he did employ his prodigious promotional talent to draw New Yorkers to the latter's exhibition. Part of Barnum's genius lay in his adroit handling of the press. To generate publicity for his attractions, he had forged a mutually beneficial relationship with the *Herald*, much as Captain Kellett seems to have done as well. In exchange for Barnum's purchases of advertising space, the *Herald* agreed to print as legitimate news the brief blurbs that Barnum wrote to excite the public's interest in his attractions.[89] With this arrangement guaranteeing him a small rectangle of space in almost every issue of the *Herald*, he unleashed a barrage of stories about Pwan, most of which were almost certainly fictitious. Unlike Kellett, Barnum was a true marketing genius who had wit at his disposal; he seldom needed to deploy cruel stereotypes about, for instance, a reputed Chinese love of rat-eating in order to generate humor.

Many of his news items revolved around the issue of class—both Pwan's class and that of her audience. Barnum portrayed Pwan as an aristocratic lady, stating repeatedly that she was "a splendid specimen of the Chinese upper ten," a person "of superior birth, position and education, besides being really pretty."[90] While promoting Pwan, these small news items simultaneously spoofed the New York press's new obsession with covering high society: balls, soirées, fashions, and outings to the opera.[91] He invented a wonderful yet absurd fiction that situated Pwan at the center of New York's haute culture. In this imaginary role, Pwan became the arbiter of good taste, able to set fashion trends for the entire city just by showing a preference for a particular style or color. After she showed a fondness for a lady wearing a pink bonnet, Barnum announced that "pink, therefore, must become fashionable."[92] Barnum would even insert French phrases into his blurbs, all to maintain the notion that a trip to see the Chinese Belle was a form of upper-class entertainment:

FASHION RULES THE WORLD—The curious lead and the crowd follow. A while ago and no one was *comme il faut* who did not go into raptures about the opera; now, no one is considered genteel whose carriage is not seen in front of the Chinese Museum, where the Chinese beauty holds court, and bewitches every visitor. She and her *suite* are all the rage.[93]

Of course, this idea that the city's elite citizenry arrived at the Chinese Museum in their carriages and attended Pwan's exhibition as they would the opera was absolutely ludicrous—but very effective. For Barnum knew that his true audience was the middle and lower classes, and he understood that the surest way to attract them to lowbrow entertainment was to characterize it as distinctly highbrow. In this way, he masqueraded a popular entertainment in the garb of aristocratic exclusivity. After announcing Pwan's upcoming engagement in London, the showman proceeded to doff his cap to himself. "Barnum," he wrote, "is an enterprising fellow."[94]

Perhaps the only part of the advertising blitz that Barnum did not fabricate was this trip to London. Seeking to capitalize on the Crystal Palace Exposition of 1851 and on the fascination for foreign cultures that it was sure to stimulate, Barnum asked one of his agents to accompany Pwan and her "suite" to London.[95] In London, they appeared alongside Dunn's Chinese Collection, which had returned from its tour of the provinces in time for the international exposition.[96]

# GEORGE WEST IN CHINA

At the conclusion of Barnum's catalog, the showman wrote, "Thus ends our Panorama—as, indeed, it may be called—of China and the Chinese."[97] Of course, he did not mean panorama here in the most literal sense of the word in which it denotes a giant painting. Yet a few years after the opening of Barnum's Chinese Museum, New Yorkers were invited to gaze on an actual panorama of China that, like the collection, also had its roots in the Cushing Mission. In addition to John R. Peters, Fletcher Webster, and Caleb Cushing, one other member of the U.S. Mission to China chose to convert his diplomatic experience into a cultural production on returning home—George R. West, the mission's draughtsman.

West's primary responsibility during the mission was to sketch Chinese scenes and important diplomatic occasions, but he appears to have spent much of his time in the same capacity as Peters—delivering messages from Cushing and Webster to Chinese officials.[98] But he still found plenty of time to escape the diplomatic community and experience China for himself. West loved to roam about by himself with his sketchpad, looking for scenes of beauty or interest. On finding them, he recorded his impressions with quick but thorough sketches made on the spot, and they would later become the basis for finished watercolor compositions. West eventually produced, in 1844, 124 paintings and sketches that, being government property, are currently held at the Library Congress.[99]

Through a twist of fate, at the conclusion of Cushing's mission George West would remain in China for six more years before finally returning to the United States. After Cushing had secured the treaty and embarked for New York in August of 1844, West remained in China with Peters, perhaps to add watercolor views to his portfolio. Unlike the wealthy Peters, however, West was a man apparently of limited financial means. He had just enough money in his possession to pay for his passage home, and in his calculations he did not account for any unforeseen complications. In December 1844, he was still in China, writing to Cushing to explain his plight. He had left Macao for the United States on the *Moslem*, only to discover in Manila that the ship was "rotten or defective in her timber." He returned to Macao to await the departure of the next available ship, during which time his "money became so reduced as not to leave sufficient [funds] to pay passage home." Finding himself stranded, West headed for Canton, where he could earn his fare by employing his skills as a painter and daguerreotypist. Presumably, foreign and Chinese clients would commission him either to paint their portraits or to use the new technology to generate photographic images of themselves.[100]

While the details are not clear, we know that at some point West shifted the purpose of his work. Instead of using his artistic abilities to earn the money for passage home, he elected to place them in the service of a far more ambitious plan. He would take advantage of the new mobility accorded to Americans by the Treaty of Wanghia and accumulate a pictorial record of the parts of China that had previously been forbidden to Western eyes—the recently opened treaty ports and the countryside surrounding them. He would become the first American since Houckgeest to capture visual images of these once restricted parts of China.

West left no records of his extensive travels through the cities, towns, and countryside of China, but we can obtain an idea of his activity from the account of B. L. Ball, an American physician who joined West on one of the latter's excursions. Like many Americans at this time, Ball longed to see the world, but he was exceptional in that he did not have to satisfy this desire by reading travelogues and visiting museums. Being independently wealthy, he possessed the means to travel almost anywhere on earth and selected China for the following reason: "I considered that China is a country as distant as any other; that it is as diverse from ours as any; that the people are as much our antipodes in dress, customs, religion &c., as in their geographical position."[101] For his grand tour, Ball craved difference not sameness, and in his mind China afforded the most dramatic escape from European-American culture.

After arriving in China in 1848, Ball passed the first months interacting with British and American merchants and missionaries in the expatriate community at the new treaty ports. In Canton, he enjoyed the company of Peter Parker,

Samuel Wells Williams (who had recently returned from his furlough), and Elijah Bridgeman, a former college classmate.[102] He also visited the various Chinese-owned shops, many of which catered to the foreign community. Inside one of these, he described the behavior of a man named Dr. Brooks, who exuded an almost childlike fascination with Chinese things.

> There were a great many oddities to be seen in the shops, especially in "Curiosity-street." The doctor manifested much curiosity, and had many curious comments to make. When he came upon something particularly different from our American side of the globe, his countenance would light up, and, turning the article over and over, he would exclaim . . . "Well, isn't that curious? Don't you think that is beautiful? Isn't it capital?" and, holding a little further off, "It is superb! Well, I do think the Chinese are the most ingenious people at carving in the world. I must take one of these home." . . . The Chinese, in the mean time, laughed, and, observing the interest he took in their works, were delighted to show him all in the shop.[103]

Ball also enjoyed these shops, but he had not traveled all the way to China to marvel at objects. He wanted to see China itself. And so one can imagine his excitement when, after traveling north to Ningbo in the summer of 1849, he met a young man who did nothing but head out into areas never before seen by foreigners—George West.

"He is engaged in sketching various scenes about Ningpoo," Ball wrote of West, "learning as much as possible about places, people, &c." Since West was planning to leave Ningbo "for an excursion into the country" and Ball also "wished to make a trip into the country," the two "concluded to go together."[104] Wanting to depart immediately, Ball and West made hasty preparations for their journey; they packed a bag of copper coins to pay for food, lodging, and transportation and hired three Chinese, two personal servants and a cook, to accompany them. Their travels took them away from the coast and inland to the Yangdang Mountains. Traveling on foot, by boat, or in hired sedan chairs, the two companions took in some extraordinary scenery as they made their way to several Buddhist monasteries and numerous small villages.

Wherever Ball and West traveled, they attracted the attention of local residents, most of whom had never seen Caucasian people before. Children would scamper to their homes and cling to their mothers in fear. Other villagers would follow the two purely out of curiosity. According to Ball, the sight of foreigners in these areas elicited in the people a sense of wonder and amazement: "They displayed as much marvellousness as we might have done at the appearance of an inhabitant from another planet." Ball described a man who would approach him rather slowly, reach out his hand rather tentatively, and touch him to determine whether he was real or merely an apparition. Another man first rubbed his fingers on Ball's face then examined his fingertips "to see if the white color came off."[105]

The mere presence of two non-Chinese was by itself sufficient to draw a crowd, and West's quick and skillful sketching added to the spectacle. At a monastery, monks congregated around the artist to watch as a likeness of their temple gradually materialized on the white paper. One group of laborers, "in their eagerness to see him draw," besieged West and "inserted their heads directly between him and the view he wished to sketch." In a "good-natured manner," West tried to push them away. Such incidents occurred frequently because, according to Ball's account, West's sketching was almost incessant. Every time the duo approached a novel sight, West would immediately begin to capture it on paper. When the physician awoke from a nap or returned from a hike, he invariably found his companion busily engaged in sketching. Like Houckgeest, Dunn, and Peters before him, West was wrapped in single-minded devotion as he pursued his project.[106]

As West's portfolio thickened, a question must have loomed in the back of the artist's mind: On returning to the United States, how would he use his unique collection of sketches? One possibility he might have considered would be to submit a series of paintings to a publisher who could convert them into a handsome album of lithographs or engravings. Had West chosen publication, he would have entered a field of Chinese views that was almost devoid of competition. The British artist Thomas Allom had recently published four elegant quartos containing about 120 Chinese scenes. However, a review in the Chinese Repository judged the pictures "more beautiful than accurate" because, unlike West, Allom had never witnessed the places he depicted: "If Mr. Allom could have been present and observed with his own eyes the scenes he has attempted to portray . . . he would have avoided some gross blunders."[107] The other artist in the field, Tingqua, was highly regarded by Americans but worked within a geographic range that was more limited than that of the peripatetic George West. The talented Chinese watercolorist worked in his studio in Canton and never offered artistic treatments of the varied landscapes and communities that existed farther to the north.[108]

A handsomely bound picture album would have had some merit, but West opted against it. Its steep price would have rendered it cost-prohibitive for most Americans. Moreover, West apparently hoped to awe his audiences with a thrilling spectacle, and a book of pictures obviously could not generate that kind of effect. After arriving in New York in 1850 or 1851, he decided to convert his hundreds of sketches into a single painting of epic proportions—a panorama of China.

## THE CHINESE PANORAMA

In the antebellum era, the panorama presented Americans with an attractive option for entertainment and instruction. This medium exposed Americans to scenic parts of the United States, natural wonders, famous battles, or views of foreign countries.[109] In fact, during the transitional period in which John Peters's collection passed to P. T. Barnum, the spacious Chinese Museum in New York was used to show Gliddon's panorama of the Nile River.[110] Audiences at these shows watched as a series of scenes glided past them while a lecturer concurrently supplied information. Panorama operators accomplished this feat first by rolling the lengthy canvas onto a large cylinder, 10 or 12 feet tall; during the course of the evening, they would slowly unwind the painting, which would become visible to the audience as it moved across the stage. A second cylinder, placed on the opposite side of the stage, stood ready to receive and roll the painting again.[111] The size of the panorama was crucial because, like today's IMAX theaters, a large canvas could provide the audience with the sensation of actually being present at the location depicted. As a result, some panoramas reached amazing proportions, measuring 12 feet in height and about a mile in length.[112]

Since the surface of West's panorama exceeded 20,000 square feet, its length probably extended more than a third of a mile.[113] Unfortunately, like nearly all panoramas, West's depiction of China has not survived to the present day. However, from the corpus of works he completed for the Cushing Mission, we can see the kinds of scenes West would have included and, from these, glean his overall view of Chinese civilization. Taken as a whole, West's pictures offer a construction of China that is positive, uncritical, and often humanistic. A general fondness for China suffuses the entire body of work, but one would not characterize it as overly idealized; rather, West seems to have captured China as it appeared on a sunny day.

His *View on Canton River* offers a pleasant scene involving junks and sampans floating on blue water; the towering pagoda leads the eye of the observer from this peaceful river activity to the vast sky above (fig. 7.3). Puntingqua's *Country Villa near Canton* shows the scenic beauty—lakes, gardens, trees, and pavilions—enjoyed by a wealthy merchant (fig. 7.4). West also turned his eyes to the working classes, where he cast a sympathetic light on their labor-intensive lives. *Chinese Blacksmiths* captures the smoky grit of a streetside occupation (fig. 7.5).And such works as *Chinese Ploughing* or *Irrigating* are imbued with a respect for those who subsist by dint of physical exertion (figs. 7.6 and 7.7). Of course, these paintings served the dual purpose of depicting the techniques and implements used by the Chinese, who were famous for their efficiency in husbandry. For this reason, West also painted any ingenious device used extensively by the Chinese, such as the abacus, that would appear novel to American eyes (fig. 7.8).

West also humanized the Chinese in such paintings as *Sampan Woman and Boat* (fig. 7.9). Beneath a blue sky filled with giant billowing clouds, this young woman breast-feeds her infant on board her sampan. Her facial expression conveys an emotion that animates nearly all women regardless of nationality or race—a mother's love and caring for her child. By selecting scenes that emphasized the universal or that transcended a specific culture, West was able to show what was human in his subjects in addition to demonstrating what was distinctly Chinese. In this way, he stood poised to make a substantial contribution to the American conception of the Chinese, and in the process he swam against two prevailing currents. First, whereas most constructions of the Chinese (even that put forward by John Peters) accentuated China's difference from Europe and America, West painted its similarity. Second, West's construction challenged a growing tendency to dehumanize the Chinese, to regard them as clownish buffoons who proudly adhered to bizarre and outdated customs. As pictures like this one reveal, West tried to reconnect the Chinese to the larger human family.

As he began this prodigious undertaking in the 1850s, China was starting to recede into the Asian background, as Americans increasingly shifted the collective focus of their gaze to Japan. In 1853, ten years after Cushing's voyage to China, Commodore Matthew Perry led another diplomatic expedition to Asia, this one designed to pry open Japan. For his official artist, Perry selected William Heine, a landscape painter originally from Dresden who was then working in a studio in New York. At the conclusion of the expedition, Heine returned to the United States with about five hundred paintings.[114] After meeting George West in New York, the two agreed to form a partnership. They would combine their experiences, resources, and artistic talents to form a single panorama, one that would whisk spectators off to both China and Japan in the same magical evening.[115]

On January 26, 1856, West and Heine unveiled their panorama in Academy Hall at 663 Broadway. Its title, *Seven Years in the Celestial Empire and the Japan Expedition*, indicated the bipartite nature of the show. Of the 57 total scenes, which required about two hours to unfurl, West accounted for 33 Chinese scenes to Heine's 24 on Japan.[116] Choosing not to speak to the audience themselves, the two artists hired three lecturers, one for China, one for Japan, and a third, a Mr. Landers, who would speak during the intermission between the two presentations.[117]

To entice people to attend, West and Heine employed a railroad motif in their advertising. They called each showing a "train," referred to audience members as "Passengers," pronounced themselves "Conductors," and labeled the entire experience "an excursion to China and Japan."[118] A reporter from the *Tribune* explored this theme of virtual travel in his review:

> A series of Panoramic Views of any country where form, perspective, color, and size contribute to imitate realities, is the next best thing to seeing the original. Indeed, when we take into consideration the sea-sickness of a voyage, and the thousand disagreeable attendants of land travel, we much prefer the panorama to the veritable thing. . . . We felt all of this on Monday night in seeing the panoramic views of China and Japan, and hearing the lectures thereupon. . . . Here we have China and Japan without the trouble of a voyage.

Understanding that West had gone to great lengths to observe China beyond the treaty ports, this writer praised the artist for showing what he called "penetralia," or "the inner life and natural scenery" of a country. He enjoyed the panorama tremendously, claimed that one could obtain from it a "better idea of these countries than any amount of ordinary reading" could provide, and highly recommended it to his readers: "All that is necessary for the viewer to do is to sit still, and the great canvas reels on, while the salient points of life and scenery . . . come like shadows."[119]

Considerable effort went into the project to promote the panorama as being able to simulate an actual trip to China and Japan, but it did not enjoy an auspicious beginning. The lectures on China appear to have been disorganized and hastily thrown together. On opening night, the gentleman responsible for China apparently apologized to the audience for his lack of preparation and admitted to having "but a day to prepare himself."[120] The *Times* liked neither the lecture nor West's artwork: "The illustrations of 'China' painted by Mr. West, did not strike us as very good, and the gentleman who explained it bungled it very badly."[121] The *Tribune*, the *Times*, and the *Herald* all agreed that, in general, the lectures were too nationalistic. "The great drawback to this exhibition is the lecturer," wrote the *Herald*, "who tells funny stories in a very melancholy manner, and is spasmodically patriotic where there is not the slightest necessity for any such displays." The *Times* believed that Mr. Landers, who spoke after China and before Japan, was excessive both in his declamations on the Americanism intrinsic to West's accomplishment and in his unrealistic ranking of West's explorations of China with the Arctic expedition of Elisha Kent Kane (whom West knew from the Cushing Mission). The *Tribune* also took issue with the lecturers' assumption that the openings of China and Japan benefited those countries. In comparing China with the outside world that forced opium on to it, the paper wrote that the "man in the moon would be puzzled to tell . . . which was the heathen."[122]

With the unpopular lecturers, West and Heine clearly had a problem serious enough to threaten the viability of their entire enterprise. Although for the most part their paintings were drawing positive reviews, the hired speakers persisted in making errors and offending people with their excessive nationalistic pride. In the face of this criticism, the two artists decided to act. They discharged the lecturers and immediately commenced their search for suitable replacements, which was no easy task. After all, how many people in the New York area were qualified to speak on either China or Japan, possessed strong oratory skills, and were able to lecture immediately, without needing time to prepare? In a re- markable stroke of apparent good fortune, they located an individual who not only met all these requirements but was qualified to speak on China and Japan at the same time. Bayard Taylor, a famous travel writer whom Heine had met on Commodore Perry's expedition to Japan, was then residing in New York.

At the urging of the New York Tribune, Bayard Taylor had sailed to China in 1853 to join Perry's squadron before it embarked for Japan. After Taylor's return, the travelogue that resulted from this experience and his earlier books on Eu- rope and the American West combined to solidify his reputation as America's most beloved travel writer. A different country or a different age might have been unlikely to confer celebrity status on a mere travel writer, but antebellum America did so with enthusiasm. Indeed, that same national yearning to ex- plore distant places that drove many Americans to Chinese museums also trans- formed Taylor into a national hero. During an extensive lecture tour that fol- lowed his return from Asia, he regularly appeared before packed auditoriums (see chapter 8).

For West and Heine, Taylor seemed like the ideal choice. His fame promised to fill the auditorium, his public speaking skills guaranteed a professional deliv- ery, and his experience in both China and Japan lent him the credibility that the previous lecturers lacked. Heine approached Taylor and formally asked him to assume the position as lecturer. For Taylor, the offer was easy to accept because he had a lecture on China and Japan already written; he would only need to modify it slightly so that it could correspond to the scenes detailed in the pan- orama. And since he possessed a favorable opinion of the Japanese, his lectures probably complemented Heine's artwork quite well. But for West, the presence of Taylor behind the podium must have been bittersweet, because, while gate receipts surely rose, Taylor's views on China were not in alignment with West's own. Whereas West had looked closely at the Chinese and discerned their hu- manity, Taylor had observed only a glaring moral depravity, and he was not bash- ful about reporting his findings. As a result, audience members at the panorama must have recognized a gross incongruity between the audio and the visual. While watching beautiful pictures of China roll by, they concurrently listened to the speaker issue a complete denunciation of the entire Chinese race.[123]

After the panorama closed later in 1856, George West left New York and headed south to Washington, D.C., where a potentially large opportunity awaited him. In the 1850s, the U.S. Capitol had become a major construction site. Since the completion of the old Capitol in 1826, the nation had added sixteen new states, including California in 1850; the resulting shortage of space and strain on facilities had compelled the government to add extensions to the building. Montgomery C. Meigs, a captain of engineers trained at West Point, was overseeing the massive project. A lover of Raphael and Michelangelo, Meigs envisioned that the walls and domes of the new interior would be adorned with paintings and frescoes executed in the style of the Italian Renaissance. He must have viewed the immigration from Italy of Constantino Brumidi, a classically trained painter, as a gift from the heavens.[124]

However, since Brumidi could not by himself handle all of the numerous painting projects needed in the extensions, Meigs needed to recruit other artists. In 1856, he hired George West to paint, from sketches drawn by Brumidi, pictures of important naval engagements on the walls of the Senate Committee on Naval Affairs. Meigs hoped that the accomplished Brumidi might serve as a mentor to West, but he found West to be rather recalcitrant and unreceptive to supervision. Besides deeming himself underpaid, West apparently had an especially high opinion of his own artistic abilities and believed Meigs was slighting him by relegating him to this role of following instructions from Brumidi. A dispute between West and Meigs arose, after which the insulted artist proposed that he destroy the three paintings he had nearly finished. After the paintings were in fact obliterated, Meigs sent other artists to paint new compositions over the last remaining traces of West's work.[125]

As the frustrated George West prepared to leave the Capitol, he must have been perplexed at how rapidly his promising career had soured. He had staked his reputation on a grand panorama that, after receiving mixed reviews, was promptly forgotten amid the unceasing parade of popular attractions in New York. And as for his humanistic construction of China, it too had been lost when Bayard Taylor confused the audience by adulterating it with his anti-Chinese vitriol. Although posterity sometimes rediscovers the brilliance of an artist overlooked in his own day, West and his panorama would never receive a reevaluation. Unlike the permanency of a published book of engravings, the Chinese panorama was an ephemeral work of art; the depiction of China existed on a cheap form of paper that would disintegrate over time. Finally, West's stint as a government-commissioned painter of the U.S. Capitol, though holding out the possibility for a modicum of immortality, had ended tragically when the dispute with Meigs left the artist in the nightmarish position of destroying his own work in anger.

When this destruction was complete, George West walked down the Capitol steps in disgust. He then promptly proceeded to pass into artistic oblivion.

# CONCLUSION

The Cushing Mission was organized to change China in two profound ways. It asked the Chinese to open more ports to American trading vessels and to open their minds to American technology. Yet this American thrust toward China triggered an unexpected reflexive action. Two of Cushing's attachés, John Peters and George West, confronted in China a complex civilization that impressed them with its beauty, ingenuity, and longevity. Instead of changing China, the two men decided instead to allocate their time, talents, and resources to the effort to change popular opinion in the United States. On returning to their homeland, Peters and West, in defiance to the condescension towards China that then suffused the mainstream, created venues that cast the Chinese in a positive light. Yet despite their admirable intentions, both young men ultimately forfeited control of their creations to two giants of antebellum popular culture. And, although P. T. Barnum and Bayard Taylor did not alter the museum and the panorama, dramatically different constructions of China emerged when control over the presentation of these shifted into their hands.

## NOTES

1. Claude M. Fuess, *The Life of Caleb Cushing* (New York: Harcourt, Brace, 1923), 1:414–15.

2. Caleb Cushing Papers (hereafter cited as CCP), box 40, folder 6–10 June 1843, Manuscript Division, Library of Congress.

3. Folder 1–10 July 1843, box 40, CCP. Cushing did return with a large collection of books in Chinese. *Catalogue of the Private Library of the Hon. Caleb Cushing of Newburyport, Massachusetts* (Boston: Sullivan Brothers, auctioneers, 1879).

4. Folder 27–31 May 1843, box 39, CCP.

5. Folder 6–10 July 1843, box 40, CCP.

6. Folder 11–16 July 1843, box 40, CCP.

7. Folder 17–21 July 1843, box 40, CCP.

8. Folder 16–26 June 1843, box 40, CCP. Caleb Cushing's "Delusions of Science" is discussed in chapter 5. *National Magazine and Republican* (March 1839).

9. Folder 11–15 June 1843, box 40, CCP.

10. Folder 11–15 June 1843, box 40, CCP. As a result of the war and subsequent treaties, the Chinese government lifted the ban on Western women in Canton.

11. Folder 17–24 July 1843, box 40, CCP.

12. Folder 9–13 May 1843, box 39, CCP.

13. Ibid.

14. Folder 27–31 May 1843, box 39, CCP.

15. Folder 20–26 May 1843, box 39, CCP.

16. Ibid.

17. The elder Peters alluded to his discussions with the president in letters to Cushing. Folder 1–10 July 1843, box 40, CCP. For Peters's position on the Common Council, see *Appendix, Containing an Account of the Commemoration of the Completion of the Erie Canal, by the Corporation of the City of New York* (New York, 1826), Harry Ransom Center, University of Texas at Austin.

18. Folder 27–31 May 1843, box 39, CCP.

19. Ibid.

20. Brooke Hindle, "The Transfer of Technology and American Industrial Fairs to 1853," in International Congress on the History of Sciences, *Proceedings, XIVth International Congress of the History of Science*, (Tokyo: Science Council of Japan, 1974), 3:146–48.

21. "The Fair of the American Institute," *Merchants' Magazine and Commercial Review* (November 1844), 446.

22. "The Eighteenth Annual Fair of the American Institute," *American Review: A Whig Journal of Politics, Literature, Art, and Science* (November 1845), 542.

23. Folder 1–8 May 1843, box 39, CCP.

24. Folder 1–10 July 1843, box 40, CCP.

25. Folder 24–31 July 1843, box 40, CCP.

26. Folder 15–24 July 1844, box 45, CCP.

27. Fuess, 1:417. Folder 23–30 April 1843, box 39, CCP.

28. Folder October 1843, box 41. CCP.

29. Ibid.

30. Folder 11–16 July 1843, box 40, CCP.

31. Folder October 1843, box 41, CCP.

32. Folder 1–10 April 1844, box 43, CCP.

33. Cushing was in Macao, where Chinese laws did not apply.

34. For Cushing's Manchu lessons, see the notebooks from his study, boxes 166–67, CCP. For Webster's troubles with his teacher, see folder 1–10 April 1844, box 43, CCP.

35. Fuess, 1:438–39.

36. Jonathan D. Spence, *The Search for Modern China* (New York: Norton, 1990), 161.

37. Folder 15–24 July 1844, box 45, CCP.

38. For an account of the incident, see Cushing's correspondence for late June and July 1844, CCP

39. Samuel Wells Williams, "A Journal of the Perry Expedition to Japan," *Transactions of the Asiatic Society of Japan* (1910), 145–48; Peter Booth Wiley, *Yankees in the Land of the Gods: Commodore Perry and the Opening of Japan* (New York: Viking, 1990), 364, 416.

40. James Polachek, *The Inner Opium War* (Cambridge: Harvard University Press, 1992), 137–41.

41. Folder 21–28 February 1845, box 48, CCP.

42. John R. Peters Jr., *Miscellaneous Remarks upon the Government, History, Religions, Literature, Agriculture, Arts, Trades, Manners, and Customs of the Chinese: As Suggested by an Examination of the Articles Comprising the Chinese Museum* (Philadelphia: G. B. Zieber, 1847), 3.

43. Samuel Wells Williams, *The Middle Kingdom: A Survey of the Geography, Government, Education, Social Life, Arts, Religion, &c., of the Chinese Empire and Its Inhabitants* (New York: Wiley and Putnam, 1848), 1:xv–xvi.

44. Folder 21–28 February 1845, box 48, CCP; and *Niles National Register* (7 June 1845).

45. Peters, 3.

46. *Boston Daily Advertiser* (17–18 October, 3–4 November 1845). Webster was still lecturing on the subject two years later and still receiving warm reviews: "All who heard Mr. Webster, can say that they know more now about the 'Flowery Nation' than they ever did before." See the same paper (4 November 1847). Webster was later killed in the Civil War at the Second Battle at Bull Run. Fuess, 1:416.

47. *Niles National Register* (1 November 1845).

48. *Niles National Register* (15 November 1845).

49. Peters, 3.

50. *Boston Daily Advertiser* (13 October 1845).

51. See Peters's catalog.

52. Peters himself may have worried that his collection offered little that was new. As if to minimize Dunn's impact, Peters claimed in the catalog that his predecessor's museum was open only "for a few months" when, in reality, it was open for nearly three years. Peters, 7.

53. *Dollar Newspaper* (31 March 1847, emphasis in original).

54. Peters, 7.

55. *Boston Daily Advertiser* (4 September 1845).

56. Peters, 112–113. Being an engineer, he wrote in a reverent tone about the Great Wall and the Imperial Canal, the two great civil-engineering projects that had dramatically altered the Chinese landscape. Peters, 20–21.

57. Peters, 17.

58. Peters, 44–45.

59. Peters, 48.

60. Spence, 165–93.

61. Peters, 200–1.

62. Ibid.

63. *Dollar Newspaper* (31 March 1847). This reporter visited Peters's museum in Philadelphia.

64. *Boston Daily Advertiser* (13 October 1845). The correct spelling is Marlboro.

65. The article from the *Mercantile Journal* was reprinted in the *Farmers Cabinet* (18 September 1845).

66. *Boston Daily Advertiser* (11 September 1845).

67. *Boston Daily Advertiser* (11 September 1845).

68. *Dollar Newspaper* (31 March 1847).

69. *A Rapid Tour around the World; or, Young Peter's Remarks to His Cousins upon the Different Nations* (Amherst, Mass.: J. S. and C. Adams, 1846), 101.

70. *Boston Daily Advertiser* (6 September 1845).

71. *With Perry in Japan: The Diary of Edward Yorke McCauley*, ed. Allan B. Cole (Princeton: Princeton University Press, 1942), 64, 77. Similarly, an American traveler in Singapore likened the architecture of a Chinese-owned house to what he had seen in "the celebrated Chinese Museums in our own country." "En Route; or, Notes of the Overland Journey to the East," *Southern Literary Messenger* (April 1854), 221.

72. *Dollar Newspaper* (31 March 1847).

73. *Public Ledger* (17 March 1847).

74. *Public Ledger* (10 March 1847).

75. *Public Ledger* (8 and 9 March 1847).

76. *Public Ledger* (17 March 1847).

77. William Elliot Griffis, *China's Story in Myth, Legend, Art, and Annals* (Boston and New York: Houghton Mifflin, 1911), vii. Griffis erroneously referred to the Chinese Museum as belonging to Nathan Dunn, when in fact he visited that of John Peters. Griffis was born in 1843, too late to have visited Dunn's collection in Philadelphia. The mistake would have been an easy one to make since the same building housed both collections.

78. Advertisements in New York papers, unlike those in Boston and Philadelphia, do not mention the two Chinese.

79. *New York Herald* (21 December 1848, 3 January 1849).

80. *New York Herald* (28 October, November 5 1849).

81. Barnum's publication refers to the death of John Peters without providing details as to the cause or the date of death: "About three years ago . . . [Barnum] placed among his world of curiosities the whole of the famous Chinese Collection, secured by the late Mr. Peters at a cost of $70,000, in China, and exhibited by him with so much effect to such crowds of wondering people." Illustrated News (29 October 1853), 57.

82. P. T. Barnum, *Ten Thousand Things on China and the Chinese* (New York: J. S. Redfield, 1850).

83. Philip B. Kunhardt Jr., et al., *P. T. Barnum: America's Greatest Showman* (New York: Knopf, 1995), 196. A. H. Saxon, *P. T. Barnum: The Legend and the Man* (New York: Columbia University Press, 1989), 99.

84. As the result of his worldwide collecting effort, Barnum asserted (with tongue firmly in cheek) that his museum compared favorably to two prestigious institutions in Europe, the Jardin des Plantes, located outside of Paris, and the British Museum in London. Barnum, *Ten Thousand Things*, 196–198.

85. "What do you know about China," Beekman Papers (Folder 2, Box 25). New-York Historical Society.

86. Barnum, *Ten Thousand Things*, 6.

87. Saxon, *P. T. Barnum: the Legend and the Man*, 152–53.

88. Arthur Bonner, *Alas! What Brought Thee Hither? The Chinese in New York, 1800–1950* (Madison: Farleigh Dickinson University Press, 1997), 1; and *New York*

*Herald* (13 April 1848). General Tom Thumb and the Chinese Lady, who was dubbed "the greatest curiosity of the day," both appeared at 315 Broadway. The Chinese Lady would appear in Chinese costume, sing and count in her native language, and eat with chopsticks.

89. Saxon, *P. T. Barnum: the Legend and the Man*, 74–75.

90. *New York Herald* (22 and 26 April 22, 3 and 6 May 1850).

91. In 1837, James Gordon Bennett announced his paper's coverage of New York's social life. *New York Herald* (17 March 1837). Michael Schudson, *Discovering the News: A Social History of American Newspapers* (New York: Basic Books, 1978), 28.

92. *New York Herald* (19 May 1850).

93. *New York Herald* (25 April 1850).

94. *New York Herald* (13 June 1850). Another tactic Barnum used was to create a false sense of urgency by announcing at the start of almost every week that Pwan was commencing her last week prior to her departure for London. She did not leave for months.

95. Barnum was probably pleased to be relieved of the Chinese family. Behind the curtains he was far from complimentary. In one letter, he wrote of the difficulty he had encountered finding an interpreter who could also "manage them properly so that they behave themselves." *Selected Letters of P. T. Barnum*, ed. A. H. Saxon (New York: Columbia University Press, 1983), 99.

96. *Illustrated London News* (10 May 1851). P. T. Barnum, *Struggles and Triumphs; or, Forty Years' Recollections* (Hartford: J. B. Burr, 1870), 366. London Times (26 October 1846).

97. Barnum, *Ten Thousand Things*, 196.

98. Folder 26–31 March 1844, box 42; and folder 1–10 April 1844, box 43. CCP.

99. Oversized box 2, CCP.

100. Folder December 1844, box 47, CCP.

101. B. L. Ball, *Rambles in Eastern Asia, Including China and Manilla* (Boston: James French, 1855), 11.

102. Ball, 104–12. In Canton, Ball noted a sudden interest in a place called "Kalyporny" that was supposedly filled with gold. See 208, 235, 241.

103. Ball, 120–21.

104. Ibid., 249–50.

105. Ibid., 285.

106. In all, the author makes twelve references to Wood's sketching. Ball, 250, 251, 252, 260, 276, 277, 278, 279, 283, 284, 288.

107. Chinese Repository (May 1847), 223–24.

108. Craig Clunas, *Chinese Export Watercolours* (London: Victoria and Albert Museum, 1984), 25–29.

109. Although West could not claim to be the first artist to paint China in a panorama, he was the first to cover the regions that became accessible in the wake of the Opium War. Robert Burford's view of Canton, the only antecedent to West's opus, never toured the United States. Burford's panorama, entitled "Description of a View of Canton, the River Tigress, and the Surrounding Country," opened in

London in 1838. See the New York Public Library for the program published for this panorama.

110. *New York Herald* (1 January 1850).

111. John L. Marsh, "Drama and Spectacle by the Yard: The Panorama in America," *Journal of Popular Culture* 10, no. 3 (winter 1976): 582.

112. Stephan Oettrermann, *The Panorama: History of a Mass Medium*, trans. Deborah Lucas Schneider (New York: Zone Books, 1997), 335.

113. *New York Tribune* (26 January 1856). The panorama probably measured 10 feet in height by 2,000 feet in length.

114. William Heine, *With Perry to Japan: A Memoir*, trans. and ed. Frederic Trautman (Honolulu: University of Hawaii Press, 1990), 10, 19.

115. To assist them in painting such a huge canvas, West and Heine hired two other artists, J. Kyle and J. H. Dallas. *New York Times* (26 January 1856).

116. *New York Times* (26 January 1856).

117. *New York Tribune* (31 January 1856); and *New York Times* (January 28, 1856).

118. *New York Tribune* (1 February 1856).

119. *New York Tribune* (31 January 1856).

120. *New York Tribune* (31 January 1856).

121. *New York Times* (28 January 1856).

122. *New York Tribune* (31 January 1856); *New York Herald* (29 January 1856); and *New York Times* (January 28, 1856).

123. *New York Herald* (1 and 6 February 1856).

124. Barbara Wolanin, *Constantino Brumidi: Artist of the Capitol* (Washington, D.C.: U.S. Government Printing Office, 1998), 35, 38, 52.

125. Wolanin, 63, 68–69; and Benjamin Perley Poore, *Perley's Reminiscences of Sixty Years in the National Metropolis* (Philadelphia: Hubbard Brothers; New York: W. A. Houghton, 1886), 493–95.

## 8. THE UGLY FACE OF CHINA

### Bayard Taylor's Travels in Asia

George West and William Heine could justifiably look to Bayard Taylor to save their panorama from financial doom because, by 1856, he had become a genuine hero and celebrity in the eyes of many Americans. Although Taylor had been well-known before joining Commodore Matthew Galbraith Perry's expedition to Japan in 1853, his reputation as "the Great American Traveler" was now solidified by that illustrious adventure.[1] He was without doubt the most famous person in his day to lecture on and write about China. He was not, however, even close to being the most qualified. That distinction belonged to Samuel Wells Williams, who also accompanied the expedition to Japan because Perry desperately needed someone possessing both knowledge of Asian customs and proficiency in Asian languages. Perry's realization that Williams fit this description perfectly came probably after reading *The Middle Kingdom*.[2]

Despite Williams's exhaustive knowledge, his example demonstrates that the most qualified do not always exercise the greatest influence. In the 1850s, more Americans learned about China from Bayard Taylor, who did not speak the language, spent a mere two months in the country, observed only parts of Shanghai and Canton, and held precious few conversations with Chinese people. In fact, Taylor was not even very particularly interested in the Chinese; he voyaged to Asia in the early 1850s partly to escape the depression that followed a tragic loss. His young wife Mary (née Agnew) had died in 1850, shortly after their marriage. When

Taylor joined the Perry expedition in 1853, he had a heavy heart, and the effects of intense and prolonged mourning were etched on his face. "There were lines that had been traced by suffering," John Sewall, a captain's clerk in the U.S Navy, wrote in his logbook, "and we learned afterward of the death of his young wife."[3]

His countrymen were examining Bayard Taylor's face just as in China and Japan he was examining the appearance of others. Since he lacked the experience, linguistic ability, and scientific expertise to make a thorough ethnographic study of the Chinese, he attempted to compensate by applying a pseudoscientific technique called physiognomy. According to the most basic claim of physiognomy, the human eye, if properly trained, could do more than observe mere surfaces; it could probe the depths and uncover the true moral nature of a person or even of an entire race. Samuel Wells Williams criticized travelers who, using "the physiognomy God has marked upon the features" of the Chinese, made devastating value judgments,[4] and Caleb Cushing had blocked efforts by phrenologists to infect his mission with their theories. But Taylor placed absolute faith in the value of physiognomy as a means to demystify the Chinese. In short, a pseudoscientific system, now discredited, undergirded Taylor's portrayal of China.

Once he had made his assessment, Taylor effectively employed three different media to disseminate his views: a popular travelogue, a fabulously successful lecture tour, and a widely read series of letters published in Horace Greeley's *New York Tribune*. Unlike Kellett, Taylor did not merely endorse popular stereotypes in his presentations. For whereas Captain Kellett sought to maximize profits by reinforcing the public's mocking attitude toward China, Taylor knew that his personal popularity guaranteed high book sales and well-attended lectures regardless of how he constructed China. After all, he, and not China, was the marketable commodity. Freed from market considerations, Taylor could dissent from the popular view and challenge Americans to see China in a new light, as Nathan Dunn, Samuel Wells Williams, John Peters, and George West had done before him. At this point, though, the similarities with his predecessors in China end. In Taylor's opinion, the Chinese demonstrated such moral depravity that they deserved not ridicule but outright condemnation.

## AN INSTANTANEOUS ETHNOGRAPHY

Philadelphia was the center for phrenology at the time of Dunn's museum, and ripples of influence emanated out to nearby towns and villages. In 1839, Dr. Thomas Dunn English of Philadelphia, then experimenting with the pseudoscience, traveled out to Chester County, Pennsylvania, to give a lecture on Franz Joseph Gall and Joseph Spurzheim. The following day, he visited the local jail to inspect the heads of the inmates. Phrenologists commonly performed examinations on criminals because a convincing demonstration that criminals had some proclivity toward unlawful behavior would lend the science some validity. The sheriff, Joseph Taylor, allowed the examinations to take place and then, on a whim, asked English to perform a reading on his fourteen-year-old son. Joseph informed English that he planned to make a farmer out of young Bayard. However, after studying the boy's head, English turned to the elder Taylor and made an augury the latter did not want to hear: The boy would resist any attempt by his father to impose the farmer's life on him because Bayard Taylor was destined to "ramble around the world." Furthermore, the lad also possessed "all the marks of a poet," and a life of physical labor would only stifle his creativity.[5]

Assuming that the above story is not apocryphal, English's head inspection would prove eerily accurate, as Bayard Taylor did become a poet of minor repute and a travel writer with a national following. However, the same prediction could have been made by anyone with access to young Taylor's scrapbook. Indeed, the articles he chose to paste into it offer us a window into the mind of an intellectually curious boy. The pages are filled with clipped newspaper and magazine stories on literature and poetry, voyages to foreign countries, and even phrenology.[6] With this strong yearning to travel and a curiosity for distant climes, Taylor's interests reflected those of his era. Like many of his countrymen, he read with a voracious appetite the accounts of explorations to uncharted parts of the globe. These works fired the young man's imagination and intensified his hunger to see the world, an ambition that rivaled his parallel ambition of becoming a poet.[7]

As Taylor reached adulthood, the presence of these two competing desires created an internal conflict. He made repeated attempts to join the ranks of America's most respected poets but failed to achieve the lofty status enjoyed by Henry Wadsworth Longfellow, William Cullen Bryant, John Greenleaf Whittier. Although some of Taylor's poems were published, these neither generated enough revenue to allow him to support himself nor enjoyed the kind of popularity necessary to lift his name out of obscurity in the literary world. While he waited for his verses to receive the recognition he believed they deserved, Taylor turned to the second of his passions, travel, in order to earn a livelihood.

After returning from a two-year walking tour through Europe in 1846, Taylor described his experiences in *Views A-Foot*, a travelogue that transformed him into a celebrity almost overnight. In the ensuing years, a trip to the American West during the Gold Rush and the subsequent publication of *Eldorado* solidified his reputation as America's great travel writer. As the ninth edition of *Views*

*A-Foot* went to the printers, Taylor expressed his astonishment at the celebrity status he had achieved in such a short time: "I am amazed—thunderstruck, almost—at the extent to which I am known and appreciated all through the United States."[8]

But Taylor soon grew uneasy with his newfound fame. As a travel writer, he found himself occupying an undesirable middle ground between the two poles, both of them more noble, of poetry and exploration. His vocation shared some of the attributes of each, but in Taylor's view it did not have the intrinsic worth of either. One needed literary talent to succeed in travel writing as well as in poetry, but Taylor revered the latter and denigrated the former as a profane waste of his artistic ability. For this reason, he looked on his loyal readers with ambivalence, appreciating their fanatical embrasure of his travelogues while resenting their cool indifference to his poetical genius. "I am known to the public not as a poet, the only title I covet, but as one who succeeded in seeing Europe with little money," Taylor confided in a friend. "Now this is truly humiliating. It acts as a sting or spur which touches my pride."[9]

If travel writing paled in comparison to the "glorious art" of poetry, it fared even worse when measured against exploration. Both the travel writer and the explorer voyaged great distances, endured harsh climes, and lived amongst foreign peoples, but only the explorer added to world knowledge in a significant way. As a mid-nineteenth-century travel writer, Taylor lived in the long shadow cast by such contemporaries as Elisha Kent Kane, the intrepid leader of two Arctic expeditions in the 1850s, who possessed the training and scientific expertise Taylor lacked.

To guide his ships to their destination, Kane knew how to use the stars in conjunction with the most sophisticated navigational instruments of his age. Having received his M.D., Kane served as the surgeon for Caleb Cushing's mission to China in 1843. And in all subsequent voyages launched under his leadership, his men could depend on him to treat their injuries and illnesses. Kane also had more than a rudimentary knowledge of chemical compounds. On one occasion, he performed the daring feat of lowering himself into the Taal Volcano in the Philippines to study its sulfurous compounds. And in the Arctic region he studied wind patterns, water currents, and magnetic fields and once even spent twelve consecutive hours with his telescope in temperatures hovering at _43 degrees Fahrenheit to observe the occultation of Saturn and Mars. With some training as a naturalist, Kane could classify previously unknown forms of plant and animal life and collect specimens for botanists and zoologists back home. Finally, he also had expertise as a surveyor, which meant he could easily map huge swaths of terrestrial space with mathematical precision.[10]

Bayard Taylor, in contrast, was quite limited. He did not know how to navigate a sailing vessel, treat anything other than a minor injury, or convert any of the natural phenomena he observed into useful knowledge. He edited the *Cyclopædia of Modern Travel: A Record of Adventure, Exploration, and Discovery, for the Past Fifty Years* (1856), which was essentially the worshipful Taylor's paean to the modern explorers. In the preface, he explained how the modern explorer, unlike his predecessor, had sophisticated instruments and scientific knowledge at his disposal: "He tests every step of the way by the sure light of science. . . . The pencil, the compass, the barometer, and the sextant accompany him; geology, botany, and ethnology are his aids."[11] Yet being very self-aware, Taylor knew that he possessed none of the expertise that he ascribed to these men. He was a travel writer, a decidedly lower form of adventurer, who, in status, prestige, glory, and heroism, occupied a position on the hierarchy well beneath that of the great scientific explorer. As such, he could do little more than arrive at a particular destination and describe what he saw. "I have relapsed into a traveler, an adventurer," he wrote to a friend from China, "seeking the heroic in actual life, yet without attaining it."[12]

Taylor's inferiority complex came to the foreground in 1856, two years after returning from China and Japan, when he traveled to Germany and met with the man to whom he had dedicated the *Cyclopædia*—the colossus of exploration himself, Alexander von Humboldt. Having retired from active life, Humboldt was engaged in writing the massive work that was to represent the culmination of his storied career. In *Cosmos*, Humboldt rather audaciously attempted the grandiose undertaking of explaining "the whole of the physical aspect of the universe in one work . . . from the nature of the nebula [of the stars] down to the geography of the mosses clinging to a granite rocks."[13] According to Taylor, nothing was beyond Humboldt's abilities. "Alexander von Humboldt is the world's greatest living man," Taylor wrote, "a throned monarch in the world of science."[14]

Face to face for the first time with the man he lionized above all others, Taylor gave into his emotions: "I had approached him with a natural feeling of reverence, but in five minutes I found that I loved him." The two quickly established an easy rapport in German, a language Taylor was fluent in,[15] and the American travel writer soon felt comfortable enough to confess his vexing concern that his "lack of severe and specific training" diminished his contribution to knowledge. Humboldt, recognizing Taylor's acute self-doubt, quite generously responded by refusing to concur. "But you paint the world as we explorers of science cannot," Humboldt assured Taylor. "Do not undervalue what you have done. It is a real service; and the unscientific traveler who knows the use of his eyes observes for us always without being aware of it." According to Humboldt, the nonscientific observer complemented the scientific work of the explorer; by using his eyes, the travel writer could add to humankind's understanding of the world in a way the explorer could not. Heartened by this vote of confidence, Taylor began to see his role in a new light. He was engaged in the noble work of constructing a "human cosmos"—a description and explication of the many types of people that inhabited the globe.[16] Even with this newfound respect for travel writing, however, Taylor would still always feel unworthy when, on the lecture circuit, his hosts introduced him as "the American Humboldt."[17]

This exchange with Humboldt is worth mentioning because it reveals a Taylor who doubted the worth of his descriptions and insights as they lacked a proper foundation in science. Perhaps to compensate for this shortcoming and to confer on his work an aura of scientific rigor, he utilized another "science," the mastery of which did not require years of training. Taylor learned the art of physiognomy, the lesser-known parent science of the more popular phrenology. In fact, he even conducted a quick physiognomical study of Humboldt's face, unbeknown to the retired explorer.[18]

Physiognomy had existed in some form for centuries, but the unique brand Taylor practiced had been developed by Johann Caspar Lavater (1741–1801) of Zurich. Lavater argueed that a perfect unity existed between the body, mind, and soul and that therefore one could ascertain the character or moral worth of an individual merely by studying the face and body. Physiognomy and phrenology shared the same assumption that intellectual and spiritual qualities were manifest in the corporeal form. Yet physiognomy did more than just predate phrenology. Phrenology would not have arisen without it. It was Lavater's theories that first inspired Franz Joseph Gall to investigate the relationship between behavior and the contours of the human head.[19]

Although Taylor never touched a single scalp in China or Japan, he performed an equivalent sort of examination by studying the skeletal and facial structures of the Chinese and Japanese people he encountered, and he used his findings to read deeply into their moral character. Physiognomy fit Taylor's needs because it lent his untrained observations some of the prestige of science, a form of validity he desperately craved. Lavater had always insisted that physiognomy was a legitimate science, arguing that, whenever "truth or knowledge is explained by fixed principles, it becomes scientific."[20] Physiognomy appealed to Taylor also because it brought his beloved art into his ethnographic study. He could use the ancient sculptures of Greece and Rome—they represented physiognomical perfection in their "Harmony" and "Proportion"—as the standard against which all human forms were to be measured.[21]

Along with the concepts of harmony and proportion, that of symmetry assumed importance in the lexicon of physiognomy and related pseudosciences. In an article on phrenology and physiognomy pasted into Taylor's childhood scrapbook, "symmetrical features" were described as the most desirable in the human form.[22] The major works of Lavater employed the term *symmetry*, as did *The Pocket Lavater*, a small handbook published after his death, that offered the basic principles in a concise format.[23] (Caleb Cushing, in denouncing physiognomy, claimed that its practitioners did little more than look for a "symmetry of countenance" in making rash judgments of people.[24]) Samuel George Morton observed in his *Crania Americana* (1839) that many tribes of North and South America were "remarkable for their perfect symmetry."[25] Taylor thought highly enough of Morton's work that he referred to the doctor's racial theories in his lectures.[26] When Taylor studied the faces and physiques of the Chinese and Japanese, he was looking for the symmetry described in these works.

Taylor's awareness of such theories is in no way surprising. In his day, American culture was steeped in pseudosciences. Editions of Lavater's seminal works were still readily available in bookstores. Other manuals or handbooks were also on the market, such as J. W. Redfield's *Outline of a New System of Physiognomy*, which simplified Lavater's voluminous teachings and illustrated their practical applications.[27] In fact, Lavater was so well known that in 1850, five decades after his death, P. T. Barnum could refer to him in a news item about the Chinese Belle, Pwan Ye Koo, that he penned for the *Herald*

> It is a curious philosophy, that of Lavatar [sic], which deduces the intellectual character of the human being from the configuration and expression of the human face. According to this philosophy, the Chinese Beauty would rank very high in the scale of mental energy, for her facial angle is remarkable and her countenance a singular admixture of the better features of the Caucasian and the native American races. Have you been to the Chinese Museum yet?[28]

That Barnum invoked Lavater in his advertisement for Pwan Ye Koo suggests he believed the paper's readers would be familiar with the name.

Ironically, one man who would not have approved of Taylor's use of physiognomy was America's most visible advocate of phrenology, Orson Fowler. Fowler entertained deep reservations about the reliability of physiognomy and periodically used the pages of his *American Phrenological Journal* to admonish his readers. Mainly, the mutability of the human face is what gave Fowler cause for concern. Whereas phrenology required its practitioners to make careful measurements of the human skull, which was fixed and unchanging, physiognomy depended on a hasty reading of the face, which underwent countless transfigurations in the course of a single day. "When one feels emotion," Fowler argued, "the muscles of the face change one's countenance depending on whether one feels at that moment love, fear, anger, suspicion, or hope." The skull, being immune to the "metamorphoses" that plagued the face, offered a "true mental index." Although Fowler did not reject physiognomy entirely, he believed it could be used responsibly only in tandem with phrenology, never in lieu of it.[29]

And so, when Taylor headed to the Far East in 1851, he carried in his mental toolkit a set of theories, a system for understanding human nature, that even a quack scientist regarded with deep suspicion. While physiognomy's merits were suspect, it clearly empowered those who believed in it. It allowed Taylor to practice a kind of instantaneous ethnography, in which he could ascertain with a mere glance the chief moral and intellectual traits of a given race. Confident in his methods, he set out to add the Chinese and the Japanese to the list of races in his grand "human cosmos." In his mind, he would superimpose his rigid geometry over their eyes, noses, lips, and cheekbones and see how these compared against the perfect aesthetic forms from his beloved world of art.

# TOURING CHINA DURING THE TAIPING REBELLION

As China opened four additional ports to commerce, merchants seeking new markets would look with high optimism on their chances of making inroads into a previously impenetrable society, as would missionaries intent on saving souls. The Opium War and the Cushing Mission had aroused America's interest in China, and now the conclusion of the War with Mexico in 1848 intensified it. After the annexation of a vast territory that included much of the Pacific coast, Americans fixed their collective gaze on Asia. With the full support of the federal government, business interests conceived of a steamship line that would connect San Francisco to Shanghai. According to preliminary calculations, a consignment of goods traveling from New York to Shanghai via Panama would arrive in forty-five days, three weeks faster than a parcel leaving London and bound for the same destination. With the establishment of such a line, the United States could control a greater portion of the China trade and thereby gain an advantage over its chief European rival in the high stakes of global commerce.

However, the success of the hypothetical enterprise depended on the cooperation of Japan, for two reasons. First, the proposed route passed right through the Japanese Isles, a course that was problematic, as Japan had been inhospitable to the surviving sailors of wrecked American whaling vessels. Second, the boilers of steamships required tremendous amounts of fuel for the transpacific journey, and Japan was believed to possess large deposits of coal. If Japan could be brought out of its self-imposed isolation and could be convinced to supply coal to steamships in transit, then the United States could become the preeminent trading power in the Pacific. With this ambition providing the impetus, the federal government appointed Commodore Matthew Perry to lead an expedition to Japan. While Perry's stated purpose was to secure better treatment for luckless American sailors marooned on Japan and to establish a coaling station, the prospect of greater intercourse with a newly opened China loomed not far behind the mission.[30]

After listening to the U.S. government's arguments in favor of the Perry expedition, Samuel Wells Williams promptly dismissed them. Assistance for marooned sailors and coaling stations provided the "ostensible reasons for this great outlay," but something larger lurked behind the expedition. And the skeptical Williams had a theory as to exactly what the true impetus was: "The real reasons are glorification of the Yankee nation &food for praising ourselves." At mid-century, America's self-confidence was surging, and this pride was now manifesting itself in foreign policy, with this audacious move of sending a "powerful squadron" to open Japan. Despite his criticism, Williams did of course agree to join the expedition, and we should not be surprised to learn his reason. God meant to use the "fear of force" inspired by Perry to jolt Japan out of self-imposed isolation; then and only could the Bible reach the Japanese people. As in the case of the Opium War, Williams disapproved of a government's action on the plane of human affairs, but on the all-important heavenly plane he discerned a divine plan: "There lies God's purposes of making known the Gospel to all nations." Perry's squadron constituted a second battering ram of God.[31]

The importance of the Perry expedition was not lost on Horace Greeley, editor of the *New York Tribune*. While Bayard Taylor was in Constantinople, Greeley sent him a communication stating that he, Taylor, was to sail for Hong Kong to join Commodore Perry's expedition. Although Perry had not offered any overt indication of his willingness to accept a civilian like Taylor, Greeley had received "indirect assurance" that he would be taken on.[32] Sure enough, Perry eventually did agree to make Taylor a temporary officer with a modest rank.[33] P. T. Barnum, who was always sensitive to the public's desires, also recognized the nation's renewed interest in Asia. Having recently purchased John Peters's Chinese collection, he now predicted that, with the launching of the Perry expedition, Japan was certain to attract the same national attention as did China. And so when Barnum heard of the dramatic change in Taylor's itinerary, he excitedly wrote to Taylor to request "drawings &sketches" (for his publication the *Illustrated News*) and oriental curiosities (for the American Museum).[34]

Taylor traveled first by steamer to Singapore, where he immediately came into contact with a Chinese settlement.

This was my first sight of a large Chinese community, and the impression it left was not agreeable. Their dull faces, without expression . . . and their half-naked, unsymmetrical bodies, more like figures of yellow clay than warm flesh and blood, filled me with an unconquerable aversion. The scowling Malay, with his dark, fiery eye, and spare but sinewy form, was ennobled by comparison, and I turned to look upon him with a great sense of relief.[35]

Taylor detested the Chinese at first sight. But more interesting than the disgust is the system of belief working behind it: the principles of physiognomy. The pseudoscience taught that the inner worth of a race manifested itself in the body, and so Taylor believed that he could focus entirely on the physicality of the Chinese and that he did not need to investigate any further into their actions, customs, or productions.[36]

After Singapore, Taylor headed to Hong Kong, where he briefly disembarked before boarding the steam-powered frigate the *Susquehanna*, bound for Macao. Although he had by this time endured two years of difficult travel, he continued to exude strength and confidence in the company of others. "His stalwart manhood impressed us," wrote John Sewall, a clerk in the U.S. Navy, after seeing the travel writer for the first time.[37] After Macao, Taylor planned to proceed next to Canton, where he would tour the famous Chinese port while awaiting the arrival of Commodore Perry. However, he revised this itinerary after the U.S. commissioner to China, Humphrey Marshall, made him the tantalizing offer to head further north. This was a rather bold proposition, as China in 1853 was in a state of tremendous upheaval caused by the Taiping Rebellion. After failing the imperial exams four times, Hong Xiuquan used the Christian theology he had read in a missionary tract to interpret his own fantastic dreams. Believing himself to be the son of God and the brother of Jesus Christ, Hong fomented in southern China a movement that, by 1853, had grown to such proportions that it posed a legitimate threat to the Qing government. Marshall decided to ascertain the true intentions of the Taipings with regard to foreigners so as to determine whether any precautions needed to be taken to ensure the protection of American interests.[38]

Marshall also enlisted Peter Parker, the medical missionary, along with several others, in addition to Taylor, for a diplomatic mission to the seat of war further north. On arriving in Shanghai on the *Susquehanna*, they received the uncertain intelligence that the Taipings had successfully captured the city of Nanjing and proclaimed it their capital. Marshall, deciding to establish contact with the Taipings in order to declare the official neutrality of the United States, ordered that the *Susquehanna* proceed up the Yangtze River to Nanjing. Unfortunately, the mission sputtered before it could get very far when the heavy steamship ran aground on a shoal. Taylor returned to Shanghai, where he found he had nothing to do except wait for Commodore Perry to reach China.[39]

Yet Taylor craved material for a future travelogue, and so, when presented with this downtime, he set out to observe Chinese life both in Shanghai and in the surrounding countryside. Although he seldom communicated with the Chinese, his desire to see the land and its people made some form of interaction inevitable. For example, during his jaunts through rural villages, he demonstrated a strange propensity to burst into Chinese homes completely unannounced. These intrusions, however, produced little in the way of new ethnographic material, for a reason he explained. "It is not advisable to be too curious, or to spend much time in inspecting Chinese dwellings, on account of their abundant vitality," he explained. "For the same reason, many features of domestic life among the lower classes must be passed over in silence." One could interpret "abundant vitality" in different ways, but most likely Taylor barged in on Chinese couples during moments of intimacy before he quietly withdrew himself from the scene.[40]

Aware of the poverty of the countryside, he often used his money to provoke amusing reactions among the Chinese. Sometimes, these activities were harmless and good-natured. For instance, he liked to purchase pastries and candy and distribute them to children. Other times, however, Taylor patronized the Chinese with games. In one instance, he climbed to the top floor of a pagoda in order to achieve a lofty vantage point from which he could view the surrounding landscape. When a crowd of beggars congregated below, he realized the situation offered a rare opportunity for entertainment. He dropped coins over the ledge and then promptly stepped backward, rendering himself invisible to the throng below. After several repetitions of these "miraculous showers," his curiosity got the better of him, and he expressed "a desire to see the beggars scramble." The beggars, identifying their mysterious benefactor for the first time, cried and waved their arms "greedily," and Taylor "enjoyed the feeling of a monarch, who scatters gold largesse."[41]

In seeing what the poor would do for money, Taylor found amusement, but the physical form of the Chinese is what continued to interest him most. In order to observe the Chinese body unclothed, Taylor on one occasion stole into a public bath, where nude bathing was common, and became something of a voyeur: He lurked in the darkness and inspected the bathers from a distance. Since it was late in the day, the water had become stale and fetid and attracted mostly people who belonged "to the lower classes." He tried holding his breath to avoid inhaling the foul air but, when the "reeking den" became more than he could bear, he darted out of the bath and into a changing room. As he observed the unclothed Chinese bodies, Taylor gathered the visual evidence required for the following physiognomical assessment:

Among the bathers in the outer room there are several strong, muscular figures, but a total want of that elegant symmetry which distinguishes the Caucasian and Shemitic races. They are broad shouldered and deep-chested, but the hips and loins are clumsily moulded, and the legs have a coarse, clubby character. We should never expect to see such figures the fine, free attitudes of ancient sculpture. But here, as everywhere, the body is the expression of the spiritual nature. There is no sense of what we understand by Art—Grace, Harmony, Proportion—in the Chinese nature, and therefore we look in vain for any physical expression of it.

The Chinese body did not hold up well against his standards, and Taylor left the bathhouse wondering whether "it is worth satisfying one's curiosity at the expense of so much annoyance and disgust."[42]

Taylor's account of the public bath provides us with the clearest articulation of his faith in the most essential tenet of physiognomy—that "the body is the expression of the spiritual nature." Pushing his theory even further, Taylor argued that if the spirit was flawed, as the Chinese spirit clearly was in his opinion, an asymmetrical physique would not stand alone as the only indicator. The flaw would corrupt essentially anything that the Chinese created, such as music, language, and architecture. For this reason Taylor expected to find all aspects of Chinese culture contaminated, and, true to this prediction, he observed precisely that. Chinese music evinced not "harmony" but "dreadful discord"; the language was "composed of nasals and consonants," and "the only symmetrical things in Chinese architecture" were pagodas, which, he asserted, probably should be credited to India, not China. So revolted was Taylor by what he saw that he felt comfortable issuing a blanket statement that could be applied to anything the Chinese made: "The wider its divergence from its original beauty or symmetry, the greater is their delight."[43]

In Taylor's view, the depravity of the Chinese even vitiated the rural landscapes in which they lived and worked. Before Taylor, the American imagination was wont to associate the Chinese landscape with charming pastoral vistas filled with hills and streams, cottages and pagodas, tea and rice fields, and picturesque farmers and fishermen. Taylor proceeded to shatter this image: "Even in the country, which now rejoices in the opening of spring, all the freshness of the season is destroyed by the rank ammoniated odors arising from the pits of noisome manure, sunk in the fields." "There is nothing striking or picturesque in the scenery of this part of China," Taylor continued, as the "country is a dead level, watered with sluggish creeks, and intersected with ditches and canals." Although the small towns and hamlets "have a pleasant rural aspect" when viewed from afar, they are "most disgusting when you draw near." The Chinese landscape that Taylor observed would never adorn blue-and-white porcelain.[44]

For his portrayal of the city, Taylor unleashed more jets of vitriol. He saw Shanghai just prior to the buildup of foreign concessions later in the 1850s; thus, it was still very much a Chinese city. Before providing the details of his promenade through the streets of Shanghai, Taylor admonished his readers to demonstrate "patience" in enduring the "disgusting annoyance" and "disagreeable features" of the Chinese. While he might like to protect them from the grim reality of Chinese life, as a "conscientious traveller" he was obliged to report what he saw.[45] In describing a group of people he dubbed "Chinese Gypsies," Taylor claimed that their "degradation is almost without parallel, and I doubt if there be any thing in human nature more loathsome than their appearance." Looking into their dens, he spied "figures so frightfully repulsive and disgusting, that we move away repenting that we have disturbed this nest of human vermin." Taylor described in revolting detail the unsanitary conditions of life in the city streets. "Porters, carrying buckets of offal, brush past us," he wrote, "and the clothes and persons of the unwashed laborers and beggars distil a reeking compound of still more disagreeable exhalations." As for the beggars, Taylor remarked that he would "almost as willingly touch a man smitten with leprosy, or one dying of the plague." To Taylor, Shanghai lacked any redeeming qualities and was remarkable only for its "horrid foulness." "I never go within its walls but with a shudder," he reported, "and the taint of its contaminating atmosphere seems to hang about me like a garment long after I have left them."[46]

Shocked by the filth and poverty of the Chinese and convinced that their physiognomies signified an interior degradation, Taylor delivered his devastating verdict: "It is my deliberate opinion that the Chinese are, morally, the most debased people on the face of the earth." He claimed that beneath the surface he had found "deeps on deeps of depravity so shocking and horrible, that their character cannot even be hinted." These "dark shadows" were sufficient "to inspire me with a powerful aversion to the Chinese race."[47]

As devastating as this assessment was, Taylor went yet further, applying it to Chinese immigration to the United States, a domestic issue there that was gathering increasing importance as the century progressed. In the 1850s, the arrival of Chinese laborers and gold miners out in the American West was just beginning to receive nationwide attention. The Chinese populations in California still amounted to only several thousand, but Taylor was ready to sound a clarion call to action. "Their touch is pollution," he said, and "justice to our own race demands that they should not be allowed to settle on our soil." In a fashion that must have been upsetting both to the immigrants themselves and to the Western business interests that coveted Chinese labor, Taylor at an early stage gave prominent voice to what would soon become a familiar argument for an exclusionary immigration policy.[48]

How can we account for his extreme view? In addition to physiognomy, the crises afflicting Shanghai in the 1850s merit attention. No doubt, Taylor did observe much poverty and squalor in and around the city. His error, though, lay in his insistence on imputing China's problems to innate racial characteristics while ignoring the unique historical circumstances in which he found himself—China was in the throes of a massive internal rebellion. While he did not witness any of the actual carnage wrought by the rebellion, as Shanghai was not attacked by the rebel armies during his brief stay, the city was still far from being immune to strife and turmoil. Along with the Taiping Rebellion that raged to the south and to the west, a related armed uprising started by the local Small-Sword Society also destabilized areas near Shanghai. As a travel writer, Taylor might have observed the devastating impact of these revolts on the people and landscape and incorporated it into his writings.

Before the onset of war, the Yangtze Valley region had been noted for the vibrant trade that flourished along its river ways. The Taiping Rebellion now disrupted commerce and caused mass unemployment.[49] Many area residents fled their farms and villages to avoid either the war or the ruthless looting practiced by armies on the move.[50] As a result, Shanghai experienced a massive influx of refugees, men and women seeking work and shelter until the various armed struggles abated. When these fugitives and castaways descended on the city, they collided with an economy and a physical infrastructure that were utterly incapable of absorbing their numbers. And so with the sudden surge in population came the inevitable concomitants: crowding, unemployment, vagrancy, extreme poverty, and disease.[51] In sum, many of the horrible scenes of filth and poverty witnessed by Taylor flowed not out of the racial character of the Chinese, as he believed, but rather out of the massive dislocation of a nation in a state of upheaval.

While enduring the chaos caused by the Taiping Rebellion, the region was also starting to feel the ill effects of the Opium War when Taylor visited. Between 1843 and 1857, the amount of opium streaming into the Shanghai area quadrupled.[52] Economically, opium traders were slowly weakening China's markets by siphoning off the nation's stores of silver. Socially, the opium trade was placing undue stress on families and communities, as individuals who had once been productive members of society were now reduced to illness and poverty through their addiction. En route to Japan, Taylor received a graphic lesson of the drug's ill effects when he watched Samuel Wells Williams's Chinese teacher, "Old Sieh," deteriorate and die:

> The latter fell a victim to the practice of smoking opium. He attempted to give it up. . . . [N]o medicines produced any effect, and he sank into a state of nervelessness and emaciation shocking to witness. His body was reduced to a skeleton, and all his

nervous energy so completely destroyed, that for a week before his death every fibre in his frame was in a state of constant agitation. His face was a ghastly yellow, the cheeks sunken upon the bones, and the eyes wild and glassy with a semi-madness which fell upon him. His whole aspect reminded me of one of those frightful heads of wax, in the museum of Florence, representing the effects of the plague.[53]

Despite witnessing Old Sieh's ghastly demise, Taylor insisted on knowing the drug through "personal experience." On arriving in Canton after the expedition to Japan, Taylor elected "to make a trial of the practice" by smoking nine pipes of opium in the home of an addict. He seems to have enjoyed the experience immensely. While under the influence of the drug, he could not control his laughter and delighted in gazing at the "brilliant colors" that "floated before my eyes," "sometimes converging into spots like the eyes in a peacock's tail, but often melting into and through each other, like the hues of changeable silk."[54]

But besides smoking opium, Taylor engaged in few other activities in Canton. Most visitors arrived in the city brimming with curiosity, but Taylor asserted that sightseeing in Canton had "very little to offer the traveller." In truth, he had had enough of the "living purgatory," as he called China.[55] "I was so thoroughly surfeited with China," he wrote, "that I made no effort to see more than the most prominent objects."[56] On departing on September 9, 1853, he wrote what was now obvious to his readers: "The reader may have conjectured that I am not partial to China, but this much I must admit: it is the very best country in the world—to leave."[57]

## "I AM CARRIED FROM PLACE TO PLACE IN TRIUMPH"

When Bayard Taylor arrived in New York on December 20, 1853, he found to his astonishment that in his absence his reputation had grown to colossal proportions. By traveling to the places others could only dream of seeing, he had become the envy of a nation. Perceptive to the desires of his readership, Orson Fowler decided to perform a phrenological examination of the conquering hero and feature his findings in an issue of the *American Phrenological Journal*. Not surprisingly, the resulting article bordered on hagiography, as Fowler found that his subject demonstrated all the attributes of the intrepid adventurer: He "courts opposition," "loves excitement and adventure," "knows nothing of fear," is "stimulated to new exertions by danger and difficulties," and is "noted for his daring and love of adventure."[58]

Taylor found his sudden fame perplexing. How was it that he had become a national celebrity when *India, China, and Japan,* the travelogue that would contain his account of the trip, would not be available in bookstores for more than a year? He soon discovered that the answer was newspapers. During the two years and four months he had been out of the country, he had mailed to the *New York Tribune* dozens of letters in which he described his experiences, and on reaching the United States those letters would take on a life of their own. Not only would smaller papers across the country lift his letters from the *Tribune* and reprint them,[59] but the *Tribune* itself enjoyed a nationwide circulation. As a result, people across the country had followed his peregrinations closely. In Milwaukee, Taylor was flabbergasted to learn that almost everyone there subscribed to the *Tribune* and had "read every one of my letters conscientiously." "I had no idea before," he confided in his mother, "that I was half so well known."[60] And in Newark, Ohio, a man informed him that he once "rode several miles through inclement weather in order to borrow a copy of the *Tribune* so his sick wife could be cheered by Taylor's letter."[61]

But as Taylor soon discovered, these people were not content just to read about his exploits in the newspapers; they wanted to meet the man himself. Not long after his return from Asia, Taylor was besieged by invitations from all over the country to come and deliver a lecture.[62] In need of money, he obliged his fans and launched a tour of the country in the spring of 1854. Over the course of more than two years, he traveled about four thousand miles and delivered 285 lectures, receiving a payment of fifty dollars for each engagement.[63] He lectured in the cities and towns of Pennsylvania, upstate New York, Ohio, Michigan, Indiana, Illinois, Wisconsin, and even Canada. And of course, toward the end of the tour, he spoke in Manhattan before crowds simultaneously watching the grand panorama of George West and William Heine.

In letters to friends and family members, Taylor offered a glimpse of his life on the lecture circuit. Every night he appeared before "crammed houses"[64] filled with legions of "worshippers."[65] Most cities treated him like royalty: "I am carried from place to place in triumph, have the best rooms at hotels," and receive "the most obsequious attention." All the adulation took him by surprise and even overwhelmed him. "The people are infatuated," he wrote, "and I can't understand why."[66] But Taylor did come to understand the motivation of his audiences quite well, writing that "most of them admire me hugely for having gotten over so much ground."[67] Indeed, people who flocked to his lectures were also animated by a yearning to explore the world, the same yearning that he was able to convert into a career. Although responsibilities at home or at work prevented them from visiting foreign lands, they could enjoy the thrill of travel vicariously through Taylor's books, letters, and lectures. He could take them to China and Japan for an evening, and they loved him for it. "Curiosity is alive," he reported in upstate New York, "to see 'The Great American Traveler.' "[68]

Wherever Taylor went the adoring crowds followed. For an engagement in Penn Yan, New York, Taylor learned of a special train coming down from Canandaigua, "solely on my account!"[69] The town of Rockford, Illinois, regaled Taylor with a serenade.[70] Indiana State College in New Albany made Taylor an honorary professor so that he could lecture in a hall reserved exclusively for faculty.[71] To flatter the traveling celebrity, audience members often told him how far they had traveled to hear him speak; distances of twenty miles or more were not uncommon,[72] and one group of men endured a seventy-mile trek, even though they had already heard Taylor lecture at a previous engagement.[73] Farmers out in rural areas often covered long distances to reach the venue, and so they did not want to leave without meeting the Great American Traveler and introducing him to their wives. Unfortunately, these poor ladies were usually "so overcome with awe" in Taylor's presence that, as he put it, "they cannot say a word."[74]

Of all of Taylor's admirers, women were often the most fanatical. When he took the stage, he observed "young ladies stretching their necks" and crying, "There he is, that's him!" On catching a glimpse of the intrepid traveler, many began to swoon and had to be carried out of the hall.[75] Other women employed aggressive tactics to attract his attention. One mysterious admirer followed him on the train as he traveled from city to city; another bought up all the tickets for the entire front row and then sat there all alone in an otherwise packed house and distracted him with seductive stares as he delivered his lecture.[76] Now that several years had passed since his wife's death, Taylor sometimes appreciated the flirtations of young women. But many women clearly repulsed him, such as the one "whose face was like a raw beefsteak, with two pickled onions upon it." That was the only physiognomical attention her visage would receive.[77]

Showered by so much adulation, Taylor griped about his "dismal popularity"[78] and referred to the audiences as "natives."[79] He found "ambitious young gentlemen" excessively tiresome when they attempted to show off their own knowledge by asking astute questions.[80] He grew aggravated by "hearing the same remarks twenty times a day" and by answering "questions that have become hideous by endless repetition!" He would sometimes "snap" at his audience out of frustration, but these outbursts provided him with little satisfaction because the people believed they were "my way of talking" and refused to take offense.[81] Most of all, he resented that his fans prized only his travel writing and ignored his beloved poetry: "I find that this business of travelling has entirely swamped and overwhelmed my poetical reputation."[82] To Taylor's complaints about the irritating people he added more about the poor food, inclement weather, head colds, and extreme fatigue. He had found a strenuous journey through Asia to be invigorating, but the trains and hotels of the American Midwest wore him out: "It is Civilization which kills, and Barbarism which cures me."[83]

## JAPAN AND CHINA COMPARED

As for the content of the lecture, Taylor gave greater emphasis to Japan. In 1854, Americans eagerly sought information on a nation that, until the Perry expedition, had effectively sealed itself off from the world. And for the parts that covered the expedition, Taylor had to rely completely on his memory, since the U.S. Navy confiscated his journal at the conclusion of the expedition and Taylor never recovered it.[84]

Before his arrival in Japan, Taylor predicted that he would detest the Japanese as he did the Chinese, but the Japanese ended up surprising him.[85] While ethnologists tended to lump the Chinese and Japanese together as "Mongolian," Taylor perceived large differences separating the two Asian peoples. In fact, he was so fascinated by his discovery that he decided to make his contrast between them the centerpiece of the lecture.[86] "Contrary to the common opinion," he informed his audience, "there are many radical differences between them [the Japanese] and the Chinese, and a running comparison of the two may not be uninteresting." Of course, for Taylor the chief differences lay in the faces and bodies of the people, and so he couched his remarks in the lexicon of physiognomy, which served to lend his lectures a scientific patina.

After establishing his most basic principle, that the "body . . . is always an expression of the spiritual nature," Taylor faulted the Chinese body for its "total want of that elegant symmetry which distinguishes the Caucasians." That the physiques were "coarse and ungraceful," never approaching "ancient sculpture," proved that the "Chinese nature" was also flawed.[87] Taylor also noted that he was not alone in holding this view, as the Japanese also looked down on the Chinese as inferior. When a contingent of Japanese officials and interpreters boarded the *Susquehanna* and saw the twenty Chinese employed by Perry, they looked at the deckhands "with a face expression of great contempt and disgust" and inquired, "Is it possible that you have Chinese among your men?" Fearing that the mere presence of Chinese would prompt the Japanese to lose respect for the mission, A. L. C. Portman, a Dutch interpreter, responded that the Chinese were merely the servants of the sailors, and the Japanese visitors were apparently satisfied by his hasty reply.

Besides demonstrating that the Japanese held the Chinese in low regard, this anecdote reminds us that Taylor did not observe all classes of people in Japan as he did in China. Ostensibly he based much of his positive assessment of the Japanese on the physiognomies of the people, but other circumstances almost certainly colored his findings. In China, Taylor had witnessed a people wracked by war and opium. Yet instead of understanding the extraordinary nature of the times, he attributed the problems he observed to an inherent racial depravity that manifested itself in the physical form of the people. But whereas Taylor could wander about Shanghai and its environs freely to see the legions of refugees and beggars, in Japan he found his mobility severely circumscribed.

Indeed, the Japanese government exerted tremendous control over his experience, deciding where he could go and whom he could meet. Consequently, Taylor met only with an impressive façade composed of the lavishly dressed members of the nobility, the dignified government officials in their scholarly attire, and the young soldiers with their chiseled bodies and handsome uniforms. Hidden from his view were the beggars, the sick, the insane, the criminals, and the destitute—the types of people who had been so visible in war-torn China. Taylor believed the doctrines of physiognomy were blind to class and thus deemed himself an impartial judge, but he could easily have allowed the impressive trappings, the comportment, and the good health of the particular Japanese people he confronted to distort his readings of the race as a whole.

For whatever reason, the Japanese fared well when Taylor applied physiognomy's principles to their countenances and physiques. Among the Japanese rowers who ferried officials and interpreters to and from the *Susquehanna*, Taylor observed many "admirable specimens of manly strength and symmetry." "They were tall, compared with the Chinese," he added, "deep-chested, and with muscular and symmetrical limbs." As for the distinguished gentleman they conveyed, Taylor was equally impressed with his facial structure: "One of their interpreters," said Taylor, "would have attracted notice in any part of the world by his regular, finely-moulded features, his large, well-balanced head, and the genial, intellectual expression of his countenance."

In enumerating the noteworthy features of the Japanese facial structure and their corresponding moral attributes, Taylor did detect one flaw, however.

> Their eyes are somewhat larger and not so obliquely set as those by the Chinese, their foreheads broader and more open, with a greater facial angle, and the expression of their face denotes a lively and active mind. Notwithstanding that spirit of cunning and secrecy, which, through the continual teachings of their Government, has become almost a second nature to them, their countenances are agreeable and expressive . . . and it was the unanimous decision of all our officers . . . that they were as finished gentlemen in their manners, as could be found in any part of the world.

In the Japanese face, Taylor descried a proclivity toward "cunning and secrecy" that he imputed to the despotic government; by indoctrinating the people, Japan's leaders had altered the mind of the people and, in so doing, had effected a parallel change in the face. Whereas Taylor had attributed problems in China to the racial makeup of the people, here, in the case of Japan, he implied that the adoption of a republican form of government would provide the antidote for this note of deceit that had entered into their features.

In fact, on several occasions in the lecture, Taylor expressed his view that a change in government could unleash the potential of the Japanese people. While studying Japanese faces, he detected untapped reservoirs of ingenuity and an openness to new ideas. These traits that he found reflected in their faces he would find manifest during demonstrations of mechanical models. The Japanese showed "a grave interest" in the miniature train's steam engine; only the "wild, unearthly shriek" of the whistle could interrupt their intense concentration. And when invited to partake in a meal served in the Western style, they "handled their knives and forks with as much dexterity as if they had never known chop-sticks." In Taylor's estimation, the typical Japanese was "the most curious and inquiring person—next to a genuine Yankee—in the world"; he would be an "inventor" if not for the restraints imposed by his own government, "which fears no enemy so much as a new idea." The government's "exclusive policy" stood in "direct opposition" to the people's will. When that "unnatural bar" was removed, the world would bear witness to "a rapid progress in all the arts which have given the Caucasian race its supremacy."

Taylor's observations convinced him that Japanese civilization was sure to transform itself in the near future. As might be expected, he was not so sanguine about China's future. While Chinese civilization sorely needed such change, he pessimistically believed the Chinese race incapable of bettering itself. The "Chinese nature," he insisted, was "so thoroughly passive" that it had produced a "mental inertia" in the people, rendering them "almost hopeless of improvement." Taylor lauded missionaries for their "zealous and devoted" attention to the Chinese, but he nevertheless judged that the entire missionary enterprise in China was futile and doomed to fail.[88] In sum, the Chinese could not help themselves, and the missionaries faced a task far too daunting even for their noble efforts to match.

Interestingly, if we revisit Taylor's exact words on this issue, we note that he said China was "almost hopeless of improvement"—that is, almost hopeless but not completely. In fact, he found cause for optimism in an event most people considered a horrible tragedy—the Taiping Rebellion. This civil war, in that it affected the lives of millions of Chinese, could succeed in spurring beneficial change. Should the Taipings emerge victorious, Taylor wrote to the *Tribune* "the probable effect will be to open all parts of China to the world."[89] Regard-

less of the rebellion's outcome, Taylor argued, massive upheaval would necessarily have a salutary effect on China, because it would break "the most profound apathy" that currently gripped Chinese culture. In this way, Taylor
enthusiastically embraced national catastrophe as the only possible agent of
change in China: "I say, welcome be the thunder-storm which shall scatter and
break up, though by the means of fire and blood, this terrible stagnation!"[90]

## CONCLUSION

Although it was a bogus science that led Bayard Taylor to his predictions, the
events of the latter half of the nineteenth century left him looking somewhat
prescient. With respect to the adoption of Western ideas and machinery, Japan
did ascend rapidly along an upward trajectory during the Meiji Revolution.
China's modernization, meanwhile, although less ambitious, was in fact indirectly caused by the Taiping Rebellion. The uprising convinced some officials
of the urgent need for Western arms and military techniques; acquisition of
these could help preserve the stability of the nation and keep the Qing government in power. The Taiping Rebellion also catapulted several capable men into
positions of power. Most notable among these was Zeng Guofan, a scholar-official
whose military leadership was instrumental in suppressing the Taipings. In the
1870s, Zeng Guofan's vision of a stronger China became Qing policy through
the launching of the Self-Strengthening Movement, which was designed to reform China's military and industrial institutions by borrowing Western ideas
and technologies. The gains achieved through the Self-Strengthening Movement were modest, but a small emanation from it touched the United States. As
is explained in the next chapter, a group of Chinese boys studying in American
schools under the auspices of the Chinese government were able to teach some
Americans, in direct contradiction of Bayard Taylor's pronouncements, that the
Chinese could indeed be innovative, forward-looking, and capable of change.

## NOTES

1. *Life and Letters of Bayard Taylor,* ed. Marie Hansen-Taylor and Horace E. Scudder (Boston: Houghton, Mifflin, 1885), 1:269.

2. Perry prepared for Asia by reading every source he could find on it. Although one cannot maintain with absolute certainty that he read Williams's *The Middle Kingdom*, it would be hard to believe otherwise, given that the book became the authoritative work on China and that Williams was asked to join the expedition. William Heine, *With Perry to Japan: A Memoir*, trans. and ed. Frederic Trautman (Honolulu: University of Hawaii Press, 1990), 6.

3. John S. Sewall, The Logbook of the Captain's Clerk: Adventures in the China Seas, ed. Arthur Power Dudden (Chicago: Lakeside Press, R. R. Donnelley and Sons , 1995), 152. Sewall participated in Perry's expeditions to Japan in 1852–53 and 1854. He published this account in 1905.

4. Samuel Wells Williams, *The Middle Kingdom: A Survey of the Geography, Government, Education, Social Life, Arts, Religion, &., of the Chinese Empire and Its Inhabitants* (New York: Wiley and Putnam, 1848), 1:xv.

5. Albert Smith, *Bayard Taylor* (Boston: Houghton, Mifflin, 1896), 19–20.

6. Joseph Taylor's daybook also contains Bayard Taylor's scrapbook. Doc. 712, Downs Collection, Winterthur Library.

7. Carl Bode, *The Anatomy of American Popular Culture, 1840–1861* (Berkeley: University of California Press, 1959), 223.

8. Bayard Taylor to John Phillips, letter, 3 August 1848, *Selected Letters of Bayard Taylor*, ed. Paul C. Wermuth (Lewisburg, Pa.: Bucknell University Press, 1997), 70.

9. Bayard Taylor to George Boker, letter, 4 April 1852, *Selected Letters*, ed. Wermuth, 95.

10. Interview on 3 September 2001 with Mark H. Metzler Sawin, author of "Raising Kane: The Creation and Consequences of Fame in Antebellum America; or, The Thrilling and Tragic Narrative of Elisha Kent Kane and His Transformation into Dr. Kane, the Hero of the Romantic Age" (Ph.D. diss., University of Texas at Austin, 2001).

11. Bayard Taylor, comp., *Cyclopædia of Modern Travel: A Record of Adventure, Exploration, and Discovery, for the Past Fifty Years* (Cincinnati: Moore, Wilstach, Keys, 1856), vii.

12. Bayard Taylor to Richard Stoddard, letter (13 August 1853), *Selected Letters*, ed. Wermuth, 110. One writer commented that the proliferation of travelogues in the antebellum era did not bring about an increase in knowledge of foreign countries: "Of all observers, the most unreliable and useless for the seeker after truth is the traveler. . . . Running hastily through a country, observing and understanding by halves, and generalizing from a remarkably limited number of ill-appreciated facts, your ambitious traveler is the least trustworthy person in the world for the manners and customs of the people." Charles Nordhuff, "The Woman's Question in China," *Ladies' Repository* (September 1859), 545.

13. William H. Goetzmann, *New Lands, New Men: America and the Second Great Age of Discovery* (New York: Penguin, 1986), 59.

14. Bayard Taylor, "Humboldt at Home," *Eclectic Magazine of Foreign Literature, Science, and Art* (March 1857), 388. Bayard Taylor, *At Home and Abroad* (New York: G. P. Putnam, 1860), 354.

15. Later in his career, Taylor translated Goethe's *Faust* from German to English.

16. Smyth, 98; Hansen-Taylor and Scudder, *Life and Letters of Bayard Taylor*, 1:327.

17. *Selected Letters*, ed. Wermuth 347.

18. "The first impression made by Humboldt's face was that of a broad and genial humanity. His massive brow, heavy with the gathered wisdom of nearly a century, bent forward and overhung his breast. . . . In those eyes you read that trust in man. . . . You trusted him utterly at the first glance. . . . His nose, mouth, and chin had the heavy Teutonic character, whose genuine type always expresses an honest simplicity and directness." Taylor, *At Home and Abroad*, 353–54.

19. John Graham, *Lavater's Essays on Physiognomy: A Study in the History of Ideas* (Berne: Peter Lang, 1979), 35; John B. Davies, *Phrenology: Fad and Science: A Nineteenth-Century American Crusade* (New Haven: Yale University Press, 1955), 7.

20. Johann Caspar Lavater, *Essays on Physiognomy* (London: William Tegg, 1869), 37–40.

21. Bayard Taylor, *India, China, and Japan* (New York: G. P. Putnam, 1855), 336.

22. Bayard Taylor's Scrapbook, contained in Joseph Taylor's daybook. Doc. 712, Downs Collection, Winterthur Library.

23. Lavater, *Essays on Physiognomy*, 350; Lavater, *Physiognomy; or, The Corresponding Analogy between the Conformation of the Features and the Ruling Passions of the Mind* (London: Thomas Tegg, 1844), 94; and Lavater, *The Pocket Lavater; or, The Science of Physiognomy* (New York: C. Wiley, 1829), 29.

24. Caleb Cushing, "Delusions of Science," *National Magazine and Republican* (March 1839), 257–58.

25. Samuel George Morton, *Crania Americana; or, A Comparative View of the Skulls of Various Aboriginal Nations* (Philadelphia: J. Dobson, 1839), 71.

26. "Dr. Morton, in measuring the internal capacity of the cranium, found it to correspond with the angle of the forehead. The scale of mental capacity, as determined by him in this manner, is as follows; commencing with the lowest:—Australian, Negro, Malay, Mongolian, Caucasian." Bayard Taylor, "Man and Climate," 28. This hand-written lecture was first delivered in 1860. Box "Lectures of Bayard Taylor," Chester County Historical Society (hereafter referred to as CCHS).

27. This book instructed readers to identify the "faculty of *Secretiveness*" in another human being by observing the nose and judging whether it resembled a Chinese nose. The Chinese, Redfield asserted, "are the most remarkable people in the world for secretiveness." J. W. Redfield, *Outlines of a New System of Physiognomy* (New York: Redfield, 1848), 12.

28. *New York Herald* (4 May 1850).

29. See two different articles entitled "Physiognomy" in the same journal: *American Phrenological Journal* 13 (1851): 7–8; and *American Phrenological Journal* 15 (1852): 7–8.

30. Peter Booth Wiley, *Yankees in the Land of the Gods* (New York: Viking, 1990), 87–88; and William L. Neumann, "Religion, Morality, and Freedom: The Ideological Background of the Perry Expedition," *Pacific Historical Review* (August 1954): 248.

31. Bayard Taylor to Frederick Williams, letter, 16 July 1853, box 1, series 1, Samuel Wells Williams Family Papers, Manuscript Collections, Yale University Library.

32. Bayard Taylor to Carter Harrison III, letter, 6 August 1852, *Selected Letters*, ed. Wermuth, 99.

33. Taylor, *India, China, and Japan*, 361.

34. *Selected Letters of P. T. Barnum*, ed. A. H. Saxon (New York: Columbia University Press, 1983), 62–63.

35. Taylor, *India, China, and Japan*, 285. Interestingly, Samuel Wells Williams observed precisely the opposite with regard to the physical nature of the Chinese: "Their form is well built and symmetrical." Williams, *The Middle Kingdom*, 1:36.

36. Taylor believed so fervently that the spirit was revealed in the human face that in India he boasted that he could "distinguish between the followers of the rival religions, without reference to any distinguishing mark of the dress, and merely the expression of the face." In Benares, he claimed that "the faces of the women" showed signs of "the teachings of missionaries." Taylor, *India, China, and Japan*, 84, 244.

37. Sewall, *The Logbook of the Captain's Clerk*, 152.

38. Taylor, *India, China, and Japan*, 287–88. Jonathan D. Spence, *The Search for Modern China* (New York: Norton, 1990), 171–78.

39. When Perry arrived, he was outraged to discover that, to handle an affair in China, Humphrey had used a steamship meant for the expedition to Japan. Taylor, *India, China, and Japan*, 297–303. Chester Bain, "Commodore Matthew Perry, Humphrey Marshall, and the Taiping Rebellion," *Far Eastern Quarterly* (May 1951): 262–70.

40. Taylor, *India, China, and Japan*, 351.

41. Taylor also paid a soldier he found "lazing about" to perform his military exercises for thirty minutes. Taylor, *India, China, and Japan*, 352–53, 355. Taylor was not the only one to toss coins from high places in order to see the ensuing scramble below; B. L. Ball notes the same pastime in his travelogue *Rambles in Eastern Asia, Including China and Manilla* (Boston: James French, 1855), 132.

42. Taylor, *India, China, and Japan*, 336–38.

43. Ibid., 352–54.

44. Ibid., 329, 350.

45. Ibid., 322.

46. Ibid., 325–29.

47. Ibid., 354.

48. Ibid.

49. For a well-researched study on the vibrant economy and culture of the region before the onset of the Taiping Rebellion, see William T. Rowe, *Hankow: Commerce and Society in a Chinese City, 1796–1889* (Stanford: Stanford University Press, 1984).

50. After touring parts of the Chinese interior, Yung Wing, the first Chinese to graduate from Yale, noted a precipitous drop in population and added that refugees had fled to Shanghai to avoid the bloodletting. Yung Wing, *My Life in China and America* (New York: Holt, 1909), 93–94, 126.

51. Linda Cooke Johnson, *Shanghai: From Market Town to Treaty Port, 1074–1858* (Stanford: Stanford University Press, 1995), 267. Kerrie L. Macphereson, *A Wilderness of Marshes: The Origins of Public Health in Shanghai, 1843–1893* (New York: Oxford University Press, 1987), 5, 21.

52. Stella Dong, *Shanghai: The Rise and Fall of a Decadent City* (New York: HarperCollins, 2000), 23. Johnson, 231.

53. Taylor, *India, China, and Japan*, 390; Samuel Wells Williams, "A Journal of the Perry Expedition to Japan," *Transactions of the Asiatic Society of Japan* (1910), 28.

54. Taylor, *India, China, and Japan*, 492–94.

55. Ibid., 477.

56. Ibid., 489.

57. Ibid., 499.

58. "Bayard Taylor. A Phrenological Character, Biographical Sketch, and Portrait," *American Phrenological Journal* 20 (1855): 3.

59. See, for example, Taylor's account of his exploration of the Japanese-controlled island of Loo Choo (now called Okinawa) in P. T. Barnum's *Illustrated News* (19 November 1853), 57. Also see Taylor's analysis of the Taiping Rebellion in the *American Republican* (7 June 1853).

60. Bayard Taylor to Taylor's mother (from Milwaukee, 16 March 1854), *Life and Letters of Bayard Taylor*, ed. Hansen-Taylor and Scudder, 1:273.

61. Bayard Taylor to George Boker, letter (from Newark, Ohio, 30 April 1854), *Life and Letters of Bayard Taylor*, ed. Hansen-Taylor and Scudder, 1:276.

62. *Life and Letters of Bayard Taylor*, ed. Hansen-Taylor and Scudder, 1:264.

63. Richard Croom Beatty, *Bayard Taylor: Laureate of the Gilded Age* (Norman: University of Oklahoma Press, 1936), 147–48.

64. Bayard Taylor to Richard Stoddard, letter (from Buffalom 5 March 1854), L 23211, Letters of Bayard Taylor, CCHS.

65. Bayard Taylor to Richard and Elizabeth Stoddard, letter (from Adrian, Michigan), 9 November 1854, Letters of Bayard Taylor, CCHS.

66. Bayard Taylor to Taylor's mother (from Milwaukee, 16 March 1854). *Life and Letters of Bayard Taylor*, ed. Hansen-Taylor and Scudder, 1:273.

67. Bayard Taylor to Richard Stoddard, letter (from Buffalo, 5 March 1854), Letters of Bayard Taylor, CCHS.

68. Bayard Taylor to James T. Fields (from Penn Yan, New York, 17 February 1854), *Life and Letters of Bayard Taylor*, ed. Hansen-Taylor and Scudder, 1:269.

69. Ibid..

70. Bayard Taylor to Taylor's mother (from Milwaukee, 16 March 1854), *Life and Letters of Bayard Taylor*, ed. Hansen-Taylor and Scudder, 1:273.

71. Bayard Taylor to Taylor's mother (from New Albany, Indiana, 23 April 1854), *Life and Letters of Bayard Taylor*, ed. Hansen-Taylor and Scudder, 1:275.

72. Bayard Taylor to Taylor's mother (from Corning, New York, 25 February 1854), *Life and Letters of Bayard Taylor*, ed. Hansen-Taylor and Scudder, 1:270.

73. Bayard Taylor to Taylor's mother (from Milwaukee, 16 March 1854), *Life and Letters of Bayard Taylor*, ed. Hansen-Taylor and Scudder, 1:273.

74. Ibid.

75. Bayard Taylor to Richard Stoddard (from Buffalo, 5 March 1854), Letters of Bayard Taylor, CCHS.

76. Bayard Taylor to Richard and Elizabeth Stoddard (from Auburn, New York, 9 November 1854), Letters of Bayard Taylor, CCHS.

77. Ibid.

78. Ibid.

79. Ibid.

80. Bayard Taylor to Richard and Elizabeth Stoddard (from Detroit, 6 March 1855), Letters of Bayard Taylor, CCHS.

81. Bayard Taylor to Richard Stoddard (from Buffalo, 5 March 1854), Letters of Bayard Taylor, CCHS.

82. Bayard Taylor to Richard Stoddard (from Buffalo, 5 March 1854), Letters of Bayard Taylor, CCHS.

83. Bayard Taylor to Richard and Elizabeth Stoddard (from Hamilton, Canada, 21 November 1854), Letters of Bayard Taylor, CCHS.

84. Smyth, 93. Taylor's Japan journal is now in the possession of Rutgers University.

85. Taylor expresses his low expectations for Japan in a letter to the New York Tribune (19 October 1853). Taylor had seen Japanese people prior to his arrival in Japan. In January 1853, a ship from Boston picked up a crew of Japanese sailors in the Pacific Ocean who had been blown far from their home by a storm. After a brief stay in San Francisco, they were taken to China, where some of them agreed to travel with the expedition to Japan. Perry believed an attempt to repatriate them would demonstrate his goodwill toward the Japanese government. Illustrated News (22 January 1853), 57.

86. Taylor's handwritten lecture is owned by the CCHS (box "Lectures of Bayard Taylor"). All subsequent quotes from his lecture come from this source.

87. In lectures, Taylor did modify the damning views on Chinese immigrants contained in the travelogue. The Chinese "who have energy enough to leave their country," he said, should "be considered as exceptional specimens, which do not represent the average of the race."

88. Taylor, India, China, and Japan, 333–34.

89. New York Tribune (2 June 1853).

90. Taylor, India, China, and Japan, 333–334.

# 9. TRADITIONAL CHINA AND CHINESE YANKEES

## The Centennial Exposition of 1876

In 1876, the United States celebrated one hundred years of independence in grand fashion: The Centennial Exposition was held in Philadelphia. Eight million people, or approximately one fifth of the nation's population, paid fifty cents each to view the finest achievements of their own as well of the twenty-five foreign countries that accepted invitations.[1] This world's fair is best remembered for offering the first major exhibition of the United States' technological prowess. Machines had been a visible part of the American landscape for decades, but after the Civil War the United States entered into a period of large-scale industrial growth. Quite fittingly, American machines seized center stage at the Centennial. The "superior elegance, aptness, and ingenuity of our machinery is observable at a glance," observed William Dean Howells as he toured America's mechanical exhibits. "Yes, it is still in these things of iron and steel that the national genius most freely speaks."[2]

Along with machines, foreign exhibits provided the other great attraction. Bayard Taylor, visiting the fair to write articles for the *New York Tribune*, observed that some of the foreign exhibits drew more attention than others. He believed he had the explanation for this disparity: "The exhibits which are accompanied by exhibitors of another race, at once recognizable in features or dress, have a double attraction to the crowd."[3] Taylor was correct. Foreign exhibitors had traversed oceans to arrange objects for public display, but visitors saw the exhibitors themselves as adding an intriguing ethnographic component to the exposition. In this way, foreign people became the unwitting participants in their nations' exhibits.

After touring the foreign exhibits, Bayard Taylor was most effusive in his praise for Japan's. Japan was enjoying a rapid ascendancy on the world stage, as two decades earlier he had predicted it would. Given his harsh views on China, he not surprisingly refused to so much as acknowledge the existence of the Chinese exhibit, which stood just a few feet away from the Japanese.[4] Shunned by Taylor, the Chinese exhibit nevertheless enjoyed resounding success, becoming one of the most popular venues at the world's fair. As visitors passed beneath the grand arching gateways, they felt as if they had been transported to the Middle Kingdom itself. Once inside, they relished the opportunity to inspect exquisite Chinese artifacts and meet genuine Chinese people.

The Centennial marked the first noteworthy exhibition of Chinese culture in the United States since the heyday of the Chinese museums in the 1830s, '40s, and early '50s. Indeed, some of the popularity of the Chinese exhibit can perhaps be attributed to this prolonged absence. Yet to fully understand the exhibit's attraction, we need to place it in context with the overarching theme of the Centennial: the celebration of technological progress. In the 1870s, the vast changes underway in the United States effected a curious resurgence in the myth of Cathay. Americans expressed a profound ambivalence about industrialization, harboring both unbridled exuberance for technological progress and wistful nostalgia for a bygone era that, in retrospect, seemed simple and pure. That China had not entered the machine age only lent its exhibit greater appeal. For in China, Americans saw a traditional culture in which skilled craftspeople continued to produce by hand objects of rare beauty. Of course, some proudly enjoyed China's lack of machinery, seeing it as helping to accentuate the technologically advanced nature of American civilization. For others, however, the Chinese exhibit offered an escape from a world that was changing too fast. Surrounded by a rich abundance of exquisite porcelain, fragrant teas, and colorful silks, guests could forget the cold, noisy, and forbidding machines and choose instead to luxuriate in timeless Cathay.

However, unlike the Cathay of old, this newer Cathay—Cathay redux—existed within restrictive boundaries. By 1876, nearly all Americans knew that China was not the pastoral paradise depicted on porcelain. They had followed China's various wars and internal rebellions in the newspapers, had read about the devastating famines that ravaged the countryside,[5] and had received Bayard Taylor's ugly version of China through his travelogue, lectures, and *Tribune* correspondence. But, although Americans could no longer naively equate the real China with mythic Cathay, in their minds China's enchanting beauty had not so much vanished as it had retreated to a smaller sector of Chinese society—the world of the elites. Americans understood that it was not so much Chinese culture that captivated them as it was Chinese high culture: sage mandarins, silk-clad merchants, delicate ladies with tiny feet, intricate carvings in ivory and jade, ornate porcelain vases, and elaborate pleasure gardens.[6] And since China appeared to resist modernization, Americans may have believed that this new iteration of Cathay, unlike the old one, would never disappear.

However, by 1876, the seeds for its destruction were already sown. Just as Americans were ambivalent about modernity, so too were the Chinese. In China, reformers and conservatives engaged in a great national debate that, quite interestingly, spilled over accidentally into the Centennial. As one of the programs initiated by reformers in the Qing government, a large group of boys was sent by China to the United States to study in New England schools. When these boys arrived at the Centennial purely as visitors, they became a de facto Chinese exhibit; for a brief period, fairgoers shifted their attention away from the timeless art objects of the official exhibit and to this group of boys in whom a striking cultural metamorphosis was taking place. The ease with which the boys were learning the English language as well as American customs, science, and technology impressed Americans and compelled them to revise their construction of China yet again.

# GATHERING, TRANSPORTING, ASSEMBLING

On receiving an invitation in 1874, the Qing government decided that China would participate in its second major international exhibition.[7] To Robert Hart, the inspector general of the Chinese Maritime Customs Service, the government delegated the enormous task of transforming this desire into a reality. Hart, who was Irish, was an employee of the Chinese government, and he carried out his duties with the interests of China, not Britain, in mind.[8] The task before him was formidable indeed, consisting of three major stages: assembling the exhibit, arranging for its transportation to Philadelphia, and structuring its presentation there so as to attract and impress visitors. To assist him in this undertaking, Hart enlisted the aid of his subordinates in the Customs Office, who included James L Hammond, of Salem, Massachusetts. And since the venue was in the United States, Hart also deemed it prudent to appoint to the traveling Chinese Commission agents from the three largest American trading firms in China: Russell and Co., Olyphant and Co., and Knight and Co.[9]

Although non-Chinese officials and merchants handled the logistics, the substance of the exhibit had to come solely from the Chinese, and several merchants from various ports volunteered to contribute their finest wares. While initial plans called for an exhibit of modest proportions, it rapidly grew in size as the list of donors lengthened.[10] One contributor in particular raised eyebrows when he announced his intention to participate. Hu Quang Yung, one of the wealthiest bankers in China, enjoyed world renown in collecting circles for his extensive holdings in Chinese art, both ancient and modern. Known in China simply as Hu Tuen Tzen (the Great Man), Hu conferred immediate prestige on China's exhibit when he agreed to display numerous items from his famous collection. Preferring to remain in his mansion in Hangzhou rather than suffer the hardships of Pacific travel, Hu dispatched his able nephew, Hu Ying Ding, to accompany the exquisite collection on its overseas journey. This second Hu, though only a young man, was himself quite accomplished, having already passed the state examinations required to become a government official. That he had also achieved proficiency in English meant he was well equipped to carry out his uncle's primary objective: to familiarize the world with the many splendors and the unique beauty of Chinese civilization.[11] And so the Chinese exhibit was assembled in a spirit of joint cooperation, with Europeans and Americans lending their assistance to what was largely a Chinese effort.

However, just because the Chinese participated did not necessarily mean that the final exhibit would offer a comprehensive explication of Chinese culture. Li Gui, a customs official who would travel to Philadelphia with the Commission, explained that the exhibit was not a mere assemblage of "curiosities" intended only to be "pleasing to the eye." Rather, it was a collection designed "to increase knowledge."[12] But with contributions coming almost exclusively from merchants, mandarins, and millionaires, the exhibit clearly emanated exclusively out of the powerful, wealthy, and learned ranks of Chinese society. It did not reflect a cross-section of life in China, because organizers clearly omitted objects that could be construed as representing laborers and farmers, who constituted the overwhelming majority of the country's population.

Yet Robert Hart and others could justify this arrangement for two reasons. First, organizers had to take Western tastes and expectations into consideration when forming the exhibit because visitors would come predominantly from the United States, of course, but also Europe, the host city being Philadelphia, on the Atlantic coast. Westerners would be the ones inspecting the objects and issuing a final verdict on the productions of China. Since most of them now believed that the beauty of China resided mainly in the possessions, costumes, lifestyle, and art of the rich and educated classes, organizers not surprisingly loaded the crates with silks, porcelain, paintings, ivory carvings, and fine teas.

The inclusion of a display devoted to the poorer sectors of Chinese society was simply not a practical option.[13]

Second, this emphasis on China's high culture was also consistent with the expectations of the Centennial. Unlike an ethnological museum, an international exposition had no pretensions about being comprehensive. While both attempted to instruct interested parties about a different culture, expositions possessed in addition an overriding commercial objective: A nation attempted to attract international business by placing on display mainly those commodities that were unique to its culture. For example, although millions of Chinese citizens wore cotton outfits, they were omitted from the exhibit because the textile industries in England and the United States could mass-produce cotton fabric at a low cost, meaning that an international market for Chinese cotton did not exist. Instead, organizers emphasized China's specialties—those objects that, for various reasons, were singularly Chinese or could not be duplicated elsewhere: porcelain because it remained one of China's top exports; tea because Western nations did not possess the proper soil and climate to grow tea trees; paintings, scrolls, and wall hangings because the artists worked within an aesthetic that was distinctively Chinese; and intricate carvings in ivory, bone, tortoiseshell, and jade because the hundreds of man-hours that these pieces required precluded their production in Western countries, where the price of labor was more dear.

In the late winter of 1876, the members of the Chinese Commission along with several carpenters set out for Philadelphia with 720 carefully packed crates, traveling first by steamer to California and then by train to the East Coast. For the second leg of the journey, their transit from west to east across the United States, they used the Transcontinental Railroad, completed just seven years earlier largely through the labor of their hard-working countrymen.[14] In a strange synchronicity, as the Commission made preparations to put Chinese civilization on display in Philadelphia, Chinese immigrants back in San Francisco were the subject of state hearings designed to weigh their usefulness against their potential menace to society. Members of both the Chinese and the white communities took the stand and offered sworn testimony on such issues as prostitution, gambling, blackmail, assassins, labor competition, opium dens, and the bribing of police officers. In stark contrast to the Chinese Commission, which carried a formal invitation from the U.S. government, Chinese immigrants found themselves defending their way of life, with a discriminatory immigration policy looming as a potential outcome.[15]

The Chinese Commission reached Philadelphia in early April and found the city festooned with banners, streamers, and the flags of participating nations.[16] On arriving in Fairmount Park, the site of the exposition, they beheld for the first time the Main Building—a vast parallelogram that measured 1,876 feet in length, 464 feet in width, and 184 feet in height. For its day, the Main Building stood as a marvel of modern architecture. With an imposing super-structure composed of wrought-iron columns and glass, the building was de-signed to be as edifying as the myriad exhibits it housed. It was also equipped with a steam elevator, a recent invention installed by the Otis Company, that could lift anyone desiring a bird's-eye view to a walkway raised 70 feet off the floor. Into this colossal edifice that itself symbolized technological progress, the Chinese Commission brought a collection consisting mainly of traditional handicrafts and works of arts.

Once inside, the Chinese, looking to establish their place at the Centennial, got off to an inauspicious start. First, they found that their allotted space in the southwest part of the building was adjacent to the exhibit from Japan; though they could not have known it at that time, this juxtaposition would ultimately yield unfavorable comparisons. Second, the Chinese discovered to their dismay that their square footage was not only significantly smaller than that allocated to Japan but also insufficient to display the contents of the 720 crates.[17] Accord-ing to Li Gui, the shortage resulted not from any unfair treatment by organizers of the world's fair but rather from China's original plan to bring a much smaller exhibit. Lacking the space for all they had brought, the Chinese sent many pieces to a local auctioneer, who promptly put them on the block.[18]

Third, and worst of all, the Chinese discovered that they had arrived on the scene very late and would have to make haste if they were going to be ready by opening day, scheduled for May 10. For newspaper reporters looking for a story in the weeks preceding the grand opening, the Main Building offered a source of unlimited fascination. Just by roving the floor, one could find people from all across the world who dressed in their native costumes and spoke in languages never before heard by most Americans. It was a modern-day Tower of Babel.

Being among the last to arrive, the Chinese attracted much of this attention as reporters provided readers with updates of their progress. "China, the latest arrival," wrote one reporter, "has a small mountain of packing-cases on her ter-ritory." Yet despite the substantial task before them, "a dozen mechanics in shirt-like blouses, skull-caps, and pigtails are putting things to rights with dili-gence and dispatch." Another reporter offered a less hopeful assessment: "Up to date of writing . . . the efforts of the Mongolians are alarmingly slow." To expe-dite the process, the Chinese hired American women to clean the objects after removing them from crates. When a vase worth $1,500 slipped from one wom-an's grasp and shattered to pieces against the floor, the Chinese were heard to utter oaths, the essence of which was easily translatable into any language.[19]

On opening day, thousands of guests gathered to listen to Theodore Thom-as's orchestra and to speeches given by important dignitaries, including Presi-dent Ulysses S. Grant. They then moved to Machinery Hall to watch the president and the Brazilian emperor Dom Pedro turn the levers that activated the Corliss steam engine, an iron-and-steel behemoth that generated the energy for all machines in the building (fig. 9.1). According to *Harper's Weekly,* at the conclusion of these ceremonies visitors began "pouring in a constant stream through the Main Building" to witness the "picturesque commingling of nationalities and costumes" that had no precedent in the United States. Visitors who flocked to the Chinese exhibit, among the most greatly anticipated of the entire exposition, found to their dismay that it was still unfinished.[20]

Any subsequent disappointment, however, disappeared when guests realized that the unfinished exhibit actually afforded as much stimulation as a complete one would have done. Here before their eyes moved the living, breathing denizens of China, all decked out in their native costumes, busily constructing "an epitome of the Flowery Land out of . . . a medley of red and gilded beams, matting and bamboo" (fig. 9.2). One writer wondered whether the exhibit's unfinished state "was not really an advantage" since "visitors could see at once the workmen and their works." He added that, although China stood at "the opposite extreme of what we call civilization," the Chinese worked with "military precision and aplomb."[21] Indeed, the crowds gathered around the unfinished Chinese exhibit were apparently so large and boisterous that Centennial organizers felt compelled to deploy a "special policeman" to prevent any disruption of the work.[22]

A few reporters did not hesitate to use the unfinished state of the exhibit to make sweeping generalizations about China's national character. One journalist construed the exhibit as symptomatic of China's lack of "goaheadativeness." This critical flaw, he argued, prevented China from joining the family of forward-looking nations, the most recent member of which happened to be China's closest neighbor in the Main Building:

> The Japanese Department . . . lies side by side with the Chinese. The oldest of Oriental Empires is thus placed in close contrast with the newest addition to the disciples of Western progressiveness. . . . Here is slow old China, with the bulk of her exhibit unpacked. The goods . . . are mainly porcelain. China is represented by china. . . . She would have made quite as good a show in this line in 1776, or even in 1476. . . . How different is it with the ambitious, striving, progressive Japan! She is all ready and obviously anxious to be seen. . . . On this side of the aisle all is life; just across the way, the almond-eyed Celestials have learned little since the days of Confucius.[23]

Indeed, the dynamic in East Asia had undergone a dramatic shift in the quarter of a century leading up to the Centennial. Before Commodore Perry's expedition to Japan in 1853, European and American whalers shipwrecked on

Japanese shores had been caged, tortured, or forced to trample on a crucifix. But in Perry's wake, this hostility to foreigners rapidly diminished, eventually giving way to a new spirit of openness. In a surprising reversal, Westerners were now invited to come to Japan in order to share their expertise and inventions with the Japanese people. As a result, the country began to rise along a steep trajectory toward a level of modernization previously found only in the West.[24] In 1876, to announce their ascendancy to the world, the Japanese brought to the Main Building a wonderful exhibit that dwarfed those of all its neighbors, including China.

If this exhibit were not spectacular enough, the Japanese also erected on the fair grounds two examples of authentic Japanese architecture, a bazaar and a traditional dwelling, both of which were so popular that only the Corliss engine attracted larger crowds.[25] One impressed visitor admitted that the exhibit had forced him to "amend his ideas" of Japan: "We have been accustomed to regard that country as uncivilized, or half-civilized at best, but we find here abundant evidences that it outshines the most cultivated nations of Europe in arts."[26] A burlesque of the Centennial written for the stage sought to lampoon Japan's swelling self-confidence. In the play, an arrogant Japanese delegate rudely dismisses one from China: "Here, off with you, Chinaman! You know nothing. Japs everybody here." The Chinese delegate, who fears the same progress of which Japan boasts, is too afraid to even enter the Otis elevator, exclaiming, "Oh, me big scared!"[27] Intended only to evoke laughter, the scene reflected Americans' perception of a shifting power structure in Asia.

## THE IMPORTANCE OF CLOTHES

One might expect that most Americans would encounter difficulty differentiating between Japanese and Chinese, but that was not the case. According to one reporter, "There are not a few individuals from these Oriental nations scattered through the mass, some in native pigtails, and some in foreign stove pipes." In making this observation, he clearly had the Chinese and the Japanese in mind.[28] As much as the exhibits themselves, the attire of the exhibitors from Asia elicited commentary from Americans. The Chinese dressed in a traditional fashion, with outfits of brocaded silk robes, petticoats, and wooden shoes; these along with their queues prompted one journalist to note, "They do seem to be a queer folk." In contrast, that same journalist observed, "You scarcely see a Jap now who is not as elegant in European clothes as anybody on the grounds." Li Gui, who closely watched his Japanese neighbors in the Main Building, observed that "were it not for their black hair and yellow skin, I could not tell them from the Westerners."[29]

However, evidence suggests that the Japanese donned Western outfits not just to show how modern they had become but to avoid harassment from the crowds. According to one reporter, foreigners were repeatedly pursued by packs of idle boys and men who "hooted and hollered" at them as if they had been "animals of a strange species." In one case, a rowdy nearly tore the silken robes off the back of a Chinese official. The regrettable result of this malicious behavior, the reporter noted, was that many foreigners had shifted to the less conspicuous American dress.[30] William Dean Howells, covering the Centennial for the *Atlantic Monthly*, found the Japanese metamorphosis disappointing because it robbed the exposition of some of its potential for color. "We saw but one Jap in his national costume," Howells lamented. "The other Japanese were in our modification of the English dress. . . . It is a great pity not to see them in their own outlandish gear, for picturesqueness' sake." As a solution, Howells proposed that exposition officials assign "a squad of soldiers" to each Japanese for his personal protection.[31]

Regardless of the true cause behind the change in Japanese dress, Americans perceived it as a Japanese attempt to imitate America. In one telling cartoon from the *Daily Graphic*, a Japanese father sends his son to the Centennial (fig. 9.3). In the first frame, he exhorts the boy, "Go, my son, go and study the civilization of the Occident." In the second frame the son has abandoned his Japanese clothes, rice-harvesting hat, and long sword in favor of a tuxedo, stovepipe hat, and cigar. He has also won the affections of an elegant young American woman, who has become his escort at the Centennial. "Dear Papa," he writes, "I am industriously studying the civilization of these Americans but it is very expensive. Please send me a bag of dollars." After just a brief taste of American life, he had become a convert.

Many reporters, as they had done with the unfinished state of the Chinese exhibit, read deep importance into the wardrobes of the two Asian nations, interpreting modes of dress as external manifestations of national ideologies. According to the *Cincinnati Daily Gazette*, the Chinese "have not budged an inch in the way of conforming to our costumes and customs." They are "an odd people," he continued, who "live under the weight of all the ages. . . . But with all their wisdom, they might learn a thing or two, if they would open their eyes." He suggested they take note of the Japanese.[32]

Another reporter made what he believed were profound insights about China and Japan after merely making a few superficial observations:

The exhibitors . . . from the Happy Isles afford a strange contrast to those of the Flowery Kingdom next to them, for the former are dressed like Americans, bear themselves in a very gentlemanly and pleasant fashion, and for the most part speak English fluently. The latter are clad in their womanish robes of silk, wear long pig-tails, and speak little if any English. The former are progressive Mongols, the latter stanch conservatives, and it is queer to see them side by side, so alike and yet so different. This shows that, though nature is much, the impulse of direction is still more. Japan is bound to be more and more progressive, and China must be more and more conservative; nor will it be very surprising should she abrogate her treaties and close her ports even in this Centennial year.[33]

Whereas the Japanese appeared "gentlemanly" in their American suits, the silk robes and queues had a feminizing effect on Chinese males, in the reporter's view.

From his observations about dress and English proficiency, he made the induction that the Japanese were "progressive" for their willingness to embrace Western ideas, while the Chinese were "conservative" for resisting the same. If this generalization were accurate, he also had strong evidence that learned behavior ("direction") supersedes innate "nature," which was determined by race, because both nations were populated by the same "Mongols." Relying entirely on the evidence of differing styles of dress, he decided the nature-versus-nurture question and could then move on to make his sweeping prediction: The Chinese would probably sever contact with the outside world. Such was the importance of clothes at the Centennial.

Other reporters, enjoying the color and the exoticism that the Chinese wardrobe provided, applauded the Chinese decision not to abandon their traditional costumes. "Look at that pig-tailed and gowned gentleman in the 'Empire of China,'" wrote one excited reporter.[34] Indeed, since China insisted on being itself and on not conforming to Western styles, William Dean Howells could still count on the Chinese enclosure to deliver the exotic experience he so coveted:

> The Chinese, whom we found in disorder and unreadiness, pushed rapidly forward during our stay, and before we left, the rich grotesquery of their industries had satisfactorily unfolded itself. We were none the less satisfied that there should be still a half-score of their carpenters busy about the show-cases; their looks, their motions, their speech, their dress, amidst the fantastic forms of those bedeviled arts of theirs, affected one like the things of a capricious dream.[35]

Howells hoped the Chinese exhibit could transport him to an oriental fantasy world, and he did not leave disappointed. What he did not fully grasp, however, was the causal relationship between the busy carpenters and his pleasurable dreamlike experience. For during the planning stage of the exhibit, Robert Hart and the other customs officers had conceived of an architectural

plan designed to evoke this exact response. The carpenters were busy transforming a blueprint on paper into a three-dimensional reality.


## A WALL AROUND CHINA


Inside the Main Building, Chinese carpenters worked steadily to bring to frui-
tion the architectural plan, the governing idea of which was virtual travel. By
erecting partitions along the perimeter of the allotted space and covering the
exhibit with a roof, they created an enclosure, unique among exhibits at the fair,
that blocked out the many distracting sights and sounds of the Main Building.[36]
In addition, at the three entrances they raised elaborate gateways, prefabricated
in Peking, that each towered more than fourteen feet in height (fig. 9.4). Over
the northern gate, the most prominent of the three, Li Gui wrote three Chinese
characters in large, bold strokes: "The great Qing state" (fig. 9.5).[37] A journalist
for the *Cincinnati Commercial* acknowledged the "potency" of these structures
in creating an immediate effect on the visitor. By referring to them as "portals,"
he implied that they actually worked to heighten the impression that one was
actually entering a foreign country and not a mere exhibit.[38]

Indeed, other visitors corroborated this sensation of virtual travel. "We entered into this country," one observer wrote, "through a tall noble gateway of
carved wood painted in dark colors, with the roof turned up, and trimmed off
with dragons like tea-chests and pagodas."[39] Rebecca Harding Davis, writing for
*Harper's Weekly*, noted that the Chinese "shut us into a different world from that
which we have known, but one which is somehow oddly familiar.[40] Likewise,
James McCabe, who compiled an entire book on the Centennial, wrote that
the exhibit conjured up the illusion of an actual trip to China: A "number of
almond-eyed, pig-tailed celestials, in their native costumes, were scattered
through the enclosure, and you might for a moment imagine that you had put
the sea between you and the Exhibition and had suddenly landed in some large
Chinese bazaar."[41] The journalist from the *Cincinnati Commercial* became so
absorbed in the Chinese department that, on completing his tour and passing
over the "threshold," he found the outside world oddly transformed: "The visitor . . . involuntarily and instantly seems to be setting forth into an entirely different world, appearing familiar, yet strangely novel."[42]

Besides creating the attractive possibility of virtual travel, the architectural
plan played an important role in visitors' experience by discouraging them from
viewing the Chinese exhibit in the context of its surroundings in the Main
Building. Robert Rydell, a historian who specializes in world's fairs, describes

America's expositions before and after the turn of the century as "triumphs of hegemony" in which the nation's "political, financial, corporate, and intellectual leaders" used their prestige to impose a specific worldview on a consenting population. Each exposition, he claims, was organized around a "cohesive explanatory blueprint" aimed at promoting and disseminating to the public American nationalism and notions about the racial superiority of Americans of European stock.

As for the Centennial, Rydell contends that organizers arranged the foreign exhibits around a "classification scheme" intended to demonstrate a firm link connecting race to the scientific and industrial progress achieved by the various participating cultures. Indeed, this agenda was clearly manifest in the American Indian exhibit, which was organized by the Smithsonian Institution rather than by the tribes themselves. By portraying American Indians as violent, depraved, and antagonistic to Western civilization, the Smithsonian implicitly justified a federal policy that involved the use of military force to suppress their resistance. If William Dean Howells's comments reflected those of the other visitors, then the exhibit achieved the desired effect. He referred to the "red man" as "a hideous demon, whose malign traits can hardly inspire any emotion softer than abhorrence." He advocated "extermination" as a viable solution.[43]

Assuming Rydell is correct in discerning a race-based hierarchical plan behind the layout of foreign exhibits, one must question the efficacy of such a plan with regard to China. The architectural apparatus encasing the Chinese exhibit had the effect of insulating it, both physically and psychologically, from its surroundings. The Chinese enclosure existed as a pocket of autonomy, impermeable to the external designs of fair organizers, inside of which members of the Chinese Commission could attempt to inculcate visitors with the view that the Chinese were an ingenious people capable of producing objects of both aesthetic beauty and practical utility—a view contrary to the Centennial's overarching purpose. Undoubtedly, some visitors imported into the enclosure prevailing opinions about the importance of Western technology and then judged the exhibit accordingly. Yet others happily relinquished their preconceptions on passing through the gateways and allowed the Middle Kingdom to explain itself on its own terms.

# THROUGH THE GATEWAY

Drawn by the promise of a novel experience, visitors came in droves to the Chinese exhibit, making it one of the most crowded in the Main Building.[44] What they found was a pleasing profusion of exquisite things with which to occupy their attention. Sir Robert Hart, his assistants, and the numerous Chinese contributors had set out to assemble an exhibit that would awe visitors with the wonderful products of China and the masterful skill of its artisans. According to Li Gui, who carefully observed the reactions of the guests, the exhibit achieved this objective convincingly: "China's productions are something that other countries' officers and visitors have never before seen. They all gasp at the beauty of everything, with some even exclaiming: 'Now we know Chinese people's ingenuity is above even that of Westerners.'"[45]

With so much to take in at one time, David Bailey, a schoolteacher from rural Ohio, expressed the great difficulty he had in describing the place: "Were I writing a book of a thousand pages, instead of one of a hundred, I could now go on and enumerate hundreds of curiosities displayed here, but as it is, I must desist."[46] "The more China is studied," observed a journalist, "the more weird, curious, suggestive and unique (from all else around) it appears to be." Though the "Celestial compartment" was not "so extensive as that of the neighboring Empire of Japan," it contained "far more than one would suppose at first, and scarcely an object will fail to repay close examination."[47]

From the ceiling, large Chinese lanterns hung, some made of bone with sides of embroidered silk. For fabrics, one could find satins, crapes, brocades, silks, shawls, nankeens, and pongees. And out of bamboo, Chinese artisans had fabricated all manner of items, including pillows, musical instruments, shoes, and even a luxurious sleeping chair (fig. 9.6). An assortment of tiny women's shoes accompanied by a model of a compacted female foot provided visitors with a glimpse of an upper-class Chinese custom they found bizarre. Although intrigued by all these, most visitors had come to see what China was most famous for—porcelain—and here they found plenty of it. The exhibit included hundreds of varieties from the best kilns in China.[48]

For tea lovers, the Chinese had brought fifty varieties, all available for purchase. An extensive array of Chinese medicines included potions that attracted all seekers of the exotic and the strange. Some guests were legitimately interested in methods of Chinese healing, but others simply took great delight in being repulsed by the tiger skulls, deer antlers, ibex horns, opium, rhinoceros bones, wild-locust pods, pulverized insects and desiccated centipedes, sea horses, lizards, and toads.[49] In addition, visitors found large bronze idols, intricate tortoiseshell carvings, fine examples of lacquerware and jade, hanging scrolls of calligraphy, and genuine relics from the Imperial Summer Palace. As for the carved wooden furniture, one reporter praised the workmanship but found the designs strange and disturbing: "The dragon crawls over everything, and where he is not there will be found some horribly ugly animal, such as could only enter the fancy of one troubled with indigestion."

The exhibit also contained dozens of statues designed to reflect the different aspects of Chinese life. A handful of these were life-size, with porcelain heads attached to wooden bodies that, being jointed, could assume any position. Guests came face to face with two mandarins, a wedding bride, a woman with bound feet and her child, a schoolmaster, a shroff (money changer), three soldiers, and a Buddhist priest with a shaved head (fig. 9.7). Along with the life-size variety, numerous smaller clay figures, most about a foot high, also populated the exhibit. Organizers had planned to exhibit these in a handful of signature scenes of Chinese life (such as a funeral procession, a wedding ceremony, and the execution of a criminal), but damage to numerous statues while en route to Philadelphia forced the Commission to abandon this scheme in favor of a single eclectic display. One observer still called them "a very amusing and at the same time very instructive feature in the Chinese exhibit" (fig. 9.8). Despite the fairly wide sampling of people and vocations, the statues did not represent China's millions of peasant farmers and laborers. "The Chinese exhibit in the Main Building," according to Rebecca Harding Davis, "illustrates only the life of the higher classes."[50]

In the ivory display, Chinese craftsmen had carved out of ivory blocks shapes that stretched the imagination—twenty-three concentric balls, for example, and an exquisitely detailed flower boat. Still more spectacular, a miniature ivory pagoda, four feet tall, rose out of a miniature garden where small figurines cavorted beneath fruit trees. Like the concentric balls, it was a miniature China within the Chinese exhibit, which was itself intended as a microcosm of the actual country. And as perhaps the most striking example of an artisan's patience and eye for meticulous detail, an elephant's tusk that was 2_ feet long bore the carved image of a Chinese city on a mountainside, complete with mulberry trees, "pumpkin-headed Celestials," temples, and "the characteristic landmarks of a Chinese city—pagodas." Although it was the result of a single man's painstaking and unerring effort over a three-year period, it could be had for the amazingly low sum of $320.

How was this possible? One observer pointed to the price of labor and the absence of machinery. "All these carvings—in fact all the articles in the Chinese section," he wrote, "were executed by hand, there being little machinery in China." Artisans in the ivory-carving trade, he explained, received a mere fifteen cents a day as compensation for their work, and this low cost of labor explains why China could sell a carving for around $300 when the same object would cost $3,000 if made in the United States. China, he implied, had found a niche by using its inexpensive work force to accomplish tasks that demanded a level of precision that Western machines were incapable of at any cost. And so China's dearth of machinery, though deemed by many a liability in the modern age, encouraged the remarkably inexpensive but exquisite handcraftsmanship that was one of China's strengths.[51]

# THE MANDARIN AND THE MACHINE

This observer's point of view represented a departure from the more standard response to China's dearth of technology: that the lack of machines in the Chinese exhibit was emblematic of vast cultural failure. Though the latter view was probably the more common of the two, many Americans clearly resisted thinking in this way. Without any intended condescension, they viewed China as the anti-Japan, a beautiful Asian nation that maintained both wonderful artistry and exotic charm by resisting the very Western ideas its island neighbor had embraced. Believing that the absence of machinery in the production process increased the beauty of the objects, these observers raved about the skill, patience, ingenuity, and eye for beauty that the Chinese craftsmen possessed:

> Every inch, every line of this work was the product not of mechanical contrivances, but of human labor directed by an unerring though somewhat incongruous sense of the beautiful, and aided by endless patience and perseverance. The entire exhibit of China was composed not of mighty engines for economizing labor, nor the apparently delicate yet actually coarse fabrics manufactured in astonishing quantities by complicated machines, but of artistically beautiful though aesthetically grotesque ornamentation, which has been cultivated until even the most ordinary articles of household use have been transformed into visions of unique beauty.[52]

Similarly, Rebecca Harding Davis identified one of the Chinese as "one of the most skillful ivory carvers in China, a man of probity and weight in his class." Were it not for prejudice and the language barrier, this Chinese craftsman and "one of the master-mechanics yonder in Machinery Hall" would realize that they "differ but little in the scope and culture of their intellects."[53]

While a stroll through Machinery Hall could certainly instill in one a sense of awe for humankind's ability to harness the forces of nature, exhibits like China's had tremendous appeal precisely because they went against the prevailing current at the Centennial. "You hear the sharp click of the telegraph telling of the restless, busy energy that has produced all this luxury," stated one visitor on his way to the exhibits of China, Egypt, and the American Indians, "and are reminded that you are not yet in Fairyland."[54] To many, the Chinese exhibit offered a preindustrial wonderland, a timeless and exotic enclave that existed inside a larger exposition devoted to change and progress. In short, for anyone who had grown weary of the worshipful reverence for technology that characterized the tone in Machinery Hall, the Chinese exhibit offered a welcome change of pace.

Although the goods the Chinese displayed were handmade rather than machine-made, one should not assume that they resisted technology. Indeed, the debate over industrialization was not purely an American phenomenon; a parallel version of it raged in China, where it took on even greater meaning because national identity itself was at stake. In 1876, the Chinese stood at a crossroads. Earlier wars with European powers and several internal rebellions had exposed the Qing dynasty's vulnerability for all the world to see. In the wake of these events, one faction in the government, recognizing the example of Meiji Japan, sought to safeguard Chinese civilization from future conflicts by mastering the same technologies that had given Western countries such an overwhelming advantage. But to the more conservative elements, this Self-Strengthening Movement, as it was called, involved making a compromise that was tantamount to cultural suicide. For once the Chinese gates opened to let Western ideas in, would they not destroy the very Confucian essence they were meant to preserve?[55]

Li Gui epitomized China's ambivalence toward modernity. In his younger years, on his way to becoming a scholar-official, he had studied and mastered the revered Confucian texts. To him, these books were not merely a means to an end, as he believed fervently both in their wisdom and in their continued relevance to Chinese society. Yet he was also a remarkably open-minded thinker, and he viewed the international exposition as an opportunity for China to perform a thorough self-evaluation with respect to its "strengths" and "defects."[56] China represented itself in a fashion Li could be proud of, but he also recognized that the exhibit lacked the one element that characterized the modern age—the machine.

Ironically, then, one of the most passionate voices criticizing China belonged not to Americans but to a Chinese official educated in the Confucian tradition. Li praised the United States for its marvelous machines and concurrently chastised conservative elements in China for their reluctance to explore anything mechanical. One reporter, implying that the Japanese took an interest in American technology while the Chinese did not, wrote that "while the Japanese are everywhere, observant, critical, apparently delighted, I cannot remember that I have seen a Chinaman in Machinery or Agricultural Halls."[57] Li's curiosity drew him to both places, and in Machinery Hall he recognized the wave of the future. In particular, the Corliss steam engine, which towered majestically over all else in its vicinity, captivated the Chinese official. He stood and marveled at the iron-and-steel colossus as its powerful walking-beams, rising and falling, efficiently meted out energy to the other machines in the hall. To Li it was nothing short of miraculous: "This giant machine does not make much noise when running, and a single person can operate it. It is truly a wonder."[58]

As Li went on to view the entire panoply of American inventions in both Machinery and Agricultural Halls, he enjoyed an epiphany reminiscent of that experienced by Henry Adams as he beheld the electric dynamo at the Paris Exposition of 1900. The path China must follow in the near future became perfectly clear. As Li examined the various machines, tools, and labor-saving devices, he envisioned their implementation ameliorating the harsh conditions in which many in China were forced to live. Hydraulic pumps would finally control China's unpredictable rivers and prevent the floods that habitually devastated the countryside. Likewise, the various farming machines seemed to have the potential to increase the food supply dramatically and thereby reduce starvation. But would China awaken to the importance of Western technology? Perhaps, but Li noted ominously that, while conservatives in the Chinese government were content to let China stand pat, the Japanese at the Centennial were busy purchasing all kinds of American machines.[59]

## THE EXHIBITORS BECOME THE EXHIBITS

As the Chinese official gazed at the various Centennial exhibits that fascinated him, he was keenly aware of the extreme interest others were taking in him. The beauty of the Chinese objects notwithstanding, Li Gui and the nine other members of the Chinese Commission discovered that, in the minds of visitors, they did not merely monitor the exhibit, they were an essential part of it. Ethnological displays would not become institutionalized in world's fairs until the 1889 Paris Exhibition and the 1893 Columbian Exposition in Chicago, but at this 1876 Centennial the members of the Chinese Commission did constitute an accidental or de facto human showcase, although their reason for attending was not to be observed. That so many visitors ventured into the Chinese enclosure with the express purpose of seeing authentic Chinese people prompted William Dean Howells to wonder "what they [the Chinese] thought of us spectators."[60]

As if in answer to Howells, Li Gui in his description of the spectators' fascination invoked the issue of class. "The Chinese the Westerners know wear short shirts and work at low ranking jobs," he wrote. "They rarely see people like us who are well-dressed and well-mannered." Indeed, as hard-working laundrymen and railroad workers had never graced the side of a porcelain vase, Americans embraced this opportunity to meet sophisticated mandarins, such as Li Gui or Hu Ying Ding, and wealthy merchants, such as Sung Sing Kung, all of whom comported themselves with grace, elegance, and refinement. Li Gui found all the attention flattering but it sometimes proved overwhelming and even smothering. "Westerners all want to talk to me," he wrote. "Wherever I go, I am besieged by people and cannot get out."[61]

All day long, Li and the others circulated through the exhibits, tirelessly fielding questions from inquisitive fairgoers. While most queries were good-natured, one reporter did attempt to provoke the Chinese, who apparently handled the situation quite wisely and simply ignored his prodding questions. "It is amazing to see how they sit back in their retreating bamboo chairs," remarked the reporter, "and how indifferent they are to all the questions with which you try to stir them up."[62]

But efforts to rile the Chinese attendants were hardly the rule. Most visitors who approached them harbored only good intentions. Children bearing notebooks and albums would seek them out and walk away delighted with several lines of classical Chinese poetry or the autograph of a genuine gentleman from the "Empire of China."[63] A woman from New Jersey approached one of the Chinese to inquire about his age, his wife, the number of children he had, and his opinion about Americans.[64] When adults made advances, it was often to ascertain information about a particular object in the exhibit (fig. 9.9). David Bailey, for example, convinced one attendant to share with him the secret technique behind the twenty-three concentric ivory balls. Other American visitors brought from home the cherished pieces of porcelain from their own collections and asked the Chinese for an assessment. To these requests, the Chinese would always lend their expertise, free of charge.[65]

Much of the interaction between Americans and Chinese involved bargaining. Nearly everything in the exhibit was for sale, and visitors enticed by the prospect of bringing a small piece of Chinese high culture into their own homes readily loosened their purse strings. For large transactions, the Chinese Commission had erected alongside the exhibit a small house, which, equipped with a six-foot couch, had the added benefit of providing temporary rest and refuge from assertive fairgoers.[66] The prices of many of the pieces soared into the hundreds and even thousands of dollars, but others could be had for pocket change. For example, for less than one dollar a visitor could outfit him or herself with a paper fan, a bamboo hat, a hand gong, and a parasol.

As far as sales were concerned, the Chinese were quite successful. By selling thousands of dollars' worth of art and commodities, the Chinese attendants reaped large profits either for themselves or for the business interests they represented. Illustrating the commercial side of the Chinese exhibit, a cartoon in *Harper's Weekly* pictured a smiling Chinese man sitting atop a throne while below him Americans eagerly wave money in attempt to buy the vases he holds (fig. 9.10). By the time the world's fair closed, the Chinese had not only sold all of their porcelain but also had accepted numerous orders for future purchases.[67]

With Americans approaching the Chinese to ask for autographs, solicit information on handicrafts, haggle over prices, and make inquiries about life in China, the Chinese exhibit became a "contact zone"—a locus of interaction between the East and the West.[68] Quite often, it was young white women who met with the male Chinese attendants inside the enclosure. A correspondent for the *Cincinnati Commercial* reported that the Chinese "are often seen sitting down with the prettiest and most dressiest young ladies, holding jolly confabs." And according to a story in the *Hartford Courant*, the frequency and intensity of these exchanges was so great as to spawn at least one nuptial. One member of the Chinese Commission had "captured the affections of a young and handsome American girl," and the two were planning to wed that winter. At a time when relationships between Chinese immigrants and white women were generally proscribed in American society, the newspaper appeared to find this interracial union charming and even befitting the spirit of internationalism and cultural understanding at the Centennial.[69]

## FLIRTING WITH BOUNDARIES

If this interracial union was not something many Americans tended to frown on, two reasons for that might be adduced. First, assuming the couple would settle in the United States, Americans could expect that the Chinese man would improve himself by undergoing the beneficial process of Americanization; he would shed his queue, his silk robes, his antiquated beliefs, and his "pagan" religion and adopt American customs, dress, ideas, and religion. Second, and more intriguingly, Americans might not object to the union because they might find themselves strangely fascinated by the prospect of becoming more Chinese themselves, even if they neither approved of that outcome nor fully understood their ambivalence about it. In this way, the stern critique of Chinese culture and the irresistible attraction to it, far from being mutually exclusive, could reside within the same person. While exhorting China to change in the modern world, individuals might at the same time have found Chinese culture so appealing that they actually could entertain the thought of becoming Chinese. In fact, in several works of popular literature from this period, we find these competing strains dueling with one another inside the minds of the characters.

One year before the Centennial, Louisa May Alcott, best known as the author of *Little Women*, published the novel *Eight Cousins* (1875). Rose, the young protagonist, meets two Chinese merchants at a New England harbor who have just arrived from China:

Mr. Whang Lo was an elderly gentleman in American costume, with his pigtail neatly wound round his head. He spoke English, and was talking busily . . . in the most commonplace way,—so Rose considered him a failure. But Fun See was delightfully Chinese from his junk-like shoes to the bottom of his pagoda hat; for he had got himself up in style, and was a mass of silk jackets and slouchy trousers. He was short and fat, and waddled comically; his eyes were very 'slanting,' as Rose said; his queue was long, so were his nails; his yellow face was plump and shiny, and he was altogether a highly satisfactory Chinaman.

Through Rose's eyes, Alcott delineates two distinct types of Chinese people. Whang Lo's language, dress, and mannerisms all bespeak a high degree of Americanization. Since his extensive contact with the Western world through commerce has eliminated what Rose feels to be authentic Chinese traits, she pronounces him a "failure." The aptly named Fun See is far more pleasant for her to regard. In contrast to his associate, he possesses all the wonderful attributes she has come to expect from someone from China, and so she can enthusiastically declare him "a highly satisfactory Chinaman."

But is he really the quintessential "Chinaman" as she professes? Raised in a wealthy merchant-class family, Fun See has always been well-fed and has never been subjected to any hard physical labor; as a result, he can grow long nails and maintain a cherubic appearance. In addition, his wealth allows him not only to attire himself in luxurious silken garments but also to dazzle Rose by presenting her with splendid Chinese handicrafts—a porcelain tea kettle and a painted fan. Fun See appeals to Rose for precisely the same reason the elite members of the Chinese Commission appealed to visitors at the Centennial. In his presence, she can enjoy the experience of becoming temporarily ensconced in the beautiful but bizarre trappings of upper-class Chinese culture.

However, Fun See's oriental exoticism proves fleeting. He has come to the United States "to be educated," and prolonged exposure to American society transforms him. Six months after Rose's initial encounter with him, she sees him again at a dinner party and finds him greatly altered in appearance. He has cut off his queue, donned American clothes, and learned English at an American school. Although the aura of enchantment has left the young Chinese merchant, Rose shows no sign of disapprobation, and her male cousins all joke that he has "improved" himself. Furthermore, when Fun See invites a white woman to dance, she is "immensely flattered by his admiration" and even signals to him that she would like a kiss; not one to disappoint, he politely obliges her request. In sum, although Rose had been pleasantly bewitched by Fun See's exotic appearance at their first meeting, both she and others agree that it is only right and proper that he become Americanized, even though this metamorphosis requires that he begin to resemble Whang Lo, the man she initially dubbed a "failure."[70]

Cherished by Rose initially for his exotic difference, the aristocratic Fun See ultimately wins the approval of his American acquaintances by learning their language and conforming to their dress and customs. In 1877, an actual situation involving a Chinese government official followed the pattern established in Alcott's fictional example.[71] An official, accompanied by both his wife and a second woman believed to be his sister-in-law, was "received with open arms" when he first took up residence in Providence. A few ministers called the man a "heathen," but the local community actually opposed the church and defended the visitor, arguing that his religion was "beautiful," and that "no man who bowed so gracefully and said such nice things could be anything but good." While the citizens saw the Chinese newcomer as strange and exotic (his wife had bound feet), they also viewed him as a man of cultivation, refinement, and learning. Indeed, it was to this lofty perception that he owed his positive reception.

As intrigued as people initially were by his novelty and difference, they nonetheless withheld their long-term acceptance of him, making that contingent on his successful adoption of American ways. The official was able to impress them simply by subordinating the Chinese elements in his physical appearance and accentuating the American. "He was an amiable gentleman," wrote the journalist who penned this story, "who dressed in the Rhode Island style" and "put up his pigtail with hairpins" in order to "conceal it under his hat." Like Fun See, the official seemed on the verge of shedding what had originally lent him such a pleasingly exotic appearance, and the community viewed this Americanization process as a worthy project. Indeed, women who had hoped to oversee his transformation personally expressed regret that he was already a married man: "More than one lady . . . took the broad general ground that for a Christian woman to marry a well-meaning Confucian . . . would be a noble exhibition of enlightened philanthropy." Apparently, Providence society was prepared not just to welcome the Chinese newcomer into the fold but even to advocate his marriage to a white woman if matrimony would accelerate his adoption of Christianity and American customs.

Interestingly, the Providence community eventually grew disillusioned with its Chinese resident. However, this change of heart occurred only after an unexpected incident brought about a disturbing disclosure regarding the marital customs of the official: The woman believed to be his sister-in-law bore him a son. Shocked and outraged, the community abruptly abandoned its "noble" project of Americanizing the official, on the grounds that some offending Chinese traits, such as bigamy, were too ingrained to be extirpated. Simply put, he was deemed to be too old and too set in his ways to ever fully embrace American ways and customs.[72]

It is important to note that, during these cultural collisions between the East and the West, the Chinese side often exerts a reciprocal, sinifying influence. In Alcott's *Eight Cousins*, for example, the Chinese character Fun See is not the only one who undergoes a transformation. The protagonist, Rose, delights not just in inspecting Chinese things but also in playfully flirting with the idea of becoming like the Chinese herself. She never crosses that line, but the act of approaching it becomes a great source of fascination and amusement. When she parts company with Fun See, she finds herself holding many of the items commonly associated with a Chinese person—a fan, parasol, and tea set—and the feeling is not at all disagreeable. "I feel as if I had really been to China," she remarks, "and I'm sure I look so." Similarly, at the Centennial, visitors purchased fans, gongs, tea sets, hats, and parasols for this same purpose of playful experimentation. Many of those who criticized China for failing to modernize would at the same time relish the opportunity to transform their wardrobes and their homes with Chinese things.[73]

In *Eight Cousins*, Alcott placed Rose's flirtation with Chinese culture on the periphery of her story. Another novelist, however, Edward Greey, boldly placed the issue at the center of his novel *Blue Jackets; or, the Adventures of J. Thompson, A.B., among "the Heathen Chinee"* (1871). When this rollicking adventure story first appeared, reviewers praised it for its realistic depiction of China. According to *Frank Leslie's Illustrated Newspaper*, the author "takes us into a country which the novelist has rarely or never visited—China." Similarly, the *New York Lantern* promised that the "reader will learn more . . . than he would from a dozen 'Travels in China.'" But what fascinated reviewers most was the love affair between the swashbuckling American sailor Jerry Thompson and the young Chinese tea-picker A-tae.[74] The novel is an early manifestation of a theme that would later appear with frequency in literature, theater, and the opera: the forbidden love between a white man and an Asian woman and that ends in the woman's tragic death.[75]

After various plot twists, Jerry Thompson finds himself having become a fugitive in China, fleeing from Chinese authorities. To render himself inconspicuous, he dissembles as a Chinese man. He adopts the Chinese wardrobe, attaches an artificial queue to the back of his head, and learns much of the language. On one occasion, he evades his pursuers by disappearing into the tea fields and posing as a hired hand; it is here that he meets the pretty tea-picker A-Tae. A true romantic, Jerry instantly falls in love and even entertains dreams of matrimony with A-tae and of a family of Chinese children. As for A-tae, she is equally smitten by the handsome stranger who, unlike the Chinese men she knows, refuses to treat her "like an inferior animal."

Yet after tantalizing readers with the intriguing possibility of interracial sex, biracial children, and an American who chooses a life of Chinese domesticity,

Greey quickly reroutes the course of the novel. The Chinese police find A-tae's brother, who leads them straight to the cave where the couple is hiding. Shocked by his sister's behavior, the brother plunges a sword into her chest. After Jerry kills the brother, he seizes the mortally wounded A-tae, holds her in his arms, and says, "I am not worthy of such love as yours, you pure lily." Before the spirit departs her body, A-tae is able to respond, "Yung-Yung-Sho, I'm-so-happy!" Then her head drops to her shoulder, signifying that she is dead.[76]

Jerry grieves for quite a while, but he eventually returns to the United States, where he finds a Caucasian wife. Still moved by his romance with A-tae and tempted by a life in China, he nonetheless decides to relegate that to the past and concentrate on his new life in America. Going further than Alcott, Greey created a protagonist who not only demonstrates a strong fascination with Chinese culture but also seriously considers "going native" before he ultimately chooses to live again among his own people. Interestingly, in the final lines of the novel, one detects in Jerry a hint of lingering dissatisfaction with his choice: "Jerry sometimes talks about his adventures . . . but never reverts to the sad fate of the poor Chinese girl. He is happy in the society of his wife and friends; and though she is not forgotten, he has no desire to dwell upon the memory of 'A-tae.'"[77] Jerry's willful determination neither to speak nor to think of A-tae suggests that she continues to haunt him. Indeed, one almost gets the impression that Greey wrote this particular ending because it was safe and proper—not because it was necessarily the ending he wanted to write.

In one final literary example, Harry French's *Our Boys in China* (1883), characters demonstrate this same ambiguous tendency to exhort China to change while at the same time exploring its seductive possibilities. The novel describes the adventures of two brothers—Scott, age fifteen, and Paul, seven—who must travel alone through China after surviving a shipwreck.[78] Before the wreck, they meet a missionary onboard the vessel who has lived in China. They express their curiosity about China and he answers all their questions. He disabuses them of certain stereotypes (the Chinese do not, for example, eat rats except in famine), but he concurs with the commonly held view that Chinese are not a forward-looking people: "They go back, back, back, and care very little for anything ahead. They hate progressive, modern notions,—railways and telegraphy are abominations in their eyes."[79]

In addition to being culturally backward, the Chinese are depicted in *Our Boys* as in need of enlightenment from Americans. In one episode, young Paul sits atop a coil of rope, preaching to a gathering of "swarthy" Asians who adopt a worshipful pose in his presence (fig. 9.11). Like his literary cousin, the angelic little Eva of Harriet Beecher Stowe's *Uncle Tom's Cabin*, Paul is a golden child who radiates a angelic glow over the more darkly complected men huddled beneath him:

Scott . . . thought he had never seen anything so beautiful in all his life as his brother Paul, at that moment, perched on the coil of rope, the silver moonlight falling softly on the golden hair, the little hands clasping his knees, the blue eyes fixed intently on . . . the three swarthy men of the Orient lying prostrate before him, as though he were a little god and they his humble devotees.

This notion of Paul being the savior of Asia appears more than once. A Chinese man on the boat named Ling becomes so devoted to Paul that he bends over and kisses the child's feet. And to protect his young master at night, Ling curls up to sleep on the floor at the entrance to Paul's quarters.[80]

After the shipwreck, the boys find themselves faced with the daunting task of traveling across the southern part of China in order to reach Hong Kong. Along the way, Paul sometimes seeks to correct the flaws he observes in Chinese society, with the pastime of cricket-fighting being the most memorable target of his moral outrage: "He had witnessed an injustice, and against it, instinctively his little heart rebelled." In an accusatory tone, Paul cries "Shame! Shame!" to the gamers and then proceeds to intrude on the contest, scoop up the insect combatants, and carry them to safety. While Scott agrees that the custom is abhorrent, he tries to temper Paul's reformist streak, believing that stern demands for change do not belong to the sphere of an outsider. "If it [China] has different customs," he explains to his younger brother, "and mean ones, we must overlook them; we are not called upon to reform all China."[81]

Curiously, despite Paul's insistence that China conform to his moral vision, it is he and not his older brother who is seduced by the culture. As the boys travel, Paul begins to absorb aspects from his Chinese environment with startling rapidity. Since the boys stay mainly in the palatial homes of Chinese prefects and governors, the ways and customs Paul internalizes are those of elite Chinese society. In this way, the ardent reformer Paul discovers that Chinese high culture is dangerously alluring. He expresses his desire to grow a queue, picks up the language with astonishing ease, and immediately takes to his new Chinese garments. In his silk outfit, French writes, Paul "began trotting about the room precisely like a Chinaman, uttering short words and simple phrases which he had already learned of the Chinese language." The "very last link" that "bound" Paul to America "seemed [to be] snapping." Indeed, the alarming sinification of Paul is a subplot of the novel. "But for his golden hair and blue eyes and pink-white skin," French writes, "one would surely have thought him a veritable Chinese." Baffled and concerned by the metamorphosis, Scott makes attempts to forestall it before it is too late. "Paul," he resolutely believes, "should not be a Chinese boy when he reached Hong Kong."[82]

Of course, the two boys exit the country before the transformation is complete, and so Paul, like Jerry Thompson, is able to return to his normal American life. Interestingly, in writing the introduction to *Our Boys in China*, French felt the need to state in unambiguous fashion his view that China needed to change. Although the boys "found some good things" among the Chinese, he summarized, "it does not at all follow that China cannot become better than she is."[83] Yet, as has been shown, those "good things" in China prove so tantalizing as to nearly lure Paul away from his American identity. And so there runs through *Our Boys in China* a subversive current that, while it cannot subvert the dominant narrative, does destabilize it as it did in *Blue Jackets*. In both novels, Americans who flirt with the idea of becoming Chinese ultimately pull back before the transformation is complete. And in *Eight Cousins* and *Our Boys in China*, Americans who are fascinated by Chinese culture end up endorsing the China's Americanization

These conflicting desires moved to the foreground of the Centennial when a group of 113 Chinese boys who, as part of an educational mission, were studying in the United States arrived in Philadelphia. Although present solely for the purpose of seeing the exhibits, these Chinese teenagers captured the attention of visitors and the press alike. Had it not been for them, enthusiasts for Chinese culture would have continued their love affair with it without having to confront the issue of modernization. Likewise, critics would have persisted in faulting the Chinese for their backwardness while extolling the virtues of the progressive Japanese. The presence of these Chinese boys at the Centennial challenged both groups to modify their views. It forced the critics to muffle their disapproval and admit that China was not as hopeless as they had previously thought. And enthusiasts had to concede that China must improve itself by following America's lead. Apparently their idealized conception of their own country as a City upon a Hill trumped their love for exoticism.

## CHINESE YANKEES

The Chinese Educational Mission (C.E.M.) was the brainchild of one man, Yung Wing. Brought to the United States by a missionary in 1847, Yung possessed, in his own words, "a great inclination to get a liberal education." Indeed, he was passionate about it, to the point where he risked alienating family members in China who did not see the value of a Western education. While residing in the United States, he maintained a correspondence with Samuel Wells Williams, whom he had known in China. Yung had great faith in Williams, trusting him to deliver money and important messages to his family. "You are better acquainted with the Chinese" than are other Westerners, Yung told Williams in a letter, adding that his own family members "put more confidence in you than [in] anybody else." In 1849, Yung tasked Williams with the difficult chore of explaining to his uncle the wisdom behind his plan to study in the United States for six additional years. This was no easy assignment, he explained to Williams, because the Chinese do not grasp "the object, the advantage, and the value of being educated. Ignorance and superstition have sealed up the noble faculties of their minds."[84]

Yung's hard work and passion for learning paid off. In 1850, he gained acceptance to the college of Samuel Wells Williams's dream—Yale. Though he found the schoolwork tough-going in the beginning, he gradually acclimated himself to the rigorous curriculum and ended up enjoying a strong academic career that included awards in English composition. The Yale experience also accelerated the pace of a personal transformation that was taking place in Yung. When he began to attend classes in 1850, he wore a long queue and Chinese tunic, but by the end of his first year both had disappeared. By the time of his graduation, he had Americanized to a great extent, even though people who did not know him still regarded him as an exotic novelty. For this reason, commencement exercises attracted a larger crowd in 1854 than it had in previous years. The additional spectators had apparently come solely to catch a glimpse of Yale's first Chinese graduate. "Being the first Chinaman who had ever been known to go through a first-class American college, I naturally attracted considerable attention," Yung later wrote, "and my nationality, of course, added piquancy to my popularity."

With his college days at an end, Yung Wing faced intense pressure to become a minister and devote his life to proselytizing the Chinese. He opted not to follow that path, however, because in his heart he knew he was meant for a different purpose. Yung was convinced that China had to change in order to survive in the modern world, but he did not believe that Christianity was the right vehicle for change. "I was determined that the rising generation of China," he wrote, "should enjoy the same educational advantages that I had enjoyed; that through western education China might become regenerated." This single goal became "the guiding star of my ambition." For many years after college, Yung worked in China, waiting for the right opportunity to bring Western learning to it.

In the 1850s and '60s, Yung Wing became a naturalized U.S. citizen, married a white American woman, and volunteered to fight for the Union Army during the Civil War.[85] In 1870, the opportunity he had been seeking at last presented itself. That year, he submitted to Zeng Guofan, a high-ranking government official, a proposal in which he volunteered to take thirty boys, twelve to fifteen years of age, to the United States every year to study in American secondary schools and colleges. As the chief architect of the Self-Strengthening Movement, Zeng subscribed to the theory that, by adopting the same technologies that had made Western nations so powerful, the Qing government could defend itself against internal rebellions and protect China's traditional culture from further foreign encroachment. In short, China must imitate the West in boats and guns but not in morals and ideas. Zeng readily approved Yung's plan because he believed the graduates would one day replace the foreign teachers in China, help revamp the military, and guide the construction of a sound industrial base. In 1872, the first detachment of thirty young boys embarked for Hartford, Connecticut, the headquarters of the C.E.M.[86]

In Hartford, B. G. Northrup, commissioner of education for the state of Connecticut, convinced Yung Wing to divide the students into groups of two and three and place them in American host families. Greater contact with Americans, he argued, would both enrich the boys' experience and expedite their acquisition of the English language. But the Chinese government, fearing the adverse effects of excessive emphasis on American culture, insisted on striking a proper balance with Chinese culture. Toward that end, Chinese teachers accompanied the students to Hartford to inculcate in them Confucian ideals and to ensure that the boys maintained high standards in their study of the Chinese classics. Yung Wing abided by this stipulation, but in his heart he considered Western learning to be of paramount importance, and his supervision of the boys might have subtly reflected this bias.[87]

In newspaper and magazine articles and in personal accounts, one never finds a negative word written on either the students in the C.E.M. or their Chinese instructors. "The students of the Mission have thus far . . . exhibited excellent ability as scholars, and . . . have been marked by their exemplary conduct," the Reverend Joseph H. Twichell said before a gathering at Yale Law School. "They have everywhere been most hospitably received. They are certainly worthy to be objects of the highest and most friendly interest to every Christian citizen in the United States."[88] Similarly, when the fourth deployment of thirty students arrived in 1875, the *New York Times* devoted a significant amount of space to a description of the latest Chinese commissioner to accompany the mission. The reporter called him "a gentleman of high and distinguished rank" and proceeded to list the honors and degrees he had earned at the most prestigious institutions in China. As for the students, he praised their sharp minds: "The boys . . . intellectually bear traces of more than ordinary capacity." He also approved of the egalitarian nature of the program—boys from poor backgrounds could, through academic achievement, earn a place next to their more privileged peers. "The poorest is arrayed in silks and satins of as fine a texture as the highest titled among them."[89]

Once situated in Hartford, the boys faced the immediate challenge of fitting in both at school and in the community. William Lyon Phelps, a classmate of some of them, looked back fondly on his experience with them. Above all else, they possessed "a genius for adaptation" that made their stay in the United States a resounding success. They excelled in their studies, learned English rapidly, forged strong and lasting friendships, and even attracted the loveliest dance partners at parties—often to the chagrin of their American classmates. Like Yung Wing's marriage to a white woman and the marriage of a member of the Chinese Commission also to a white woman, these dance combinations did not elicit public outrage, a response corroborated by the conjugal interest that several Providence women expressed in the Chinese official living there.[90] According to Phelps, the boys also pursued athletics with a competitive spirit, learning both football and baseball. In football, the boys would tie their queues around their heads before stepping onto the playing field so as not to tempt opposing tacklers.

> I can well remember, when we used to 'choose up sides' at football, how the first choice invariably went to Se Chung, a short thick-set boy, built close to the ground, who ran like a hound and dodged like a cat. What Se Chung had in grace and speed, Kong had in bull strength. Built broad and strong, eternally good-natured and smiling, he would cross the goal line, carrying four or five Americans on his shoulders. In baseball, Tsang was a great pitcher, impossible to hit.

Looking back on his experience with the boys, Phelps did not think he had "ever known a finer group of boys or young men."[91]

Before the students made the trip to Philadelphia, visitors there were already familiar with the C.E.M. because samples of the boys' academic work had been on display in the Main Building. The Centennial included an international competition in which judges from several countries assessed the achievements of participating states and nations in such categories as manufactures, medicines, handicrafts, machinery, and the arts. In his state's entry in the category "Educational Systems, Methods, and Libraries," Dr. Northrup included the schoolwork of the Chinese students, and it received accolades from the judges:

> Considering the age of the pupils, the difficulties inseparable from the pursuit of studies in a foreign language . . . and the shortness of their term of study, the results presented were very remarkable. In one point of view, these specimens of Chinese pupils' work were the most interesting objects shown in the whole Exhibition, representing . . . that the most populous nation in the world, until so recently refusing intercourse with the other nations, has not only revolutionized her commercial policy but has actually organized an educational commission . . . and sent them to this newest of the nations . . . at the expense of the empire. It means a dawn of a new era in Asiatic civilization.[92]

Up to this point, the Chinese had inspired mostly comments to the effect that, while they were capable of creating stunning beauty in their handicrafts, they were also conservative, hidebound, and locked in the misty past. All of a sudden, some were beginning to regard China as a progressive Asian nation much like Japan.

Not surprisingly, the boys became the center of attention the moment they arrived in Philadelphia on August 22, 1876. Symbolic of the partial nature of their Americanization was their attire, which combined American with Chinese elements (fig. 9.12). To augment the educational experience, notable professors volunteered to give them guided tours and lectures. Yet despite the trip's ostensible purpose of exposing the boys to the highest attainments of world culture, the students quickly discovered that they themselves had become a second, though unofficial, Chinese exhibit. As they moved about, they attracted crowds of curious onlookers and newspaper reporters. According to the *Daily Graphic*, whenever the students paused to rest, they were immediately "pounced upon and interviewed." The "bright, intelligent looks on their faces," wrote a reporter for the *New York Tribune*, "show that their thirst for knowledge is just as keen as that of boys who do not have almond-shaped eyes, or wear their hair in a braided string."[93]

The upwelling of support for the Chinese students culminated on August 24, in Judges' Hall, where each of the boys received the rare honor of a formal introduction to President Ulysses S. Grant. After Grant had shaken the hands of all 113 students, everyone congregated in a larger room and listened to speeches marking the occasion. The most substantial words were delivered by Joseph Roswell Hawley, ex-general of the Union Army and former governor of Connecticut, who was serving as president of the Centennial Commission. Six years earlier, Hawley had delivered a speech in which he voiced his opinion on the controversial "Chinese question." Although decidedly against any restrictions on immigration, he admitted to wishing that the Chinese who came were "in a better condition" and had "a better education in regard to American institutions."[94] Now he found himself standing before a large group of Chinese boys who perfectly matched his ideal specifications; in the precise areas where he had observed shortcomings among Chinese immigrants—degree of Americanization, level of education, and overall refinement—these boys were strong.

This is "the strangest audience I have ever addressed," Hawley remarked as he scanned the several rows of youths, "and yet, it fills me with pleasure to see your bright faces." Twenty-five years earlier it was "a matter of wonder to see one of your countrymen" in the United States, but now it was within the power of these boys both to change China for the better and to effect a mutually beneficial relationship with the United States:

We are a great and ingenious people, as you may see in our machinery. You will study it, and when you go home you can tell your country men what you have seen, and may invent some new labor-saving device . . . of your own. After you have spent your years of probation here you will go home and will be a power in your land, and we will know each other better, and can exchange our knowledge and become better friends.

Hawley could have delivered a few perfunctory remarks and stepped down from the podium, but he chose instead to share his vision of what the long-term effect of the C.E.M. should be: nothing less than a new China remade according to the American example. Rather than merely acquiring the latest ideas and inventions of the United States, China should adopt the American inventive spirit itself and use it to develop new machinery of its own. In this way, Hawley's goals surpassed those of the Self-Strengthening Movement out of which the C.E.M. had initially sprung and according to which the Chinese mind was, as an essential tenet of that movement, to remain inviolable to external influences. But in Hawley's far-reaching vision, American ideas would actually penetrate the Chinese mind and utterly transform it. He foresaw a colossal American ally across the Pacific, populated by Chinese Yankees, that would exchange ideas and inventions with the United States. After these prophetic words, the next speaker rose and added that next time China should send girls too.[95]

If Li Gui understood the full implications of Hawley's speech, it probably filled him with grave concern. As progressive as his thinking was, he would have wondered whether the Americanization process, once set in motion, could be halted before one's entire thinking became subsumed by it. Could Western ideas coexist peacefully with Chinese ideas inside a single mind, or would the former eclipse the latter, undermine traditional Confucian morals, and leave Hawley's Chinese Yankees as the undesirable yet inevitable result? With these vexing thoughts in mind, Li singled out some of the older boys and posed question after question relating to Confucianism. In this way, he sought to determine whether their absorption of American "technical knowledge" had precluded a traditional Chinese education. To his relief, the boys passed his test, indicating that Chinese values had not suffered as a result of the sudden and powerful infusion of Western ideas.[96]

# CONCLUSION

On November 10, 1876, Ulysses S. Grant stood before a crowd and officially announced, "I now declare the International Exhibition of 1876 closed."[97] In a

gesture of goodwill, both the Chinese government and Hu Quang Yung be-
queathed many of the remaining pieces of the Chinese exhibit to the Philadelphia Museum of Art, which was established in the wake of the Exposition.[98]
The showing made by Japan was remarkable, of course, but it did not prevent
most American visitors from thinking highly of the China they encountered in
Philadelphia—regardless of which China that was. In an odd twist of events,
Americans at the Exposition were exposed to two versions of the Chinese empire, traditional China and Yankee China, neither of which accurately represented the actual country. The official Chinese exhibit, displaying mostly objects that only the wealthy could afford, reflected the lifestyle of only a tiny
stratum, the uppermost stratum, of Chinese society. As for the students of the
C.E.M., they offered Americans a pleasing glimpse of Yankee China, which,
being purely hypothetical, did not exist except as a possibility in the future.

## NOTES

1. Dee Brown, *The Year of the Century: 1876* (New York: Charles Scribner's Sons,
1966), 2, 12. Richard Nicolai places the attendance figure at 10 million, or one in every
four Americans. *Centennial Philadelphia* (Bryn Mawr, Pa.: Bryn Mawr Press, 1976), 84.

2. William Dean Howells, "A Sennight of the Centennial," *Atlantic Monthly* (July
1876), 96. A sennight is one week.

3. Bayard Taylor, "Foreign Pavilions and Booths," *New York Tribune* (22 August
1876).

4. Ibid.

5. The year 1876 marked the onset of one of the worst famines in modern Chinese
history. See *Cincinnati Commercial* (31 July 1876); North China *Herald* (22 March
1877).

6. When Bayard Taylor went to "inspect the dwelling of a Chinaman of the better
class," even he was modestly impressed. India, China, and Japan (New York: Putnam,
1855), 334.

7. China had participated in the 1873 exposition in Vienna. *The I. G. in Peking:
Letters of Robert Hart Chinese Maritime Customs, 1868–1907*, ed. John King Fair-
bank, Katherine Frost Bruner, and Elizabeth Macleod Matheson (Cambridge:
Belknap Press, 1975), 99.

8. Contrary to the mistaken assumption that the Office of Chinese Maritime Customs Service only served the interests of Western nations trading in China, Chinese
authorities approved of the arrangement, received substantial revenue from it, and
were responsible for both appointing the Western officials and paying their salaries.
*The I. G. in Peking*, 5–6.

9. The traveling Commission included James Hart, Robert Hart's son who served as commissioner at Canton; Alfred Huber, a French customs official; and James Hammond, the commissioner at Swatow. The three companies were represented in Philadelphia by Edward Cunningham (Russell and Co.), W. W. Parkin (Olyphant and Co.), and F. P. Knight (Knight and Co.). *The Catalogue of the Chinese Imperial Maritime Customs Collection, at the United States International Exhibition, Philadelphia, 1876* (Shanghai: Inspector General of Chinese Maritime Customs, 1876); *The Philadelphia Inquirer* (4 April 1876);*The I. G. in Peking,* 72, 212–13.

10. For a list of these companies, see United States Centennial Commission, *Reports and Awards,* ed. Francis A. Walker (Philadelphia: J. B. Lippincott, 1877), 27. Several are also mentioned in the *Philadelphia Public Ledger's* lengthy description of the Chinese exhibit (21 April 1876).

11. Frank H. Norton, *Illustrated Historical Register of the Centennial Exhibition, Philadelphia, 1876* (New York: American News Company, 1879), 244–47; J. S. Ingram, *The Centennial Exposition, Described and Illustrated* (Philadelphia: Hubbard Brothers, 1876), 571–73.

12. Li Gui, *New Account of Traveling around the World* (Hunan People's Publisher, 1980), 8–9. Li Gui's writings, which are in Chinese, have been translated by Minhui Wang Haddad for use in this chapter.

13. Pearl Buck once wrote that, regrettably, the "beauty of China" is lodged in the possessions of the "wealthy and leisured." The "poorer and more ignorant classes" have no access to it. "Beauty in China," *Forum* (March 1924), 334. Several years later, Buck would describe beauty in the lives of common people in her book *The Good Earth* (1931).

14. Edward C. Bruce, *The Century: Its Fruits and Its Festivals, Being a History and Description of the Centennial Exhibition, with a Preliminary Outline of Modern Progress* (Philadelphia: J. B. Lippincott, 1877), 95.

15. *Chinese Immigration: The Social, Moral, and Political Effect* (Sacramento, Calif.: State Printing Office, 1876). Richard Dillon, *The Hatchet Men: The Story of the Tong Wars in San Francisco's Chinatown* (New York: Ballantine Books, 1962), 79–110.

16. *The Philadelphia Inquirer* (4 April 1876); Brown, 114.

17. According to the *Authorized Visitor's Guide to the Centennial Exhibition,* the Japanese had 17,080 square feet at their disposal, and most other nations occupied between 1,000 and 5,000 (Philadelphia: J. B. Lippincott, 1876). The Chinese exhibit filled 8,844 square feet. *Catalogue of the Chinese . . . Collection.*

18. Li Gui, 8–9. Advertisement, Thomas Birch and Son, auctioneers, *Philadelphia Public Ledger* (4 May 1876).

19. Taken from a newspaper article pasted into the scrapbook of the Philadelphia Centennial, Library Company of Philadelphia. In most clippings, the name of the newspaper and the date of the article have literally been cut out. For this reason, readers are referred to the scrapbook itself as the source of information. See also Ingram, 576. As with other international expositions, the Chinese workers in Philadelphia were almost certainly a part of the Chinese Commission and sent by Robert Hart.*The I. G. in Peking,* 250–53.

20. Rebecca Harding Davis wrote that on opening day "the great American people had for the first time rushed in upon" the Chinese ("Odd Corners at the Exposition," *Harper's Weekly* [25 November 1876]). "The Centennial," *Harper's Weekly*, (20 May 1876), 413; "Our Centennial," (27 May 1876), 422; Nicolai, 16.

21. Bruce, 112 (italic in original).

22. *Cincinnati Commercial* (25 May 1876).

23. "Fogyism and Progress," *Cincinnati Daily Gazette* (24 May 1876).

24. Walter A. McDougall, *Let the Sea Make a Noise—: A History of the North Pacific from Magellan to MacArthur* (New York: Basic Books, 1993), 270–72.

25. Brown, 298.

26. James McCabe, *The Illustrated History of the Centennial Exhibition* (1876; reprint, Philadelphia: National Publishing Company, 1976), 417.

27. Nathan Appleton, *Centennial Movement, 1876: A Comedy in Five Acts* (Boston: Lockwood, Brooks, 1877), 28–29.

28. Scrapbook of the Centennial, Library Company of Philadelphia.

29. *Cincinnati Daily Gazette* (30 May 1876); Li Gui, 10.

30. Scrapbook of the Centennial, Library Company of Philadelphia.

31. Howells, 97.

32. *Cincinnati Daily Gazette* (8 July 1876).

33. Scrapbook of the Centennial, Library Company of Philadelphia.

34. *Cincinnati Commercial* (25 August 1876).

35. Howells, 96–97.

36. Although in his letters Robert Hart said little about this particular construction project, he wrote voluminously about the Chinese exhibit at the Health Exhibition of 1884 in London. Clearly, Hart had a talent for arranging a space in a way that would grant Westerners the oriental experience they craved. For the London exhibit, Hart even agreed to send along a "Tea-House" that, though seeming Chinese, was unlike anything in China because it was modeled on the Western idea of how a Chinese teahouse should look—not an authentic structure. "The English idea of the Chinese Tea-House," Hart explained, "has nothing corresponding to it in China except that there are buildings in which people can . . . drink tea: if we could supply you with one of them bodily, you would indeed have a slice out of the real life of China, but English sightseers would neither eat nor sit in it, and the Committee would very soon beg us to move it out."*The I. G. in Peking,* 516–20.

37. Sung Sing Kung, a merchant who worked at the exhibit, sold the gateways to the Philadelphia Museum of Art at the end of the Centennial (Accession files for 1876 Exhibition, Office of the Registrar, Philadelphia Museum of Art). On another gateway, Li Gui wrote "Treasury of Heaven" on the top and, down the side, couplets: "Treasures gathered from eighteen provinces, the craftsmanship is superb" and "Celebrate the Centennial, the friendship is everlasting" (Li Gui, 8–9).

38. *Cincinnati Commercial* (May 25, 1876).

39. *Josiah Allen's Wife as a P.A. and P.I., Samantha at the Centennial* (Hartford, Conn.: American Publishing Company, 1877), 439. See also Norton, 87.

40. Rebecca Harding Davis, "Odd Corners at the Exposition."

41. McCabe, 418–19.

42. *Cincinnati Commercial* (25 May 1876).

43. Robert Rydell, *All the World's a Fair: Visions of Empire at American International Expositions, 1876–1916* (Chicago: University of Chicago Press, 1984), 2–3, 21–22, 24–26. One should note that Howells did not lump all American Indians together indiscriminately. In fact, he called the Apaches and the Comanches "red savages" because he believed their presence threatened the existence of the Pueblos, whom he saw as a "peaceful and industrious people" (Howells, 103).

44. James Dale, *What Ben Beverly Saw at the Great Exposition* (Chicago: Centennial, 1876), 76.

45. Chang-fang Chen, "Barbarian Paradise: Chinese Views of the United States, 1784–1911" (Ph.D. diss., Indiana University, 1985), 128. Li Gui, 8–9.

46. David Bailey, *"Eastward Ho!" or, Leaves from the Diary of a Centennial Pilgrim* (Highland County, Ohio: The Highland News Office, 1877), 72.

47. *Cincinnati Commercial* (25 May 1876).

48. The following description of the Chinese exhibit draws from several sources: Norton, 244–47; Ingram, 573–75, 580–84; The *Philadelphia Public Ledger* (21 August 1876); and the Scrapbook of the Philadelphia Centennial, Library Company of Philadelphia.

49. Americans were starting to visit the handful of Chinese physicians practicing in the United States at this time. According to a newspaper story, one physician in New York "enjoyed a very large patronage, many of the richest ladies of the city being among his credulous patients." The journalist wrote that the Chinese doctor used medicines such as "serpents" and "revolting salves" to treat his patients. Another doctor moved to New York from New Orleans, where he had been "very successful," with "many white persons being among his patients." "Chinese in New-York," *New York Times* (26 December 1873). To attract non-Chinese patients, the first doctor mentioned above placed advertisements in the *New York Times* (6 July 1870).

50. Rebecca Harding Davis, "Odd Corners at the Exposition."

51. Ingram, 571. According to Neil Harris, inexpensive labor allowed Asian nations to produce commodities that Europe and the United States could not duplicate despite their sophisticated machinery. "All the World a Melting Pot? Japan at American Fairs, 1876–1904," in *Mutual Images: Essays in American-Japanese Relations*, ed. Akira Iriye (Cambridge: Harvard University Press, 1975), 34–35.

52. Ingram, 573. A Philadelphia journalist echoed this sentiment. The United States was more technologically advanced than China, he wrote, but the latter showed "a marvelous skill, an individuality of design and delicacy of manipulation in their hand-work deserving of attentive study" (*Philadelphia Public Ledger* [12 May 1876]).

53. Rebecca Harding Davis, "Odd Corners at the Exposition."

54. McCabe, 340–41. The telegraph office was situated in the west end of the Main Building, very close to the Chinese exhibit (*The Philadelphia Inquirer* [28 April 1876). To another reporter, a trip to the Chinese enclosure was tantamount to time travel: "It is with venerable admiration that the eye dares to roam . . . over teapots, out of which Confucius himself may have often sipped the fragrant leaf decoction. . . . All

these things as one meanders about the tangle, are not only queer, but quite thrilling to think of—carrying us back to the cradle of the race" (*Cincinnati Commercial* [25 May 1876]).

55. Jonathan Spence, *The Search for Modern China* (New York: Norton, 1990), 216–20.

56. Li Gui, 128.

57. "The Chinese Display in the Main Building," *Cincinnati Daily Gazette* (8 July 1876).

58. Li Gui, 26–27.

59. Li Gui, 25–27, 36–38; Henry Adams, *The Education of Henry Adams* (New York: The Modern Library, 1931), 380–81.

60. At later world's fairs, ethnological exhibitions often took the form of "native villages." Paul Greenhalgh, *Ephemeral Vistas: The Expositions Universelles, Great Exhibitions, and World's Fairs, 1851–1931* (Manchester: Manchester University Press, 1988), 82–86. Howells, 96–97.

61. Li Gui, 7–8.

62. *Cincinnati Daily Gazette* (8 July 1876).

63. *Cincinnati Commercial* (25 August 1876).

64. Rebecca Harding Davis, "A Rainy Day at the Exposition," *Harper's Weekly* (18 November 1876).

65. Bailey, 71. To determine the origin of a particular piece, one individual presented it to a Chinese attendant who "spoke a few words of English." The latter replied, "No, No, not China—not China—don't know—maybe Europe—not China" (Annie Trumbull Slosson, *The China Hunters Club, by the Youngest Member* [New York: Harper and Brothers, 1878], 263).

66. McCabe, 418–19.

67. Some antiques and silks remained because of the hefty price tags they carried (Li Gui, 9). A high tariff on imported silks might have dampened sales in that department (Francis Walker, *The World's Fair: A Critical Account* [New York: A. S. Barnes, 1878], 42).

68. Mary Louise Pratt uses this term (*Imperial Eyes: Travel Writing and Transculturation* [London and New York: Routledge, 1992], 6).

69. *Cincinnati Commercial* (2 June 1876); *Hartford Courant* (23 August 1876).

70. Louisa May Alcott, *Eight Cousins; or, The Aunt-Hill* (1875; reprint, Cleveland: World, 1948), 68–77, 200.

71. "A Chinese Mystery," *New York Times* (23 August 1877).

72. Another distinguished Chinese gentleman residing in the Northeast also found the local community welcoming: "A Chinese citizen of credit and renown, temporarily residing in Connecticut, contemplates becoming naturalized to the great Republic. He has married a daughter of the Pilgrims, and has assumed other obligations . . . to the land of the free and the home of the brave." *New York Times* (11 April 1875). Quite possibly, this individual was Yung Wing, discussed later in this chapter.

73. Alcott, 73–74.

74. The edition consulted for this description included numerous excerpts from book reviews—Edward Greey, *Blue Jackets; or, the Adventures of J. Thompson, A.B.,*

*among "the Heathen Chinee"* (Boston: J. E. Tilton, 1871), The Phillips Library. Peabody Essex Museum, Salem, Mass.

75. All of the various permutations of *"Madame Butterfly"* share this basic plot. John Luther Long, a Philadelphia lawyer, first published his story *"Madame Butterfly"* in the *Century Magazine* (January 1897). Inspired by both Long's story and Pierre Loti's romance *Madame Chrysantheme* (1888), the dramatist David Belasco wrote the theatrical drama *Madame Butterfly*, which first appeared on the New York stage in 1900. Later that year, Belasco took the play to London, where Puccini saw it on opening night. Almost immediately, the composer and the dramatist reached an agreement whereby Puccini would produce an opera by the same name. His *Madame Butterfly* opened in New York in 1906. David Belasco, *Six Plays* (Boston: Little, Brown, 1929), 3–8.

76. Greey, 113, 126–46.

77. Greey, 236.

78. Harry French, *Our Boys in China: The Thrilling Story of Two Young Americans, Scott and Paul Clayton Wrecked in the China Sea, on their Return from India, with their strange adventures in China* (New York: Charles Dillingham, 1883).

79. French, 39.

80. French, 29–33.

81. French, 224–27.

82. French, 184–85, 313.

83. French, vii–viii.

84. Yung Wing to Samuel Wells Williams, letter, 13 April 1849, box 1, series 1, Yung Wing Papers, Manuscript Collections, Yale University Library.

85. Since his offer to enlist occurred late in the war, he was cordially turned away, although the gesture was appreciated (Yung Wing, My Life in China and America [New York: Holt, 1909], 38–41, 158–59, 222, 255).

86. Yung Wing, 39–40; Yung Shang Him, *The Chinese Educational Mission and Its Influence* (Shanghai: Kelly and Walsh, 1939), 4–5, 8; Bill Lann Lee, "Yung Wing and the Americanization of China," *Amerasia* (March 1971), 25–29.

87. Edwin Pak-Wah Leung, "The Making of the Chinese Yankees: School Life of the Chinese Educational Mission Students in New England," *Asian Profile* (October 1988), 402, 410; Bill Lann Lee, 25–29, 31.

88. An address by Rev. Joseph H. Twichell, delivered before the Kent Club of Yale Law School, 10 April 1878, reprinted in Yung Wing, 271.

89. "Chinese Students," *New York Times* (28 November 1875).

90. According to the *New York Times* (9 January 1882), one student who fell in love with a white American girl in Connecticut corresponded with her after returning to China. Chinese officials learned of the affair and promptly beheaded the student. Given its sensational nature, this story may be false.

91. Phelps became a noted writer and professor at Yale University. The experience inspired in him an interest in China that lasted throughout his life. In the 1930s, he publicly championed Pearl Buck, pronouncing her "the ablest living interpreter of the Chinese character" (Peter Conn, *Pearl Buck: A Cultural Biography* [Cambridge:

Cambridge University Press, 1996], 156). William Lloyd Phelps, *Autobiography with Letters* (New York: Oxford University Press, 1939), 83–85; Edwin Pak-Wah Leung, "The Making of the Chinese Yankees," 406, 408.

92. United States Centennial Commission, *Reports and Awards* (Group 27), 24.

93. *Daily Graphic* (31 August 1876); *Hartford Courant* (25 August 1876); *New York Tribune* (25 August 1876); Edwin Pak-Wah Leung, "China's Quest from the West: The Chinese Educational Mission to the United States, 1872–1881," *Asian Profile* (December 1983), 531.

94. *New York Times* (5 July 1870).

95. Philadelphia Inquirer (25 August 1876).

96. Edwin Pak-Wah Leung, "China's Quest from the West," 531.

97. Brown, 290.

98. See letter from Colin Jamieson, indicating that the Chinese commissioner has been authorized, presumably by the Chinese government, to donate the remnants of the trade collection (Archives of the Philadelphia Museum of Art). Also, the accession files for the 1876 Exhibition in the Office of the Registrar (PMA) contain records of the items given to the museum by Hu Quang Yung. Hu's career ended in financial ruin in 1884 after an economic panic precipitated the collapse of his corner of the silk market *The I. G. in Peking*, 513).

# CONCLUSION

In 1795, Andreas Everadus van Braam Houckgeest made his memorable appearance before the Chinese emperor Qianlong. In 1874, Samuel Wells Williams found himself in the same position. The American minister to China, B. P. Avery, had official business to transact with the emperor, and he required Williams's services as an interpreter. Houckgeest had followed Chinese protocol by engaging in the prescribed *kowtow*, but that was a formality Williams could dispense with. The previous year, the foreign community in Peking had settled this issue with the Qing government. For the aging American missionary, this singular experience before the monarch was symbolic of the changes that had taken place in China over the course of the century. When he had first arrived in Canton in 1833, he was considered a "foreign devil" by the Chinese and was granted few rights or privileges by Qing officials. Now, in 1874, he and Avery were received "on a footing of perfect equality with the 'Son of Heaven.'" To what did he attribute this dramatic shift? Over the previous half century, China had sustained several massive collisions with foreign powers and the people's national pride was consequently deflated in a manner that Williams regarded as beneficial. The continual humbling of the Chinese, he hoped, would ultimately render them more receptive to the Word of God. After four decades in China, Williams continued to believe that God's will was moving China inexorably (if slowly) in the direction of Christianity.[1]

Williams was less optimistic about the news coming out of the United States, where Chinese immigrants and the white population were clearly not "on a footing of perfect equality." Williams had often criticized the morals of the Chinese, but he nevertheless always understood their worth and firmly believed in their potential. And so he was horrified by the acts of violence committed against Chinese living and working in the American West. The clarion call for the exclusion of Chinese immigrants then echoing through the halls of the U.S. government reached his ears in Peking and left him feeling ashamed of his own country. Williams decided he must return home to teach deluded Americans about the true worth of Chinese civilization, as he had done in the 1840s. History, it seems, was beginning to repeat itself.[2]

The poor treatment of Chinese immigrants heavily influenced Williams's decision to leave China, but declining health and weakening eyesight were also contributed to it. The stalwart missionary who had always enjoyed good health and physical vigor was simply growing old. In fact, members of the foreign community playfully called him Nestor, in reference to the elderly Greek sage in Homer's *Iliad*. On October 25, 1876, Williams departed China for good, forty-three years to the day after his initial arrival in Canton. "Whatever good or evil I've performed in my time in China must now remain," He wrote. "God can make their effects a part of His blessed plan."[3]

Shortly after arriving home, Williams received gratifying news from the institution he had longed to attend as a youth. Yale College had decided not only to confer on him the degree of master of arts but also to create a faculty position for him. He would be the first to occupy the Chair of Chinese Language and Literature. Although the position was largely honorary, given Williams's age and health, it nevertheless held the distinction of being the first of its kind in the United States.[4] And since James Dwight Dana was already a member of the Yale faculty, the childhood friends from Utica were at last reunited. Since the college library's holdings were devoid of Chinese texts, Williams worked with Yung Wing to effect the transfer from China of a sizeable library of Chinese books, totaling 1,280 volumes. The Yale Library now had an East Asian collection.[5] In 1878, Williams delivered his first lecture and remarked later that the "audience was good," despite a heavy snowstorm and a presentation that he described as less than "exhilarating."[6]

Since his teaching responsibilities hardly taxed him at all, Williams devoted substantial time and energy to the plight of the Chinese living in the United States. By the late 1870s, the so-called "Chinese question" had become the topic of a national debate. The anti-Chinese movement began in California, where most of the Chinese population in America lived and worked. After the market crash of 1873 threw many Americans out of work, demagogues like Dennis Kearney, who claimed to speak for the interests of white labor, castigated industries for letting white workers go and hiring in their stead less-expensive Chinese immigrants. Kearney simultaneously used incendiary language to incite unemployed white workers, prodding them to channel their rage toward the Chinese. At political rallies and in the newspapers, the Chinese were painted as human vermin who took industrial jobs from deserving white Americans, added nothing to society, and sent all their earnings back to China.

One might expect capitalists to put forward an alternative narrative, but men like Leland Stanford, the California railroad magnate, were too often cowed by this populist uprising; they usually relented against the intense pressure of agitators by releasing Chinese workers from their jobs. In 1877, Kearney started the Working Man's Party, whose members rallied under the slogan "The Chinese must go!" In 1878, Kearney took his anti-Chinese campaign onto the national stage. Although pro-business politicians in the Republican Party might have been expected to defend the Chinese, their pragmatism instead dictated that they too adopt an anti-Chinese platform. Many joined in the ruthless scapegoating of the Chinese so as to secure some of the anti-Chinese vote and keep pro-labor candidates from reaching office. In 1882, this tragic drama culminated in the passage of the Chinese Exclusion Act. A nation that had once criticized China for its hostility toward foreigners proceeded to build its own Great Wall out of legislation.[7]

Interestingly, as this story was unfolding, Williams drew a parallel between the current mistreatment of Chinese in the United States and the predicament of foreigners in Canton a half century earlier. Both minority groups were unwanted, condescended to by officials, and dispossessed of their rights. He believed that the behavior of both countries was xenophobic and wrongheaded but that the present American hostility toward the Chinese was far more egregious: "And how much greater is our offense against them than theirs was against us." Filled with indignation, Williams stepped forward as an advocate for Chinese immigrants in the late 1870s and early 1880s. He gave talks on the subject, published several articles that refuted the arguments of the anti-Chinese demagogues, took a trip to Washington to address Congress, and even sent a letter to President Rutherford B. Hayes to argue against the exclusion of Chinese immigrants. This letter, written by Williams, was signed by dozens of members of the Yale faculty.[8]

As with the furlough in the 1840s, Williams's largest project was of a literary nature. Throughout his career, Williams had witnessed the passing of many missionaries, most of whom had died in obscurity. Each death had provoked in him troubled speculation as to the meaning of a missionary's life. Exactly what lasting influence did missionaries have? Would decades of sacrifice be utterly forgotten by future generations? Did the relatively small number of Chinese converts negate a lifetime of dedicated service? Williams tried to dismiss these

questions by constantly reminding himself that God, not his fellow human beings, would ultimately determine the value and meaning of his long career as a
missionary.[9] However, he still possessed that overweening pride. In an effort
both to explain Chinese culture to a new generation of Americans and also to
ensure the survival of his name for posterity, Williams revisited that great work
that had established his reputation three decades earlier. He decided to revise
*The Middle Kingdom*.

The revision proved to be no easy task, given that Williams needed to update
his statistics, include an account of events (such as the Taiping Rebellion) that
had taken place since 1847, and incorporate new knowledge that had become
available since the first edition. As Williams proceeded to add more content to
a two-volume work previously criticized for its excessive size, he admitted to
having "difficulty in digesting my material in my mind." What was worse, he
even began to question the viability of his project. "China," he confided to his
diary, "is too big a subject to put into two octavo vols." Williams, it appears, was
starting to realize that the grand dream of describing all of China in a single
work was perhaps, in the end, pure folly.[10] Despite these doubts, however, the
indomitable Williams persevered. After all, China had always attracted individuals of great ambition who coveted large challenges—and Williams was no
different.

By 1881, though, health problems that the author summed up as "age, weakness, and decay" signaled that he was running out of time. For the first time,
he confronted the "disturbing" possibility that he would die before completing
the revision. *The Middle Kingdom*, he wrote, "looms up larger than ever, a
mountain too high for me to climb." As his motor skills began to deteriorate,
Williams found he could not hold his hand steady enough to write legibly. And
that wonderful stamina and energy that had sustained him for four decades in
China now seemed utterly "used up." In his diary, he called on God to lend
him additional strength: "May God graciously preserve me to finish this revision, if it will be helpful to his cause in China." Yet quietly, he began to prepare himself for what he called "the final disappointment." On January 26,
1881, fate dealt him a devastating yet expected blow—Sarah Walworth Williams died. In his diary, a shaken Williams bid her farewell: "Dear wife of my
life, mine for one third of a century, adieu till we meet on the Sea of Glass."[11]
In January 1882, his already slow progress on his book came to a crashing halt
when a fall on a slippery sidewalk resulted in a broken arm. Williams's dream
was now in jeopardy.[12]

As Williams confronted the likelihood that his final act would end in failure,
a good friend of his found himself also in the unfortunate position of watching
his grand dream unravel. In 1876, Yung Wing had issued a bold statement. By
bringing the Chinese boys of the C.E.M. to the Centennial, he had challenged

the tired stereotype associated with his country of birth, that it was old-fashioned, backward, hidebound, inflexible, and averse to technology. In Philadelphia, Yung had showcased a fresh Chinese character before American eyes—young, quick-witted, brave, athletic, adaptable, and oriented toward the future. One year after the Centennial, the experiment continued to thrive. A pleased Yung Wing proudly reported to his friend Samuel Wells Williams that "our Chinese students are making commendable progress."[13]

Later that decade, however, the wheels started to come off. Yung Wing had pinned his hopes and dreams on the C.E.M., but now he was increasingly drawn away from it. The Chinese government, recognizing that Yung's unique abilities and experiences made him useful as a diplomat, began to hand him assignments in international affairs unrelated to the C.E.M. Since these duties often called him away from Hartford, the government reduced his position there to that of associate minister and dispatched a man named Wu Zideng to serve as his successor. When Minister Wu arrived in Hartford, he found to his great consternation not only that the students refused to *kowtow* in his presence but also that several had converted to Christianity and cut off their queues. Soon Peking received from Wu alarming reports in which he accused Yung Wing of elevating the goal American education to status of top priority while permissively allowing the boys to grow lackadaisical in their Chinese studies.

Yung Shang Him, one of the students, later wrote his account of the controversy. Minister Wu, whom he called "a bigoted and fanatical conservative," made the charge that the boys were being "Americanized and denationalized, and that they would do no good, but positive harm, to China, if they were allowed to finish their studies." When Yung Wing heard of the calumnies spread by Wu, he defended his role with the C.E.M. and argued vociferously for its continuance—but to no avail. Even a petition signed by many notable Americans, including Samuel Wells Williams, and a letter from former President Ulysses S. Grant to Li Hongzhang, the powerful protégé of the late Zeng Guofan, could not forestall the breakup of the Mission. The students were recalled to China in 1881.[14]

According to Mark Twain, a friend of Yung Wing's and a signer of the petition, the "order came upon him with the suddenness of a thunderclap. He did not know which way to turn." After the Mission's recall, Yung for the most part remained in the United States with his American wife, living out his years in despair.[15]Back in China, the students faced a serious reentry crisis owing to the negative publicity surrounding a bold experiment now labeled a failure. Once regarded as China's best and brightest, the boys were now viewed by most as damaged goods. Consequently, they were treated with contempt, eyed with suspicion, and placed in poor living conditions. For employment, officials assigned them low-paying government jobs with scant responsibility, making them little more than "office coolies," in the words of Yung Shang Him. According to Yung, it was only through "spunk and determination" that in subsequent years he and many of his peers were able to rise to prominence as doctors, diplomats, professors, and the heads of telegraph, railroad, and mining companies.[16]

Back in Hartford, citizens collectively mourned the loss of the C.E.M. as one would a death in the family. The *Connecticut Courant* printed an epitaph for the Mission that carried a portentous message: "The Educational Mission, though now in ruins, has not utterly perished from the earth. Its influence survives; no imperial decree can abolish that. The bright lads who are unwillingly going back to China carry ideas among their own luggage. And an idea is more dangerous . . . than a cargo of dynamite." Years after the recall, an unidentified Chinese man apparently wandered into a junk shop in Connecticut and found the sign board for the C.E.M. He promptly bought it "so that it might not get into an American Museum to become a permanent reminder of China's disgrace in the abandonment of a magnificent enterprise."[17]

In nearby New Haven, Samuel Wells Williams continued his race against the clock. Since he no longer possessed the physical energy and mental acuity of his youth, his efforts to write and revise were progressing at a frustratingly slow pace. But unlike the sad saga of Yung Wing's C.E.M., this story would have a happy ending. Late in 1881, Williams's son, Frederick, looked over the work his father had completed thus far and discovered the extent to which the author was struggling. The added chapters were, in Frederick's words, "a confused and prolix narrative." Fortunately, Frederick agreed to assist his father with the editing, and, with his much needed help, the retired missionary was able to see the massive project through to completion.[18]

And it was massive. When the publisher released the revised edition of *The Middle Kingdom* in October 1883, it had grown by a full third since its previous incarnation and now totaled more than 1,600 pages. Although blindness prevented Williams from reading his own completed work, he enjoyed holding the two volumes in his hands and feeling their substantial weight. As with the first edition, Williams still cared deeply about the verdict rendered by readers and critics. "He made no pretence of concealing his interest in the press notices of his work," Frederick observed, "which were read to him as they appeared." One review in particular that Frederick clipped out of The Critic must have cheered his father's spirits:

Those whose conception of China is that of a land of rat-eaters need . . . conversion. No one can now inform himself about the Chinese without seeing in them a civilized nation. Not to know China as civilized argues ourselves barbarians. It would also be well if the average American, and especially the average Congressman, could learn one thing—viz: that we are not in any danger of a Mongolian deluge. . . . In spite of advanced years and feeble health, our author may yet live to see the absurd and un-American bill repealed.[19]

With the publication of the revised Middle Kingdom, Williams's final act of loyal service to God was complete. And since he would now be remembered as perhaps the nineteenth century's greatest expert on China, his intellectual legacy was also secured. And so Williams had succeeded in satisfying that great pride that had always existed in a state of tension with his religious mission. Having nothing left to accomplish, the aged missionary promptly entered into rapid decline. That he had survived so long led Frederick to suspect that the hand of Providence had intervened: "It seemed as though his life had been spared to see the consummation of this important endeavor, after which he faded gradually away." On February 16, 1884, Williams died in his bed without suffering. After the funeral was held on the Yale campus, his body was removed to Utica, where he was buried next to his wife.[20]

At the time of Williams's death, the Exclusion Act had been in effect for two years and was already reducing the number of immigrants from China. The hopeful prediction in the Critic, that Williams might "live to see the absurd and un-American bill repealed," proved to be naively optimistic: The law was renewed in 1892 for ten additional years and then made permanent in 1902. Its unfortunate influence endured all the way until 1943, when it was repealed during the Second World War. A question worth considering centers on the role played by the cultural productions covered in this study. What was the relationship between the mainstream attitudes that enabled the passage of the Exclusion Act and the museums, panoramas, lectures, books, and travelogues that were designed to teach Americans about China?

More often then not, that relationship was adversarial. Those involved in the project of educating the public about China confronted audiences that, for the most part, did not present them with a tabula rasa on which they could inscribe their own views. Most Americans had a preexisting attitude toward China and Chinese people, an attitude formed during their interactions with an almost infinite number vernacular references to China that appeared in sermons, newspapers, books, political speeches, everyday expressions and idioms, and jokes exchanged in casual conversation. Because most people were comfortable with their prejudices, the challenge facing most of the individuals discussed in this book was to construct China in a way that could subvert the status quo so that something more enlightened, at least in their opinion, might assume its place.

After the Catholic missionaries' rosy portrayal of Chinese civilization had won wide acceptance, Houckgeest sought to puncture it in his account. Similarly,

Nathan Dunn attempted to administer a dose of realism to an American public that for decades had been enthralled by the myth of Cathay. And after the Opium War, Samuel Wells Williams, John Peters, and George West each tried to change the popular view that the Chinese were a laughably absurd people. Even Bayard Taylor refused to conform to the mainstream view; to him, the Chinese were not a harmless and comically unprogressive people but rather a vile race that needed to be kept away from American shores. Taylor offered this construction two decades before Dennis Kearney began to provoke anti-Chinese sentiment in California. Finally, Yung Wing, the organizers of the Chinese exhibit at the Centennial, and Samuel Wells Williams all made valiant efforts to combat the mainstream's paranoid call for Chinese Exclusion in the 1870s and 1880s. The pattern that emerges is one in which popular stereotypes were contested rather than reinforced. Although Captain Kellett clearly intended to reap a profit by feeding the public's appetite for mockery, his Chinese junk stands out as an exception, not the rule.

Given this pattern of contestation, I do not believe that constructions of China either caused or contributed much to the popular mindset that favored Exclusion. In fact, it is more likely that the diverse nature of these constructions provided a countervailing influence against anti-Chinese sentiment in America in a way that strengthened resistance to that sentiment. Although the resistance to it ultimately failed, a large number of Americans did decry the acts of bigotry against Chinese immigrants, did defend the right of those immigrants to live and work in the United States, and did register their disapproval of the anti-Chinese movement as it approached its crescendo in 1882.[21] In other words, while the writers, painters, collectors, diplomats, and missionaries discussed in this book did not possess either the power or the uniformity of voice necessary to quell the anti-Chinese movement, they did, when taken as a group, succeed in keeping competing views of China alive in the public discourse. In sum, their books, exhibits, lectures, and paintings probably did not provide the intellectual foundation for the anti-Chinese monolith erected in 1882. These cultural productions might, however, have worked to destabilize the same.

In fact, their intellectual contributions often left lasting impressions when approached by open-minded Americans. They were even able to inspire some people to devote their entire careers to the study of China. In hindsight, although Samuel Wells Williams did very little actual teaching at Yale, the university's decision to create the Chair of Chinese Language and Literature for him appears to mark an important shift. The chair signaled that the day of the amateur ethnologist was drawing to a close. Houckgeest (merchant and diplomat), Nathan Dunn (merchant), John Peters (engineer and diplomat), George West (painter and diplomat), Bayard Taylor (poet and travel writer), and Samuel Wells Williams (naturalist, printer, and missionary) had all traveled to China for reasons unrelated to ethnography. Brought to China by their careers, usually they studied China simply because their interest in it had compelled them to do so. Toward the end of the nineteenth century, however, the study of China was becoming increasingly a specialized field reserved for trained experts bearing the appropriate credentials—professional anthropologists and sinologists possessing academic or curatorial positions in universities and museums. The generational succession in the Williams family perfectly encapsulates this transition. Exposed to Asia by his father, Frederick Wells Williams went on to become professor of modern oriental history at Yale.

This new generation of experts were often inspired and shaped by their amateur forebears. In the case of Frederick Wells Williams, the chain of influence is of course obvious. However, other experts who lacked bloodlines also acknowledged the continued relevance of the previous generation. For example, the German-born anthropologist Berthold Laufer probably knew more about Asia than any other Westerner at the turn of the century. He had a doctoral degree, could read ten Asian languages, and held a curatorial position at the American Museum of Natural History as well as a teaching post at Columbia University. In 1901, the American Museum, looking to increase its Chinese holdings, sent Laufer on an extensive collecting expedition to China. Seeing the obvious relevance of past exhibits, Laufer studied the catalog from the Chinese exhibit at the Centennial. Once in China, he specifically requested that Samuel Wells Williams's *The Middle Kingdom* be mailed to him. Laufer knew precisely what he was asking for: the revised edition of a book written more than half a century earlier by a missionary with no formal ethnographic training. He deemed it worthy of consultation nevertheless.[22]

In some cases, the older generation of amateurs had an even more profound impact on the new specialists. For the Far Eastern expert William Elliot Griffis (1843–1928), it provided the spark that ignited a lasting interest in Asia. Like many of the figures discussed in this work, Griffis believed that the American public grossly misunderstood Chinese culture. In 1881 he wrote a textbook on China, Korea, and Japan for use in the Chautauqua Society in western New York. At a time when much of the popular press was busy reviling China, while many Americans were clamoring for the exclusion of its immigrants, Griffis insisted on calling China "one great nation, worthy of our respect, and even our emulation."[23]

By 1911, neither his views on China nor his views on the American public had undergone much change. For this "great country and civilization," he wrote, referring to China, most ordinary people exhibited only "dense ignorance" by erroneously insisting on seeing only "monotonous inflexibility" in the Chinese character. Like many of his predecessors, Griffis hoped to rectify the situation by writing a book—in his case, *China's Story in Myth, Legend, Art, and Annals* (1911). The task of writing a preface to it prompted Griffis both to contemplate everything he knew about China and to try to understand how he had come by all this information. Toward this end, he decided to compile a comprehensive inventory of knowledge, a personal epistemology that would explore any and all interactions with China that had taken place over a lifetime of nearly seventy years.[24]

Griffis proceeded to perform what amounted to an archeological excavation of his mind, an endeavor that involved digging down through the various strata of images, ideas, impressions, and memories of all kinds. Passing through the most recent levels, he noted his association with Chinese people who had provided him with key insights into their culture. In particular, he recalled Yung Wing, the Yale-educated Chinese American who had organized the C.E.M. Continuing his dig, Griffis arrived at the layer composed of the various China experts he had known personally and the influential books these learned individuals had written. Here was Samuel Wells Williams, the American missionary and author of the comprehensive and authoritative Middle Kingdom. Penetrating all the way to his childhood years, Griffis encountered the grand Chinese Museum of John Peters, its wonderful array of objects, its statues placed instructively in dioramas, and the two Chinese men, T'sow Chaong and Le Kawhing, who had patiently answered the questions of a curious boy. On reaching bottom, he found his very earliest impressions of China—vague mental images formed by the old China trade. His grandfather, a merchant navigator who journeyed to Canton in the late eighteenth century, brought back numerous "pretty curiosities" that captivated the young Griffis. And his father, a mariner who also plied the waters of the Pacific, regaled him with accounts of his voyages to the Far East. These stories and objects, firing the imagination of the young boy, had "provoked a desire to know more about the mighty hermit nation."[25]

Griffis also asked himself whether, from these myriad influences, a single source was able to rise above the others to assume the privileged position of defining his attitude toward China. The answer was no. One's acquaintance with "a single person, or book," he observed, was "worth but little" when attempting to comprehend "so vast and varied a land as China." In Griffis's view, these sources worked collectively to shape his overall understanding of China. Even the older images, including those that dated back to his early childhood years, had never entered into a dormant state even as information that was more recent and more reliable became available. And so, quite remarkably, an object that a Cantonese artisan had crafted during the reign of Qianlong continued to exert its influence over a man who was then witnessing the collapse of the Qing dynasty and the formation of a republic.

Also following the tumultuous events in China was Berthold Laufer, who by 1911 had taken a curatorial position in anthropology at the Field Museum in

Chicago. China had once been so mysterious as to cast a spell over dreamy Westerners from afar. As one who had been entranced, Laufer could look back with nostalgia on the days when the ethnographer in China confronted a rich and unique civilization that had developed without much discernible influence from the West. Those days were now gone. The once remote country that had captivated the wide-eyed Houckgeest as he sketched it from his palanquin was now teeming with foreigners from Europe, Japan, and the United States. Vast railroad and mining projects were altering the Chinese landscape; overzealous missionaries sought the eradication of Chinese customs that impeded the advance of Christianity; and a parasitical international community in the port cities treated the local residents as subhuman as it relentlessly pressed China for more and more trading privileges. Given these profound changes, Laufer could only mourn at the passing of a magical era in which China had inspired true wonder in those who beheld it with an open mind. "The romance of China has died away," he wrote, "with the end of the Chivalrous Manchu dynasty."[26]

## NOTES

1. Samuel Wells Williams, *The Middle Kingdom: A Survey of the Geography, Government, Education, Social Life, Arts, Religion, &., of the Chinese Empire and Its Inhabitants* (New York: Charles Scribner's Sons, 1883), 1:xiii–xiv.

2. Frederick Wells Williams, *The Life and Letters of Samuel Wells Williams, LL.D.* (New York: G. P. Putnam's Sons, 1889), 414–15.

3. Frederick Wells Williams, 416–20.

4. In 1879, three years after Yale had established its professorship in Chinese Studies, Harvard followed suit by hiring Ko Kun-hua from China. Professor Ko and Samuel Wells Williams enjoyed a strong, but short, friendship. Professor Ko died the following year. Frederick Wells Williams, 450–53.

5. See list of Chinese titles: Box 17, series 2, Samuel Wells Williams Family Papers, Manuscript Collections, Yale University Library. Hereafter, this collection will be cited as SWWFP. This was not the first time Williams had brought about the transfer of Chinese books to American institutions. In 1869, he orchestrated an exchange of texts between the United States government and the Chinese government. See Tsuen-hsuin Tsien, "The First Chinese-American Exchange of Publications," *Harvard Journal of Asiatic Studies* (1965): 19–30.

6. Samuel Wells Williams to Robert Stanton Williams, letter, 1 February 1878, box 14, series 2, SWWFP.

7. See Andrew Gyory, *Closing the Gate: Race, Politics, and the Chinese Exclusion Act* (Chapel Hill: University of North Carolina Press, 1998).

8. Frederick Wells Williams, 414; Samuel Wells Williams to Robert Stanton Williams, letters, 1 and 6 February 1878, box 13, series 2, SWWFP; and Samuel Wells Williams to Henry Blodgett (Peking), 7 February 1878, box 13, series 2, SWWFP. See Faculty of Yale College to President Rutherford B. Hayes, 21 February 1879, letter, box 13, series 2, SWWFP.

9. Frederick Wells Williams, 420.

10. See entries for 9 and 10 March 1881, "The National Diary 1881," box 14, series 2, SWWFP.

11. Entry for 26 January 1881, "The National Diary 1881," box 14, series 2, SWWFP.

12. Samuel Wells Williams to Sophia Gardner Williams Grosvenor Gray, letter, 17 January 1882, box 13, series 2, SWWFP.

13. Yung Wing to Samuel Wells Williams, letter, 19 February 1877, Yung Wing Papers. Manuscript Collections, Yale University Library.

14. Bill Lann Lee, "Yung Wing and the Americanization of China," *Amerasia* (March 1971): 31; Yung Shang Him, *The Chinese Educational Mission and Its Influence* (Shanghai: Kelly and Walsh, 1939), 10–11; *Mark Twain's Letters*, ed. Albert Bigelow Paine (New York: Harper and Brothers, 1917), 1:391-392; and Thomas E. La Fargue, *China's First Hundred* (Pullman: State College of Washington, 1942), 43–49. Samuel Wells Williams discusses his role in writing the letter in a diary entry dated 22 October 1881, "The National Diary 1881," box 14, series 2, group 547. Williams also describes the C.E.M. in *The Middle Kingdom* (New York: Charles Scribner's Sons, 1883), 2:739–741.

15. Edwin Pak-Wah Leung, "The First Chinese College Graduates in America: Yung Wing and His Educational Experiences," *Asian Profile* 16, no.5 (October 1988): 458.

16. In addition, all the subtle transformations that had taken place in the students' general comportment rendered them out of place in China. Yung Shang Him recalled that, while walking through a country village and dressed in appropriate Chinese attire, a pack of boys followed him and called out "fan kwai" (foreign devil). Puzzled by the taunt, he related the incident to a friend, who explained that "your manly bearing and the style of your walk . . . made you appear so different to others." Yung Shang Him, 14–16.

17. William Hung, "Huang Tsun-Hsien's Poem 'The Closure of the Educational Mission in America,'" *Harvard Journal of Asiatic Studies* 18 (June 1955): 61, 73.

18. Frederick Wells Williams, 449.

19. *Critic* (November 1883). See "Reviews of the Middle Kingdom," box 16, series 2, SWWFP.

20. Frederick Wells Williams, 460–61.

21. Philip S. Foner and Daniel Rosenberg, *Racism, Dissent, and Asian Americans from 1850 to the Present: A Documentary History* (Westport, Conn.: Greenwood Press, 1993), 1–7.

22. Berthold Laufer to Franz Boas, letter, 10 April and 1 March 1902, Anthropology Archives, American Museum of American History. See also the chapter devoted to

13

Berthold Laufer in John Haddad, "The Romance of China: Excursions to China in U.S. Culture: 1776–1876" (Ph.D.diss., University of Texas, 2002).

23. William Elliot Griffis, *Asiatic History: China, Corea, Japan, Chautauqua Textbooks* 34 (New York: Phillips and Hunt, 1881), 3–4.

24. William Elliot Griffis, *China's Story in Myth, Legend, Art, and Annals* (Boston and New York: Houghton Mifflin, 1911), vii.

25. We have no way to know whether the majority of Americans understood China in as eclectic a fashion as did Griffis. However, in the 1950s, Harold Isaacs interviewed nearly two hundred panelists to test their understanding of China. He found that, on the subject of China, the minds of his interviewees were littered with an odd assortment of images that, when taken together, did not add up to a single cohesive vision. Harold R. Isaacs, *Images of Asia: American Views of China and India* (New York: Capricorn Books, 1962), 47. Isaacs's book illuminated the American mind in the 1950s, and, unfortunately, no earlier scholar conducted a systematic survey of the nineteenth century to provide us with a comparable snapshot. In the only earlier study, one hundred Princeton students were asked to describe the Chinese, along with other racial groups, by choosing from a pool of eighty-four adjectives. The wide range of responses prompted the researchers to conclude the following: "Apparently the general stereotype for the Chinese among eastern college students is fairly indefinite, for the agreement on typical Chinese characteristics is not great." Daniel Katz and Kenneth Braly, "Racial Stereotypes of One Hundred College Students," *Journal of Abnormal and Social Psychology* 28 (October–December 1933): 282–87.

26. The Manchu dysnasty and the Qing dynasty are the same. Berthold Laufer, "Modern Chinese Collections in Historical Light: With Especial Reference to the American Museum's Collection Representative of Chinese Culture a Decade Ago," *American Museum Journal* 12 (April 1912), 137.

# BIBLIOGRAPHY

## PRIMARY SOURCES

### Archives, Libraries, and Collections

American Philosophical Society
Chester County Historical Society
Free Library of Philadelphia
Haverford College, Special Collections
Historical Society of Pennsylvania
Library Company of Philadelphia
Library of Congress (Reading Rooms: Rare Book and Special Collection,
Manuscript, Newspaper and Current Periodical, Prints and Photographs)
New York Public Library
New-York Historical Society
Peabody Essex Museum, East Asian Exports
Philadelphia Museum of Fine Arts
Smithsonian Museum of American History, Warshaw Collection of Business
    Americana

University of Texas at Austin, Humanities Research Center
Winterthur Library and Downs Collection
Yale University, Manuscript Collection

## Newspapers

*Alta California*
*American Magazine*
*Boston Courier*
*Boston Daily Advertiser*
*Boston Herald*
*Boston Post*
*Brooklyn Eagle*
*Cincinnati Commercial*
*Cincinnati Daily Gazette*
*Daily Graphic*
*Daily Times and Dispatch*
*Dollar Magazine*
*Dollar Newspaper*
*Farmers' Cabinet*
*Florida Trend*
*Hartford Courant*
*London Morning Chronicle*
*London Times*
*Louisville Courier-Journal*
*New York Clipper*
*New-York Commercial Advertiser*
*New-York Daily Advertiser*
*New York Evening Post*
*New York Herald*
*New York Journal of Commerce*
*New York Sun*
*New York Times*
*New York Tribune*
*New York World*
*Niles National Register*
*Philadelphia Inquirer*
*Philadelphia Saturday Courier*
*Pittsfield Herald*
*Poulson's American Daily Advertiser*

*Public Ledger*
*South China Morning Post*
*Utica Observer*


## Journals and Magazines


*American Journal of Science and Arts*
*American Museum Journal*
*American Phrenological Journal*
*American Republican*
*American Review: A Whig Journal of Politics, Literature, Art, and Science*
*Appletons' Journal of Popular Literature, Science, and Art*
*Art Union*
*Atlantic Monthly*
*Century Magazine*
*Chinese Repository*
*Collier's Weekly*
*De Bow's Commercial Review of the South and West*
*Eclectic Magazine of Foreign Literature, Science, and Art*
*Family Magazine*
*Forum*
*Fraser's Magazine*
*Galaxy*
*Harper's Bazaar*
*Harper's Weekly*
*Illustrated London News*
*Independent*
*Journal of American Folk-lore*
*Ladies' Repository*
*Lady's Book*
*Leslie's Weekly*
*Merchants' Magazine and Commercial Review*
*Modern Priscilla*
*Museum of Foreign Literature, Science, and Art*
*National Magazine and Republican*
*New-York Mirror*
*North American Review*
*North China Herald*
*Southern Literary Messenger*
*Southern Quarterly Review*

*Transactions of the American Ethnological Society*
*Transactions of the Asiatic Society of Japan*
*United States Magazine and Democratic Review*
*Vanity Fair*

## Books

Abeel, David. *Journal of a Residence in China, and the Neighboring Countries.* New York: Leavitt, Lord, 1834.

Adams, Henry. *Education of Henry Adams.* New York: The Modern Library, 1931.

*Aladdin; or, the Wonderful Lamp.* London: Hardy, 1789.

Alcott, Louisa May. *Eight Cousins; or, The Aunt-Hill.* Cleveland: World, 1948.

Alcott, William, *Tea and Coffee.* Boston and New York: George W. Light, 1839.

Appleton, Nathan. *Centennial Movement, 1876: A Comedy in Five Acts.* Boston: Lockwood, Brooks, 1877.

*As a Chinaman Saw Us: Passages from his Letters to a Friend at Home.* New York: D. Appleton, 1905.

Bailey, David. *"Eastward Ho!" or, Leaves from the Diary of a Centennial Pilgrim.* Highland County, Ohio: Highland News Office, 1877.

Ball, B. L. *Rambles in Eastern Asia, Including China and Manila.* Boston: James French, 1855.

Barnsely, Edward R. *History of China's Retreat: Paper Read by Edward R. Barnsley before the Bucks County Historical Society at Doylestown, Pa., May 6, 1933.* Briston, Pa.: Bristol Printing Company, 1833.

Barnum, P. T. *Ten Thousand Things on China and the Chinese.* New York: J. S. Redfield, 1850.

——. *Struggles and Triumphs; or, Forty Years' Recollections.* Hartford: J. B. Burr, 1870.

——. *Selected Letters of P. T. Barnum.* Edited by A. H. Saxon. New York: Columbia University Press, 1983.

Barrett, Walter. *The Old Merchants of New York City.* New York: Carleton, 1862.

Belasco, David. *Six Plays.* Boston: Little, Brown, 1929.

Bowen, Daniel. *A History of Philadelphia . . . Designed as a Guide to Citizens and Strangers.* Philadelphia: Daniel Owen, 1839.

Bruce, Edward C. *The Century: Its Fruits and Its Festivals, Being a History and Description of the Centennial Exhibition, with a Preliminary Outline of Modern Progress.* Philadelphia: J. B. Lippincott, 1877.

Buckingham, J. S. *The Eastern and Western States of America.* 3 vols. London: Fisher, Son, 1842.

California Legislature, Senate, Special Committee on Chinese Immigration. *Chinese Immigration: The Social, Moral, and Political Effect.* Sacramento: State Printing Office, 1876.

Camehl, Ada Walker. *The Blue-China Book Book: Early American Scenes and History Pictured in the Pottery of the Time*. 1916. Reprint, New York: Dover, 1971.

Carnegie, Andrew. *The Autobiography of Andrew Carnegie*. Edited by John C. Van Dyke. 1920. Reprint, Boston: Northeastern University Press, 1986.

*Catalogue of the Chinese Imperial Maritime Customs Collection, at the United States International Exhibition, Philadelphia, 1876*. Shanghai: Inspector General of Chinese Maritime Customs, 1876.

*Catalogue of the Private Library of the Late Hon. Caleb Cushing of Newburyport, Massachusetts*. Boston: Sullivan Brothers, auctioneers, 1879.

Clark, Francis E. *Our Journey around the World*. Hartford, Conn.: A. D. Worthington, 1894.

Combe, George. *Notes on the United States of North America, during a Phrenological Visit in 1838-39-40*. Vol. 1. Philadelphia: Carey and Hart, 1841.

Comer, T. *Favorite Melodies from the Grand Chinese Spectacle of Aladdin or the Wonderful Lamp; as Produced at the Boston Museum*. Boston: Prentiss and Clark, 1847.

"*Commonwealth v. Nathan Dunn*," *Reports of Some of the Criminal Cases on Primary Hearing, before Richard Vaux, Recorder of the City of Philadelphia: Together with Some Remarks on the Writ of Habeas Corpus and Forms of Proceeding in Criminal Cases*. Philadelphia: T. and J. W. Johnson, 1846.

Coolidge and Wiley, *The Boston Almanac for the Year 1850*. Boston: B. B. Mussey, 1850.

Dale, James. *What Ben Beverly Saw at the Great Exposition*. Chicago: Centennial, 1876.

*A Description of the Royal Chinese Junk, "Keying."* London: J. Such, 1848.

Bentley, William. *The Diary of William Bentley, D.D., Pastor of the East Church, Salem, Massachusetts*. Salem: Essex Institute, 1905.

Downing, C. Toogood. *The Fan-qui in China, 1836–1837*. London: Henry Colburn, 1838.

Dunn, Nathan. "*Ten Thousand Things Chinese*": *A Descriptive Catalogue of the Chinese Collection in Philadelphia*. Philadelphia, 1839.

Earle, Alice Morse. China Collecting in America. New York: Scribner's Sons, 1892.

Farmer, Little, and Company. *The Later Specimens and Reduced Price List of Printing Types*. New York, 1879.

Forbes, Robert Bennet. *Personal Reminiscences*. Boston: Little, Brown, 1882.

——. *Remarks on China and the China Trade*. Boston: Samuel N. Dickinson, 1844.

*The Arabian Nights*. Translated by Edward Forster. London: W. Savage, 1810.

French, Harry W. *Our Boys in China: The Thrilling Story of Two Young Americans, Scott and Paul Clayton Wrecked in the China Sea, on Their Return from India, with Their Strange Adventures in China*. New York: Charles Dillingham, 1883.

Gilchrist, A. S. *Book of Specimens of Printing Types, Cuts, Ornaments, &c., Aast at the Knickerbocker Type Foundry of A. S. Gilchrist*. Albany, 1857.

[Goodrich, Samuel G.] *Peter Parley's Tales about Asia*. Philadelphia: Desilver Jr. and Thomas, 1833.

——. *Manners and Customs of Nations*. Boston: G. C. Rand, Wm. J. Reynolds, 1844.

Greele and Willis. *Specimen of Printing Types and Metal Ornaments, Cast at the New England Type Foundry by Greele and Willis.* Boston, 1831.

Greey, Edward. *Blue Jackets; or, The Adventures of J. Thompson, A.B., among "the Heathen Chinee."* Boston: J. E. Tilton, 1871.

Griffis, William Elliot. *Asiatic History: China, Corea, Japan.* Chautauqua Textbooks 34. New York: Phillips and Hunt, 1881.

——. *China's Story in Myth, Legend, Art, and Annals.* Boston and New York: Houghton Mifflin, 1911.

*Grocer's Companion and Merchant's Hand-Book.* Boston: New England Grocer Office, 1883.

*Guide to Tea Drinking.* New York: Pekin Tea Company, 1845.

Hansen-Taylor, Marie and Horace E. Scudder, eds. *Life and Letters of Bayard Taylor.* Boston: Houghton, Mifflin and Company, 1885.

Harrison, Carter. *A Race with the Sun.* New York: G. P. Putnam's Sons, 1889.

Hawks, Francis L. *Narrative of the Expedition of an American Squadron to The China Seas and Japan, Performed in the Years 1852, 1853, and 1854, Under the Command of Commodore M. C. Perry, United States Navy.* Washington, D.C.: A. O. P. Nicholson, printer, 1856.

Hawthorne, Nathaniel. *The House of Seven Gables.* Oxford: Oxford University Press, 1991.

Heine, William. *With Perry to Japan: A Memoir by William Heine.* Translated and edited by Frederic Trautman. Honolulu: University of Hawaii Press, 1990.

*Hints to Young Tradesmen and Maxims for Merchants.* Boston: Perkins and Marvin, 1838.

Hobart and Robbins. *New England Type and Stereotype Foundry.* Boston, circa 1850.

Hodges, Nan, ed. *The Voyage of the Peacock: A Journal by Benjamin Ticknor, Naval Surgeon.* Ann Arbor: University of Michigan Press, 1991.

Holt, Hamilton. *The Life Stories of Undistinguished Americans.* New York: Routledge, 1990.

Howland, Paul. *Specimen Book of Printing Types.* New Bedford, 1884.

Hughes, Sarah Forbes, ed. *Letters and Recollections of John Murray Forbes.* New York: Arno Press, 1981.

Hunter, W. C. *The Fan Kwei at Canton before Treaty Days, 1824–1844.* 1882. London: Kegan Paul, 1882. Reprint. Taipei: Ch'eng-wen, 1965.

Ingram, J. S. *The Centennial Exposition, Described and Illustrated.* Philadelphia: Hubbard Bros., 1876.

James Connor and Sons. *Specimens of Printing Types and Ornaments, Cast by James Connor and Sons.* New York, 1855.

Jenkins, Walter. *Bryant Parrott Tilden of Salem, at a Chinese Dinner Party.* Princeton: Princeton University Press.

Johnson, L. *Specimen of Printing Types and Ornaments Cast by L. Johnson.* Philadelphia, 1844.

Holley, Marietta. *Josiah Allen's Wife as a P.A. and P.I.: Samantha at the Centennial.* Hartford, Conn.: American Publishing Company, 1877.

Keating, John. *With General Grant in the East.* Philadelphia: Lippincott, 1879.

Kidder, D. P., ed. *The Chinese; or, Conversations on the Country and People of China.* Department of Rare Books, Library of Congress. New York: G. Lane and C. B. Tippett, 1846.

King, Caroline Howard. *When I Lived in Salem, 1822–1866.* Brattleboro, Vt.: Stephen Daye Press, 1937.

Langdon, William. *"Ten Thousand Chinese Things": A Descriptive Catalogue of the Chinese Collection, Now Exhibiting at St. George's Place, Hyde Park Corner, London.* London, 1842.

Laufer, Berthold . "Modern Chinese Collections in Historical Light: With Especial Reference to the American Museum's Collection Representative of Chinese Culture a Decade Ago." *American Museum Journal* 12 (April 1912).

Lavater, Johann Caspar. *The Pocket Lavater; or, The Science of Physiognomy.* New York: C. Wiley, 1829.

———. *Physiognomy; or, the Corresponding Analogy between the Conformation of the Features and the Ruling Passions of the Mind.* London: Thomas Tegg, 1844.

———. *Essays on Physiognomy.* London: William Tegg, 1869.

Li, Gui. *Huan you diqiu xin lu* (New account of traveling around the world). Hunan People's Publisher, 1980.

Leland, Charles. *The Pidgin English Sing-Song; or, Songs and Stories in the Chinese-English Dialect.* Philadelphia: J. B. Lippincott, 1876.

Loines, Elma, ed. *The China Trade Post-Bag of the Seth Low Family of Salem and New York.* Manchester, Maine: Falmouth Publishing House, 1953.

MacKellar, Smiths, and Jordan. *Print Types, Borders, Ornaments, and All Things Needful for Newspaper and Job Printing Offices Made by MacKellar, Smiths, and Jordan.* Philadelphia, 1880.

Mayer, Brantz. *A Nation in a Nutshell. Pamphlet, Department of Rare Books, Library of Congress.* Philadelphia: Brown, Bicking, and Guilbert, 1841.

McCabe, James. *The Illustrated History of the Centennial Exhibition. 1876.* Reprint, Philadelphia: National Publishing Company, 1976.

Mills, Brothers, and Co. (New York). *Catalogue of Canton Fans, Grass Cloths, and Fancy Goods Now Landing from the Ship" Howard," from Canton . . . June 5th, 1832.* Boston: Childs Gallery, 1968.

Moreau De Saint-Mery, M. L. E. *An Authentic Account of the Embassy of the Dutch East-India Company, to the Court of the Emperor of China, In the Years 1794 and 1795 . . . Containing a Description of Several Parts of the Chinese Empire, Unknown to Europeans; Taken from the Journal of Andr&ecute$ Everard Van Braam.* 2 vols. London: Lee and Hurst, 1798.

Morton, Samuel George. *Crania Americana; or, A Comparative View of the Skulls of Various Aboriginal Nations.* Philadelphia: J. Dobson, 1839.

Niemcewicz, Julian Ursyn. *Under Their Vine and Fig Tree: Travels in America in 1797–1799, 1805, with Some Further Account of Life in New Jersey.* Elizabeth, N.J.: Grassmann, 1965.

Norton, Frank H. *Illustrated Historical Register of the Centennial Exhibition, Philadelphia, 1876.* New York: American News Company, 1879.

312 *Bibliography*

Nye, Gideon. *Tea: And The Tea Trade.* New York: Geo. W. Wood, 1850.

Nye, Gideon. *The Morning of My Life in China: Comprising an Outline of the History of Foreign Intercourse from the Last Year of the Regime of Honorable East India Company, 1833, to the Imprisonment of the Foreign Community in 1839.* (Transcript of a lecture delivered in Canton, 31 January 1873.) Canton, 1873.

Odel, George C. D. *Annals of the New York Stage.* New York: Columbia University Press, 1931.

*People and Customs in Different Countries.* Uncle Oliver's Books for Children. Auburn, N.Y.: Oliphant and Skinner, 1837.

*People of China; or, A Summary of Chinese History.* Philadelphia: American Sunday-School Union, 1844.

*Peter Piper's Tales about China.* Albany, N.Y.: R. H. Pease, n.d.

Peters, John R., Jr. *Miscellaneous Remarks upon the Government, History, Religions, Literature, Agriculture, Arts, Trades, Manners, and Customs of the Chinese: As Suggested by an Examination of the Articles Comprising the Chinese Museum.* Philadelphia: G. B. Zieber, 1847.

Phelps, William Lyon. *Autobiography with Letters.* New York: Oxford University Press, 1939.

Planché, J. R. *Extravaganzas of J. R. Planché, Esq.* Edited by T. F. Dillon Crocker and Stephen Tucker. 5 vols. London: Samuel French, 1879.

Poore, Benjamin Perley. *Perley's Reminiscences of Sixty Years in the National Metropolis.* Philadelphia: Hubbard Brothers; New York: W. A. Houghton, 1886.

*Punch's Guide to the Chinese Collection.* London: Punch Office, 1844.

Shaw, Samuel. *The Journals of Major Samuel Shaw, the First American Consul at Canton.* Edited by Josiah Quincy. Taipei, Ch'eng-wen, 1968.

*Rapid Tour around the World; or, Young Peter's Remarks to His Cousins upon the Different Nations.* Amherst, Mass.: J. S. and C. Adams, 1846.

Redfield, J. W. *Outlines of a New System of Physiognomy.* New York: Redfield, 1848.

Robb, Alexander. *Specimen of Printing-Types and Ornaments Cast by Alexander Robb.* Philadelphia, 1846.

Roorbach, Orville A., ed. *Bibliotheca Americana: Catalogue of American Publications, Including Reprints and Original Works, from 1820 to [January 1861].* 4 vols. New York: Peter Smith, 1939.

Sewall, John S. *The Logbook of the Captain's Clerk: Adventures in the China Seas.* Edited by Arthur Power Dudden. Chicago: Lakeside Press, R. R. Donnelley and Sons, 1995.

Shaw, Samuel. *The Journals of Major Samuel Shaw, the First American Consul at Canton.* Edited by Josiah Quincy. Taipei, Ch'eng-wen, 1968.

Shearer, F. E., ed. *The Pacific Tourist: An Illustrated Guide.* New York: J. R. Bowman, 1879.

Shuck, Henrietta. *Scenes in China; or, Sketches of the Country, Religion, and Customs, of the Chinese.* Philadelphia: American Baptist Publication Society, 1853.

Silliman, Benjamin. "Mr. Dunn's Chinese Collection." *American Journal of Science and Arts* (January 1839).

————. *Mr. Dunn's Chinese Collection in Philadelphia*. Pamphlet, Department of Rare Books, Library of Congress. Philadelphia: Brown, Bicking, and Guilbert, 1841.

Sturge, Joseph. *A Visit to the United States in 1841*. London: Hamilton, Adams, 1842.

*Tales from the Arabian Nights' Entertainments, as Related by a Mother for the Amusement of Her Children*. New York: Edward Walker, 1848.

Taylor, Bayard. *Views A-Foot; or, Europe Seen with Knapsack and Staff*. London: Wiley and Putnam, 1847.

————. *A Visit to India, China, and Japan, in the Year 1853*. New York: G. P. Putnam, 1855.

————. *A Visit to India, China, and Japan, in the Year 1853*. New York: G. P. Putnam, 1859.

————. *At Home and Abroad*. New York: G. P. Putnam, 1860.

————, comp. *Cyclop3⁄4dia of Modern Travel: A Record of Adventure, Exploration, and Discovery, for the Past Fifty Years*. Cincinnati: Moore, Wilstach, Keys, 1856.

Tiffany, Osmond, Jr. *The Canton Chinese; or, The American's Sojourn in the Celestial Empire*. Boston: James Monroe, 1849.

Tocqueville, Alexis de. *Democracy in America*. Translated and edited by Harvey C. Mansfield and Delba Winthrop. 1835. Chicago: University of Chicago Press, 2000.

Twain, Mark. *Mark Twain's Letters*. Edited by Albert Bigelow Paine. New York: Harper and Brothers, 1917.

Tyng, Charles. *Before the Wind: The Memoir of an American Sea Captain, 1808–1833*. Edited by Susan Fels. New York: Viking Penguin, 1999.

United States Centennial Commission. *Reports and Awards*. Edited by Francis A. Walker. Groups 2 and 27. Philadelphia: J. B. Lippincott, 1877.

Wainright, Nicholas B., ed. *A Philadelphia Perspective: The Diary of Sidney George Fisher Covering the Years 1834–1871*. Philadelphia: Historical Society of Pennsylvania, 1967.

Walker, Francis. *The World's Fair: A Critical Account*. New York: A. S. Barnes, 1878.

Wells, L. T. *Specimens from the Cincinnati Type Foundry*. Cincinnati, 1852.

White, John T. *Specimen of Modern Printing Types at the Foundry of John T. White*. New York, 1839.

Williams, Frederick Wells. *The Life and Letters of Samuel Wells Williams, LL.D., Missionary, Diplomatist, Sinologue*. New York: G.P. Putnam's Sons, 1889.

Williams, Samuel Wells. *The Middle Kingdom: A Survey of the Geography, Government, Education, Social Life, Arts, Religion, &c., of the Chinese Empire and Its Inhabitants*. 2 vols. New York: Wiley and Putnam, 1848.

Wood, William W. *Sketches of China: With Illustrations from Original Drawings*. Philadelphia: Carey and Lea, 1830.

Longfellow, Henry Wadsworth. *Works of Henry Wadsworth Longfellow*. Edited by Samuel Longfellow. 10 vols. Boston: Houghton, Mifflin, 1886.

Yung, Shang Him. *The Chinese Educational Mission and Its Influence*. Shanghai: Kelly and Walsh, 1939.

Yung, Wing. *My Life in China and America*. New York: Holt, 1909.

SECONDARY SOURCES


*Journal Articles*


Bain, Chester. "Commodore Matthew Perry, Humphrey Marshall, and the Taiping Rebellion." *Far Eastern Quarterly* (May 1951).

Carpenter, Charles H. "The Chinese Collection of A. E. van Braam Houckgeest." *Magazine Antiques* (February 1974).

Dirlik, Arif. "Chinese History and the Question of Orientalism." In "Chinese Historiography in Comparative Perspective," edited by Axel Schneider and Susanne Weigelin-Schwiedrzik. Special issue, *History and Theory* 35 (December 1996).

Downs, Jacques M. "Fair Game: Exploitive Role-Myths and the American Opium Trade." *Pacific Historical Review* 41 (May 1972).

Godden, Geoffrey. "The Willow Pattern." *Antiques Collector* (June 1972).

Hawes, Dorothy. "To the Farthest Gulf: Outline of the Old China Trade." *Essex Institute Historical Collections* 77 (April 1941).

Hummel, Arthur. "Nathan Dunn." *Quaker History* 59, no. 1 (1970).

Hung, William. "Huang Tsun-Hsien's Poem 'The Closure of the Educational Mission in America.'" Harvard Journal of Asiatic Studies 18 (June 1955).

Jenkins, Lawrence Waters. "An Old Mandarin Home." *Essex Institute Historical Collections* 71 (April 1935).

Katz, Daniel and Kenneth Braly. "Racial Stereotypes of One Hundred College Students." *Journal of Abnormal and Social Psychology* 28 (October-December 1933).

Kuo, Ping Chia. "Canton and Salem: The Impact of Chinese Culture upon New England Life during the Post-Revolutionary Era." *New England Quarterly* 3 (1930).

Leath, Robert A. "'After the Chinese Taste': Chinese Export Porcelain and Chinoiserie Design in Eighteenth-Century Charleston." *Historical Archeology* 33, no. 3 (fall 1999).

Lee, Bill Lann. "Yung Wing and the Americanization of China." *Amerasia* (March 1971).

Leung, Edwin Pak-Wah. "China's Quest from the West: The Chinese Educational Mission to the United States, 1872–1881." *Asian Profile* 11, no. 6 (December 1983).

——. "The First Chinese College Graduates in America: Yung Wing and His Educational Experiences." *Asian Profile* 16, no. 5 (October 1988).

——. "The Making of the Chinese Yankees: School Life of the Chinese Educational Mission Students in New England." *Asian Profile* 16, no. 5 (October 1988).

Lorence, James. "Organized Business and the Myth of the China Market: The American Asiatic Association, 1898–1937." *Transactions of the American Philosophical Society* 71 (1981).

Mahler, Jane Gaston. "Huguenots Adventuring in the Orient: Two Manigaults in China." *Transactions of the Huguenot Society of South Carolina* 76 (1971).

Marsh, John L. "Drama and Spectacle by the Yard: The Panorama in America." *Journal of Popular Culture* 10, no. 3 (winter 1976).

Neumann, William L. "Religion, Morality, and Freedom: The Ideological Background of the Perry Expedition." *Pacific Historical Review* (August 1954).

Sellers, Charles Coleman. "Peale's Museum and 'The New Museum Idea.'" *Proceedings of the American Philosophical Society* 124, no. 1 (November 1980).

Worthy, Edmund H., Jr. "Yung Wing in America." *Pacific Historical Review* (August 1965).

Wright, Conrad Edick. "Merchants and Mandarins: New York and the Early China Trade." In *New York and the China Trade*. Edited by David Sanctuary Howard. New York: New-York Historical Society, 1984.

## Books

Adas, Michael. *Machines as the Measure of Men: Science, Technology, and Ideologies of Western Dominance*. Ithaca: Cornell University Press, 1989.

Alderson, William T., ed. *Mermaids, Mummies, and Mastodons: The Emergence of the American Museum*. Washington, D.C.: American Association of Museums, 1992.

Aldridge, Owen. *The Dragon and the Eagle: The Presence of China in the American Enlightenment*. Detroit: Wayne State University, 1993.

Alexander, Edward. *Museum Masters: Their Museums and Their Influence*. Nashville, Tenn.: American Association for State and Local History, 1983.

Altick, Richard D. *The Shows of London*. Cambridge: Harvard University Press, Belknap Press, 1978.

Barnard, Harry. *The Story of the Wedgwood Willow Pattern Plate*. Hanley, England: Catalogue Printers. Josiah Wedgwood and Sons published this guide book to Wedgwood porcelain.

Beatty, Richard Croom. *Bayard Taylor: Laureate of the Gilded Age*. Norman: University of Oklahoma Press, 1936.

Bode, Carl. *The Anatomy of American Popular Culture, 1840–1861*. Berkeley: University of California Press, 1959.

Bonner, Arthur. *Alas! What Brought Thee Hither? The Chinese in New York, 1800–1950*. Madison, N.J.: Farleigh Dickinson University Press, 1997.

Brown, Dee. *The Year of the Century: 1876*. New York: Scribner, 1966.

Caplan, Aaron. "Nathan Dunn's Chinese Museum." Master's thesis, University of Pennsylvania, 1986.

Chen, Chang-fang. "Barbarian Paradise: Chinese Views of the United States, 1784–1911." Ph.D. diss., Indiana University, 1985.

Christman, Margaret C. S. *Adventurous Pursuits: Americans and the China Trade*. Washington, D.C.: Smithsonian Institute Press, 1984.

Chu, Doris. *Chinese in Massachusetts: Their Experiences and Contributions*. Boston: Chinese Culture Institute, 1987.

Clunas, Craig. *Chinese Export Watercolours*. London: Victoria and Albert Museum, 1984.

Conn, Peter. *Pearl Buck: A Cultural Biography*. Cambridge: Cambridge University Press, 1996.

Conn, Steven. *Museums and American Intellectual Life, 1876–1926*. Chicago: University of Chicago Press, 1998.

Conner, Patrick. *George Chinnery, 1774–1852: Artist of India and the China Coast*. Woodbridge, Suffolk, England: Antique Collectors' Club, 1993.

Copeland, Robert. *Spode's Willow Pattern and Other Designs after the Chinese*. New York: Rizzoli, 1980.

Cox, Warren. *The Book of Pottery and Porcelain*. New York: L. Lee and Shepard; distributed by Crown, 1944.

Crossman, Carl. *The China Trade: Export Paintings, Furniture, Silver, and Other Objects*. Princeton, N.J.: Pyne Press, 1972.

——. *The Decorative Arts of the China Trade: Paintings, Furnishings, and Exotic Curiosities*. Woodbridge, Suffolk, England: Antique Collectors' Club, 1991.

Curtis, Julia B. *Chinese Porcelains of the Seventeenth Century: Landscapes, Scholars' Motifs, and Narratives*. New York: China Institute Gallery, 1995.

Davies, John B. *Phrenology: Fad and Science: A Nineteenth-Century American Crusade*. New Haven: Yale University Press, 1955.

Davis, Nancy Ellen. "The American China Trade, 1784–1844: Products for the Middle Class." Ph.D. diss., George Washington University, 1987.

Degler, Carl N. *In Search of Human Nature: The Decline and Revival of Darwinism in American Thought*. New York: Oxford University Press, 1991.

Dennett, Tyler. *Americans in Eastern Asia: A Critical Study of the Policy of the United States with Reference to China, Japan, and Korea in the Nineteenth Century*. New York: Macmillan, 1922.

Dong, Stella. *Shanghai: The Rise and Fall of a Decadent City*. New York: HarperCollins, 2000.

Dulles, Foster Rhea. *The Old China Trade*. Boston and New York: Houghton Mifflin, 1930.

Fitzsimons, Raymund. *Barnum in London*. New York: St. Martin's Press, 1970.

Foner, Philip S., and Daniel Rosenberg. *Racism, Dissent, and Asian Americans from 1850 to the Present: A Documentary History*. Westport, Conn.: Greenwood Press, 1993.

Forbes, Crosby. *Hills and Streams: Landscape Decoration on Chinese Export Blue and White Porcelain: A Loan Exhibition from the Collection of the China Trade Museum*. Washington, D.C.: International Exhibition Foundation, 1982.

Forster, John. *The Life of Charles Dickens*. London: Cecil Palmer, 1928.

Fuess, Claude M. *The Life of Caleb Cushing*. New York: Harcourt, Brace, 1923.

Goetzmann, William H. *New Lands, New Men: America and the Second Great Age of Discovery*. New York: Penguin, 1986.

Goetzmann, William H., and William N. Goetzmann. *The West of the Imagination.* New York: Norton, 1986.

Goldstein, Jonathan. *Philadelphia and the China Trade, 1682–1846: Commercial, Cultural, and Attitudinal Effects.* University Park: Pennsylvania State University Press, 1978.

Graham, John. *Lavater's Essays on Physiognomy: A Study in the History of Ideas.* Berne: Peter Lang, 1979.

Greenblatt, Stephen. *Marvelous Possessions: The Wonder of the New World.* Chicago: University of Chicago Press, 1991.

Greenhalgh, Paul. *Ephemeral Vistas: The Expositions Universelles, Great Exhibitions and World's Fairs, 1851–1931.* Manchester, England: Manchester University Press, 1988.

Gyory, Andrew. *Closing the Gate: Race, Politics, and the Chinese Exclusion Act* Chapel Hill: University of North Carolina Press, 1998.

Haller, John S. *Outcasts from Evolution: Scientific Attitudes of Racial Inferiority, 1859–1900.* Urbana: University of Illinois Press, 1971.

Hao, Yen-p'ing. "Chinese Teas to America—A Synopsis." In *America's China Trade in Historical Perspective: The Chinese and American Performance.* Edited by Ernest R. May and John King Fairbank. Cambridge: Committee on American-East Asian Relations of the Department of History in collaboration with the Council on East Asian Studies, Harvard University; distributed by Harvard University Press, 1986.

Harris, Neil. *Humbug: The Art of P. T. Barnum.* Boston: Little, Brown, 1973.

———. "All the World a Melting Pot? Japan at American Fairs, 1876–1904." In *Mutual Images: Essays in American-Japanese Relations.* Edited by Akira Iriye. Cambridge: Harvard University Press 1975.

Hart, Robert. *The I. G. in Peking: Letters of Robert Hart, Chinese Maritime Customs, 1868–1907.* Edited by John King Fairbank, Katherine Frost Bruner, and Elizabeth MacLeod Matheson. Cambridge: Harvard University Press, Belknap Press, 1975.

Hevia, James L. *Cherishing Men from Afar: Qing Guest Ritual and the Macartney Embassy of 1793.* Durham, N.C.: Duke University Press, 1995.

Hindle, Brooke. "The Transfer of Technology and American Industrial Fairs to 1853." In International Congress on the History of Sciences, *Proceedings, Fourteenth International Congress for the History of Science.* Tokyo: Science Council of Japan, 1974.

Honour, Hugh. *Chinoiserie: The Vision of Cathay.* New York: E. P. Dutton, 1961.

Hornung, Clarence P., and Fridolph Johnson. *Two Hundred Years of American Graphic Art: A Retrospective Survey of the Printing Arts and Advertising since the Colonial Period.* New York: George Braziller, 1976.

Hudson, Frederic. *Journalism in the United States, from 1690 to 1872.* New York: Harper and Brothers, 1872.

Hume, Ivor Noël. *Pottery and Porcelain in Colonial Williamsburg's Archaeological Collections.* Williamsburg, Va.: Colonial Williamsburg, 1969.

Isaacs, Harold R. *Images of Asia: American Views of China and India.* New York: Capricorn Books, 1962.

Jiang, Qian. "Samuel Wells Williams and the Attitudes of U.S. Protestant Missionaries toward the Opium Trade and the Opening of China, 1830–1860." Master's thesis, University of Toledo, 1992.

Johnson, Linda Cooke. *Shanghai: From Market Town to Treaty Port, 1074–1858.* Stanford: Stanford University Press, 1995.

Kaiser, Andrew T. "S. Wells Williams: Early Protestant Missions in China." Master's thesis, Gordon-Conwell Theological Seminary, 1995.

Kastner, Joseph. *A Species of Eternity.* New York: Knopf, 1977.

Keswick, Maggie. *The Chinese Garden: History, Art, and Architecture.* New York: Rizzoli, 1978.

King, H. H. *A Research Guide to China-Coast Newspapers, 1822–1911.* Cambridge: Harvard East Asian Research Center, 1965.

Kingston, Maxine Hong. *China Men.* New York: Vintage Books, 1977.

Kunhardt, Philip B., Jr., et al. *P. T. Barnum: America's Greatest Showman.* New York: Knopf, 1995.

La Fargue, Thomas. *China's First Hundred.* Pullman: State College of Washington, 1942.

Layton, Thomas. *The Voyage of the "Frolic": New England Merchants in the Opium Trade.* Stanford: Stanford University Press, 1997.

Lazich, Michael C. *E. C. Bridgman (1801–1861), America's First Missionary to China.* Lewiston, N.Y.: Edwin Mellen Press, 2000.

Lee, Jean Gordon. *Philadelphians and the China Trade, 1784–1844.* Philadelphia Philadelphia Museum of Art, 1984.

Lee, Robert G. *Orientals: Asian Americans in Popular Culture.* Philadelphia: Temple University Press, 1999.

Franklin, Benjamin. *The Autobiography of Benjamin Franklin: A Genetic Text.* Edited by J. A. Leo Lemay and P. M. Zall. Knoxville: University of Tennessee Press, 1981.

Lo, Hsiang-Lin. "Portrait of a Chinese Diplomat of the Last Manchu Emperors Sir Chentung Liang Cheng." In Chinese Historical Society of America, *The Life, Influence, and the Role of the Chinese in the United States, 1776–1960: Proceedings, Papers of the National Conference Held at the University of San Francisco July 10, 11, 12, 1975.* San Francisco: Chinese Historical Society of America, 1976.

Macphereson, Kerrie L. *A Wilderness of Marshes: The Origins of Public Health in Shanghai, 1843–1893.* New York: Oxford University Press, 1987.

Malefijt, Annemarie de Waal. *Images of Man: A History of Anthropological Thought.* New York: Knopf, 1974.

Margolin, Victor, Ira Brichta, and Vivian Brichta. *The Promise and the Product: Two Hundred Years of American Advertising Posters.* New York: Macmillan, 1979.

McCauley, Edward Yorke. *With Perry in Japan: The Diary of Edward Yorke McCauley. Edited by Allan B. Cole.* Princeton: Princeton University Press, 1942.

McDougall, Walter A. *Let the Sea Make a Noise—: A History of the North Pacific from Magellan to MacArthur.* New York: Basic Books, 1993.

Meserve, Walter J. *Heralds of Promise: The Drama of the American People during the Age of Jackson, 1829–1849.* New York: Greenwood Press, 1986.

Miller, Stuart Creighton. *The Unwelcome Immigrant: The American Image of the Chinese, 1785–1882*. Berkeley: University of California Press, 1969.

Moy, James S. *Marginal Sights: Staging the Chinese in America*. Iowa City: University of Iowa Press, 1993.

Nicolai, Richard R. *Centennial Philadelphia*. Bryn Mawr, Pa.: Bryn Mawr Press, 1976.

Oettrermann, Stephan. *The Panorama: History of a Mass Medium*. Translated by Deborah Lucas Schneider. New York: Zone Books, 1997.

Perry, John Curtis. *Facing West: Americans and the Opening of the Pacific*. Westport, Conn.: Praeger, 1994.

Pratt, Mary Louis. *Imperial Eyes: Travel Writing and Transculturation*. London: Routledge, 1992.

Quintner, David. *Willow! Solving the Mystery of Our Two-Hundred-Yyear Love Affair with the Willow Pattern*. Burnstown, Ontario: General Store Publishing House, 1997.

Reynolds, David S. *Walt Whitman's America: A Cultural Biography*. New York: Vintage Books, 1996.

Rhoads, Edward J. M. *Manchus and Han: Ethnic Relations and Political Power in Late Qing and Early Republican China, 1861–1928*. Seattle: University of Washington Press, 2000.

Riddle, Ronald. "The Cantonese Opera: A Chapter in Chinese-American History." In Chinese Historical Society of America, *The Life, Influence, and the Role of the Chinese in the United States, 1776–1960: Proceedings, Papers of the National Conference held at the University of San Francisco, July 10, 11, 12, 1975*. San Francisco: Chinese Historical Society of America, 1976.

Rowe, William T. *Hankow: Commerce and Society in a Chinese City, 1796–1889*. Stanford: Stanford University Press, 1984.

Rydell, Robert W. *All the World's a Fair: Visions of Empire at American International Expositions, 1876–1916*. Chicago: University of Chicago Press, 1984.

Said, Edward. *Orientalism*. New York: Pantheon, 1978.

Sawin, Mark H. Metzler. "Raising Kane: The Creation and Consequences of Fame in Antebellum America; or, The thrilling and Tragic Narrative of Elisha Kent Kane and His Transformation into Dr. Kane, the Hero of the Romantic Age." Ph.D. diss., University of Texas at Austin, 2001.

Saxon, A. H. *P. T. Barnum: The Legend and the Man*. New York: Columbia University Press, 1989.

Schudson, Michael. *Discovering the News: A Social History of American Newspapers*. New York: Basic Books, 1978.

Seaburg, Carl, and Stanley Patterson. *Merchant Prince of Boston, Colonel T. H. Perkins, 1764–1854*. Cambridge, Harvard University Press, 1971.

Sellers, Charles Coleman. *Mr. Peale's Museum*. New York: Norton, 1980.

Siržn, Osvald. *Gardens of China*. New York: The Ronald Press Company, 1949.

Slosson, Annie Trumbull. *The China Hunters Club, by the Youngest Member*. New York: Harper and Brothers, 1878.

Smyth, Albert. *Bayard Taylor*. Boston: Houghton, Mifflin and Company, 1896.

Spence, Jonathan D. *The Chan's Great Continent: China in Western Minds*. New York: Norton, 1998.

———. *The Search for Modern China*. New York: Norton, 1990.

Stanton, William. *The Leopard's Spots: Scientific Attitudes toward Race in America, 1815–1859*. Chicago: University of Chicago Press, 1960.

Stocking, George W. *Victorian Anthropology*. London: Collier Macmillan, 1987.

———, ed. *The Shaping of American Anthropology, 1883–1911: A Franz Boas Reader*. New York: Basic Books, 1974.

Takaki, Ronald. *Strangers from a Different Shore: A History of Asian Americans*. Boston: Little, Brown, 1989.

Taylor, Bayard. *Selected Letters of Bayard Taylor*. Edited by Paul C. Wermuth. Lewisburg, Pa.: Bucknell University Press, 1997.

Tchen, John Kuo Wei. *New York before Chinatown: Orientalism and the Shaping of American Culture, 1776–1882*. Baltimore: Johns Hopkins University Press, 1999.

Thill, Joan Kerr Facey. "A Delawarean in the Celestial Empire: John Richardson Latimer and the China Trade." Master's thesis, University of Delaware, 1973.

Trachtenberg, Alan. *The Incorporation of America: Culture and Society in the Gilded Age*. New York: Hill and Wang, 1982.

Trowbridge, Thomas R., ed. "The Diary of Mr. Ebeneezer Townsend, Jr." *Papers of the New Haven Historical Society*. Vol. 4. New Haven, 1888.

Tsu, Andrew Yu-yue. "The Use of Leisure Time among the Chinese Immigrants of the New York City." Master's thesis, Columbia University, 1910.

Tuan, Yi-fu. *Escapism*. Baltimore: Johns Hopkins University Press, 1998.

Twain, Mark. *Mark Twain's Weapons of Satire: Anti-Imperialist Writings on the Philippine-American War*. Edited by Jim Zwick. Syracuse, N.Y.: Syracuse University Press, 1992.

Wakeman, Frederic. *Strangers at the Gate: Social Disorder in South China, 1839–1861*. Berkeley: University of California Press, 1966.

Walsh, William. *The Rise and Decline of the Great Atlantic & Pacific Tea Company*. Secaucus, N.J.: Lyle Stuart, 1986.

Warner, John. *Tingqua: Paintings from His Studio*. Hong Kong: Hong Kong Museum of Art, 1976.

Wermuth, Paul C. *Bayard Taylor*. New York: Twayne, 1973.

Whitehill, Walter Muir. *The East India Marine Society and the Peabody Museum of Salem: A Sesquicentennial History*. Salem, Mass.: Peabody Museum, 1949.

Wiley, Peter Booth. *Yankees in the Land of the Gods: Commodore Perry and the Opening of Japan*. New York: Viking, 1990.

Williams, Dave, ed. *The Chinese Othe,r 1850–1912: An Anthology of Plays*. Lanham, Md.: University Press of America, 1997.

Wilson, Arthur Herman. *A History of the Philadelphia Theatre, 1835–1855*. Philadelphia: University of Pennsylvania Press, 1935.

Wines, E. C. *Hints on a System of Popular Education*. Philadelphia: Hogan and Thompson, 1838.

———. *A Peep at China in Mr. Dunn's Chinese Collection.* Philadelphia: Ashmead, 1839.

Wolanin, Barbara. *Constantino Brumidi: Artist of the Capitol.* Washington, D.C.: U.S. Government Printing Office, 1998.

Wood, Gordon S. *The Radicalism of the American Revolution.* New York: Knopf, 1992.

Zweig, Paul. *Walt Whitman: The Making of the Poet.* New York: Basic Books, 1984.

ABOUT THE AUTHOR

**John Rogers Haddad** teaches classes on American culture at Penn State Harrisburg, where he is associate professor of American studies and literature. He currently resides in Hershey, Pennsylvania, with his wife Catherine an his two children, William and Elizabeth.

Printed in the United States
129246LV00003B/1-84/P

9 780231 130943